NewVegetarian Classics:
Entrées

by
Mary F. Taylor

photographs by Diane Farris

The Crossing Press, Freedom, CA 95019

In this book I have pulled together the work, training, and inspiration of years. Attempting to thank all of the people who have contributed means reaching as far back as 1972 and my time training in France. Without the knowledge and inspiration offered me when I first trained at L'École des Trois Gourmandes, I would never have begun this book. My thanks to Julia Child, Simone Beck, and their assistant Camille Cadier. Since then there are many people who have offered support, guidance, and enthusiasm for this project.

First I am indebted to The Crossing Press for giving me the opportunity to pursue this dream, in particular Elaine Gill for her clarity and continued support. I also thank Dennis Hayes for his enthusiasm, Karen Narita for her humor and patience, and Amy Sibiga for her eye for design.

Many friends and family members have helped immeasurably by offering support, tasting and testing recipes, and giving perspective when needed, and I would like to thank you all. In particular I am grateful to my parents, Carol and Frank Taylor, to Kimmer Maracus, Cindy and Tristan Watson, Barbara Bowerman, Anne Harper, Becky Buntyn, Jia Gottlieb and Eileen Martin, and Catrine Truillon. A special thanks goes to Doris Houghland and the staff of the Peppercorn for their generous use of props as well as to Marilyn Asse for her collector's eye. Thank you also to the consumer information department at the University of California at Berkeley Wellness Letter and to Nancy K. Weirs at Spectrum Naturals who provided critical background information about fat in the diet. Thanks also to Diane Farris for her understanding of food as art and to my assistants Desirée Sanchez and Melanie Gillum for testing recipes and standing up to a computer with a personality.

Finally many thanks to Karen Hirt for all of her help with the most precious ingredient of all, and of course to my husband Richard Freeman and our son Gabriel for their unyielding support.

Library of Congress Cataloging-in-Publication Data

Taylor, Mary F.
    New vegetarian classics : entrees / Mary F. Taylor.
        p. cm.
    Includes index.
    ISBN 0-89594-738-2 (pbk.)
    1. Vegetarian cookery.   2. Entrées (Cookery)   I. Title.
TX837.T38 1995   94-48011
641.8'2—dc20   CIP

Table of Contents

For Richard whose understanding of the palate rivals any.

Introduction

It is estimated that the average American cook has a repertoire of twelve to fifteen recipes from which to draw for the focal point of all home-cooked meals. The number may seem small, but if you stop to count your own "family favorites," you may find that you rely on fewer than you imagine. Why so few?

We are creatures of habit. It is simple to fill our grocery carts with the same items week after week in order to shop, pay the grocery bills and prepare meals without any unwelcome surprises. In addition, cooking is time-consuming enough when you know exactly what steps to follow without the attention and thought new recipes demand. Also, we may cook the same things repeatedly because they are made from familiar ingredients.

When I first became interested in vegetarian cooking, it was unfamiliar ingredients that presented the biggest challenge. Garbanzo beans, seitan, and (heaven forbid) tofu were beyond my comprehension. I barely knew how to identify them, let alone transform them into an edible meal. But I was drawn to vegetarian foods out of curiosity because I had never enjoyed the taste of meat. Having trained and worked in the food business for years, I already knew how to cook (or so I thought). I had no problem with classic dishes such as Pâté Brisée, Boeuf Bourguignon, or a Hollandaise Sauce. When I began to explore the use of vegetarian ingredients as alternatives in some of the world's most classic meat-based dishes, an entirely new realm of cooking presented itself. By applying classic cooking methods and techniques to vegetarian ingredients, my attempts to create new vegetarian dishes became more interesting and multidimensional. Not that I invented anything, I simply found a way of translating what I already knew into the medium of nonmeat ingredients. This, with attention to the use of fresh vegetables, whole grains, low-fat ingredients, and an eye for design is what *New Vegetarian Classics* is all about.

Entrées is an unusual collection of vegetarian recipes that are, for the most part, low fat and simple to prepare. Ingredients lists are often long, but once you read through the steps involved in preparation, you will see that most can be assembled in stages with only a few last-minute finishing touches. For each recipe I list yield, preparation time (prep) and, when applicable, cooking time. Prep time includes all work involved in preparing ingredients for final assembly and cooking. For example, peeling vegetables, combining ingredients for a marinade, or cooking a stuffing would all be considered Prep Time. In some recipes you may be instructed to carry out two tasks at once. In all such cases one task, such as draining tofu or reducing a liquid, requires only a brief period of setup and little or no surveillance. Combining ingredients and cooking them just before serving is considered Cooking Time. Many recipes also list a Cook's Note. If a recipe requires an unsupervised resting period (for soaking beans, marinating, pressing tofu, etc.), the time required will be noted in the Cook's Note.

The first two chapters of the book are an introduction to vegetarian ingredients and the fundamental theories and techniques that make cooking an art. Chapter 3 is a collection of recipes that elaborate on these fundamentals. Each is intended to demonstrate precise cooking methods and is designed to be inspiration for experimentation as much as it is to be followed exactly by the book. The recipes in Chapter 3 could serve as a new repertoire—with limitless variation—of vegetarian entrées. Recipes in Chapter 4 are light, yet filling. They are simple in one of two ways. Either they are fast to prepare—start to finish—or they work well prepared in stages in a few short 10- to 15-minute blocks of time over the course of a day or so, before the final cooking. Chapter 5 contains recipes modeled after classic meat-based recipes such as Boeuf Bourguignon or traditional pot pies. The recipes in Chapter 6 are the most festive in appearance and style. Though a few are very quick to prepare, the majority of recipes in this chapter require more work than other recipes in the book. In Chapter 7 you will find accompaniments and components for many of the recipes found in the other chapters. In addition to general guidelines and prototype recipes for salads, as well as vegetable and grain side dishes, the chapter contains recipes that can be used as a component in many entrées such as tofu "cheeses" and seitan as well as a selection of versatile sauces.

All recipes are designed to be healthy. They are made from whole grains and whole foods with attention to the natural flavor and beauty that each ingredient brings to a dish. Most recipes are low in fat and because I use very few dairy products, cholesterol is generally extremely low. In recipes that call for foods to be cooked in fat as one of the first steps of the recipe, you may "sauté" in stock or juice instead of fat to lower fat content. The only caution I give here is that on some occasions the loss of flavor will alter the depth of the dish considerably. (See page 18 for information on the role of fat in cooking.) Though I exercise extreme caution in adding fat and other high-fat ingredients to the recipes that follow, they are not eliminated entirely. Instead each recipe is an effort to balance a wide range of ingredients gracefully. And this is my understanding of what a healthy diet is: an approach to eating and cooking in which the food is treated with high regard as it is prepared and relished with the same respect and enthusiasm as it is eaten. It is in this spirit that I have written this book.

1 • Making It Easy

In this chapter I give some basic information about the tools, materials and organizational approach that help to make cooking easy and relaxing. A truly positive cooking experience is culminated by the food being eaten and enjoyed—when a dish actually contributes to someone's good health. So the final section of this chapter addresses the challenge of how to eat a healthy diet without sacrificing flavor.

A comfortable, well-organized work space and good, dependable equipment are essential to an enjoyable cooking experience. In terms of kitchen comfort, lighting is critical. Good general lighting in addition to that directed at work and cooking space (without glare in the eyes) is usually best. Avoid soft or fluorescent lighting, and be careful to avoid shadows.

Having equipment, ingredients, and work space easily accessible and countertops at the right height are also very important. It seems you can never have too much counter space, and a heatproof countertop next to the stove (onto which hot pans may be transferred without damage) is essential. When organizing ingredients and equipment, let common sense prevail. Everything should be arranged for a smooth flow of movement as you prepare and cook. For example, knives should be stored near the cutting space, cooking spoons next to the stove, and pots, pans, and lids easy to reach. If possible—without overcrowding valuable work space—store small equipment, such as a food processor or toaster oven, out and ready to use. Keep in mind that cooking is an art and it becomes infinitely more enjoyable if you do not have to interrupt the creative process in order to recall where you might find one thing or another.

With regard to equipment, there are only a few pieces that are essential for preparing vegetarian entrées. Once you have a good set of knives, pots and pans, and a few odds and ends like cooking spoons, whisks, and strainers, anything is possible. Wait to buy a piece of equipment with a very specific use, such as a pasta machine, until you find yourself frequently needing it. The following is a list of basic equipment that will simplify the preparation of recipes in this book.

Essential Equipment

Knives. Good knives are of supreme importance in a kitchen. Your knife is an extension of your hand and fingers when you cook, so it must fit your grip perfectly, be balanced, and sharp so that you can manipulate it accurately. When selecting knives, look for those of high-quality construction. Pay close attention to how the knife feels in your hand. It should feel sturdy without being overly heavy. When you hold a large knife above the work surface, it should feel balanced—the tip of the blade should not feel as though it is being pulled downward. The tail of the knife (the continuation of the blade into the handle) should reach to the end of the handle. (You will be able to see the tail as a metal dot at the end of the handle or a steel band will be visible all the way around the upper and lower perimeter of the handle). The handle should be of high-quality wood or wood mixed with plastic. Most important, the blade itself should be made of a high-carbon/stainless steel blend, or high-quality carbon steel. These are durable and can be sharpened easily at home with a good sharpening steel, though a carbon steel blade stains easily and may eventually pit.

For a good basic set of knives I recommend having one or two all-purpose, large kitchen knives; a 10- to 12-inch French chef's knife and/or an 8- to 10-inch Japanese style cleaver. (Knife length is measured by the length of the blade.) You also need one or two small 3- to 4-inch straight-edged paring knives for peeling and fine work. Finally, an 8- to 10-inch wavy-edged knife is indispensable for cutting citrus, tomatoes, and bread.

Cultivate the habit of rinsing and drying your knives each time you finish cutting. This keeps the blade in good shape and inhibits the spread of germs. Never wash good knives in the dishwasher. Always store them in a knife block or on a magnet to avoid having them jostled around—and dulled—in a drawer.

A good knife sharpener is essential, too. Knives should be sharpened each time you cook. A hard-steel, medium-grained, 16- to 18-inch sharpening steel with a protected handle is a good, all-purpose choice. To sharpen, hold the knife at a 20-degree angle to the steel and draw gently, but without applying excessive pressure over the surface of the steel. Alternate sides of the blade as you sharpen, stroking it down one side of the steel, then on the reverse side of the blade and steel. Do not press hard as you draw the knife over the steel. Sharpening is a means of realigning the molecules on the edge of the blade, so you must work as patiently and carefully as if you were shaping sand into a sharp-edged wall with your hands.

Cutting Board. Good knives should be used on a good cutting surface in order to maintain their edge as long as possible. Having more than one cutting surface is often a blessing, especially when a recipe requires a great deal of vegetable prep, so I recommend having two or three laminated hardwood cutting boards that are no smaller than 12 by 18 inches.

A cutting board should be thoroughly cleaned at least once a week. To do so, scrape off all food with a sturdy dough scraper or pancake turner. Rub the board with lemon juice and salt to remove stains. Rinse with water and dry immediately. Never wash wooden boards with soap or in the dishwasher as the wood will deteriorate.

Pots and Pans. Choose pots and pans with heavy, flat (non-ribbed) bottoms so that foods cook evenly without burning. The best are made of a material that conducts heat well and is thick enough so that heat can be controlled and foods do not burn easily. Copper and aluminum are excellent heat conductors, but they react with and discolor some foods, so they should be avoided unless lined with another material, such as stainless steel or tin. Heavy-gauge anodized aluminum with an interior stainless steel coating makes excellent all-purpose cookware. For less expensive alternatives, enameled cast-iron or double-layered, copper-lined stainless steel are good for most purposes.

Seven or eight basic pots and pans should serve you well. You will need a large stockpot or Dutch oven for making stocks, cooking beans, and making large quantities of oven-baked entrées. The volume of your largest pot will depend on whether you normally cook for two or ten, but a 4-quart capacity is the minimum. A separate 5- to 6-quart pasta pot with an inner steamer basket is extremely useful for cooking pasta, preparing stocks, and steaming vegetables. A pressure cooker is invaluable for preparing beans and accomplishing many other cooking tasks quickly. If you get one, a 6-quart capacity and a quick release valve is advisable. You will also need some smaller pots for cooking sauces, sautéing and steaming small amounts of food. A 1-quart and a 3-quart heavy-bottomed saucepan, and a 10- to 12-inch sauté or frying pan should do. In addition it is helpful to have a 12- to 14-inch heavy-gauge wok for stir-frying and steaming. A heavy cast-iron crêpe pan can be used for preparing crêpes and for sautéing small amounts of foods. All pots and pans should have tight-fitting lids.

Other Equipment and Supplies

Baking Pans/Dishes. You should have at least two shallow baking pans for marinating foods and baking. One 9- by 9-inch and one 9- by 13-inch Pyrex or stainless steel pan are sufficient. You will also need at least two heavyweight baking sheets. Local restaurant supply stores are a good source for these, just be certain that they fit the size of your oven. One broiling pan and a pizza pan are also good additions to your kitchen. At least one large (8-cup) and four individual (1 1/2-cups) ramekins and/or gratin dishes for preparing baked dishes and casseroles will also come in handy. Finally, one large (9-inch) and several small (4-inch) pie plates will allow latitude in presentation style.

Bowls. Preparation is simplified when you have assorted sizes of stainless steel and/or hard plastic mixing bowls, in addition to several small bowls for pre-measuring ingredients as you cook.

Citrus Juicer. For juicing lemons, limes, and small oranges, you should have either a plastic or glass countertop juicer that fits all sizes of citrus or a hand-held teardrop-shaped lemon juicer (available in wood or plastic).

Cooking Spoons. Equip your kitchen with assorted beech or boxwood spoons in various shapes and lengths, including at least one flat-faced (rounded or squared end) spoon for scraping the bottom edge of a soup pot, and one spaghetti fork or plain wooden fork for removing pasta from cooking water. You may also find that one or more stainless steel cooking spoons, and a Chinese-style set of wok utensils—a ladle and shovel—come in handy.

Dough Scraper. A rectangular stainless-steel, sturdy-bladed dough scraper is invaluable for clearing the work space, moving piles of prepared ingredients, and cleaning the cutting board.

Food Processor, Blender. It is nice to have both, but if you get only one, I suggest a processor. Larger volumes can be processed in a processor, and it can be used for chopping, grating, and slicing foods. When buying a processor, I recommend an 8-cup bowl unless you always cook for a crowd. (A large-capacity bowl will not always work when chopping or beating small quantities.) For smaller jobs and for certain ingredients such as pastes, a blender is preferable to a processor. I recommend blenders with glass jars and as few control buttons as possible.

Garlic Press. Choose a heavy-gauge stainless-steel press with small holes and a self-cleaning system for adding garlic to marinades and dishes that require little cooking.

Graters. Two graters are useful: a 6-sided stainless-steel stand-up grater; and a hand-cranked Mouli grater with replaceable grating disks.

Kitchen Aprons and Towels. At least three cotton aprons and eight cotton kitchen towels are essential. Wearing one towel looped around your apron waist tie and having towels hanging at convenient spots around the kitchen save time and promote neatness.

Measuring Equipment. Reliable measuring equipment is essential. Have one set of measuring spoons, Pyrex liquid measuring cups in 1-, 2- and 4-cup capacities, and a set of stainless-steel dry measuring cups.

Parchment Paper. Parchment is oven-safe paper used for lining molds and for wrapping foods to be baked "in parchment." Dioxin-free parchment is available at some natural foods markets.

Pastry Brushes. You need one 1-inch natural bristle, wooden-handled brush for brushing pastry, glazing and painting butter, a basting brush with moderately soft bristles, and a long-handled, firm-bristled basting brush for grilling. Wash brushes by rubbing the ends of the bristles vigorously against the palm of your hand in hot, soapy water. Rinse well and dry with bristles hanging down, but without the weight of the brush on the bristles.

Pepper and Nutmeg Mills. For optimal flavor, using freshly grated pepper and nutmeg is always recommended in the recipes that follow. Select mills with stainless steel mechanisms.

Rubber Spatulas. Several sturdy but flexible rubber-bladed spatulas on wooden or plastic handles simplify mixing and transferring foods from containers.

Salad Spinner. A number of models are available, the best is a plastic bucket with a basket that fits inside so that greens or herbs may be washed in the bucket, then dried in the spinner in or out of the sink.

Steamers. A 5- to 6-quart pasta pot with an inner steamer basket that doubles as a steamer for all sorts of foods is an excellent investment. A collapsible steamer rack that fits various sizes of pots will give you latitude in steaming. Finally, a Chinese bamboo steamer—at least three tiers high with a lid—is a must for cooking steamed dishes, such as Ginger Scallion Tofu (page 72). Bamboo steamers impart a delicate bamboo scent into foods that are steamed in them in addition to the fact that the lid absorbs droplets of condensation, preventing water from dripping back down onto the foods. For a makeshift steamer, arrange 4 chopsticks across the bottom of a wok so that they form a large grid pattern. Place a heatproof plate or bowl—containing the food to be steamed—on this frame. Fill the wok with water to 1/2 inch of the plate, then secure with a tight-fitting lid before steaming.

Storage Containers. Glass and/or plastic storage containers in assorted sizes—from 1 cup to 3 quarts—all with tight-fitting lids—are essential. Use them for freezing, refrigerating, and storing prepared ingredients.

Strainers. You need one 12- to 14-inch, medium-mesh stainless-steel strainer for straining pasta, steamed vegetables, and grains; one 8-inch fine-mesh stainless-steel strainer for straining sauces for finer texture; and a small tea strainer for citrus juice and dusting dry ingredients.

Swivel-Bladed Vegetable Peeler. A stainless-steel rotating blade on a sturdy metal handle is essential. The swivel action provides best control.

Teakettle. An all-purpose teakettle for adding water to dishes as they cook is necessary.

Whisks. You should have two sauce whisks (long and narrow) with tinned or stainless-steel wires, one measuring 6 inches and the other 10 inches, and one balloon whisk (full and rounded) for beating egg whites to firm peaks.

Ingredients

The difference between an exquisite dish and a rather ordinary one more often lies in the quality of ingredients used than in the skill of the cook, or even the recipe used. There is no match for ingredients that are at their peak of freshness. The best method of learning to select for quality is to pay attention to ingredients each time you use them; to notice how they feel, smell and look (both raw and cooked) when they taste the way you like them.

Below I give some general guidelines for selecting high-quality ingredients. In addition, I have elaborated on a few ingredients that are indispensable to preparing vegetarian entrées. For information about other and less common ingredients, please consult the Glossary of Ingredients (page 190).

Guidelines for Selecting Produce

Though ultimately taste is the final judge, we often engage all of our other senses to assess produce before we perceive its flavor. For example, if you are choosing an apple from a tray of fruit, you spot one with good color that looks plump and juicy. As soon as you touch it you know whether it has the desired firmness and as you bring it close to your mouth, its sweet smell becomes noticeable. You then bite through it and can actually hear the sound of its crunchy texture before the first drop of juice alerts your taste buds to its flavor. Of course you might only observe all of this if you concentrate fully on the food and slow the eating process down beyond reason. But we use the same step-by-step assessment (albeit subconscious) every time we choose a food.

For the most part, fruits and vegetables should appear plump, giving the impression that their juices are bursting at the skin. Produce should feel appropriately firm. Avoid fruits and vegetables that are limp or those with extreme soft spots, bruises, mold, or if they feel unevenly firm when gently squeezed. Most produce smells very distinctive when it is at its peak of freshness and when it is beginning to fail. The appealing smell of juicy, dark red strawberries is enticing, just as the musty smell of sprouts that are beginning to go bad or mushrooms that have passed their peak is repulsive. Trust your nose.

One note of caution: Though you must judge produce by its appearance, do not be deceived into thinking that the prettiest is always the best. Some organic fruits and vegetables have minor blemishes but they may be the best choice for quality, freshness, and taste. (See page 15 for more information on organic foods.) Be aware that some organic produce may have worms or aphids living on them which should be removed. For instance, in the summer it is not uncommon to find a particular type of grey-green aphids hiding on kale leaves or broccoli tops. These aphids are so similar in color and form to the broccoli florets that you might overlook them. (If by chance you do, you will recognize their musty flavor when the vegetable is cooked.) To remove most pests from produce, simply rinse and gently rub the produce in many changes of water until no pests are visible on the produce and none float in the water. If you cannot rinse them off in several changes of cold water you may try soaking the produce in salty water for 30 minutes, then rinsing again in plain water before cooking.

Generally speaking, most fruits are best stored in a well-ventilated spot at a cool room temperature until they are ripe. All fruits will remain reasonably fresh once ripe, if they are refrigerated. (This does not apply to bananas.) It is especially important to keep soft ripening fruits, such as peaches and plums, chilled after ripening as they perish quickly.

A few vegetables, namely onions, garlic, shallots, potatoes and winter squash, are, like fruits, best stored in a cool, well-ventilated basket or storage pantry. Most other vegetables must be refrigerated to maintain freshness. Some, such as greens and mushrooms, do well if they are trimmed, washed, dried, and then wrapped loosely in a plastic bag lined with a paper towel. (See pages 34 and 35 for instructions on storage of greens and mushrooms.) Store most other vegetables, loosely wrapped, in the vegetable bin of the refrigerator and wait to clean or trim them until as close to the time you are to use them as is practical. No raw food should be stored in a sealed plastic bag or airtight plastic container. (Do not twist or tie plastic bags shut.) Condensation will build up inside the container and speed spoilage. Freshly picked herbs, as well as stalks of lemon grass, maintain optimal freshness if trimmed then refrigerated with the base of their stems in a container of water. Avocados and tomatoes, like fruit, should be ripened at room temperature, then refrigerated.

All fruit and vegetables called for in the recipes that follow should be peeled unless otherwise indicated. I recommend peeling for two reasons. First, it is not uncommon for chemical residue from pesticides to remain on the skin of commercial produce. In addition, though the skin of fruit adds fiber, in many dishes the texture and visual appeal are greatly compromised when the skin remains. Because the recipes include so much fiber to begin with, the added amount given by the skin of most produce is inconsequential. Some vitamins may be lost by peeling, but for the most part, the same reasoning applies—the recipes are well balanced nutritionally so they already contain good amounts of most vitamins.

Healthy Guidelines for Selecting Other Ingredients
Dried Beans

Beans are also referred to as legumes because they are members of a family of flowering leguminous plants which produce large, protein-rich seeds. These seeds (the bean), when combined with grains, seeds or dairy products, provide a complete protein (one containing all 18 essential amino acids). Consequently, beans are the mainstay ingredient in vegetarian cuisines throughout the world. In addition to their protein, beans are good sources of iron and B vitamins and, except for soybeans, are low in fat. They are also high in fiber and contain no cholesterol.

Most beans are available dried, though some, such as soybeans, favas, and limas, may be bought fresh or frozen. Beans are inexpensive and may be stored, dried, in airtight containers at room temperature indefinitely. Different varieties of beans offer a wide range of flavors and textures. Some, such as chickpeas, are rugged and exceptionally dominant while others, such as mung beans, are subtle and delicate. In the recipes that follow, beans of similar nature may be substituted for one another without problem. If you want to substitute beans with less similar characteristics for one another, be aware that you might need to increase or decrease cooking times and/or the amount of liquid required for cooking. Also, spicing might need to be adjusted to suit the taste of the bean.

There are a number of good methods for cooking beans, and once you incorporate cooking beans into your monthly cooking routine, you can always have some on hand in the freezer. Use the following guidelines:

1. Before measuring, beans should be "picked over" to remove all rocks and debris. You should pour them out on a flat basket or cookie sheet. Tilt the basket at about a 30 degree angle. Allow the beans to roll down to the bottom edge of the basket, as you carefully search through for foreign matter. Most commercially produced beans are relatively free of rocks or debris, whereas some produced by smaller farms or supplied through international markets may contain a fair amount of foreign matter.

2. Once picked over, place the beans in a fine mesh strainer and rinse well in cold water. Split beans, lentils, peas and various forms of small "dal" (Indian-style beans) may stick together and clump when wet, so they should not be rinsed until just before transferring to a soaking or cooking liquid.

3. After washing, beans may be placed in a large bowl and covered with cold water (4 cups water per cup of beans) then soaked overnight. This will speed up their cooking and aid in digestibility. As a time-saving device, they may be "quick soaked." To do this, place beans in a large pot of water (4 cups per cup of beans) and bring them to a boil. Cook them for 3 minutes, then cool in their liquid before proceeding with a recipe.

4. There are several methods for cooking beans. In the recipes that follow I usually do not specify a method, but call for cooked beans as having a stash of cooked beans on hand (either freshly cooked or frozen) is essential if you cook beans on a regular basis. Boiling beans is the simplest method, requiring the least amount of equipment. To boil beans, for each cup of dried beans, add 4 cups of water and spices of your choosing to a large heavy-bottomed pot. (Diced onion, garlic, bay leaf and peppercorns are a versatile preliminary seasoning. Adding 2 teaspoons of oil per cup of beans may improve texture and reduce foaming. Do not add salt, miso, tamari, soy sauce or acidic foods such as lemon, tomato or vinegar, to the first cooking or the beans will be tough.) Bring the beans to a boil, skim and discard foam that rises to the surface, then reduce to a simmer and cook, covered, until tender (usually 1 1/2 to 2 hours). Garbanzos, soybeans, and cannellini beans will take up to an hour longer. Black-eyed peas and anasazi beans cook more quickly and can be cooked without presoaking as can split peas and most dal.

Other methods for cooking beans follow. The same cleaning and seasoning principles apply no matter what method is used. In a slow cooker use the 4 to 1 ratio of water to beans and cook on high for 1 hour, then 8 to 10 hours on low. To oven bake, use a 5 to 1 ratio of water to beans. Bring the water and beans to a boil on top of the stove for 20 minutes, then bake at 350°F. for 4 to 5 hours. In a pressure cooker, use the 4 to 1 ratio of water to beans. Bring the beans and water to a boil, then skim off any foam. Lock the lid in place and cook the beans on medium heat for 30 to 45 minutes, or on high heat for 8 to 35 minutes. (For an excellent resource on pressure cooking, see *Cooking Under Pressure* by Lorna J. Sass.)

Whatever method of cooking beans you use, I advise cooking large quantities as a time-saving device. You may then use a small amount for a recipe and freeze the rest for later use. There are also a number of high-quality organic canned beans available. Using precooked beans will greatly reduce cooking time. If you use beans that are precooked, you may wish to adjust seasonings that would have been cooked into the dried beans in a preliminary stage of the recipe.

Grains

In many vegetarian main-course dishes, grains play a critical supportive role. The rice served with lightly broiled tofu gives both variety in texture and balance in protein as does the tortilla that wraps the beans. The grain may come in the form of bread or pasta, or it may be served as the whole cooked grain. A wide range of whole grains is readily available in bulk at natural foods grocery stores. You may find as many as 10 varieties of rice—each with a different flavor and tendency towards stickiness—as well as millet, barley, quinoa, and so on. Whole grains may be cooked by boiling, steaming, pressure cooking, or long soaking. The most common method is as follows:

1. Place the grain in a bowl, cover with cold water, and rub the grain between your fingers to remove all talc and surface dirt. Drain the grain through a fine mesh strainer, then return it to the empty washing bowl. Again cover it with cold water and rinse it well by rubbing, then strain it a second time. Continue this washing and straining process until the water runs clear.

2. Place the grain and 2 to 3 times its volume of liquid (water and/or stock) along with any flavorings such as salt, minced onion, or garlic in a heavy-bottomed saucepan. Be sure to use a pan that will allow room for the grain to expand. (Most grains double or triple in volume, though millet and barley expand to 4 times their original volume.)

3. Place over high heat and bring to a boil. Stir once, then cover, reduce to a simmer and cook undisturbed until the grain is tender and the liquid is absorbed.

4. Fluff the grain by tossing it with the tines of a fork. Set aside, covered, until ready to use.

Noodles

Many varieties and shapes of noodles are called for in the recipes that follow. For the most part, you may substitute different noodles for those recommended; however, the balance of the recipe may be altered slightly. For instance, if you substituted udon noodles for angel hair in the tofu "sausage" with angel hair recipe (page 40), the colors would be very different and you would need to have bright-colored vegetables to complement the noodles. Also, because udon are slightly thicker than angel hair noodles, you might want to break the tofu into larger pieces so that the textures would feel balanced. Substituting one very different shaped noodle for another may have a radical effect (good or bad) on the recipe.

Noodles made from various flours (corn, quinoa, artichoke, etc.) are interesting to experiment with. Traditional Italian noodles are usually made from wheat or semolina flour. They may or may not contain eggs—check the label if this is a concern. Those that do not contain eggs are usually labeled "cholesterol free." Noodles made from alternative flours may also contain wheat, so check labels for a complete list of ingredients if wheat is problematic in your diet.

Oils

One of the most effective steps you can take to reduce fat in your diet is to select high-quality oils for cooking. The notion may sound contradictory, but because most high-quality oils are superior in flavor to those of lesser quality, smaller amounts produce the desired effect and therefore you can use less. When selecting an oil you must consider its flavor, its consistency (light or thick), and how it is produced. The smell and taste of the best-quality oils are reminiscent of the nut or seed from which they are extracted. Depending on the type of oil and how saturated it is, it may feel more or less light as it coats your tongue. Of course, flavor and consistency are difficult to judge without tasting an oil, so experience must be your guide.

The way an oil was produced may be stated on the label. Most are manufactured through one of three processes: by use of a chemical solvent ("solvent extraction"), "mechanical" or "expeller pressing," or "cold pressing." An oil may then be "refined" as a means of removing a variety of naturally occurring materials to produce an oil that can withstand higher heat without burning. Most mass market oils are extracted through the use of chemical solvents and many are treated with chemical preservatives or defoaming agents during the refining process. Most small companies that produce "natural" oils which are labeled "mechanically pressed" or "expeller pressed" are made with little or no chemical treatment to speed up the extraction process. Another term that sometimes appears on oil labels is "cold pressed." The term is often misapplied as true cold pressed oils are produced by a mechanical batch-pressing process in which the temperatures remain below 120ºF. and hydraulic presses or refrigerated in-line cooling devices are used on expeller presses. *Spectrum Naturals* (an oil manufacturer in Petaluma, California) produces four varieties of high-quality, cold-pressed oils. The extraction method for olive oils is seldom stated on the label as they are so soft that they need not be heated in the preliminary stages of extraction.

The term "high oleic oil" also sometimes appears on oil labels. This is an indication of the molecular makeup of the oil and has nothing to do with the manufacturing process. High oleic oil has been associated with lower cholesterol levels in some populations and lower rates of some forms of cancer.

Another concern of many consumers is rancidity in oil. Oils become rancid (spoiled) after prolonged contact with air, light, and/or heat. A rancid oil usually has a strong, unpleasant odor and a sharp flavor. (The oil in nuts and seeds also becomes rancid under the same conditions. A rancid nut or seed will have a similar unpleasant taste.) Refined oils become rancid less easily than those that are non-refined, however it is more difficult to detect rancidity in refined oils because their flavor and odor bodies have been removed. It is best to buy oil in small quantities and store it in a cool, dark place. If oil will not be used within 2 months of purchase, it is best refrigerated.

In the recipes that follow I always specify a particular type of oil, but vegetable oils may be used interchangeably in most instances. The exceptions to this are that toasted sesame oil has such a distinctive flavor that it is best used only in small amounts for added flavor, and oils with low smoking points should not be used for frying over high temperatures. When choosing which oil to use in a dish consider how the oil will taste with other ingredients in the recipe and whether or not the oil would be typically used in the cuisine from which a recipe is inspired. For instance, olive oil is most appropriate in a Mediterranean-style dish and peanut oil would be good in a curry. Whatever oil you choose, it should lend a subtle tone of integrity to a dish, never dominate it. Having at least three distinctly different types of oil to choose from when you cook will give you the capacity to arrive at very different and distinctive flavors in dishes you prepare. I recommend having a mild-tasting vegetable oil with a relatively high smoking point.

Refined peanut oil with a smoking point of 450°F. or refined canola oil with a smoking point of 400°F. are good choices. Also select a high-quality olive oil which smokes between 325°F. and 350°F. and serves well for light sautéing.

Olive oil has become an increasingly popular choice as a basic oil. Its fruity flavor, rich aroma and smooth consistency lend a rich, satisfying quality to salads as well as cooked dishes. It has a low smoking point which makes it appropriate for sautéing, but it cannot tolerate the higher temperature required to stir-fry. The oil extracted from the olives' first pressing is called "virgin" olive oil. "Extra virgin" olive oil is considered the best, with the finest flavor and the lowest acid content. "Fine virgin" and "plain virgin" olive oils also come from the first pressing, but they have respectively higher acid contents. "Pure" olive oil is the least desirable, as it is that from the second pressing and often tastes very strong, but not smooth and fruity. It may have a slightly bitter taste, though an attempt is usually made to remove it by washing the oil in hot water or treating it with chemicals. Olives grown in different climates and soils may have noticeably different flavors and—like grapes grown in different vineyards—may yield oils of equally different flavors, colors and aromas. The fact that olive oil can range in character from very fruity and green to mellow and gold is one reason for its popularity. But it is also considered one of the most "heart healthy" choices because its particular monounsaturated makeup is associated with lower cholesterol levels.

Toasted sesame oil is good to have on hand to use in Oriental-style dishes. Its aroma—the appealing scent that often first strikes you as you enter a Chinese restaurant—whets the appetite and adds sparkle to the surface of foods when added. Because it is so dominant in character, toasted sesame oil is best used in very small amounts (1 to 2 teaspoons), added only as a finishing touch to a dish.

Cook's Note: An oil's "smoking point" is the temperature at which it begins to smoke and once an oil smokes it may soon burn. Burned oil has an unpleasant, penetrating flavor and its molecular structure begins to break down, releasing free radicals—unattached molecules that bond easily with oxygen. (Free radicals have been associated with aging.) An oil's smoking point rises when it is refined as impurities that burn are removed in the process. For more information on the fat content in oils, see the chart on page 18.

Dairy Products

All foods that are derived from milk may be referred to as dairy products. Dairy products play an important role in many vegetarians' diets because, except for butter, they are a good source of protein and calcium. Dairy products are also readily available and, when first experimenting with vegetarian foods, dairy products such as cheese and yogurt may seem more familiar—less alienating—than other nonmeat alternatives. Dairy products can broaden the range of potential textures and flavors within vegetarian dishes, but too much of them may cause problems.

First, in spite of the positive nutritional contribution of dairy products (protein and calcium), many are high in fat. Yogurt, milk, and some cheeses are available in reduced or nonfat form, but most cheeses, butter, and other whole-milk products are often one of the highest contributors of fat in a vegetarian diet. In addition, dairy products, and eggs are the only source of cholesterol for vegetarians. A high-fat diet may contribute to higher serum cholesterol levels, and this risk is increased in diets also high in cholesterol. A balanced vegetarian diet includes a wide range of foods—beans, grains, lots of fresh fruit and vegetables—so that moderate amounts of cheese, other dairy products, and eggs pose no risk. But if cheese sandwiches, omelettes, yogurt and pizza become the mainstay, a vegetarian diet could be extremely high in fat and quite unhealthy.

Many people experience an increase in mucus when high-fat dairy products or excessive amounts of any dairy products are included in the diet. Current medical research shows no direct connection between mucus production and consumption of dairy products. Nonetheless, many people who experience chest or nasal congestion find some relief when they reduce their intake of dairy products.

Another problem some people experience with milk is the inability to properly digest the milk sugar lactose. For lactose to be properly absorbed into the system, it must first be broken down by an intestinal enzyme called lactase. In most populations, lactase levels are high at birth, then slowly after the age of two the levels drop. In some people lactase virtually disappears with age. People with this enzyme deficiency are said to be "lactose intolerant." Those with severe lactose intolerance may experience gas, abdominal cramping, or bloating after eating non-cultured liquid milk products. For most others, small amounts of lactose-containing foods are not a problem, especially if consumed with other foods. In severe cases of lactose intolerance, all sources of lactose (milk, cream, evaporated milk, dry milk powder, ice cream as well as yogurt, buttermilk, and sweet acidophilus milk that do *not* contain active cultures) must be avoided. Soft and hard ripened cheeses as well as buttermilk, yogurt, sour cream, and acidophilus milk that contain live lactobacilli cultures are usually tolerable to those who are lactose-intolerant.

Finally, there is growing concern as to the effect that commercial dairy products may have on our health. Residue from the antibiotics, parasiticides and growth hormones the cows themselves are given may be transmitted to people through their milk. More importantly, the diets fed to commercial cows are under scrutiny because residue from anything the animals ingest may end up in the milk. Commercial feed is made from grain that may be highly treated with herbicides, pesticides, and other chemicals as is commercial hay (which comprises about 50% of most dairy cows' diet). Organic cheese, milk and yogurt have recently become available in some parts of the country. One of the biggest organic milk production companies (Horizon Organic dairy products) now supplies organic milk and yogurt on the East and West Coasts and many parts of the central United States. Organic dairy products are made from milk produced by cows that eat 100% organic grain and hay, live on farms that have been certified organic (the land itself is not treated with chemical fertilizers, pesticides, etc.), and the cows are given no growth hormones. If antibiotics or other medications are given to the cows, their milk is not used for two years. As with all organic foods, the best way to support existing manufacturers and encourage others to work towards supplying organic products is to buy organic foods and ask for it at your local markets.

There is also concern that residue from some milk cartons may enter the milk as the milk rests in the carton. Buying milk sold in glass containers or transferring cartoned milk to a glass pitcher (with a lid) can lessen this risk.

The most commonly used dairy products in the recipes that follow are cheese and butter. Nondairy substitutes for both (oil for butter, soy cheese for cheese) will always function in the recipes. When I suggest using a dairy product it is always for a specific effect in a recipe that is most effectively attained with the suggested ingredient. The same basic principle applies to using dairy products as to oil; select for quality and use sparingly.

Eggs

The egg has gone in and out of favor over the past few decades. Years ago it was considered the model source of protein, against which the protein in other foods was measured. Later, fat and cholesterol became matters of national concern, and eggs quickly fell out of favor. The fear of eggs tapered off when we began to remind ourselves that dietary cholesterol is more of a concern in an overall high-fat diet than it is on its own. So the idea of an egg now and then became acceptable. Then we became aware of how much salmonella was spread through consumption of eggs and, again, eggs were relegated to the unwanted list. Where does all this leave us with regard to including eggs in the diet?

From a diner's point of view it is very simple. If you choose to include eggs in the diet, do so in moderation. An average of one or two eggs a week (including those in baked goods, breadings, prepared and packaged foods) is reasonable for most of us. Never eat raw eggs, and discard eggs with even a hairline crack in the shell through which harmful bacteria can spread.

From a culinary standpoint, eggs are one of the most complex ingredients to be found. The white (main protein portion) is used in soufflés, custards, baked goods, cakes and meringues to give unparalleled lightness. It is also used to glaze baked goods, clarify stocks and, when mixed with a small amount of oil, may be used effectively without the yolk in many baked goods or even omelettes. The yolk (which contains some protein as well as fat and cholesterol) is used as an emulsifier—holding liquids in suspension—which can bind and it gives foods a rich and creamy quality. (For a more detailed understanding of the egg and its culinary properties, consult *On Food and Cooking* by Harold McGee.) Because of the egg's versatile and unique culinary function, I include a handful of recipes in this book that call for eggs.

From the standpoint of the shopper, we must look for keys to quality. Eggs are graded according to quality of the white and yolk. AA eggs are the highest grade with the thickest whites and strongest yolks. Grading is not an indication of freshness. As a matter of fact, eggs age at similar rates, most quickly over the first two days after being laid. Eggs may also be categorized according to size (extra large, large, etc.). Recipes contained in this book have been tested using extra large eggs. Eggs also come with either white or brown shells. Shell color is largely determined by the type of chicken that laid the egg, so either color is a good choice.

Whatever the grade, the best choice is always the freshest. The best method for judging an egg's freshness is to crack it open and look at it. A very fresh egg will have a yolk that is rounded and high in shape. As an egg ages, contact with the air in the shell causes the white to become less able to support the weight of the yolk and the yolk spreads out flatter. As it is not reasonable to crack eggs open before you buy them, the best means of insuring freshness is to buy eggs from a reputable market with a fast turnover.

You may find "free range" and "fertile" eggs at local markets. Those labeled "free range" are produced by chickens who do exactly that: they wander around their barnyard, rather than being caged in an overcrowded coop. They are usually not given antibiotics or other medications and are often fed organic grain. Free range eggs are usually more expensive than commercially produced eggs, but a good value. Fertile eggs are also likely to be from free range chickens, but the eggs have been fertilized by the male. Some people feel it beneficial to eat a food with such a "strong life force" and, for exactly the same reason, others would just as soon have non-fertilized eggs.

Salt

Salt is another ingredient that has been under scrutiny by health professionals during the past decade or so. It began when the link between salt and an increase in hypertension and high blood pressure became clear. A practical move seemed to be to reduce salt intake as a precautionary measure. Many of us did so and recognized that once the palate is sensitized to lower levels of salt, a small amount can accentuate flavors without dominating a dish.

Years after salt's ill effects became recognized, however, research showed that not all people are sensitive to its ill effects. In fact, even some people with hypertension or high blood pressure are not sensitive. That is not to say we should heavily salt foods, it simply means that using small amounts of salt sensibly as we cook may be reasonable in terms of health and, on occasion, preferable in terms of taste. From a culinary standpoint, salt used sparingly can bring out and harmonize flavors in many dishes.

The question of sea salt as opposed to mined salt sometimes arises. Many people feel that the trace minerals present in sea salt make it superior to other salts. An interesting note is that because most salt manufacturers use the least expensive form of salt available, most salt sold in this country is sea salt, though many brands do not specify their source.

A Note About Organic Foods

Organic foods are those grown without the use of chemical pesticides and herbicides. Organic farmers rely on crop rotation, soil management, and crop selection to produce foods in the "cleanest" environment possible. The result is not only that the food produced is free of possibly harmful residue from chemical treatment, but so is the land and runoff that joins the local groundwater system. Hence both consumers and the environment benefit from organic farming methods.

Large supermarkets often have small sections of organic produce, but local farmers' markets and natural foods stores usually offer a wide range of organic foods. Many food manufacturers are producing various types of organic foods—from flours and grains to canned beans and convenience foods. At the time of the writing of this book, only two large dairy farms producing organic milk and milk products exist in this country (see dairy products, page 12), but the number of farmers employing organic methods is growing exponentially. The best way to encourage farmers and food manufacturers to produce organic foods is to buy them.

Stocking Your Pantry

The single most effective means I have found of offering variety at mealtime is to have a well-stocked pantry. First, having a varied stash of dried goods is critical; they serve as the base for many dishes. It is good practice to have four or more types of dried beans to use as the base for sauces, stews or salads; several types of rice; a variety of shapes and styles of pasta; and four or five whole grains. It is sensible to stock one or more types of flour, as well as cornstarch or kuzu, to use as a thickener in sauces.

Dried spices are essential, and those you should keep depend on your personal taste. Store dried spices in a cool, dark place and buy only as much as you are likely to use within six months. After a year, most spices become flat and are best replaced.

High-quality bouillon cubes are good to have in a pinch, when fresh stock is unavailable. Having several forms of sweeteners allows for versatility. A selection of nuts and seeds as well as one or two types of nut or seed butters allows for depth in recipes.

A well-stocked condiment shelf should include mustard, three types of oil (page 11), soy sauce or tamari, and three or more types of vinegar. You should also stock pickled ginger, olives, and two or more types of miso, in addition to other items like capers and pickled peppers that you find yourself using on a regular basis.

I recommend using fresh foods as often as possible, but in a pinch certain canned or packaged foods can save the day. Two or three types of canned beans, high-quality whole peeled tomatoes, tomato paste and peeled green chilies, as well as sweet red peppers are ingredients that will aid in assembling meals in less than 15 minutes. Seitan Mix (from Arrowhead Mills) makes seitan available within minutes, and shelf-safe boxes of tofu can be useful in preparing sauces or using in place of eggs.

Always have onions, shallots, garlic, and ginger on hand as one or more of them can serve as the beginning of virtually any dish you can imagine.

Finally, have an assortment of prepared items that you have made yourself. These can be the most valuable of all. Stock, sauces, and cooked beans can be frozen in 1-cup containers. Tempeh freezes very well, so having an extra batch of it or frozen tofu is helpful. Pesto (page 176), peeled peppers (page 35), and most marinades can be stored in the refrigerator or freezer and can serve as the base for sauces or as a directing flavor in many dishes. Minced garlic and ginger can be refrigerated for 2 weeks if covered completely with oil. You can then dip into them when you stir-fry or sauté, or use their soaking oil as you cook.

Most fresh produce can be cleaned and refrigerated in loosely wrapped plastic bags ready to use in an instant. You may also refrigerate or freeze baked onions or garlic (page 36), puréed baked potatoes or sweet potatoes to use for sauces, and reduced stocks—which serve as a sort of homemade bouillon cube. Finally, as you cook, do not hesitate to make double batches of whole recipes (half to freeze) or of the grain or bean component of the recipe. Either may be dressed with a salad dressing, or stored plain, then they may be incorporated into a meal a few days later.

What Is a Healthy Diet?

No diet is healthy for everyone. People differ remarkably with respect to what foods seem to contribute to a state of well-being, and as an individual's health evolves, so do dietary needs. While human nutrition is a relatively new science and there are many aspects of it that are not thoroughly understood, it makes sense to eat foods that have been adulterated as little as possible—choosing organic and whole foods while staying away from highly processed foods, artificial ingredients, and chemical additives. It also makes sense to eat a wide range of foods, none to excess.

The amount of fat we consume in our diet is a matter of great concern. Diets high in fat, particularly saturated fat, have been linked with a number of health problems including an increased incidence of heart disease, obesity, and some forms of cancer. Experts agree that a diet with no more than 25 to 30% calories from fat is sensible for overall good health. But what does all this mean, and how can it be incorporated into everyday eating? The overview below may help clarify the subject. For more information about diet, nutrition and health, I recommend consulting Jane Brody's books on diet and nutrition as well as *Good Food: A Shopper's Guide to Eating Well* by Margaret Wittenberg.

What Is Fat?

Fat is a calorie-dense nutrient found in some foods. In cooking, the term "fat" may be used in a general sense to denote the source of fat—butter, oil or animal fat—contained in a dish. "Fat" is also used specifically in reference to more saturated fats such as butter or lard. "Oil" refers to that which is extracted from nuts, seeds, or beans, and it is always liquid at room temperature.

In simple nutrition terms, fats and oils are both classified as triglycerides and differ from each other in melting point. All fats are composed of combinations of molecular structures called fatty-acid chains. A fatty-acid chain is made up of a series of carbon molecules that have bonded together. Each carbon has three sides not connected to a neighboring carbon to which a hydrogen molecule may bond. When a chain of carbons has a hydrogen on every available side, it is called saturated.

Some carbon chains contain double bonds between one or more of the carbons. This double-bonding eliminates an available spot onto which a hydrogen could bond, and the chain is then referred to as unsaturated. If a chain has one such double bond, it is called monounsaturated. If two or more double carbon bonds exist, the chain is called polyunsaturated.

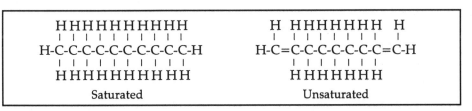

All oils and fats are composed of a combination of fatty acids—some saturated, some unsaturated. Those with a higher percentage of saturated chains are called saturated and those with more unsaturated chains are called unsaturated. Animal fat tends to be more highly saturated than fat derived from plants (with the exception of coconut oil and palm kernel oil). Saturated fat is solid at room temperature and unsaturated fat is liquid. You might wonder how margarine and shortening, both produced from unsaturated vegetable oil, can be solid at room temperature? It is because they have been "hydrogenated." In the process of hydrogenation, an oil is exposed to hydrogen while being heated under high pressure. A tiny bit of nickel is added to the oil as a catalyst (it is later filtered out). The result is that double bonds between carbons break down, allowing the carbons to bond to the hydrogen that is present. The oil is artificially saturated and is, therefore, solid at room temperature. Because the process changes the molecular structure of fats, I recommend caution in using any hydrogenated fats in the diet.

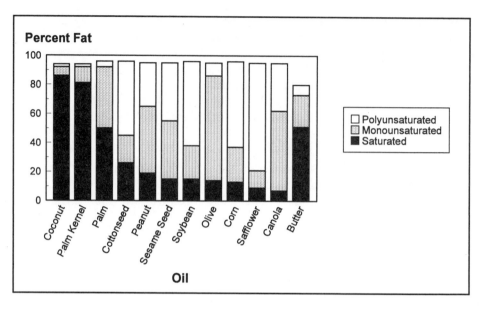

Why Use Fat?

Certain vitamins (A, D, E and K) are fat-soluble, which means they cannot be assimilated into the system without the presence of some fat. Also, vegetable oils are rich sources of linoleic acid, an essential fatty acid that is not synthesized by the body and, therefore, must be consumed. Nonetheless, only a very small amount of fat is necessary to serve these functions and maintain good health.

When we cook, fat functions in several important—and different—ways. In pastry doughs, for example, fats added to dry flour weaken the bonding capacity of gluten molecules which when bonded contribute to a dough's elasticity. As such, fat affects a dough's flakiness. Fats also can help lighten batters and contribute tenderness and moisture to baked goods.

Another important culinary function of fats is to produce a crisp skin on a food cooked in it. Fat can be heated to a much higher temperature than water before it boils (depending on the type of fat, its boiling point ranges from 500°F. to 750°F.), so when a food is dropped into hot (375°F.) fat, the surface of the food cooks quickly. Liquids inside the food are temporarily sealed in by the cooked "skin." Immediately after a food is added to hot fat, however, the temperature of the fat drops. So if the food is left to cook in the fat, osmosis begins and liquid from inside the food seeps out as fat is drawn in, resulting in greasy-tasting food. The amount of fat a food absorbs may be reduced if a food remains in the fat for a very brief time and is then removed as in stir-frying. The outside layer of the food begins to cook, but before the temperature of the fat drops and osmosis begins, drawing fat into the food, the food is removed. This is the underlying principle behind stir-frying.

Another gastronomic function of fats is to mellow and harmonize flavors. This is most noticeable when fat is added to a food without cooking as in the case of oil in salad dressing or butter creamed into a filling.

The sensation of eating fat is an interesting one. Fat coats the inside of the mouth when we eat, giving a sensation of satiation and satisfaction. Once you begin reducing the amount of fat you eat, say using low-fat milk instead of regular milk, you are likely to become more sensitive to this coating sensation and high-fat foods may seem greasy and distasteful. By the same token, when just a small amount of fat is present, the richness and sense of satisfaction it can lend to a dish may become more apparent. Using fat to add grace (rather than heaviness) to a dish requires a delicate touch and precise attention to the ingredients contained in the dish. When it comes to using fat, moderation is the key.

How Much Fat?

How much fat is too much? To some degree the question must be answered on an individual and daily basis. For someone with a history of heart disease, a virtually fat-free diet may be recommended. For most of us, eating a balanced, low-fat diet (about 30% calories from fat) is reasonable.

If you strive to make every mouthful of every meal derive less than 30% of its calories from fat, you may feel deprived and your diet can be difficult to maintain. It is also time-consuming to calculate your fat consumption for every meal. Consider instead the simple approach to lowering fat in the diet by *thinking* before you eat. If you have at the forefront of your awareness the dangers of too much fat, while at the same time understanding the culinary contribution of fat, you can decide when and where in your diet it is appropriate to add fat. By learning to identify high-fat foods and including only small amounts of them in your routine diet, you can then liberate yourself to eat simply and sensibly, sandwiching higher fat meals between those that are low in fat.

Identifying high-fat foods is relatively simple. Nuts, seeds, coconut, avocados, soy beans, oil, butter, cheese, whole milk dairy products and eggs are higher in fat than most other whole vegetarian foods. Prepared and processed foods are often high in fat (check labels). If the feeling and taste of fat overpowers any subtle quality of a food, too much fat is present. Use fat with moderation, if at all, as you cook and avoid it as much as possible in foods you do not prepare.

What Are Fat Calories?

Fat molecules are extremely efficient at storing energy, so that each gram of fat contributes about 9 calories to the diet (about twice that of a gram of carbohydrate or protein). Consequently, calories from fats can add up quickly. For example, if you prepare a simple ratatouille (vegetable stew) by steaming the vegetables rather than frying them in oil before simmering them together, each large serving will contain about 120 calories with 0% fat calories. If instead you sauté the vegetables first (the traditional method of preparation), the calories per serving may as much as triple with 65% fat calories. So although in both instances you would be eating a relatively healthy dish, the second version would be far beyond the recommended fat percentage. To calculate the percentage of fat calories, multiply the total grams of fat by 9 (the number of calories in one gram of fat). Take that number and divide it by the total number of calories in the food. For example, an average whole milk yogurt contains 200 calories and 9 grams of fat, so the calculation for it would be:

9 (grams) x 9 (calories) = 81 calories from fat $\dfrac{81 \text{ (calories from fat)}}{200 \text{ (total calories)}} = 40\%$ fat calories

Another question that arises for many people trying to control fat in their diet is how many grams of fat are appropriate. To calculate grams of fat divide 30% of your ideal caloric intake by 9 (the number of calories in one gram of fat). As an example, let's say you average 1,800 calories a day; 30% of that is 540, so 60 grams of fat is the maximum you should have.

What About Cholesterol?

After fat, the next most pressing dietary concern is cholesterol. The term applies to both serum cholesterol (that produced in the body) and dietary cholesterol (that found in food). Research indicates that in addition to a high-fat diet, one high in cholesterol can contribute to heart disease. Although high intake of dietary cholesterol can raise cholesterol levels, other factors such as an overall high-fat diet (especially one high in saturated fat), heredity, and stress seem to contribute to high cholesterol as well.

Dietary cholesterol is found only in animal products, so for a vegetarian the only sources of cholesterol are dairy products (butter, cheese, milk, etc.) and eggs. A vegan diet, which does not include either dairy products or eggs, is free of dietary cholesterol. A vegetarian who eats mainly cheese and other dairy products could consume a high-cholesterol (and high-fat) diet.

What About Protein?

Many people considering a vegetarian diet are concerned about getting enough protein without meat. It is a legitimate concern. In order for protein to be synthesized by the body, 22 amino acids must be present. All except 8 of these can be manufactured by the body. Those that cannot are called "essential amino acids" and they must be supplied through the protein consumed in the diet. Animal protein supplies all essential amino acids, whereas most plant sources of protein contain some, but not all. If even one essential amino acid is missing, protein cannot be fully synthesized. Therefore, many people concluded a number of years back that unless plant proteins were combined properly—foods weak in some essential amino acids combined with foods strong in those that were missing—a vegetarian diet (especially one that did not include dairy products) ran the risk of being protein-deficient. Hence the notion that beans (strong in some amino acids) should be combined with grains (strong in complementary amino acids) became a popular solution to the vegetarian protein requirement. This is certainly not a bad habit to cultivate and is actually traditionally part of many cuisines—beans wrapped in a tortilla, tofu served with rice, or dal with rice. In addition, from a gustatory perspective, combining beans and grains usually gives a much more satisfying feel to the diner than either one does alone.

In recent years, however, it has become clear that although plant protein is not as "complete" as animal protein, it would be almost impossible for a vegetarian diet that is made up primarily of whole foods and meets caloric requirements not to provide ample protein—and appropriate amino acids—even when foods are not consciously combined for the purpose of protein complementing.

A great deal of the original concern over vegetarian protein deficiency was due to the fact that our nutritional standards were set for and by a culture that eats a predominantly meat-based diet. The most sensible approach, therefore, is to include one rich source of protein (beans, soy foods, or dairy products) in each meal and to accompany it with other foods that provide additional forms of protein (vegetables and grains). For more information on vegetarian protein consumption, see *A Vegetarian Sourcebook* by Keith Akers.

A healthy diet *is* a highly individual and personal matter, one that evolves with lifestyle and other aspects of our health. Ultimately the signals your own body gives you as to what feels healthy must be your guide—this is simply an awareness that must be constantly cultivated.

2 • The Fundamentals

What do you want for supper? How about a fat, juicy slab of tofu? Somehow, the notion doesn't quite hit the spot, does it? Unlike the meat in a traditional Western entrée, the major source of protein in most vegetarian dishes is usually not what springs to mind when contemplating supper. In vegetarian dishes, the main source of protein is usually very mild in character and depends on spicing and cooking treatment in order to make the dish a success. So relying on the image of plain tofu or beans for inspiration can be disastrous. But there are virtually no limits to the types of vegetarian dishes you can create if you understand the nature of the foods you are working with and the process of creating a recipe that appeals to what you feel like eating.

In this chapter we explore the fundamentals of creating interesting vegetarian entrées. First, we examine how a dish is constructed—the elements that successfully draw the ingredients of a dish together. Next, we review basic cooking methods and techniques that help to make cooking enjoyable so that the ingredients can shine in their individual glory.

There are five elements that contribute to a successful dish and, within a successful recipe, these elements are harmoniously balanced. It is useful to look at the elements separately as a means of gaining insight into which ingredients comprise them and how each functions within a dish. The first element that comes to mind when you are creating a dish is its "character," its tastes and aromas. The character is the root of inspiration. Next you can consider the "form" the dish will take. This usually is determined mostly by the main source of protein that will be in the dish (tofu, beans, etc.). "Structure" (the next element) is given to a dish by the vegetables, pastas, grains or other ingredients added to complement the form and support the character. Sometimes a sauce or enrichment is necessary to give "balance" or act as a liaison between parts in a dish. Finally, the way in which a dish is presented offers the element of "beauty" that invites the diner to take part in the meal.

Tastes and Aromas: The Element of Character

When we stop for a moment to consider what it is we *feel* like eating, tastes, textures and aromas are at the root of desire. The feeling that arises (it starts somewhere deep in the belly and blossoms in the back of the mouth) is the "character" we are searching for in a particular dish. In its simplest form, one ingredient springs to mind—the sweet taste of corn or the smooth texture of tofu. Sometimes a general blending of flavors and aromas, such as Chinese food or curry, appeal. Or we may have the urge for a particular dish that has a striking combination of tastes and textures, such as pasta with pesto sauce.

The first element to consider whether following a recipe or designing a dish is the dish's character, which is determined by the sensual qualities of the seasonings and ingredients it contains. Once you experience the character of a dish, all of your senses hook in, the process flows and you no longer have to think about every step of preparation as you cook. In my experience, this is when I can cook with true enthusiasm and creativity.

The way to hook into a dish's character is simply to empty the palate. When preparing a recipe, if you concentrate on the ingredients and how they are assembled, with your palate empty, the recipe should make sense. It will quickly become apparent what effect is being sought by combining the ingredients in the order listed, and what the final dish is likely to look, smell and taste like. With this information, the recipe should be easy to follow. (This is why reading through an entire recipe before beginning is often recommended).

When creating an original recipe, if you focus on what really sounds good to eat, you can then build on whatever it is that strikes your fancy. For example, imagine that kale is what attracts you. Are you drawn to its crunchy texture when lightly steamed, or to puréed kale as part of a sauce? Is the thought of its simple, unadorned flavor appealing, or does it sound better coupled with certain spices or another ingredient? Do you imagine it steaming hot or at room temperature? These are the questions that, when answered, will establish the character you seek. In this way you can build on the nature of the ingredients, slowly and carefully layering onto your palate the combination of tastes, textures, aromas and temperatures that you find appealing. The result should be a dish that is absolutely perfect for your tastes.

Taste and aroma are usually more critical than texture and temperature with regard to character. Within a dish there are the taste and aroma of the main ingredients themselves, plus those contributed by spices and seasonings you may add. A tenet of French cooking, one that contributes to the refined quality for which it is renowned, is that no single ingredient should ever overpower a dish and no ingredient should obscure another. That is not to say that strong ingredients are taboo or that a dish should not have the distinctive flavor of a particular ingredient. Quite the contrary. It means that ingredients should never be combined if they conflict in any way with each other. The timing of when you sense the flavor of an ingredient, as well as the flavors themselves, must be carefully calculated. Combining the mild taste of artichokes, for example, with the powerful bite of lemon can be successful because the strong taste of lemon drops off quite quickly in the mouth, whereas artichokes are notorious for their mild flavor and lingering aftertaste.

The character of a dish is directed by the flavors of the main ingredients—the protein, vegetables and grain used. When you add a crunchy vegetable or a light-colored grain, the addition of contrasting or complementary textures or colors will make sense. As you add one support flavor—vinegar, for example—others, like lemon juice, become less appropriate. With this sort of interplay in mind, you can discern which flavors you want and then what aromas, textures and temperatures will support the character.

Good cuisines worldwide apply the same principle, as centuries of culinary tradition have evolved intricate balances of native flavors that work. In her book, *Ethnic Cuisine*, Elizabeth Rozin sheds interesting light on how absolutely distinctive subtle changes of ingredients can be in identifying classic cuisines. She postulates that a number of "flavor principles" exist to characterize cuisines, and that slight variations in these principles make neighboring cuisines recognizably different. One simple example she offers is that soy sauce—rice wine—gingerroot are typical of China (with additional subtle variations according to region), whereas soy sauce—sake—sugar are typical of Japan. This type of attention to the successful interplay of flavors is at the root of understanding character in a dish.

The Main Protein: The Element of Form

The main source of protein contained in an entrée gives the dish "form" in the sense that form defines something as recognizable. A dish can be dominated by its form, as in the case of a marinated broiled tofu or a seitan roast, in which case its form is simple, similar to that of many main-course meat dishes. Alternatively, the main protein can play a supportive role, as in the case of pasta with beans or B'stilla, in which case the form is more of a backdrop upon which the character plays and around which other elements are built.

The four main sources of protein predominantly used in dishes in this book are tofu, tempeh, seitan and beans. Some recipes also include cheese and I occasionally incorporate eggs. Tofu, tempeh and seitan tend to be more dominant in form, whereas cheese and eggs (except in the case of soufflés) are generally more supportive in form. Beans are the most versatile main source of protein with regard to form, working equally well as the main focus—in baked beans, for example—as they do as a background ingredient, as in Fluffy Bean Cakes (page 81).

One substantive difference, when working with tofu, tempeh, seitan or beans (rather than meat) is that they must all be prepared to a greater or lesser degree before beginning a recipe. Tofu is usually pressed, tempeh steamed, seitan simmered, and beans precooked. In effect you must make the "meat" of the dish before you even begin preparing a recipe. This added step can be a hurdle when you are first learning to work with vegetarian recipes, but once you become accustomed to thinking ahead far enough in advance to prepare them at your leisure, working ahead of time can become second nature. Another notable trait of vegetarian protein sources is that, except for cheese, their texture is usually as critical, if not more so, than their taste.

Tofu is particularly interesting because, depending on the style used, whether or not it is pressed or frozen and how it is cooked, its texture can be extremely different. Firm tofu that has been pressed and steamed is very similar in texture to a firm-fleshed fish. A very fresh, soft tofu can be scrambled and will seem almost like eggs, whereas tofu that is frozen, pressed, and crumbled is similar in texture to ground meat. Puréed silken tofu, when mixed with strong flavors, and thinned with a flavorful stock, results in a creamy, rich-tasting sauce.

Tempeh and seitan are more unidimensional in texture, though both can produce slightly different effects depending on how they are cut. Tempeh's dense, granular texture is interesting if slabs are cubed or diced before cooking. The slabs may also be sliced in half horizontally, then cut into thin strips for a lighter effect. When crumbled or grated, tempeh gives a parallel effect to ground meat in stuffings and stews. No matter how the tempeh is cut, it is best used in recipes that require at least 20 minutes of cooking to increase its digestibility. Steaming tempeh for 15 minutes before marinating or adding it to a recipe also facilitates its ability to absorb flavors. Seitan is usually precooked (simmered) before adding it to a recipe. This step produces the finest texture and allows the seitan to absorb flavor from the broth in which it is precooked.

Beans offer a unique composite of textures, with no two beans being alike. Each can be evaluated in terms of its shape and the interplay of the whole-bean texture with other ingredients in the dish. It can also be considered in terms of how mealy, dry, or moist its interior is—compare the crunchy texture of garbanzo beans to smooth pinto beans, for instance. Finally, bean textures vary depending on their thickness. A lentil as compared to a kidney bean, for example, has a very low ratio of meat to skin.

Eggs and cheese are unlike the other main proteins used in vegetarian entrées. Neither requires precooking (though eggs must be cooked before consumption) and their flavors—especially various types of cheese—are far more distinctive. The most important factor to keep in mind when cooking either eggs or cheese is that their textures become radically altered when cooked, and that cooking them too fast, too much, or not enough can be disastrous. (Again, this is in direct contrast to working with precooked ingredients which—other than soft tofu—are relatively indestructible.)

Eggs have a delicate capacity to bind, emulsify, and lighten foods. These all have to do with the protein structure of both yolks and whites. Protein molecules bond together—coagulate—to produce a thickened effect. Coagulation is most notably influenced by changes in heat. Gentle, even temperatures result in a desirable smooth and creamy cooked effect, whereas heating too quickly or overheating can cause eggs to become rubbery or to curdle. In addition to heat, the presence of salt or acid—even excess air bubbles—can alter molecular structure and cause coagulation. Egg yolks are also sometimes used in emulsified sauces such as a mayonnaise or hollandaise. In an emulsified sauce, tiny droplets of oil or butter are held in suspension within the water of the egg. The result is a sauce that is smooth, thick and creamy. I include only one sauce of this nature in this book—as a demonstration of the technique (Béarnaise, page 180)—because eggs are high in fat. Finally, the foaming effect of egg whites is remarkable, producing unmatched lightness in body and fluffiness in baked goods and soufflés. When beating egg whites, it is important always to work with very clean utensils and to separate the eggs carefully as even a tiny drop of fat or egg yolk will decrease the volume of the beaten whites.

Cheese, the final main protein included in the recipes, is used both for flavor and texture. Cheeses vary notably in character from hard, like Parmesan, to unripened, like ricotta; and from very pungent, like Gorgonzola, to mild, like mozzarella. Strongly flavored cheeses are usually added in small amounts to act as a punctuation of taste in a dish. Most often the characteristic flavor of a strong cheese and its salty quality are one of the first sensations to hit the palate, but they often drop off or change quickly in taste, leaving room for the other flavors in the dish to surface. Mild cheeses are more often added for the texture they contribute. When heated, the protein in cheese (casein) coagulates and separates from the fat and water that are present. This can cause cheese to become tough, chewy or—as in the familiar image of a slice of pizza being lifted from the pan—stringy. For this reason, cheese is often added just before serving or it is baked directly into a slow-cooked dish. Hard, well-ripened cheeses, like Parmesan, can stand higher temperatures than soft cheeses; and those with higher fat content are more easily blended into sauces. However cheese is used in cooking, it must be handled with care for the most desirable effect.

Even though the texture of the main protein is critical to determining the form of a dish, the taste is relevant to how that form will be constructed. Because tofu, tempeh and seitan are mild in flavor, they are often marinated or blended with strong-tasting sauces, spices, or salt at an early phase of a recipe. Though beans offer slightly more intensity and variety of flavor, they too are often combined with onion, garlic or seasonings when precooked. (However, if dried beans are given their first cooking in a liquid that contains salt or a highly acidic ingredient—such as tomatoes or lemon juice—the bean will be tough.) Beans may also be marinated before being stirred into a dish at the end, as a means of adding depth.

Vegetables and Grains: The Element of Structure

Fresh produce, grains, pasta, as well as nuts and seeds, contribute the simple though vital element of structure to vegetarian entrées. The structure is similar to the support beams and inner walls of a building. In the early stages of design and construction, they could be placed almost anywhere, but once the blueprint is made and the form determined, the best structure is usually obvious and without too many options. So it is with the creation of a dish. The character and inspiration are born, the form is decided upon, then the main body of ingredients—the structure—can be determined. Good structure ensures that a dish will be interesting to eat. When the texture, color, shape, and flavor of the structural ingredients are varied and complementary to each other and the main protein, then each bite of the dish is lively and appealing. If the structural ingredients are monotonous or inconsistent with the character of the dish, then the dish may be boring or confusing. Many dishes could be successful either with a minimal amount of structure, as in the case of Rosemary Orange Tofu (page 53), whereas others, like Penne with Beans (page 39), are dependent on a number of structural ingredients in order for them to work well. In many dishes the precise structure can be varied (rice instead of millet, or mixed vegetables instead of broccoli), but generally speaking the proportion of structural ingredients to those that determine form should remain consistent if the dish is to retain its character.

The most critical role structural ingredients play is to determine how a dish is cooked and what shape it will take. The inspiration of a flavorful couscous mixture as the carriage for a tofu-based orange sauce (page 130), for example, could have taken various structural turns. As it is, I suggest serving it as a stuffing for steamed artichokes, but it serves equally well baked in a winter squash or layered in a tofu loaf.

The structure is an important and playful element in a dish and probably the simplest to successfully vary when first adapting recipes. The key to understanding how to change structure is to determine what function the current structure serves and to experiment with structural ingredients of similar function: for example, vegetable for vegetable or grain for grain. The types of questions useful in understanding structure are as follows: Do the vegetables or grain serve as contrasting texture or form for the main protein or sauce? Which vegetables complement the character of the dish and would typically be served in the cuisine from which the flavors of the dish were inspired? What effect is achieved by cooking the dish in the prescribed manner of the recipe? The answers to these sorts of questions will clarify the structure of a dish and make obvious possible variations.

Sauces and Enrichments: The Element of Balance

Sauces unify the elements of a dish, and enrichments such as oil, nut butters, milk or cream, smooth out rough edges. Together they transform ordinary dishes into memorable, balanced works of art. Understanding the classic principles of saucing is essential to creating unique and varied vegetarian entrées because of the depth and refinement sauces can contribute to a dish. In developing sauce recipes for this book, I drew from two systems. First, the classic French system in which the sauce is usually prepared separately from the dish and often includes stock obtained from the same type of meat as is in the dish. Classic French sauces may be categorized into families, depending on how they are thickened and what serves as the main source of liquid. Though many are absolutely dependent on meat stock or meat glaze (reduced stock) for effect—so they cannot be directly transferred to vegetarian recipes—their categorization is helpful in understanding sauces in general. First, French sauces can be grouped as dark or light in color and warm or cold in temperature. All sauces fall within these categories, which may then be subdivided into what are often called "families." Members of the same family of sauces are thickened in the same way and usually contain the same type of liquid. "Mother" sauces are considered the prototype for a family; minor additions (an ingredient or spice) to the mother sauce produce the rest of the family. Once you know what a particular mother sauce is, you can understand, through a sort of cook's shorthand, how to prepare any member of the family by simply knowing what is added to its mother. Warm light mother sauces include Béchamel (roux—cooked flour and fat—base with milk), Velouté (roux base with stock), and Hollandaise (flavored egg yolks used to emulsify melted butter). Warm dark sauces include Demi-Glace (browned roux base with rich stock or meat glaze) and Tomato. Cold sauces include mayonnaise and vinaigrettes. The final family, simply referred to as butter sauces, incorporates butter as the main ingredient. Composed butter is that into which one or more ingredients or spices are added. Escargot Butter, for example (that which is stuffed into snails before baking), is butter into which garlic, lemon juice and parsley are added. Composed butters are usually melted directly onto a food at the table or just before removing from the heat. In the second type of butter sauce, plain butter is whisked into a reduced stock or liquid just before serving and is called a "mounted" butter sauce.

The second system of saucing, more typical of the Orient, relies less heavily on stocks and more on seasonings and flavors obtained from marinating and cooking the ingredients contained in the dish. Oriental-style sauces are usually prepared as part of the dish as it cooks, rather than separately. Light stocks are sometimes used, and though rich coconut milk may be included in the liquid for a sauce, it is unusual for an enrichment to be added at the end of cooking. For consistency, cornstarch, kuzu, or arrowroot mixed with water may be added.

Both the Oriental and French systems of saucing also include some sauces, like Indian chutney or French coulis, that are composed of raw or minimally cooked and roughly chopped fruits or vegetables.

I found the challenge of making sauces perplexing when I began working with vegetarian ingredients. Having trained in France and apprenticed with a

Chinese chef, I wondered how sauces comparable to the classics could possibly be made without meat-based stocks. Sauces, after all, are such an important part of French cuisine that in many restaurants a "saucier" (sauce chef) enjoys high rank in the kitchen hierarchy. The starting point for many sauces is a good stock and a rich, full-tasting vegetarian stock will enable you to make quality sauces.

What makes a stock good? Quite simply there are three basic rules to follow. First, always use fresh ingredients. Many people have the mistaken idea that a stock can be a sort of catch-all for kitchen trimmings, leftovers, or any food found buried in the corner of the vegetable drawer that isn't quite rotten enough to go directly to the compost. A stock made with stale or low-quality ingredients will, at best, taste uninteresting, but is more likely to taste stale. Second, try to understand the ingredients, then handle them properly and balance their flavors in a stock to achieve well-rounded tastes. For example, the inner layers of leeks are often filled with dirt, so they must be well cleaned; spinach will become grassy and bitter-tasting with long cooking; and more than a couple of stalks of celery can overpower many stocks. Any ingredient you might consider adding to a stock will have idiosyncratic qualities that must be considered before it is added. Third, use a high ratio of vegetables to liquid to produce a rich, full-tasting stock.

In Chapter 7, I include three basic stock recipes with a number of variations. Throwing together a stock usually takes no more than 15 minutes. It can then take care of itself until time to strain, after which it can be frozen for up to 3 months. Until you get into the habit of preparing stock on a regular basis, the process may seem too laborious. So begin with an exquisite stock (try porcini or ginger) one lazy afternoon to give yourself a sense of how simple it actually is. Your efforts will be rewarded with enough stock to make sauce for 8 to 10 dishes. Having stock in the freezer is like money in the bank because the inspiration for and preparation of any number of dishes has already begun.

On the other hand, never let the fact that you do not have homemade stock on hand stop you from preparing most dishes. (Any recipes in this book that hinge critically on the exact stock listed have notes as to how to approximate the desired flavor.) You may, in a pinch, use high-quality salt-free vegetable bouillon cube. If you choose the commercial route, be careful! Many brands of bouillon cubes, pastes and canned stocks are very salty and so dominant in flavor that any dish made from them will be overpowered and will taste like all others made with the same stock. Taste any prepared stock before you add it to a dish, then adjust seasonings accordingly. You are looking for a sauce that is unified or smooth in flavor with distinctive character. In this way the sauce can cleanly complement a dish rather than compete with it.

Good texture is essential to the success of a sauce. A sauce designed to be part of a dish is predominantly some sort of liquid which is given body, by one means or another, so that it can "nap" (coat) the main ingredients of the dish. The speed with which a sauce runs off ingredients when poured over them is its napping quality. A sauce may be very light—creating just a film over the surface, or more dense—seeming to briefly pause in its continuous flow over ingredients. Whatever the napping quality, a sauce, in Alma Lach's words, "should have body but not thickness" and should by no means be pasty or oily.

There are various methods for obtaining the desired texture in a sauce. Thickeners such as flour, cornstarch, or root starches, such as kuzu or arrowroot, may be added. This method of obtaining consistency is probably the simplest and most common throughout the world. When flour is used, it works best mixed with some form of fat. (Without fat it tends to leave a grainy residue in a sauce.) Though most forms of flour will thicken, the smoothest effect is obtained with wheat flour (preferably unbleached white). Other flours, especially rice flour, often result in a very grainy undertone, regardless of how much additional fat or enrichment is added. When using flour for consistency, the most common and effective method of incorporating it is to first cook the flour in fat. This flour-fat base is called a "roux." The roux may be cooked slowly for 1 to 3 minutes before the liquid is added. The sauce may then be simmered for 10 minutes or more to mellow the flavors and ensure that all raw-grain flavor is cooked from the flour. This is called a "white roux" and serves as the base for a standard white sauce or gravy. A roux that is cooked slowly for 15 to 45 minutes before the liquid is added will turn a beautiful brown (from very light to the color of chocolate). Its nutty flavor and color will impregnate the sauce which is usually cooked for at least 30 minutes after the liquid is added as a means of increasing depth and unifying flavors. When a roux is browned, careful attention must be given to remove any bits of overly cooked or burned flour before whisking in the liquid. Depending on the ratio of flour to fat, and the volume of liquid added, a roux-based sauce may be light or quite thick. Slightly more flour must be added to a browned roux than to a white roux to obtain the same degree of thickness, as the flour loses some of its thickening quality when browned. In either case, gradually whisking in warm or room temperature liquid is the best insurance for a smooth, lump-free sauce.

As a general rule, for a light but not watery sauce, I recommend using 1 tablespoon of fat, 2 tablespoons of flour and 1 cup of liquid. Roux-based sauces were traditionally the most common type of sauce in French and French-inspired cuisines. They are very stable and versatile so they provided chefs with great latitude. Many modern chefs have decreased their use of roux-based sauces, opting for lighter (though not necessarily lower-fat), quicker methods for preparing sauces. Thickeners traditionally used in the Orient have become more popular. Starches such as cornstarch can be mixed with cold water then stirred into a sauce at the end of cooking. They require no fat, little cooking and can produce a clear, glistening sauce. Too much of these thickeners, though, can result in a thick or lumpy sauce. In addition, starch-thickened sauces are not as stable as those that are roux-based, so they are not as appropriate for recipes that require advanced preparation. This form of sauce-making is easy and light but may lack depth.

Perhaps the most common "modern" type of sauce is a "reduction." As the name indicates, a reduction is a sauce in which the main liquid is reduced in volume (by boiling). As the liquid evaporates, the sauce automatically becomes slightly more syrupy in consistency. More importantly, the flavors become more pronounced because they are not as highly diluted by the presence of water. (When preparing a reduced sauce, be extremely careful to use a base that is unsalted or very lightly salted, otherwise the salt will become overpowering.) Reductions may be used as is, or may be enriched by whisking in butter, cream, soy cream, yogurt or puréed squash. Another modern method of preparing sauces is to simply purée solid ingredients. This type of sauce (for example, Asparagus Sauce for Stuffed Shells, page 152), is particularly successful with vegetarian dishes because it tends to be simple in flavor. When puréeing a sauce, it is best to include some form of starch—potato, rice, etc.—in the base in order to give the sauce a body that does not easily separate.

To "finish" a sauce or a simple reduced stock, you may wish to whisk in a small amount of an enrichment—butter, oil, cream, soy cream or a nut or seed butter. In addition, a finely puréed vegetable, minced fresh herb, scallions, tomato paste, or puréed baked garlic may be added. Any sauce may be strained through a fine-mesh strainer to refine its consistency. This technique is commonly used when a sauce consists mainly of puréed vegetables as uneven bits of the purée can then be removed, but it is also useful when preparing other sauces to produce a more finished quality. (If you plan to strain a sauce, wait to whisk in final flavorings such as minced herbs so as not to strain them back out.)

When preparing a sauce or adding an enrichment to a dish, the same basic principles of flavoring, balance, and texture development apply as they do when considering other elements of a dish. A sauce should support and complement a dish. Its texture should be supportive rather than a main focus. A sauce should be memorable, but should never overpower or distract from other features of the dish.

The Finishing Touch: The Element of Beauty

The final concern to a cook—presentation—is the first element to strike the diner and invite a taste. But presentation is not only of last-minute regard. From the moment the first ingredient is added, the tone for the look of a dish is established. All ingredients thereafter must fit like pieces of a puzzle if the dish is to look well thought out and balanced. The beauty of a dish encompasses both the way the ingredients are designed—their inherent shape, how they are cut, balance in color and form—as well as the final presentation—their arrangement on the plate.

In its simplest form, the presentation of a dish feels balanced. Consider the fundamental makeup of most Chinese dishes as a perfect example. The dish usually contains one main protein ingredient and a number of vegetables. The main protein ingredient usually stands out in shape and possibly arrangement on the plate. "Structural" ingredients, the vegetables, are usually cut to complement each other and the shape of the main ingredient (usually all shredded or cut into large pieces, not some shredded and others cubed), with a few garnishes added to pull the design together (perhaps scallions scattered on top). In a Western-style dish, equivalent balance is essential. A stew, for example, usually has ingredients of equal size and shape with possibly a simple garnish added just before serving. This sort of balance in presentation is calming to the eyes and is also functional. When similar ingredients are cut into similar-sized pieces, they are more likely to cook in the same amount of time.

The second consideration when designing the look of a dish is how to get all the ingredients fully cooked, at the right temperature and arranged attractively on the plate. If a recipe is to be cooked in one vessel, some ingredients may need to be cut into different shapes or thicknesses in order for the dish to cook evenly. This sort of single pot dish may look attractive simply turned out onto a plate, or you may wish to ring it with noodles or a grain, or arrange it next to a nicely cut vegetable as a side dish. For a modern presentation of casseroles and one-pot dishes, try preparing the dish as individual servings. Small ramekins of Eggplant Parmesan, for example, can be far more visually appealing than a large casserole spooned out family style at the table.

Many dishes require that ingredients be cooked separately, then combined at some stage—if only on the service plate—before being brought to the table. When ingredients are prepared separately, the cook has more control over how each ingredient cooks in addition to more latitude for innovative design. Vegetables can be arranged to visually optimize shape and color and sauces may be poured where they look best, rather than coating every ingredient equally. This type of light, fresh recipe and delicate plate presentation is typical of "nouvelle cuisine." It can be beautifully executed or carried to a tiresome extreme.

Attempting to serve every meal as though you were running a ritzy restaurant in L.A. could be bothersome—especially for your family. Playing with the presentation of the food you cook, however, is a marvelous way of slowing down before you eat and it is helpful as a means of appreciating the work of art you have created. In most great cuisines, presentation plays a paramount role. In Japan, for example, the precise bowl that a food is served in and how that dish is garnished are often considered part of the recipe itself. Attention to detail in presentation is far less a part of American heritage perhaps because embedded deep in our culinary psyche is the image of the wagon train cook slopping a spoonful of grub onto our plate. But we have certainly evolved quite splendidly from the wagon train to L.A., and the following pointers may be helpful as you develop your own personal touch for presenting foods you prepare.

Try to match the presentation to the style of the dish. Simple Mexican dishes, for example, look appropriate on rustic plates with vegetables roughly chopped and a thick sauce coating the main ingredient. A Chinese- or Japanese-style dish often appears light with a delicate sauce and brightly colored vegetables cut in interesting shapes to catch the eye. Decide well ahead of time whether you plan to arrange food on individual plates or to serve family style from one large platter. This decision will affect the overall presentation, both in terms of how individual ingredients may be cut and the number of garnishes, such as sprigs of parsley, you need. Third, consider whether or not the dish lends itself to being decoratively arranged on the service plate, or if it would work well simply turned out onto the plate. As contrasting examples, Saffron Broiled Tofu which is served on a bed of arame (page 190), demands to be arranged, whereas Tofu "Scallops" (page 71) start to look overworked if they get much more attention than simply turning them out onto serving plates. Keep your presentation balanced. Include ingredients that have contrasting colors and shapes, arrange foods in simple designs, use garnishes as punctuation marks, and select a service plate that complements the look of the dish. As with flavoring, exercise restraint in presentation. When considering presentation of a dish, as when looking for the answer to a scientific problem, always check the simplest solution first.

Finally, look at each plate as a whole before you bring it to the table. Check first the overall look of the food and make any last-minute additions. Also check for ingredients that seem out of place, such as clumsy or ill-placed garnishes, drips of sauce on the edge of the plate, and so on. Presenting foods beautifully can be extraordinarily satisfying to both cook and diner. When you consider cooking as art, you may find, as I do, that even the simplest presentation—a nicely arranged plate of sliced vegetables—will give you great joy.

Methods and Techniques

"Methods" and "techniques" are to students of classical cooking the foundation of the curriculum. The terms overlap and are often used interchangeably. A subtle differentiation I make between them here is to emphasize ways of cooking or handling food when I refer to a method, and the mastery of a technical skill when I speak of technique. Steaming would therefore be a "method" of cooking and cutting foods into julienne would be a "technique." Once you understand fundamental methods and techniques, you can cook. More importantly, you have the tools you need to begin creating your own recipes and developing your own style of cooking. Jacques Pepin, in his classic work, *La Méthode,* sums it up succinctly when he states that the techniques and methods covered are "processes" that "will not teach you recipe-making but will teach you how to cook."

Basic Knife Techniques

Handling knives properly and with ease is perhaps the single most important skill when it comes to efficiency and pleasure in kitchen work. Developing good knife skills also takes more practice than any other kitchen technique.

Consider the knife an extension of your arm and hand. I first understood this while working in a Chinese restaurant and I noticed how often I put my cleaver down as compared to the chef. He used the sharp edge of the blade, in the ways I was used to, for slicing, chopping and such. But he didn't stop there: he used the tip of the cleaver for detail work; the rear tip of the cleaver for cracking hard ingredients or working slowly through very firm ingredients; and he used the broad side of the blade for flattening ingredients, for scooping vegetables from the work surface, and transferring them to a bowl. Perceiving the knife as an extension of the body, as he did, is extremely helpful because when the knife is "your hand" you can begin to feel whatever ingredient the knife is in contact with, as if you are really touching it. You can actually sense the resistance of the ingredient the knife is cutting through if you notice the subtle changes in vibration in the knife handle. This depth of feel facilitates accuracy in strength and angling of a cut.

Relax! Again, it wasn't until I worked in a professional kitchen that I understood the importance of relaxed knife handling. By ten in the morning (three hours into a thirteen-hour workday), I was exhausted while everyone else was just beginning to wake up. I was getting a whole body workout just chopping up a couple of cloves of garlic, and in a restaurant you may go through ten heads of garlic in a day. With a resilient grip and a relaxed wrist, forearm, and shoulder, you can use a knife for hours without fatigue. Why is that important in a home kitchen? Because being relaxed as you cook will help you enjoy the work which, in turn, affects every aspect of cooking.

There are a few specific movements for knife handling that apply to virtually every cutting technique. First, for best control the grip itself should feel balanced. This balance depends on having a knife handle that fits your hand comfortably and a quality knife that is designed for balance, with the blade neither too heavy nor too light in proportion to the handle. Second, depending on the design of the knife, you may need to "choke" the blade in order to execute some movements. For example, when using a cleaver to slice, it is best to grasp the knife where the blade and handle join, but for mincing, holding the cleaver by the middle of the handle facilitates a more relaxed, balanced chopping motion. A small French paring knife, which is used for fine work, can become very much like a sharp extension of the forefinger if you choke the blade and then place your forefinger along the backside of the blade.

Finally, the relationship between how you hold whatever it is you are cutting and the knife is critical. When holding food off the counter to perform a detail work such as shaping or peeling, the food should be held in place loosely so that it moves, as if dancing in step with the movement of the knife. By contrast, when working with a chef's knife or cleaver to slice, dice, chop, or cut into julienne, the food should be stable on the work surface. When cutting a round-sided ingredient, such as a carrot, it may be helpful to stabilize it by cutting a thin strip off the length of one side of the ingredient, so that it rests evenly on the work surface. To facilitate even, smooth cutting, hold the knife in one hand and secure the ingredient on the counter, holding it with the fingertips of your second hand. By bending these fingers at the first knuckle, you can position your middle finger so that the top front edge of its second joint comes in contact with the broad side of the blade of the knife. This knuckle then becomes a gauge as you cut, determining how thick a slice you can make. If in this process you place the thumb of your second hand towards the back of the ingredient you are cutting, you can then use your thumb to gently push the ingredient towards the knife, like a log through a sawmill, every time you make a cut. The knife blade can rest on the counter, tip down, and by rocking it back and forth, allowing the ingredient to slide under, you can chop, slice, dice and shred foods in a relaxed manner. Most methods of cutting require this same basic technique. Hold the knife firmly and perpendicular to the work surface and cut with determination. To cut very firm vegetables, such as jicama, it may be easier to use the rear third of the blade (near the handle) because more weight/strength may be applied. Very soft ingredients, such as tomatoes, are best cut using a wavy-edged knife and a sawing motion. For detailed descriptions of specific cutting methods (slicing, dicing, etc.) please see the Definitions of Terms (page 188).

Mincing is the only method of cutting ingredients that requires a notably different technique. To achieve fine, even-sized pieces, an ingredient is first cut into relatively small pieces and then minced. Depending on the original shape of the ingredient, the technique for getting it into these small pieces may vary (see variations below), and depending on whether you are using a cleaver or a chef's knife, the technique of mincing itself is also different. To mince with a chef's knife, position the mound of ingredients to be minced on the cutting surface 8 to 10 inches in from the edge of the counter so that you will have good leverage when working. Hold the handle of the knife with a balanced grip and position it, ready to cut, over the mound. Rest the fingertips of your second hand on the dull side of the tip of the blade, fingers straight, and rest the side of the heel of that hand on the counter. This secures the knife in place and creates a pivot point for the knife tip. Then simply chop with the blade held in place, moving it back and forth across the mound of ingredients. Periodically stop mincing and, using the blade as a scoop, flip ingredients from the bottom of the pile to the top and reshape the mound. The only difference when mincing with a cleaver is that it can be a one-handed operation. Because the blade is straight and most of its cutting edge comes in contact with the cutting board , one downward chop will cut through a long line of ingredients (as opposed to a chef's knife which is slightly curved and has only about 1 inch of surface that is in contact with the cutting board at any given time). It works well, therefore, when mincing with a cleaver to chop back and forth across the mound—almost like a fast hammering motion. The mound must be turned and reshaped for even mincing. If you mince in this way, being relaxed is essential unless you are interested in self-torture. Regardless of the type of knife you use, because ingredients are minced finely, they must be dry when the mincing begins. It is natural for their juices to be released to some extent during mincing, but if they are wet when you begin to mince, they will become soggy and will not mince evenly. Bear in mind, also, that the finer you get the initial tiny pieces, the smaller and more evenly you will be able to mince the ingredient before it begins to release so much of its liquid that mincing should stop.

To mince garlic, peel each clove by placing it on the counter and gently slapping it with the flat side of a large knife or cleaver. The skin will peel off easily and you can cut the clove in half from tip to root end. With the tip of a paring knife, remove and discard the germinating core (if there is one). Then make thin slices from the root end to the tip of each half clove, leaving the root end intact to hold the slices in place. Next place the clove flat side down on the cutting board and make thin slices, again from root to tip so that you have tiny matchstick-shaped pieces, attached at the root end. Cut tiny dice by slicing across these cuts. Then proceed with mincing as described above. If you are mincing 4 or more cloves of garlic, you may use the food processor. For this technique, clean all cloves and remove their germinating sections. Fit the processor with the metal chopping blade. With the motor running, drop all of the cloves of garlic at once into the processor through the feed tube. Within a few seconds the garlic will end up on the sides of the bowl. Scrape it off and process again for another few seconds. This method produces a larger, more uneven effect, but it is simple and may be practical when time is limited.

Shallots and onions can be minced by hand in the same manner as garlic. To mince them in a processor, first slice them (if you have a very thin slicing blade, use it), then fit the processor with the metal chopping blade and, using an on-off motion, mince the shallot or onion, being sure to scrape down the sides of the bowl between pulses.

To mince ginger, peel it, then cut it into thin pieces. Stack the pieces and cut them crosswise into thin matchstick strips, then cut these into tiny dice and proceed with mincing. Ginger may also be grated but does not work well in a processor.

To mince mushrooms, slice a cap horizontally into thin rounds, retaining the shape of the cap. Still keeping the shape of the mushroom, cut down through the cap to form matchstick strips, then cut these into tiny dice.

To mince parsley, chervil, cilantro, or other soft-stemmed, curly herbs, wash and dry them well. Put the stalks together into a bunch with root ends together. Arrange the leafy ends of the stems into a compact pile, and hold them in place, close to the edge of the pile. Press firmly enough to hold them close together, but not so much that you crush them. Then cut through the leaves as if you were slicing thin slices. Proceed with the general method for mincing. For both parsley and cilantro, the stems may or may not be included as you mince by hand. To mince most other fresh herbs, remove the leaves from the stems, then stack them in a bunch and proceed as above. Basil is an exception. As it bruises so easily, basil is usually shredded or finely chopped.

To mince scallions, line them up all facing in the same direction. Cut off their roots, but do not leave the root end intact. Trim the green ends as necessary to leave only fresh, crisp tops. Peel the scallions, removing the thin, slightly slippery layer on each. Again line them up facing the same direction. Lay the broad side of a cleaver or chef's knife on one end of the scallions, then slap the knife onto the onions and immediately as it hits, slap the blade with your free hand. The scallions should be flattened. Move the knife up to the other end of the scallions and slap again to flatten. Place your second hand on top of the smashed scallions to hold them in place, then using a sawing action, slice the scallions in half horizontally, moving your second hand to keep the scallions in a neat row. Finally, cut the scallions crosswise into tiny pieces. Scallions are best minced by hand rather than in a processor.

Basic Food Prep Techniques

To clean greens such as spinach, kale, or chard, fold a leaf in half lengthwise, top sides touching. Grasp the leaf with one hand holding your thumb along the bottom edge of the stem on one side of the leaf and your fingertips along the bottom edge of the stem on the other side. With your second hand, pull the stem from the bottom of the leaf to the tip. Drop the leaf into a large bowl of cold water, discard the stem and repeat the de-stemming with the remaining leaves. Wash the leaves in several changes of water. Between water changes, lift the leaves out of the water and place them in a strainer or salad spinner basket. Empty the water and rinse out the bowl before filling again with fresh water and adding the spinach. Do not pour the water over the spinach to drain or the dirt (and insects) that rinsed off will be poured back onto the leaves. Once no residue remains in the water when the spinach is lifted out, spin the leaves dry in a salad spinner. Place a paper towel in the bottom of a plastic bag. Add the dry leaves—very loosely packed—and refrigerate, loosely folded shut, for up to 5 days. For larger volumes of leaves, it may be necessary to layer in half the leaves, cover with a second towel, then add the remaining leaves.

To clean a leek, trim the roots even with the bottom, leaving the root end intact. Cut off the tough upper green section, then peel off the tough outer layers of the leek. Beginning about 1 inch from the root end, cut through the leek lengthwise from bottom to top. Turn the leek 90 degrees and make a second cut. Place the leek under cold running water and rinse very well, rubbing inside and out on each layer to remove all dirt. Be certain to rinse the bottom core as dirt often gets lodged deep inside leeks.

To clean button mushrooms, select mushrooms that are absolutely fresh with tightly closed caps and no discoloration. Cut off the stems even with the bottom of the caps. Place the caps in a mesh strainer and rinse under a thin stream of cold running water, tossing and rubbing the mushroom caps constantly. Work quickly to remove all dirt so that the mushrooms are under the water for as little time as possible. Immediately place the caps, stem side down, on a clean, dry kitchen towel or paper toweling. Pat the tops of the caps to remove excess water, then allow the mushrooms to dry at room temperature for 20 minutes or longer. (Do not let the mushrooms get so dry that they become squeaky to the touch.) If the caps are so wet that the towel gets very wet within a few minutes, transfer the mushrooms, stem side down, to a second dry towel before drying. Once dry, transfer the mushrooms to a plastic bag lined with a paper towel. Cover loosely and refrigerate for up to 4 days. (This method works beautifully for fresh, closed-capped mushrooms. If you select mushrooms that are not absolutely fresh, they will not last but can be cleaned before use in the same manner.)

To peel and seed a tomato, using a paring knife, make a shallow cross cut—just through the skin—in the blossom end of the tomato. Carve a cone-shaped piece around the stem, then remove and discard the stem. Bring 1 quart of water to a rolling boil. (If peeling more than 1 tomato, have enough water to comfortably hold the tomatoes so that water circulates around them all.) Lower the tomato into the water and cook, stirring once or twice, until the skin at the cross mark begins to peel back, about 30 seconds. Immediately remove the tomato to a strainer and, holding it blossom side up, run cold water over it. As soon as the tomato is cool enough to handle, stop the water and remove the peel. Slice the tomato in half horizontally, then gently squeeze the seeds out of each half.

To toast nuts, preheat the oven to 375°F. Arrange the nuts on a dry baking sheet and place in the center of the oven. Bake, stirring occasionally, until brown to the core, about 10 to 12 minutes. Immediately transfer the nuts to a bowl or clean countertop (they will continue to cook and will burn if left on the sheet). To remove the skin from hazelnuts or walnuts, turn the warm nuts onto a clean kitchen towel, fold the towel over the nuts and rub.

To roast a pepper, first wash it well to remove all dirt and dust, paying special attention to the area around the stem. Preheat the broiler to high. Place the pepper on a baking sheet about 4 inches from the flame. Allow the pepper to cook, turning several times, until it is blistered on all sides. (Use a towel or tongs to turn the pepper; a fork may pierce the meat and allow the juices and steam to escape.) Immediately transfer the pepper to a brown paper bag and fold the bag shut to seal in the steam and encourage the skin to separate from the meat. When the pepper is cool enough to handle, hold it over a bowl and, with a paring knife and your fingers, peel off all skin. Allow the juices to drop into the bowl. Tear the pepper in half, then scrape out and discard the seeds and stem. Cut the pepper into the desired shape, place it in a plastic container and strain the juices over it, then cover tightly. The pepper will keep for 2 to 4 days, if refrigerated. If you wish to keep the pepper longer, cover it with oil, then cover and refrigerate for up to a week. Peppers in oil may also be frozen for up to 2 months. Whether refrigerated in pepper juice or oil, you may wish to add a smashed, peeled clove of garlic to the container for additional flavor.

To oven-roast vegetables, preheat the oven to 375°F. Place the vegetable on a baking sheet and bake until soft when squeezed. For a slightly more moist effect, a small amount of oil may be drizzled over the surface of the vegetable before baking (this seals in the moisture slightly), or they may be baked in a covered baking dish. Baked vegetables are often used as components of recipes. For example, oven-baked onions acquire a sweet caramelized quality and the cloves of whole heads of baked garlic can be used as a paste to flavor sauces or dressings. Baked sweet potatoes, winter squash, and eggplant serve beautifully as nonfat thickeners for sauces.

Methods of Judging "Doneness"

The idea of throwing spaghetti against the wall and having it stick was one of the images that drew me into cooking at an early age. (Unfortunately, if it does stick, the spaghetti is so overcooked that toothless babies are among the few to whom it appeals.) Judging when ingredients are properly cooked, however, is usually far more restrained, and indicators of "doneness" vary from one to the next.

The best method to judge "doneness" is to feel an ingredient: to poke it with a fork, bite it, or "cut" into it with a fingernail. All are ways to sense resistance and you may find one method easier to interpret than another. (I use them all, depending on the ingredient. I poke potatoes, bite pasta and feel broccoli with my thumbnail.) How well done an ingredient should be is, ultimately, a matter of personal taste, but the following general pointers may be helpful in judging when a food is cooked to optimum flavor.

Firm vegetables, such as broccoli, green beans, and carrots, should be crisp on the surface and just beginning to soften beneath that. More porous vegetables such as potatoes, summer squash, or whole mushrooms should be an even texture throughout, cooked to accentuate their texture and no more. Pasta and grains are good cooked until they present a slight resistance—without seeming hard—when bitten into ("al dente"). Beans are best cooked al dente if you want them to remain intact and more so if the desired effect is that they be smooth or puréed. Each ingredient is different and, depending on the recipe for which it is intended, the same ingredient might be better more or less well done. Ultimately you must get to know the ingredients, know how they respond to various cooking methods, and pay close attention to them as they cook.

Basic Cooking Methods

Most of the recipes that follow are prepared using only a few cooking methods, notably steaming, stir-frying, sautéing and broiling. Though they are all straightforward, they must be executed precisely for best results. Below I have elaborated on the most commonly used cooking methods called for in recipes included in this book. For information about other cooking methods, consult the Definitions of Terms (page 188).

Steaming is a versatile cooking method commonly used in China and other parts of the Orient, but unusual in classic French recipes. The underlying principle is that foods be placed in a hot, sealed steam bath to cook quickly. Foods cook thoroughly, and their texture is usually less disturbed than it might be if the ingredient were sautéed or boiled. Foods remain moist and plump, and aromas are often drawn out of neighboring ingredients in the steamer to be absorbed by one another. Vegetables retain their vibrant colors and appealing textures when steamed until just tender, but if overcooked, they turn soggy and become dull in color (army green broccoli or yellowish cauliflower, for example). Steamed vegetables will continue to cook if left covered in a steamer that has been turned off, so if they are not to be served immediately, they should be immediately transferred to a strainer and placed under a gentle stream of cold water to stop their cooking. Once cool, they should be drained on a clean kitchen towel.

Various sorts of steamers are available at any cookware store (page 6), but regardless of the type you use, the method is always the same. To steam a food, fill the steamer pot with enough water to come to about 1/2 to 3/4 inch from the bottom of the steamer rack. Cover the steamer pot and bring the water to a boil. Place the food in the steamer rack and add this to the pot, then immediately cover tightly to seal in the steam. It is important that the food be placed into an environment that is already steaming to ensure that the exterior of the food begins to cook immediately, allowing the interior to retain moisture.

If the ingredient requires long steaming—such as an artichoke—check the water level periodically to be sure that it does not boil away. If it does, you will smell a burning odor, the bottom of the pan will become scorched, and the food will become inedible with an unpleasant smoked flavor. The molecular structure of most pans will become damaged if they are burned in this way. If this happens a number of times, the pan will pit and need to be replaced.

Sautéing and **stir-frying** are related cooking methods, the former more typical of Western-style dishes, the latter of dishes with Oriental influence. Both terms are very literal: sauté, meaning "to jump" in French (the foods jump around the pan when cooked), and stir-fry, a simple description for the procedure. They are used when cooking ingredients that have been cut into small pieces and are to be cooked (or partially cooked) quickly. When using either method, all ingredients—including sauce mixtures and final garnishes—should be prepared and arranged next to the stove before you begin.

Sauté food in a sauté pan or skillet in which you heat a small amount of fat over a medium high flame until hot, but not smoking. An ingredient may be sautéed in this way for a brief time before another ingredient is added or the heat may be reduced slightly allowing the ingredient to cook gently for a longer period of time.

To stir-fry, place a wok over a high flame. When it is hot, add the oil (use an oil with a high smoking point) and heat for about 15 seconds. Immediately add the ingredient(s) and cook, tossing constantly. The best tools for tossing foods in a wok are a Chinese shovel and ladle designed to accompany a wok. Hold the shovel and ladle face to face, touching the bottom of the wok, at the sides of the food in the wok. The tool handles should point up out of the wok. Draw the shovel and ladle together, picking up as much of the ingredient as possible, then flip the pieces of the ingredient over and drop them back into

3 • New Family Favorites

Penne with Roasted Peppers, Beans, and Basil

Yield: 4 servings • Prep Time: 25 minutes • Cooking Time: 30 minutes

Porcini mushrooms used both in the stock and added to the dish itself give this pasta dish an intense flavor and aroma. Use this same procedure for preparing any number of bean and pasta dishes, using pinto or anasazi beans and adding various vegetables such as marinated artichoke hearts, steamed broccoli, or grated raw carrots just before turning out onto the serving plate.

3 tablespoons olive oil
1 1/3 cups diced red onion
4 large cloves garlic, sliced
8 ounces button mushrooms, sliced
1/2 ounce dried porcini mushrooms, soaked, then drained
1/2 cup dry Madeira or white wine
3/4 cup porcini stock (page 163) or mushroom stock (page 163)
1/2 teaspoon crushed dried oregano
3/4 teaspoon salt
1/8 teaspoon black pepper
1 yellow or green bell pepper, seeded and sliced
3 red bell peppers, roasted (page 35)
1 1/2 cups cooked cannellini or kidney beans
6 ounces penne noodles
1/4 teaspoon red pepper flakes (optional)
1/3 cup minced fresh basil
Freshly grated Parmesan

1. In a large skillet, heat the olive oil over medium-high heat until hot, but not smoking. Add the onion and cook, stirring constantly, for 1 minute. Reduce the heat to medium and continue to cook until soft, about 8 minutes. Add the garlic and mushrooms and continue to cook, stirring often until the mushrooms begin to soften, about 3 minutes. Stir in the Madeira and cook briskly for 1 minute, then add the stock, oregano, salt, and pepper. Continue to cook, stirring occasionally, for about 10 minutes. Add the beans and both yellow and roasted red peppers. Continue to cook for 5 minutes to warm through. If the pasta has not cooked, remove this sauce from the heat and set aside until just before serving. This step may be completed up to an hour before serving if covered and left at room temperature.

2. Meanwhile, cook the penne in rapidly boiling water until it is al dente. Drain immediately and run hot water over it briefly, then shake the strainer and allow the pasta to drain for a moment as you finish cooking the sauce.

3. Just before serving, stir the basil and pepper flakes into the sauce. Warm for about 30 seconds, then taste and adjust the seasonings. (The sauce should taste slightly oversalted, as the pasta will tone it down.) Pour the hot sauce into a large serving dish. Add the pasta, toss well, and serve immediately. Pass the Parmesan.

Variation

1. Use 12 ounces button mushrooms and no porcini. Omit the Madeira and use light vegetable stock (page 162) in place of the porcini stock. Stir 1/3 cup pesto (page 176) or miso pesto (page 176) into the sauce with the peppers. Finish the recipe as described above.

Cook's Note: To cut down on prep time, the red peppers may be roasted, peeled and sliced up to 3 days in advance, and the button mushrooms may be cleaned several days ahead (page 35). The beans may be cooked several days ahead, or you may use frozen or canned beans. Up to 6 hours before serving, the yellow and green peppers, as well as the mushrooms, may be sliced. All should be refrigerated in airtight containers.

Spinach Fettuccine with Cauliflower and "Gorgonzola" Cream Sauce

Yield: 4 servings • Prep Time: 35 minutes • Cooking Time: 30 minutes

1 small head cauliflower (about
   1 1/2 pounds)
4 ounces tofu "Gorgonzola"
   (page 173) or true Gorgonzola
   cheese
2 tablespoons olive oil
1 cup minced shallots
1 teaspoon minced garlic
1/2 cup dry white wine
2 cups mushroom stock (page 163)
1 cup sliced cremini mushrooms
1 small red pepper, diced
1/4 teaspoon salt
1/8 teaspoon white pepper
3 tablespoons minced fresh
   Italian parsley
3 tablespoons minced fresh mint
6 ounces spinach fettuccine
Freshly grated Parmesan
   or soy "Parmesan"

For those wishing to avoid cheese, tofu "Gorgonzola" replaces the true cheese exceptionally well in this flavorful pasta dish. You may, of course, go with the original cheese, which results in a far more rich dish.

1. Trim and discard all tough leaves and stem pieces from the cauliflower, then cut the head into small florets. You should have about 5 to 5 1/2 cups. Set this aside. Break the "Gorgonzola" into small pieces and place it in a small bowl.

2. Heat the olive oil in a 12-inch skillet over medium high heat until hot, but not smoking. Add the shallots and sauté, stirring constantly, for 1 minute. Reduce the heat to low and continue to cook, stirring often, until the shallots are soft and translucent, about 8 minutes. Increase heat to medium, add the garlic and cauliflower. Cook for 2 minutes, tossing often.

3. Stir the wine into the cauliflower mixture, allowing it to sizzle and steam so the alcohol evaporates. Add the stock, then cover and simmer, stirring occasionally, for 10 minutes. Stir in the mushrooms, red pepper, salt, and pepper. Cover and continue to cook until the cauliflower is just tender, about 5 more minutes. Remove from the heat and stir in the Gorgonzola, parsley, and mint. Taste and adjust the seasonings. Keep the sauce warm while preparing the noodles.

4. Meanwhile, bring 3 quarts of water to a rolling boil. Stir in the fettuccine and cook until al dente, 1 to 8 minutes, according the the package directions. Drain the noodles into a strainer, then shake them several times to remove as much excess water as possible. Immediately turn them out onto a large serving platter. Pour the sauce over the noodles and toss to mix. Top with grated Parmesan and serve immediately.

Variation

1. For a richer sauce, combine the gorgonzola with 1/4 cup crème fraîche (page 172), or soy cream (page 171) and 1/4 cup mushroom stock (page 163) before adding in step 3.

Cook's Note: To cut down on last-minute prep time, you may prepare the dish through step 3 up to 6 hours in advance, then rewarm the sauce as the noodles cook.

Angel Hair with Tofu "Sausage," Fennel, and Sun-Dried Tomatoes

Yield: 4 servings • Prep Time: 25 minutes • Cooking Time: 20 minutes

2 tablespoons olive oil
2 cups thinly sliced red onion

This angel hair pasta recipe is light yet extremely satisfying. The taste of fennel, from the seeds in the "sausage" and fresh fennel bulb, has a lingering, full effect.

1. In a 12-inch skillet, heat the oil over medium high heat until hot, but not smoking. Add the onion and toss until it is coated with oil. Reduce the heat slightly and continue to cook, stirring often, until it is translucent, about 10 minutes. Add the stock and tofu "sausage," then increase the heat slightly and simmer for 5 minutes.

2. Drain the sun-dried tomatoes and slice them. Stir them into the skillet along with the tomatoes and the garlic. Cook at a low boil, stirring often, for about 10 minutes or until the liquid just covers the tofu. This sauce may be prepared up to an hour in advance if left covered at room temperature.

3. Meanwhile, bring a large pot of water to a rolling boil. Cook the pasta according to the package directions, stirring occasionally, until it is al dente. Immediately transfer the pasta to a large strainer and shake it to drain as much water as possible. Transfer it to a serving platter.

4. As the pasta cooks, stir the fennel, peas, and basil into the skillet with the sauce. Heat for 1 minute. Pour the sauce mixture over the pasta and toss to combine. Sprinkle pine nuts on top and serve Parmesan alongside.

2 cups mushroom vegetable stock (page 163)
1 pound tofu "sausage" (page 166)
10 sun-dried tomatoes, soaked in water
1 1/2 cups peeled, seeded and diced tomatoes (2 medium)
2 cloves garlic, minced
6 to 8 ounces angel hair pasta
1 1/2 cups sliced fennel bulb
1/2 cup peas (may use frozen)
1/3 cup shredded fresh basil
1/4 cup toasted pine nuts (page 35)
Freshly grated Parmesan, optional

Variation

1. Just before serving this pasta dish, stir 1/3 cup crème fraîche (page 172), tofu "cream" (page 171), or milk into the tofu "sausage" mixture as an enrichment.

Pesto-Stuffed Winter Squash

Yield: 4 servings • Prep Time: 25 minutes • Cooking Time: 1 hour

As the squash bakes, the house is filled with the mouthwatering aroma of pesto. The filling can be prepared quickly without prior cooking and the squash can be stuffed up to 24 hours in advance.

1. Halve the squash lengthwise, then scrape out and discard their seeds. With a wavy-edged knife, slice a thin round of skin (about 1 by 2 inches in size) from the bottom of each half so that the squash will rest evenly on the work surface. Arrange the squash halves in a shallow baking dish and preheat the oven to 375ºF.

2. In a mixing bowl, combine the tempeh, carrot, celery, onion, pesto, celery seeds, and enough water or yogurt to just bind the mixture and lighten it. Divide the filling evenly among the squash. Pour boiling water into the pan around the squash, so that it comes about 1/4 of the way up the sides of the squash. Cover the pan with a lid or foil and bake until the squash is tender, about 1 hour. During the last 15 minutes of cooking, remove the lid from the pan and sprinkle the cheese over the squash. Continue to cook until the cheese is melted. Remove the baking pan from the oven and place the squash on a cake rack to cool for 5 minutes before serving.

2 acorn or delicata squash
8 ounces tempeh, crumbled
1/2 cup finely diced carrot
1/4 cup finely diced celery
1/4 cup minced white onion
1/4 cup pesto (page 176) or miso pesto (page 176)
1 teaspoon celery seeds
3 tablespoons water or plain nonfat yogurt
1/3 cup grated soy mozzarella or Monterey Jack (optional)

Warm Pasta Salad

Yield: 4 servings • Prep Time: 45 minutes • Cooking Time: 45 minutes

8 ounces tempeh, crumbled
1/4 cup soy sauce
3 tablespoons balsamic vinegar
5 tablespoons olive oil
3/4 teaspoon dried thyme
1/2 teaspoon dried oregano
1 tablespoon minced garlic
2 cups broccoli florets
1 tablespoon honey
3 tablespoons champagne
    vinegar
1/3 cup light vegetable stock
    (page 162)
2 teaspoons crushed fennel seeds
1 teaspoon salt
1/8 teaspoon black pepper
6 ounces fusilli pasta
Pinch of red pepper flakes
4 cups curly endive leaves, torn
    into pieces
1 cup chopped radicchio
6 sun-dried tomatoes, drained and
    quartered
1 cup sliced red bell pepper
2/3 cup sliced fennel bulb
12 cherry tomatoes, halved
1/3 cup shredded basil leaves

For a quick and simple supper, this satisfying salad includes baked crumbled tempeh, which some think resembles bacon.

1. In a small, shallow baking pan (such as a pie plate), combine the tempeh, soy sauce, balsamic vinegar, 1 tablespoon of the oil, 1/2 teaspoon of the thyme, the oregano, and 1 teaspoon of the garlic. Mix well and allow to marinate at room temperature for 1 hour.

2. Preheat the oven to 350°F. Bake the tempeh, turning several times, until most of the liquid has evaporated and the tempeh is browned, about 20 minutes. Remove from the oven and set aside. The tempeh may be prepared up to 3 days in advance if refrigerated in an airtight container.

3. Meanwhile, place the broccoli in the top rack of a steamer over rapidly boiling water. Cover and cook until it is just tender, about 8 minutes. Immediately transfer the broccoli to a strainer and place it in the sink under cold running water to stop its cooking. When cold to the touch, turn the broccoli out onto a clean kitchen towel to drain. The broccoli may be prepared ahead and drained, then refrigerated in an airtight container for up to 2 days.

4. Combine 3 tablespoons of the oil with the honey and 1 tablespoon of the champagne vinegar in a small mixing bowl. Stir in the stock, fennel seeds, 1/2 teaspoon salt, pepper, and remaining 2 teaspoons of minced garlic. Set aside.

5. Bring 2 quarts of water to a rolling boil. Add the remaining 1/2 teaspoon of salt. When the water returns to the boil, stir in the pasta. Cook according to packaged instructions, until it is al dente. Drain the pasta immediately and place it in a wide pasta platter. Drizzle the honey and oil mixture and the red pepper flakes over the pasta and toss to coat evenly. If the vegetables are not quite ready, cover the bowl to keep the pasta warm.

6. Meanwhile, heat the remaining 1 tablespoon oil in a 12-inch skillet. Add the endive and cook, tossing constantly, until it is coated with oil, about 30 seconds. Add the remaining 2 tablespoons vinegar and cook for another minute. Stir in the radicchio, sun-dried tomatoes, tempeh, broccoli, pepper, fennel, and cherry tomatoes. Cook only long enough to warm through, about 1 minute. Add this vegetable mixture to the pasta along with the basil and toss well. Serve at once.

Cook's Note: The tempeh is best marinated for at least 1 hour before proceeding with the recipe.

Basic Polenta

Yield: 2 1/2 cups • Prep Time: 2 minutes • Cooking Time: 25 minutes

Polenta is a form of corn grits, widely used in Italian cooking. It may be served straight from the pan, lightly seasoned with butter, salt, and pepper, or accompanied by a sauce. It also serves beautifully as a foundation for more complex presentations such as pies or layered dishes. Shaped polenta is best prepared a day or so in advance, as are most fillings and sauces that would accompany an elaborate polenta dish. With this in mind, polenta becomes a terrifically versatile element in many recipes.

The best method for preparing basic polenta requires time and relaxed attention, but it is well worth the investment. Though there are a few polenta quick mixes, the traditional method of cooking and stirring for 25 minutes produces polenta that is unmatched in its creamy, homogeneous texture.

3 cups water or stock
1/4 teaspoon salt
1 cup polenta

1. In a 2-quart saucepan, combine the water and salt, then bring it to a boil. Pour the polenta into the boiling water, in a thin stream, stirring constantly as you pour. Allow the polenta to return to the boil, stirring constantly, then reduce the heat to medium low and continue to cook, stirring constantly, working the spoon back and forth across the bottom and around the corners of the pan, until the polenta is extremely creamy, about 25 minutes.

2. Remove the polenta from the heat and season it to taste. Serve immediately or transfer the cooked polenta to a shallow mold or baking dish, then spread evenly and cool. Cover with a layer of plastic wrap touching the surface and refrigerate for up to 3 days. Return the cooked polenta to room temperature before proceeding with a recipe.

Variations

1. Add 2 tablespoons snipped chives and 1/4 teaspoon nutmeg to the polenta just before pouring out into a mold or serving.

2. Add up to 1/2 bulb puréed baked garlic (page 36) to the polenta just before serving or pouring into a mold.

3. For a slightly creamier polenta, stir 2 tablespoons butter or olive oil into the cooked polenta just before serving or pouring into a mold.

Polenta "Salmon" with Greens and Mustard Sauce

Yield: 4 servings • Prep Time: 55 minutes • Cooking Time: 20 minutes

1 recipe Basic Polenta (page 43)
2 slices fresh peeled beet
2 tablespoons butter
1/4 teaspoon nutmeg
Pinch cayenne
1/4 cup arame (page 190)
1 lemon
1 tablespoon olive oil (optional)
6 cups kale leaves
15 sorrel leaves
10 ounces firm silken tofu
4 teaspoons Dijon-style mustard
1/2 cup light vegetable stock
 (page 162) or
 kombu stock (page 163)
Salt and pepper to taste

The color of polenta when cooked with beet bears a remarkable resemblance to cooked salmon. It, of course, is dissimilar in taste and texture, but when served in combination with a mustard sauce and sorrel, flavors that complement true salmon, the deception to eye and mind are complete.

1. Prepare the polenta according to directions on page 43, with the following adjustments. Just after you add the polenta to the water and have stirred it to combine, add the slices of beet and continue to cook until the polenta has turned a dark salmon color, about 10 minutes. Remove the beet and finish cooking, then remove the polenta from the heat and stir in the butter, nutmeg and cayenne. Stir vigorously, then transfer it to a 9-inch square baking dish. Spread the polenta out evenly (dampen your fingers with water to prevent them from sticking to the polenta), then cool for 5 minutes. Lay a piece of plastic wrap over the polenta, touching its surface, then refrigerate until firm. The polenta may be prepared up to 3 days in advance.

2. Preheat the oven to 375°F. Place the arame in a small bowl and cover with boiling water. Set this aside for 20 minutes, then drain. Grate the zest from the lemon and place it in a small bowl, then juice the lemon and set both aside. Remove the polenta from the pan (it should come out in one piece if loosened around the edges and on the bottom with a metal spatula). Break the polenta into rough-edged rectangles measuring about 2 1/2 inches by 1 inch. Lightly oil a baking sheet with the olive oil and place the polenta on this, then brush the pieces with additional oil. (If you prefer not to use oil, line the baking sheet with parchment.) Chop the kale into large pieces. Remove and discard the stems from the sorrel, then stack the leaves on top of each other and shred them into 1/4-inch-wide strips. Set these aside.

3. Place the polenta in the center of the oven and bake until very lightly browned around the edges, about 15 minutes. Meanwhile, place the kale in the top of a steamer over rapidly boiling water. Drizzle about 1 tablespoon of lemon juice over the kale and toss. Cook, stirring once or twice, until it is just tender, about 8 minutes. Add the arame and continue to cook for 2 minutes. Transfer the kale to a large serving platter. Add the sorrel and toss, then arrange the polenta over this. Keep this warm while preparing the sauce.

4. Drain the tofu and place it, with the mustard, in a blender or food processor fitted with the metal chopping blade. Heat the stock until boiling, then with the motor running, pour the stock into the blender. Purée, scraping down the sides of the beaker as necessary, until the sauce is very smooth. Add the reserved lemon zest and season to taste with salt and pepper. Drizzle a small amount of sauce over the polenta and kale, then serve the dish at once with additional sauce alongside.

Cook's Note: The polenta must be prepared at least 8 hours before proceeding with the recipe, so allow yourself time. Also, the protein source in this is the tofu in the sauce, so if you choose to serve this with an alternative, non-protein-based sauce, you might add a cup of cooked chickpeas to the kale for the last few minutes of cooking.

Spinach-Stuffed Polenta with Light Miso Sauce

Yield: 4 servings • Prep Time: 1 hour • Cooking Time: 45 minutes

I once attended a culinary meeting in New York at which Giuliano Bugialli orchestrated a wonderful dinner for hundreds of attendees. As an appetizer he served a delicate polenta dish accompanied by a light anchovy sauce. The miso sauce here was inspired by that memorable meal.

1 recipe Basic Polenta (page 43)
4 1/2 teaspoons minced garlic
2 tablespoons minced fresh
   parsley
3 pounds fresh spinach
1 tablespoon olive oil
1 cup diced onion
2/3 cup dulse (page 190)
   (optional)
1 teaspoon honey
1 1/2 cups light vegetable stock
   (page 162)
1 tablespoon red wine vinegar
Salt and pepper to taste
1/2 cup grated soy mozzarella
   or skim-milk mozzarella
2 teaspoons kuzu (page 192)
1/4 cup mellow white miso
1/8 teaspoon dried red chili flakes
   (optional)
1/4 cup minced fresh mint

1. Prepare the polenta according to directions on page 43 with the following adjustments. When the polenta is fully cooked, remove it from the heat and stir in 1 1/2 teaspoons garlic and the minced parsley. Stir vigorously to mix, then transfer it to a 10- by 15-inch baking sheet. Spread the polenta out evenly to about 1/2-inch thickness (dampen your fingers with a small amount of water to prevent them from sticking to the polenta), then cool for 5 minutes. Lay a piece of plastic wrap over the polenta, touching its surface, then refrigerate until firm. The polenta may be prepared up to 3 days in advance.

2. Remove and discard the stems from the spinach. Clean and dry the leaves, then chop them finely. Heat the oil over medium heat in a 9-inch nonstick skillet. Add the onion and cook briskly, stirring constantly, until all pieces of onion are coated with oil, about 1 minute. Reduce the heat to medium low and continue to cook, stirring often, until the onion is translucent, about 10 minutes. Increase the heat to medium and add the spinach. Cook, stirring constantly until all leaves are wilted, about 2 minutes. Reduce the heat slightly and add the remaining tablespoon of garlic, the dulse, honey, and 1/2 cup of stock. Cook, stirring often, until all of the stock has evaporated, about 8 minutes. Stir in the vinegar and season to taste with salt and pepper. This filling can be prepared up to 3 days in advance if refrigerated in an airtight container.

3. Preheat the oven to 375°F. Remove the polenta from the pan by loosening it with a metal spatula. Cut it into 24 rectangles or triangles that are approximately equal in size. Place half of the pieces, smooth side up, on the work surface. Top each piece with filling, dividing it evenly among them. Sprinkle 1/4 cup of the grated cheese over the filled polenta slices. Top each with a second piece of polenta of about the same size. These top pieces should also be placed smooth side up. Sprinkle the remaining cheese over the polenta, then transfer them to a baking sheet. Bake until the cheese is melted.

4. Meanwhile, prepare the sauce. Crush the kuzu with a fork, then place it in a 1-quart saucepan and mix it with the remaining 1 cup of stock. Bring this to a boil, whisking constantly. Place the miso in a small mixing bowl and gradually whisk in the stock. Return this to the saucepan and warm, but do not boil. Stir in the chili flakes and mint.

5. To serve, spoon a small amount of sauce onto individual serving plates. Place 3 pieces of polenta on each. Serve immediately with additional sauce alongside.

Cook's Note: The polenta must be cooked, then chilled for at least 3 hours. Allow yourself time for this.

Mexican Rose Polenta with Tomatillo Sauce

Yield: 4 servings • Prep Time: 1 hour • Cooking Time: 15 minutes

1 recipe Basic Polenta (page 43)
1/4 cup fresh tomato salsa
   (page 182) or use high-quality
   bottled salsa
10 ounces Gina Marie cheese,
   mild goat cheese, or tofu
   cottage cheese" (page 172)
2 red bell peppers, roasted
   (page 35), and chopped
1 1/2 tablespoons olive oil
3/4 pound tomatillos
1 cup diced white onion
1 tablespoon minced garlic
2 teaspoons ground cumin
1/2 teaspoon salt
1 serrano pepper, seeded and
   minced
1 lime, cut into wedges
1/2 cup chopped cilantro
24 small sprigs cilantro

Rounds of polenta (turned a rusty rose color when flavored with tomato salsa) sandwich a creamy cheese filling, and are topped with a spicy tomatillo sauce. For a nondairy version, replace the cheese with tofu "cottage cheese."

1. Prepare the polenta according to directions on page 43 with the following adjustments. Bring only 2 3/4 cups water to a boil, then proceed with the recipe and cook the polenta for 15 minutes. At this point, stir the salsa into the polenta and continue to cook for 10 minutes. Once cooked, pour the polenta into a 14-inch pizza pan and spread it out to about 1/2-inch thickness. (Dampen your fingers with water as you work to prevent the polenta from sticking.) If you do not have a pizza pan, you may use 1 or 2 rectangular baking sheets, although for efficiency in cutting, a circular sheet works best. Allow the polenta to cool for 5 minutes, then cover with a piece of plastic wrap touching its surface. Chill until firm, for at least 1 hour. The polenta may be prepared ahead and refrigerated, tightly covered, for up to 3 days.

2. Using a 2 1/2-inch round cookie cutter, or a glass of the same diameter, cut 24 rounds from the polenta. Place the cheese in a small bowl and cream it until smooth. Divide the cheese among 12 of the rounds, forming a smooth, flat round of cheese on each piece of polenta. Top each of these with roasted pepper and a second piece of polenta, placing the top piece rough side up. Transfer the polenta rounds to a lightly oiled baking sheet and brush their tops with oil. The rounds may be prepared to this point up to 8 hours in advance if refrigerated, tightly covered. Return to room temperature before baking.

3. Warm a large cast-iron skillet over high heat until a drop of water skips across its surface. Place the tomatillos in the pan and cook quickly, tossing often, until they just begin to brown and sizzle. Immediately remove them from the heat and, when cool enough to handle, rub off and discard their husks. Quarter the tomatillos and place them in a food processor fitted with the metal chopping blade. Add the onion, garlic, cumin, salt and serrano pepper. Purée until very smooth. Transfer this sauce mixture to a 2-quart saucepan and simmer for 5 minutes. The sauce may be prepared up to 2 days in advance if refrigerated in an airtight container. Rewarm before serving.

4. Preheat the oven to 425°F. Place the baking sheet on the top rack of the oven and bake, uncovered, until the cheese is soft and the tops are lightly browned.

5. To serve, spoon a small amount of sauce onto individual serving plates. Arrange 3 warm polenta rounds on each plate, on top of the sauce. Drizzle additional sauce over the rounds and garnish each with sprigs of cilantro. Serve.

Variations

1. Soak 1 ancho pepper in hot water until soft. Drain the pepper, then pull off and discard its stem and seeds. Purée the pepper in a blender until smooth, adding 1 tablespoon of its soaking liquid. Add the cheese and blend this with the pepper. Use this for the cheese in the recipe, above.

2. Replace the tomatillo sauce with ancho pepper sauce (page 181).

Cook's Note: The polenta requires time to chill, so it is best to space preparation of this dish over two or more days.

Pecan Tofu in Cornmeal Crêpes

Yield: 4 servings • Prep Time: 45 minutes • Cooking Time: 20 minutes

The delicate cornmeal crêpes are filled with a delightfully light combination of tofu and squash and gracefully complemented by an interesting sweet corn sauce.

1. Prepare the cornmeal crêpes according to directions on page 171. Thaw the tofu, then press or squeeze as much water from it as you can. Crumble the tofu and set it aside.

2. In a skillet, combine the red wine, soy sauce, garlic and mirin, and stir to mix. Bring to a boil over medium heat. Add 1 cup of stock, the squash and tofu, then cook, stirring constantly until the squash is soft and most of the liquid has evaporated, about 10 minutes. Stir in 1 cup of corn and continue to cook for 2 minutes. Remove from the heat and stir in 2 tablespoons of the minced scallions. Set this filling aside.

3. Meanwhile, prepare the sauce. In a 2-quart saucepan, combine the remaining 1 3/4 cups stock, 2 1/2 cups of corn, leeks, eggplant, rice syrup, salt, pepper, and turmeric. Bring this to a boil, then reduce to a simmer and cook, stirring often until the eggplant is very soft, about 15 minutes. Transfer the sauce to a blender and purée until very smooth, scraping down the sides of the bowl as necessary. Return the sauce to a pan and stir in the milk or soy milk along with the chives and nut butter. Taste and adjust the seasonings.

4. Place the crêpes speckled side down on the work surface. Divide the tofu filling among the crêpes. To roll the crêpes, place a strip of filling from one side to the other, in the center of each crêpe. Fold one unfilled edge of the crêpe over the filling, then roll the crêpe over towards the other unfilled edge so that a double layer of crêpe forms a seam on the bottom.

5. Preheat the oven to 375°F. Put about half of the sauce in the bottom of a large gratin dish. Arrange the crêpes, seam side down, on the sauce. Cover the dish with a lid or aluminum foil and bake until the crêpes are piping hot, about 15 minutes. Remove from the oven and sprinkle the reserved 2 tablespoons scallions and the pecans over the center of the crêpes. Serve.

Cook's Note: This recipe requires tofu which has been frozen for at least 24 hours. Before beginning to prepare the filling you must thaw the tofu for at least an hour.

12 cornmeal crêpes (page 171)
1/2 pound firm tofu, frozen
1/4 cup dry red wine
1/4 cup soy sauce
1/2 teaspoon minced garlic
1 tablespoon mirin
2 3/4 cups light vegetable stock (page 162)
1 zucchini squash, diced
Kernels from 4 ears of sweet corn (about 3 1/2 cups)
1/4 cup minced scallions
2 cups chopped leeks
1/2 cup cubed eggplant
2 tablespoons rice syrup (page 193)
1/2 teaspoon salt
1/8 teaspoon white pepper
1/8 teaspoon turmeric
1/2 cup milk or soy milk
2 tablespoons snipped chives
1 tablespoon pecan or almond butter (page 167)
1/4 cup toasted pecans, chopped

Seitan Cutlets

Yield: 6 cutlets • Prep Time: 25 minutes • Cooking Time: 15 minutes

3 tablespoons uncooked bulgur (cracked wheat)
3 cups (firmly pressed) grated cooked seitan (24 ounces) (page 184)
1/4 cup minced scallions
1/3 cup puréed silken tofu (3 ounces)
1/3 cup cooked sweet brown rice
1/4 cup uncooked oatmeal
1/4 cup sesame seeds
1/2 teaspoon salt
1/8 teaspoon pepper
2 teaspoons Italian seasoning
2 tablespoons minced fresh parsley
2 cloves garlic
1 tablespoon olive oil

While developing recipes for this book, I tried repeatedly without success to come up with a cutlet recipe that had a desirable texture. On a whim one day I combined some leftovers I happened to have on hand and was shocked at the success. So plan your leftovers for this treat. You will need cooked seitan (which may be frozen, then thawed to use in this recipe), bulgur and cooked sweet rice.

1. Rinse the bulgur and place it in a small bowl. Cover it with 1/4 cup boiling water and stir, then cover and set aside for at least 30 minutes to plump and soften.

2. Drain the seitan. (Save the seitan juices to add to another sauce or a soup.) Grate the seitan in a food processor or by hand. You should have about 2 cups of tightly packed seitan. Place this in a large mixing bowl and add the softened bulgur, scallions, tofu, rice, oatmeal, and sesame seeds. Stir well to mix evenly. Add the salt, pepper, Italian seasoning, and parsley. Press the garlic into the mixture through a garlic press. Blend thoroughly. Divide the mixture into 6 even portions, then press each into a 3/4-inch-thick patty or cutlet shape. The cutlets may be prepared ahead to this point, if wrapped airtight and stored in the refrigerator. They can also be frozen for up to 2 months if you are using seitan that has not been previously frozen. To cook frozen cutlets, thaw completely before continuing with the recipe.

3. Heat the oil in a 10-inch skillet over medium heat. Place the cutlets in the pan and cook for 1 minute, shaking occasionally, to prevent sticking. Lower the heat slightly and continue to cook until the cutlets are golden brown on the bottom, about 1 minute. Carefully flip each cutlet and continue to cook until golden, about 2 more minutes. Serve immediately with caper sauce (page 179) or fresh salsa (page 182).

Variations

1. Omit the Italian seasoning. Add 1 tablespoon minced gingerroot and 2 tablespoons tamari to the cutlet mixture. Serve with the Almond Raisin Sauce which accompanies the tempeh and broccoli recipe on page 87.

2. Prepare as in original recipe. Serve as a burger on a bun with standard condiments.

3. Prepare as in the original recipe. Serve with light tomato sauce (page 175).

Tamales

Tamales, a Mexican classic, vary from one household to the next. The common thread is a base of tamale (masa) dough that, when garnished with a flavorful topping, wrapped in corn husks and steamed, fills the air with a heavenly scent. The best are light and spongy, never heavy, and are delicious served with tomato salsa (page 182) and tomatillo salsa (page 182) or ancho pepper sauce (page 181).

Diana Kennedy, an undisputed expert on the cuisines of Mexico, recommends mixing the masa dough (made from lime-treated cornmeal or Quaker Quick Grits and lard) until a small piece floats when lowered into cold water. This, she says, is the key to obtaining the best texture. I have approximated the consistency of lard by recommending the substitution of butter (or margarine) and either or both oil and cream cheese. These fillings do not consistently float as the lard-based nonvegetarian dough does.

Corn and Pinto Tamales

Yield: 8 servings • Prep Time: 30 minutes • Cooking Time: 45 minutes

The simple bean filling used in these tamales can double, on its own, as a bean salad.

20 dried corn husks
2 Anaheim peppers, roasted and peeled (page 35), or 1/2 cup diced roasted red pepper
1 cup cooked pinto beans
1 1/2 cups fresh corn kernels
1/2 teaspoon dried oregano
2 tablespoons balsamic vinegar
1 1/2 teaspoons salt
1 teaspoon ground cumin
2 cups masa harina or Quaker Quick Grits
6 tablespoons butter
2 tablespoons canola oil
1 to 1 1/4 cups light vegetable stock (page 162)
1 1/4 teaspoons non-aluminum baking powder (optional)
1/2 cup grated Monterey Jack cheese or soy mozzarella

1. Place the corn husks in a large bowl and pour boiling water over them to cover. Set aside for at least 4 hours, or overnight.

2. Roughly chop the Anaheim peppers and place them in a mixing bowl. Add the beans, corn, oregano, vinegar, 1/2 teaspoon of salt, and the cumin. Mix well and set aside for at least 20 minutes. This topping may be prepared up to 24 hours in advance if refrigerated in an airtight container.

3. Meanwhile, prepare the masa dough. If using Quick Grits, grind them in a coffee grinder until very fine. Mix in the remaining 1 teaspoon of salt. If using masa harina, simply stir in the salt. In a separate bowl, beat the butter with an electric mixer until it is very light. Gradually add the oil, beating constantly. Continue to beat this mixture for 1 minute. Heat the stock until warm, then alternately add the grits and warm stock to the butter mixture, pouring each in gradually and beating constantly. You should begin with about 1/4 cup of grits, then some stock, then grits and finally stock. Once both are added, continue to beat for 3 to 4 minutes, then stir in the baking powder.

4. To fill a tamale, tear 16 thin strips from 3 or 4 corn husks to use as ties. Set these aside. To fill each husk, lay it flat on a clean work surface. Place about 1 to 1 1/2 tablespoons of the masa dough in the center of the husk and spread it out into a thin layer that is rectangular in shape and is about 3 inches from the broad end and 2 inches from the narrow end of the husk. Top this with 1 to 1 1/2 tablespoons of bean filling, spreading it out to cover the masa. Sprinkle a scant tablespoon of cheese over the filling. Fold one side of the husk over the filling, then the second side. Fold the narrow end of the husk up over the filling, then bring the broad end down, forming a waterproof, rectangular-shaped package. (An alternative, possibly simpler method of shaping tamales is to fill in the same manner, then fold the corn husk over the filling lengthwise, as above. Instead of folding the ends down over the filling, simply twist both ends in opposite directions and tie each in place with strips of husk.) Place the tamale, standing upright with its broad side up, in the top of a steamer. Fill the remaining husks and arrange them neatly in the steamer. The tamales may be prepared to this point up to 24 hours in advance, if refrigerated. They may also be frozen, wrapped airtight in a storage container. If frozen, they should be thawed before steaming.

5. Place the steaming rack over, not touching, rapidly boiling water. Seal and cook for 45 minutes. Check the water level periodically, adding more as necessary. Serve with fresh salsa (page 182) or ancho pepper sauce (page 181).

Cook's Note: The corn husks must be soaked for at least 4 hours.

Sweet and Spicy Pepper Tamales

Yield: 8 servings • Prep Time: 35 minutes • Cooking Time: 45 minutes

This light and tasty tamale is filled with sweet and hot peppers, goat cheese, pecans, and raisins and perfumed with cilantro, garlic, cinnamon, and oregano.

16 to 20 dried corn husks
1 pound red bell peppers, roasted
1 ancho pepper, softened in hot water
1 white onion, quartered
1 yellow bell pepper, diced
2 cloves garlic, halved
1 jalapeño pepper, seeded and minced
3 tablespoons orange juice
2 teaspoon ground cumin
1 1/2 teaspoons salt
1 teaspoon cinnamon
1/4 teaspoon dried oregano
1/3 cup pecans, chopped
1/4 cup raisins
2 cups masa harina
1 1/4 teaspoons non-aluminum baking powder
6 tablespoons butter
1 to 1 1/4 cups light vegetable stock (page 162)
6 ounces tangy goat cheese, crumbled
1/4 cup chopped cilantro

1. Place the corn husks in a large bowl and pour boiling water over them to cover. Set aside for at least 4 hours, or overnight. Tear 1 or 2 husks lengthwise into thin strips. Set these aside as ties for the tamales.

2. Peel the red peppers, then remove and discard their stems and seeds. Place the peppers in a blender or food processor fitted with the metal chopping blade. Purée. Drain the ancho pepper, then remove and discard its stem and seeds. Add it to the roasted pepper along with the onion. Blend briefly, until the onion is roughly chopped. Transfer this filling mix to a bowl and stir in the yellow bell peppers, garlic and the jalapeño. Add the orange juice, cumin, 1/2 teaspoon salt, cinnamon, and oregano. Stir in the pecans and raisins, then blend well and set aside.

3. Place the masa harina in a mixing bowl and stir in the remaining teaspoon of salt and baking powder. In a separate bowl, beat the butter with an electric mixer until it is very light. Continue to beat this mixture for 2 minutes. Heat the stock until warm, then alternately add the masa harina and warm stock to the butter mixture, pouring each in gradually and beating constantly. Once both are added, continue to beat for 3 minutes.

4. To fill a tamale, flatten a corn husk out on a clean work surface. Place about 2 1/2 tablespoons of the filling in the center of the husk and spread it out into a thin layer that is rectangular in shape and is about 3 inches from the broad end and 2 inches from the narrow end of the husk. Top this with about 1 1/2 tablespoons of pepper filling and place 1 tablespoon of cheese and a sprinkling of cilantro on top of this. Fold 1 side of the husk over the filling, then the second side over this to encase the filling. Twist the ends of the husk to seal and tie each end securely with a piece of husk. Place the tamale in the top of a steamer. Fill the remaining husks and arrange them alongside in the steamer. Place the steaming rack over, not touching, rapidly boiling water. Seal and cook for 45 minutes. Check the water level periodically, adding more as necessary. Serve warm with tomatillo salsa (page 182).

Cook's Note: The corn husks must be soaked for at least 4 hours.

Mixed Vegetable Tamales

Yield: 8 servings • Prep Time: 30 minutes • Cooking Time: 45 minutes

These tamales have a very simple vegetable and cheese filling.

16 to 20 dried corn husks
1 cup diced white onion
1 cup diced red bell pepper
1 cup diced green bell pepper
1 1/2 cups fresh corn kernels

1. Place the corn husks in a large bowl and pour boiling water over them to cover. Set aside for at least 4 hours, or overnight. Tear 1 or 2 husks lengthwise into thin strips. Set these aside as ties for the tamales.

2. In a mixing bowl, combine the onion, bell peppers, corn, jalapeño pepper, garlic, cumin, oregano, pumpkin seeds, and 1/2 teaspoon salt. Mix well. This topping may be prepared up to 24 hours in advance if refrigerated in an airtight container.

3. In a small bowl, combine the masa harina with the remaining teaspoon of salt. In a separate bowl, beat the butter and cream cheese with an electric mixer until it is very light. Gradually add the oil, beating constantly. Continue to beat this mixture for 2 minutes. Heat the stock until warm, then alternately add the grits and warm stock to the butter mixture, pouring each in gradually and beating constantly. Once both are added, continue to beat for 2 to 3 minutes, then stir in the baking powder.

4. To fill a tamale, flatten a corn husk out on a clean work surface. Place about 2 tablespoons of the masa dough in the center of the husk and spread it out into a thin layer that is rectangular in shape and is about 3 inches from the broad end and 2 inches from the narrow end of the husk. Top this with 1 1/2 to 2 tablespoons of vegetable filling, spreading it out to cover the masa. Sprinkle 1 tablespoon of cheese over this. Fold 1 side of the husk over the filling, then the second side over this to encase the filling. Twist the ends of the husk to seal and tie each securely with a strip of husk. Place the tamale in the top of a steamer. Fill the remaining husks and arrange them neatly in the steamer. The tamales may be prepared to this point up to 24 hours in advance, if refrigerated. They may also be frozen. If frozen, they should be thawed before steaming.

5. Place the steaming rack over, not touching, rapidly boiling water. Seal and cook for 45 minutes. Check the water level periodically, adding more as necessary. Serve with fresh salsa (page 182) or ancho pepper sauce (page 181).

Cook's Note: The corn husks must be soaked for at least 4 hours.

1 jalapeño pepper, seeded and minced
1 teaspoon minced garlic
2 teaspoons ground cumin
1/2 teaspoon dried oregano
3 tablespoons pumpkin seeds
1 1/2 teaspoons salt
2 cups masa harina
4 tablespoons butter
2 tablespoons cream cheese
2 tablespoons canola oil
3/4 cup vegetable stock (page 162)
1 1/4 teaspoons non-aluminum baking powder
1/2 cup grated Monterey Jack cheese or soy mozzarella

Simple Steamed Vegetables

When you need to get supper on the table in less than 30 minutes, make steamed vegetables with a sauce. The recipes that follow include some pleasing combinations, but you can vary the vegetables depending on what you have on hand. Whatever vegetables you choose, be certain to use a large enough steamer to accommodate the ingredients included. (See page 6 for more information on steamers.) Be sure to select a variety of vegetables—paying attention to differences in flavor, color, and textures. Also, steam the vegetables the appropriate length of time so that each is cooked to just the right degree of tenderness.

Selecting the vegetables is simple. Be certain they are absolutely fresh; being cooked in an unadorned manner, they will show any flaws, and those flaws will dominate the dish. Also, choose some that are predominantly sweet (red bell peppers, carrots, beets, etc.); only one, or at most two (and in that case they must complement one another), with a dominant flavor (broccoli, kale, sorrel, etc.); and one or more that have a less dominant flavor but give a lot to the dish in terms of fullness and texture (potatoes, yellow squash, mushrooms, etc.). This will give you a balance in taste and texture.

A general rule of thumb for cooking a variety of vegetables in the same steamer is that vegetables should be added to the steamer, one type at a time, depending on which is more or less porous. The shape and size into which vegetables have been cut also contribute to the length of time cooking they will require. For example, carrot, a relatively nonporous vegetable, is usually added close to the beginning of steaming. But if it is cut into thin rounds or grated, it may need to be added at the very end of cooking.

Steamed Vegetable Medley
with Sesame Scallion Sauce

Yield: 4 servings • Prep Time: 25 minutes • Cooking Time: 18 minutes

2 medium size carrots, roll cut
   (page 189)
1 small head cauliflower, cut into
   florets
3 leeks, chopped
1 small bunch broccoli (about 1
   pound), top cut in florets, stems
   peeled and cut in 3/4-inch
   pieces
1 pound firm tofu, cubed
1 yellow summer squash, cut
   lengthwise into 1 1/2-inch strips
1 red bell pepper, cut in triangles
1/2 cup tamari
1/4 cup minced scallions
2 teaspoons minced garlic
1 teaspoon minced gingerroot
2 tablespoons cider vinegar
1 tablespoon sesame oil
2 tablespoons black and/or white
   sesame seeds

1. Fill a steamer with enough water to come to just below the bottom of the steamer rack or basket. Bring the water to a boil with the rack in place, then add the carrots, cover and cook until they darken slightly in color, about 2 minutes. Add the cauliflower and leeks, stir once, then cover and continue to cook until the cauliflower are just beginning to soften, about 4 minutes Add the broccoli, tofu and squash. Stir, then cover and cook until the broccoli is a vibrant green and just barely tender, about 6 minutes. Add the red pepper, cover and continue to cook until it is tender, about 3 minutes. Immediately remove the steamer rack from the steamer and remove the lid. The vegetables may rest at room temperature briefly.

2. Meanwhile, combine the tamari, scallions, garlic, ginger, vinegar, and sesame oil. Warm to just below the boil, then pour the sauce into a sauce boat. Toss the vegetables and tofu to mix them evenly, then transfer them to a serving bowl. Sprinkle the sesame seeds on top and serve immediately.

Mexican-Style Steamed Vegetables

Yield: 4 servings • Prep Time: 30 minutes • Cooking Time: 30 minutes

8 ounces tempeh, cut in small
   cubes
1 yellow potato, cubed
1 1/2 cups green string beans, ends
   trimmed
1 red bell pepper, seeded and
   sliced
1 yellow bell pepper, seeded and
   sliced
1 cup julienne-sliced jicama
1 recipe fresh salsa (page 182)

This unusual combination of flavors—steamed vegetables plus tempeh and tomato salsa—is highly successful. Serve it with warm tortillas or over fluffy Mexican rice (page 159).

1. Place the tempeh in the steaming rack of a steamer over rapidly boiling water. Steam, covered, for 5 minutes. Add the potatoes and continue to steam for 2 minutes. Add the green beans and steam until they are almost tender, about 15 minutes. Stir in the peppers and jicama and steam until the beans are tender, no longer than 5 minutes. Immediately transfer the vegetables to a serving bowl and toss to combine. Serve with warm tortillas and salsa on the side.

Cook's Note: Prepare the tomato salsa as the tempeh and vegetables steam or up to 24 hours in advance.

Steamed Vegetables with Spicy Miso Sauce

Yield: 4 servings • Prep Time: 20 minutes • Cooking Time: 15 minutes

1 1/2 cups carrots, roll cut
   (page 189)
6 shiitake mushrooms, softened
   in hot water

This simple steamed vegetable dish combines the flavors and textures commonly used in Japanese cooking. Here the vegetables are accompanied by tiny bits of tofu and are served with a fiery miso sauce.

1. Place the carrots and mushrooms in the top rack of a steamer over rapidly boiling water. Cover and cook until the carrots begin to darken in color, about 4 minutes. Add the broccoli, tofu and bok choy. Stir once, then cover and continue to cook until the broccoli looks vibrant and is almost cooked, about 6 minutes. Add the celery, cover and cook for 2 minutes, then add the baby corn, snow peas, and water chestnuts. Cover and cook for about 1 minute or until the snow peas are puffed and very green. Immediately turn the mixture out into a serving bowl and toss to mix evenly, then top with walnuts or nori and cilantro.

2. Meanwhile, in a small saucepan, combine the miso, vinegar, syrup, ginger, wasabi powder, and the chili paste with garlic. Whisk in the water to make a smooth paste. Warm this sauce to just below the boil, then transfer it to a sauce boat and serve alongside the vegetables.

3 cups broccoli florets
3/4 pound firm tofu, cut in tiny dice
2 cups chopped bok choy
3/4 cup diagonally sliced celery
3/4 cup baby corn
3/4 cup snow peas, strings removed
1/2 cup sliced water chestnuts
1/4 cup chopped walnuts and/or 3 tablespoons crumbled nori
Fresh cilantro sprigs
1/3 cup light miso
3 tablespoons rice vinegar
2 tablespoons rice syrup (page 193)
2 teaspoons minced gingerroot
2 teaspoons wasabi powder
2 teaspoons chili paste with garlic
3/4 cup water

Rosemary Orange Tofu

Yield: 4 servings • Prep Time: 5 minutes • Cooking Time: 18 minutes

When time is limited or the tastes of your guests are unknown, choose this simple marinated broiled tofu. It may be cooked indoors or on the grill.

1. Drain the tofu and slice it into 1/2-inch-thick slabs. If time allows, place the tofu on a clean kitchen towel, cover with a second towel and place a small cutting board on top. Press firmly, then allow the tofu to drain for 30 minutes. (You may skip this step, but the tofu will be slightly watery in texture.) Once pressed, cut the slabs into 1-inch-wide strips.

2. In a 9-inch square baking pan, combine the tamari and orange juice. Crush the rosemary leaves between the palms of your hands and add them to the tamari mixture. Also add the garlic by pressing it through a garlic press. Stir to combine this marinade, then place the tofu in a single layer in the pan. Turn the slices to coat them on both sides. Cover and refrigerate, turning the tofu several times, and marinate for at least 2, but no longer than 24, hours.

3. Preheat the broiler to high. Broil the tofu in its marinade, placing it about 5 inches from the heat. When it begins to brown around the edges and has small, crisp spots (about 8 minutes) turn the slices of tofu and broil it on the second side until browned, about 5 minutes. Serve immediately.

1 pound firm tofu
1/4 cup tamari
3/4 cup orange juice
1 tablespoon dried rosemary leaves
2 cloves garlic

Variations

1. Replace the orange juice with 1/2 cup rice vinegar and omit the rosemary. Add 2 tablespoons of honey and 2 teaspoons minced gingerroot to the marinade. Proceed with the recipe as described above.

2. Follow the above variation, but stuff the tofu slices with a thin layer of wasabi paste before marinating. Sprinkle chopped nori over the tofu before serving.

3. Cube the tofu then follow the marinating instructions above. Skewer the tofu with mixed vegetables and/or tempeh and seitan, then cook under the broiler or on the grill.

Cook's Note: The tofu is best pressed for 30 minutes and marinated for at least 2 hours.

Middle Eastern-Style Tofu Kabobs

Yield: 6 servings • Prep Time: 30 minutes • Cooking Time: 25 minutes

1 1/2 pounds firm tofu
1 medium-sized yellow onion
3 cloves garlic
1 1/4 teaspoon salt
1 teaspoon minced gingerroot
1 teaspoon ground coriander
1/4 teaspoon cayenne pepper
1/4 teaspoon dried ground ginger
1/4 teaspoon cinnamon
2 tablespoons tomato paste
1 tablespoon honey
2 tablespoons red wine vinegar
12 scallions
12 mushrooms
12 cherry tomatoes
1 1/4 cups whole wheat couscous
2 1/3 cups light vegetable stock
　　(page 162) or water
1 cucumber, peeled, seeded, and
　　diced
1/4 cup currants
1/4 cup chopped almonds
　　(optional)
1/3 cup minced fresh mint

The same general principle for making all kabobs applies to these: have a strong or concentrated marinade for the main ingredient, then assemble skewers with ingredients of complementary color, taste and texture. These kabobs are absolutely wonderful grilled outdoors and served with a whole-grain flatbread and sliced raw vegetable salad. Try a salad of peppers, fennel, red onion, romaine, green olives, Greek peppers, feta and fresh mint with a drizzling of olive oil.

1. Drain the tofu and slice it into 1 1/4-inch-thick slabs. Place them on a clean kitchen towel with a second towel on top. Put a light cutting board over the tofu with a heavy skillet or several 1-pound cans on top. Press gently, then allow the tofu to drain under this weight for 30 minutes.

2. Peel and quarter the onion and cloves of garlic, then place them in a blender or food processor fitted with the metal chopping blade. Add 1 teaspoon salt, the gingerroot, coriander, cayenne pepper, ground ginger, and cinnamon. Blend, scraping down the sides of the beaker, for about 1 minute, or until roughly chopped. Add the tomato paste, honey, and vinegar, then continue to purée, scraping down the sides of the beaker as necessary, until this marinating mixture has formed a smooth paste.

3. Cut the pressed tofu into 1 1/2-inch cubes and place them in a single layer in a shallow baking dish. Rub the marinade into the tofu, turning the pieces to coat both sides. Cover and allow it to marinate for at least 8 hours, better yet a full day.

4. If you are using wooden skewers, soak them in hot water for 20 minutes before threading. Trim the root ends from the scallions and remove tough upper and outer stalks. Wipe the mushrooms clean with a damp kitchen towel, then trim the tough outer part from each stem, leaving the stem attached to the cap. Thread the tofu and alternating vegetables (scallions, mushrooms, and cherry tomatoes) onto the skewers, beginning and ending with the tofu. To skewer each scallion, spear it just above the root end to secure it in place, then skewer another ingredient over the scallion. Next, wrap the scallion over this ingredient and skewer it in place. (You may find it easier to steam the scallions for 3 minutes before skewering, though their texture will be less crisp after broiling.) Once all kabobs are formed, place them on a broiling rack. They may be refrigerated, covered, for up to 3 hours before proceeding with the recipe.

5. Preheat the broiler to high. Broil the kabobs, turning once, until the tofu has begun to brown and the tomatoes are soft, about 10 minutes. Meanwhile, place the couscous in a mixing bowl. Bring the stock to a boil. Add the remaining 1/4 teaspoon of salt, then pour this over the couscous. Stir once, then cover the bowl with a plate and set aside for 15 minutes. Once all stock is absorbed, fluff the couscous with a fork and mix in the cucumber, currants, almonds, and mint. Mound the couscous in the center of a large serving platter and top it with the kabobs. Serve at once.

Cook's Note: The tofu is best if pressed for 30 minutes and then marinated overnight.

Chinese-Style Barbecued Seitan Roast

Yield: 8 servings • Prep Time: 25 minutes • Cooking Time: 3 hours

Seitan is delicious when bathed, as in the traditional style of Chinese barbecued pork roast, in an aromatic mixture of hoisin sauce (available in Asian markets), garlic, and scallions.

2 1/2 cups uncooked seitan (page 184)
5 cups water
1 teaspoon salt
1/4 teaspoon black pepper
1/8 teaspoon cayenne
4 cloves garlic, sliced thin
1 1/2 tablespoons minced ginger-root
1 4-inch piece kombu (page 192)
1 3-inch cinnamon stick
1/2 cup soy sauce
2 tablespoons peanut oil
5 tablespoons hoisin sauce
1/4 cup dry white wine
2 tablespoons honey
1 tablespoon minced garlic
1 teaspoon chili paste with garlic
1/3 cup minced scallions

1. Prepare the seitan according to directions on page 184. Shape it into 3 large sausage-shaped pieces, making them as long as the pot in which they will be cooked can tolerate. In a large Dutch oven or saucepan, combine 4 cups of water, the salt, pepper, cayenne, sliced garlic, 1 tablespoon ginger, kombu, cinnamon, 1/4 cup soy sauce, and the peanut oil. Bring this mixture to a boil, then reduce to a very low simmer. Add the seitan and cook covered, stirring occasionally to prevent the seitan from sticking, for 1 hour. Do not allow the liquid to boil as the seitan cooks or its texture will become airy and unpleasant. Remove from the heat and allow the seitan to cool in its cooking liquid. The seitan may be prepared up to 4 days in advance if refrigerated, in the liquid, in an airtight container. It may also be frozen for up to 2 months.

2. Remove the seitan from its cooking liquid, then strain the liquid into a saucepan and reduce it to 1 cup. In a shallow baking dish, combine the hoisin sauce, wine, honey, minced garlic, chili paste, scallions, and remaining 1/4 cup soy sauce and 1/2 tablespoon ginger. Mix well, then add the reduced cooking liquid. Stir again and add the seitan. Turn to coat well, then cover and allow to marinate, turning several times for at least 2 hours or overnight.

3. Preheat the oven to 375°F. Place the pan of seitan, uncovered, on the center rack of the oven for 30 minutes. Turn the seitan several times as it cooks. Serve the roast sliced thin, drizzled with its marinade. (Thin the marinade with up to 1 cup water, if desired.) Alternatively, use the seitan in one of the following recipes.

Cook's Note: The seitan must be simmered for 1 hour, then cooled in its cooking liquid. It must then marinate in the hoisin sauce marinade for at least 2 hours.

Barbecued Seitan Salad

Yield: 4 servings • Prep Time: 20 minutes • Cooking Time: 10 minutes

1/3 recipe Barbecued Seitan Roast (page 55)
1/4 cup cooking marinating liquid from Barbecued Seitan Roast
1 cup light vegetable stock (page 162) or water
1 teaspoon cornstarch + 2 teaspoons cold water
1/4 cup minced scallions
1 1/2 tablespoons canola oil
1 tablespoon minced gingerroot
1 tablespoon minced garlic
1 to 2 dried red chili peppers
8 fresh shiitake or button mushrooms, sliced
1 1/2 cups sliced celery (cut on the diagonal)
2 cups chopped bok choy
2 cups mung bean sprouts
1 cup yellow bell pepper, sliced
1 cup grated carrot
4 cups shredded romaine lettuce
1/4 cup minced cilantro (optional)
1/4 cup toasted walnuts, chopped (optional)

One of the numerous ways to use Barbecued Seitan Roast (page 55) is to mix it into a salad. Slices of the seitan are tossed in with stir-fried vegetables, then served with rice or tortillas.

1. Slice the seitan into 1/4-inch-thick pieces and set them aside. In a 1/2-quart saucepan, combine the cooking liquid from the seitan roast with the stock. Bring this to a boil, then reduce to a simmer and cook, stirring occasionally for 5 minutes. Stir the cornstarch paste into this sauce and bring it to a boil. Remove the sauce from the heat and stir in the scallions and sliced seitan.

2. Heat a 12-inch wok over medium high heat then add the oil and heat until hot, but not smoking. Add the ginger, garlic, and red chili peppers. Cook, tossing constantly, until the peppers darken in color, about 1 minute. Add the mushrooms and continue to cook, stirring constantly, for 1 minute. Reduce the heat slightly and continue to cook, stirring often, until the mushrooms soften, about 5 minutes. Return the heat to medium high and add the celery and bok choy. Cook, tossing often, until the celery turns a bright green, about 2 minutes. Add the bean sprouts and yellow pepper, then toss for about 1 minute, or until the sprouts plump slightly. Immediately remove the skillet from the heat and add the carrots, lettuce, and cilantro.

3. Mound the salad on individual plates or 1 large serving platter. Rewarm the sauce briefly, then pour it over the salad, arranging the seitan on top. Garnish with walnuts and serve at once.

Simple Stir-Fries

Almost any food can be stir-fried, but here I concentrate on presenting a basic formula for a main course grain-based stir-fry. Any grain can serve as the base of a stir-fry, if it can be cooked so that it is fluffy. Lightly cooked millet works well, but other grains, sticky rice or barley, for example, can be disastrous in stir-fries. The method is a simple one to experiment with, and the three prototype recipes that follow may serve as inspiration.

Stir-Fried Rice Mediterranean Style with Fava Beans and Artichoke Hearts

Yield: 6 servings • Prep Time: 25 minutes • Cooking Time: 20 minutes

2 cups basmati or long-grain brown rice
4 1/2 cups light vegetable stock (page 162)

The rich taste of fava beans adds body and a sprinkling of pine nuts adds a rich texture to this simple stir-fry. I use basmati rice here, though it is not typical of Italian dishes. You may use sun-dried tomatoes, not packed in oil, for fewer calories from fat.

1. Rinse the rice well in several changes of cold water, until the water runs clear. Leave it in the strainer to drain as you bring 4 cups of stock to a boil in a 3-quart saucepan. When the stock is boiling, stir in 1/4 teaspoon of salt and the rice. Return to a boil, stirring once or twice, then cover and reduce to a simmer. Cook, covered, until the rice is just tender and most of the liquid is absorbed, about 25 minutes. Immediately transfer the rice to a strainer and run cold water over it to stop its cooking. Toss the rice in the strainer with your fingertips as the cold water runs through it to cool it quickly. Use as little water as possible. Do not allow the rice to become soggy. As soon as most of the rice is cool to the touch, turn it out onto a clean kitchen towel to drain. Cover it with a second towel and allow it to rest at room temperature for 15 minutes. The rice may be used immediately, or it can be refrigerated in an airtight container for up to 3 days.

2. Grate the zest from the lemon and set it aside, then slice the lemon in half. Rinse the artichokes then, with a wavy-edged knife, saw off about 1/2 inch from the top and stem of each artichoke. With a paring knife, trim off all tough outer leaves (each artichoke will be about half its original size), then cut each in half lengthwise. As you work, rub each artichoke with a generous coating of lemon juice on all cut surfaces to retard discoloring. (If you are using frozen artichokes, skip this step.)

3. In a 12-inch skillet, heat 1 tablespoon oil over medium high heat until hot, but not smoking. Add the onion and cook, stirring constantly, until all pieces of onion are coated with oil, about 1 minute. Reduce the heat slightly and add the artichokes. Toss to coat with oil, then stir in the garlic, oregano and remaining 1/2 cup stock. When the liquid boils, reduce the heat to a simmer. Cover and cook, stirring often, for 5 minutes. Add the zucchini, then continue to cook, stirring frequently, until the artichokes are just tender, about 5 more minutes. Transfer the cooked vegetables to a bowl.

4. Preheat the broiler to high. Heat the remaining 2 tablespoons of oil in the skillet over high heat until very hot, but not smoking. Add the rice and cook, stirring constantly, until the rice begins to pop, about 1 1/2 minutes. Stir in the wine vinegar, remaining salt, pepper flakes, and yellow pepper. Continue to cook, stirring constantly, for about 1 minute, or until the bell pepper is warm. Add the cooked vegetables, beans, and sun-dried tomatoes. Continue to cook, stirring constantly, until the mixture is just warmed through. Remove the stir-fry from the heat and stir in the lemon zest and tarragon.

5. Transfer the rice to a heatproof serving platter. Sprinkle the cheese over the surface of the rice then place the platter under the broiler briefly, until a delicate brown crust forms on top. Remove from the broiler, sprinkle with pine nuts and serve immediately.

Cook's Note: Fresh fava beans may be cooked in 4 minutes, but require time to shell and peel. You may cook and peel them up to 3 days in advance.

1 1/4 teaspoons salt
1 lemon
6 fresh or frozen baby artichokes
3 tablespoons olive oil
1 cup diced white onion
2 cloves garlic, minced
1/2 teaspoon dried oregano
1 small zucchini, diced
3 tablespoons white wine vinegar
1/4 teaspoon dried chili flakes
1/2 cup diced yellow bell pepper
1 cup cooked fava beans (page 96) or use baby limas or cannellini beans
8 oil-packed sun-dried tomatoes, drained and chopped
3 tablespoons chopped tarragon leaves
3 tablespoons grated Parmesan
2 tablespoons toasted pine nuts (page 35)

Quinoa with Anasazi Beans

Yield: 4 servings • Prep Time: 35 minutes • Cooking Time: 8 minutes

The quinoa is light and fluffy with a slightly earthy quality. It is complemented by the rich, sweet flavor of anasazi beans.

1 lemon
1 3/4 cup cooked anasazi or
   azuki beans
3/4 teaspoon salt
1 teaspoon ground cumin
1 teaspoon ground coriander
1/4 cup minced scallions
2 teaspoons minced garlic
1 cup quinoa
3 cups water
1 tablespoon canola oil
3/4 cup diced carrot
1/2 cup diced celery
1/2 cup diced onion
1 tablespoon curry powder
1 teaspoon garam masala
   (page 191)
1 jalapeño pepper, minced
2 teaspoons minced gingerroot
3 tablespoons soy sauce
1 1/2 cups alfalfa or mung
   bean sprouts
1 teaspoon toasted cumin seeds
3 tablespoons minced cilantro
2 tablespoons minced fresh mint
1/4 cup chopped peanuts
   (optional)

1. Grate the zest from the lemon into a small bowl, then squeeze in the juice. Add the beans, 1/2 teaspoon salt, the ground cumin, coriander, scallions, and garlic. Mix well and set aside for at least 20 minutes to marinate. (The beans can be marinated, covered and refrigerated, for up to 24 hours.)

2. Place the quinoa in a bowl and cover it with cold water. Rub it between your fingers to clean it, then drain it through a fine mesh strainer and rinse again. Repeat this several times until the water runs absolutely clear. (If the quinoa is not sufficiently rinsed it will have a strong, earthy taste.) In a 1 1/2-quart saucepan, bring the water to a boil. Add the remaining 1/4 teaspoon of salt and stir in the quinoa. Reduce the heat to a simmer, cover and cook until all grains have popped open and are just barely tender, about 15 minutes. As the quinoa cooks, occasionally scrape down grains of quinoa from the sides of the pan. When done, immediately drain the quinoa and run cold water over it to stop its cooking. Toss the quinoa with your fingers until it is cool, then stop the water and allow it to drain thoroughly. The quinoa may be cooked up to 3 days in advance if thoroughly drained, then refrigerated in an airtight container.

3. In a 12-inch wok or skillet, heat the oil over medium high heat until hot, but not smoking. Add the carrots, celery, and onion. Toss well, until all are lightly coated with oil, about 1 minute. Add the curry powder and garam masala. Continue to cook, tossing constantly, to release the curry flavors. Stir in the jalapeño and ginger and toss briefly. Add the quinoa along with the beans and their marinade. Cook, tossing constantly, until the quinoa begins to make a popping sound, about 2 minutes. Pour the soy sauce over the quinoa and toss, then add the sprouts and toss again. Remove the quinoa from the heat and top with the cumin seeds, cilantro, and mint. Toss again, then turn out onto a serving platter. Sprinkle the peanuts over the quinoa and serve at once.

Fluffy Millet with Marinated Tempeh

Yield: 4 servings • Prep Time: 45 minutes • Cooking Time: 18 minutes

Millet is a wonderfully versatile grain that can take on many forms, depending on how it is handled. Here delightfully light and fluffy millet, seasoned with cardamom and cinnamon, serves as the base of the dish. The topping is a dusting of sweetly seasoned toasted millet.

2 cups uncooked millet
3 cups water
1/2 teaspoon salt
1 tablespoon butter or oil
2 teaspoons maple sugar
1/4 teaspoon cayenne pepper
8 ounces tempeh
5 tablespoons tamari
2 tablespoons balsamic vinegar
1 tablespoon honey
1 tablespoon canola oil
1 dried red chili pepper
2 cups chopped kale leaves
4 cardamom pods, crushed
1/2 teaspoon cinnamon
1 tablespoon minced garlic
1 teaspoon minced gingerroot
1 cup diced red bell pepper
1/2 cup minced scallions
1/2 cup fresh or frozen peas
1/4 cup chopped basil leaves

1. Rinse the millet well in several changes of cold water. Remove 1/2 cup and transfer it to a clean kitchen towel. Spread this out and allow it to dry thoroughly. In a 1 1/2-quart saucepan, bring the water to a boil. Stir in 1/4 teaspoon of the salt and the remaining 1 1/2 cups of millet. Bring this to a boil, then reduce to a simmer, cover and cook, stirring occasionally, until the grains of millet have popped open and are light and fluffy, about 25 minutes. Immediately transfer the millet to a strainer and run cold tap water over it to stop its cooking. As it cools, toss the millet with your fingers to distribute the cold water. Once cold to the touch, allow the millet to drain thoroughly in the strainer. It may be prepared ahead, fully drained, then refrigerated in an airtight container for up to 3 days.

2. Melt the butter in a small skillet. Add the remaining 1/4 teaspoon of salt, the maple sugar, and cayenne pepper. Stir to blend, then add the uncooked 1/2 cup of millet and cook, stirring constantly, until the millet begins to crisp and brown. Immediately turn the millet out onto a plate lined with paper towels to drain and cool. Set this aside. This toasted topping may be prepared up to 24 hours in advance if stored in an airtight container at room temperature.

3. Crumble the tempeh into small pieces and place it in a mixing bowl. Add the tamari, the balsamic vinegar and honey. Stir to combine, then cover, refrigerate and allow the tempeh to marinate for at least 20 minutes, or up to 24 hours.

4. In a 12-inch wok or skillet, heat the oil over medium high heat until hot, but not smoking. Add the chili pepper and toss until it darkens, about 1 minute. Stir in the kale, cardamom, cinnamon, garlic, and ginger. Cook, tossing constantly until the kale wilts, about 2 minutes. Add the tempeh, along with its marinade. Reduce the heat slightly and continue to cook, tossing constantly, until the kale is tender, about 5 minutes. Add the fluffy millet, red pepper, and scallions. Return the heat to medium high and continue to cook, tossing constantly, until the millet is warmed through, about 2 minutes. Mix in the peas and basil, then cook for another minute. Turn out onto a serving platter and sprinkle the maple sugar-spiced millet on top. Serve at once.

Variation

1. To increase the nutty flavor of the dish, try toasting the 2 1/2 cups millet in a dry skillet over high heat (shaking the pan constantly after the millet is added and cooking only until it is lightly browned) before boiling it. Proceed with the recipe as above.

Cook's Note: The tempeh is best marinated for 20 minutes. Allow time for this.

Scrambled Tofu

When I first began eating vegetarian foods, I recall finding Scrambled Tofu in virtually every small vegetarian restaurant I came across. I found the name very confusing because I expected scrambled tofu to be a nondairy version of scrambled eggs. Though sometimes the tofu was crumbled and visually resembled overcooked, dried-out pieces of scrambled egg, it was often presented simply cubed, looking nothing like eggs. Also, I could find very little resemblance in the taste of scrambled tofu from one restaurant to the next, although turmeric was often added to give an egg-like color.

When I began working on this series of cookbooks, I decided it was time for me to begin making my own tofu from scratch in order to understand the process and shed light on this mainstay ingredient. The first time I made it, I took some that was very soft and fried it with simple flavors (tamari, pickled ginger and toasted sesame oil). Though the flavor was not that of traditional scrambled eggs, the texture was virtually identical! Suddenly I understood the evolution of the mystifying term "Scrambled Tofu" which had been perplexing to me for years. For this reason alone I encourage you to make tofu from scratch (page 164) and use it in the recipes that follow.

Simple Scrambled Tofu

Yield: 4 servings • Prep Time: 20 minutes • Cooking Time: 15 minutes

1 pound firm tofu
2 teaspoons olive oil
1 cup diced red onion
1 cup sliced mushrooms
1 cup peeled, seeded, and chopped tomatoes (page 35) or 1 16-ounce can chopped tomatoes, drained
1 teaspoon minced garlic
Pinch of dried thyme
2 1/2 tablespoons tamari
3 tablespoons minced fresh parsley, dill or basil

1. Drain the tofu and cut it into 1/2-inch cubes. Set them aside on a clean kitchen towel to drain as you prepare the rest of the ingredients.

2. In a 10-inch nonstick skillet, heat the oil over medium high heat. When the oil is hot, but not smoking, add the onion and cook, stirring constantly, for about 30 seconds. Reduce the heat to medium low and continue to cook, stirring often, until the onion begins to wilt, about 5 minutes. Add the mushrooms and continue to cook, stirring often, until they begin to release their juices, about 5 minutes more. Add the tomatoes, garlic, thyme, and tamari and stir to combine. Reduce the heat slightly and mix in the tofu and fresh parsley. Continue to cook, stirring often, until the mushrooms are completely softened and the taste of garlic is no longer raw, about 5 minutes. Serve immediately.

Sweet and Spicy Scrambled Tofu

Yield: 4 servings • Prep Time: 25 minutes • Cooking Time: 20 minutes

1 pound soft tofu
3 tablespoons canola oil or ghee (page 191)
1 cup diced yellow onion
1 small sweet potato, peeled and cut in small dice
2 teaspoons minced gingerroot
2 teaspoons ground cumin

This scrambled tofu variation is excellent for either brunch or dinner. Serve it, as suggested below, over bean sprouts with Garlic Crostini (page 167) on the side.

1. Drain the tofu and crumble it with your fingers into 1/2- to 3/4-inch pieces. Place the tofu in a strainer and allow it to drain over the sink as you prepare the rest of the ingredients for the dish.

Broccoli and Black Beans with Cashew Sauce
(page 94)

Tofu "Scallops"
(page 71)

Corn and Pinto Tamales
(page 49)

Rosemary Orange Tofu
(page 53)

Soba Noodles with Dipping Sauce
(page 146)

Potato Crust Pizza
(page 68)

Eggplant Steaks with Madeira Sauce
(page 112)

Idlis with Tomato and Tamarind Chutneys
(pages 103, 183, 184)

2. In a 10-inch skillet, heat 2 tablespoons of the oil or ghee over medium high flame until hot, but not smoking. Add the onion and toss quickly to coat evenly with the oil. Reduce the heat to medium low and continue to cook, stirring often, until the onion is translucent, about 10 minutes. Add the sweet potato and continue to cook, stirring frequently, until the potato just begins to soften, about 5 minutes.

3. Return the heat to medium high and add the ginger, cumin, cinnamon, salt, turmeric, hing, and molasses. Cook for 2 minutes, stirring constantly, then add the tomato, green pepper, and tofu. Stir, then reduce the heat to low, and cook for 2 minutes.

4. Squeeze and rub the tamarind with your fingertips to separate the seeds from the pulp. Press the pulp and soaking water through a tea strainer into the skillet. Continue to cook, stirring often until the flavors have merged, about 5 minutes. Remove the tofu from the heat and stir in the cilantro.

5. Heat the remaining oil or ghee in a small skillet until hot, but not smoking. Add the serrano peppers and mustard seeds. Cook, stirring constantly, until the seeds pop and darken, about 1 minute. Stir these into the tofu and toss well.

6. Arrange 3 crostini on individual serving plates with points touching opposing sides of the plate. Mound 1/2 cup of the sprouts in the center of each plate and divide the tofu evenly among the plates, placing it on top of the sprouts. Serve immediately.

1 1/2 teaspoons cinnamon
1 teaspoon salt
1/4 teaspoon turmeric
1/4 teaspoon hing (asafoetida) (page 192)
2 teaspoons molasses
1 cup chopped tomato
1 medium green pepper, seeds removed and diced
1 walnut-sized ball tamarind (page 195), softened in 1/4 cup boiling water
1/4 cup minced cilantro
2 to 3 serrano peppers, seeded and sliced into rounds
1 teaspoon brown mustard seeds
12 crostini (page 167)
2 cups fresh mung bean sprouts

Scrambled Tofu with Sun-Dried Tomatoes

Yield: 4 servings • Prep Time: 20 minutes • Cooking Time: 20 minutes

A simple tofu preparation that is delicious as a filling for crêpes or served with rice.

1. Drain the tofu and cut it into 1-inch-thick slabs. Place on a clean kitchen towel with a second towel on top. Gently press the tofu to extract some of the water, then allow the tofu to rest for 20 minutes. Drain the sun-dried tomatoes, saving their liquid, then shred the tomatoes into 1/4-inch-thick slices. Set aside.

2. In a 12-inch skillet, heat the olive oil over medium high heat. Add the leeks and cook, stirring constantly, until they just begin to soften, about 1 minute. Reduce the heat to low and add the garlic. Continue to cook, stirring often, until the leeks are very soft and the thinnest parts of them are translucent.

3. Turn the heat to medium high and add the chopped mushrooms. Cook, stirring and tossing constantly until all of the mushroom pieces have been lightly coated with oil, about 2 minutes. Add the wine and cook, shaking the pan occasionally, until the steam dies down and the smell of alcohol evaporates, about 1 minute. Drain the porcini mushrooms, saving their soaking liquid, and add them along with the sun-dried tomatoes to the skillet.

4. Combine the strained soaking liquid from the mushrooms with the tomato-soaking liquid. Measure out 3/4 cup of this and add it to the skillet. Stir in the oregano, salt, nutmeg, and the tofu. Mash the tofu against the sides of the skillet so that it breaks into rough, small shapes. Continue to cook, stirring often, until only a thin coating of liquid remains, about 10 minutes.

5. Stir the olives into the tofu mixture and warm through. Remove it from the heat and stir in the arugula or the basil. Taste and adjust the seasonings. Serve.

1 pound soft tofu
10 sun-dried tomatoes, softened in hot water
1 tablespoon olive oil
3 leeks, cleaned and chopped
2 teaspoons minced garlic
1/2 pound button mushrooms, chopped
1/4 cup dry white wine
1/2 ounce porcini mushrooms, softened in hot water
2 teaspoons minced fresh oregano or 1/2 teaspoon dried
1/4 teaspoon salt
1/8 teaspoon nutmeg
4 green Greek olives, pitted
8 Kalamata olives, pitted
1/2 cup shredded arugula leaves or 1/3 cup shredded basil leaves

Breakfast-Style Scrambled Tofu

Yield: 4 servings • Prep Time: 20 minutes • Cooking Time: 20 minutes

Because this dish resembles true scrambled eggs in appearance, it is a good choice for breakfast. By any name, it makes a quick and simple main course for a meal.

1 pound soft tofu
2 tablespoons olive oil
1 1/2 cup diced leek, or 1 cup diced white onion
4 cloves garlic, sliced thin
6 ounces mushrooms, sliced
1 teaspoon salt
1/4 teaspoon black pepper
1/4 teaspoon turmeric
1 teaspoon tamari
1/4 teaspoon paprika
1/4 teaspoon nutmeg
1 tablespoon lemon juice
1 teaspoon Dijon-style mustard
1 teaspoon fresh thyme, minced, or 1/4 teaspoon dried
3 tablespoons snipped fresh chives
4 chive blossoms, if available

1. Drain the tofu and, with your fingertips, crumble it into 1/2-inch pieces. Set this aside in a strainer set over the sink and allow it to drain for 15 minutes.

2. In a 12-inch skillet, heat the oil over medium high heat until very hot, but not smoking. Add the leeks and sauté, stirring constantly, until all of the pieces are coated with oil. Reduce the heat slightly and continue to cook, stirring frequently, for 5 minutes. Add the garlic and mushrooms then continue to cook, tossing often, until the leeks are very soft, about 7 minutes.

3. Add the tofu to the skillet and toss. Increase the heat slightly and stir in the salt, pepper, turmeric, tamari, paprika, nutmeg, lemon juice, mustard, and thyme. Continue to cook, stirring often, until the tofu is heated through and the flavors have merged, about 5 minutes. Stir in the chives, then taste and adjust the seasonings. Serve at once, garnished with the chive blossoms.

Variation

1. Replace the mustard with 1 tablespoon tahini and instead of thyme, use 2 teaspoons toasted cumin seeds. Omit the chives and stir 1/4 cup minced cilantro into the tofu just before serving.

Curried Tofu Scramble

Yield: 4 servings • Prep Time: 10 minutes • Cooking Time: 15 minutes

Curry's strong burst of flavor is a welcome addition to tofu. Mung bean sprouts and cashews add interesting texture and balance the taste.

1 pound soft tofu
1 cucumber
1 teaspoon salt
1 1/2 tablespoons peanut oil or ghee (page 191)
1 stalk celery, cut in small dice
2 tablespoons curry powder (or to taste)
1 cup chopped tomato
2 teaspoons honey or 2 tablespoons raisins
1/2 cup mung bean sprouts
1/4 cup minced scallions
1/4 cup fresh or frozen peas
2 tablespoons chopped cashews
4 sprigs fresh mint

1. Drain the tofu and cut it into 1-inch-thick slabs. Place them on a clean kitchen towel and place a second towel on top. Gently press the tofu to extract some of the water, then allow it to rest for 10 minutes.

2. Peel the cucumber, then cut it in half. Scrape out and discard the seeds, then slice the cucumber into 1/4-inch-thick half circles. Place the slices in a colander and sprinkle with 1/4 teaspoon of salt. Allow this to "sweat" for about 10 minutes

3. In a 12-inch skillet, heat the oil or ghee over medium high heat until hot, but not smoking. Add the celery and cook, tossing constantly, for about 30 seconds. Stir in the curry powder, reduce the heat to medium and continue to cook, stirring often until the curry has released its flavor and the celery is beginning to soften, about 5 minutes. Add the tomato and cook to just soften, about 2 minutes.

4. Crumble the tofu with your fingers as you add it to the skillet. Stir in the honey or raisins, remaining 3/4 teaspoon salt and continue to cook, stirring and crumbling the tofu as you work, until all of the juice from the tomato has evaporated, about 5 minutes.

5. Quickly toss the bean sprouts, scallions, and peas into the tofu and heat just long enough to warm through. Taste and adjust the seasonings. Transfer the scrambled tofu to one large plate or 4 individual dinner plates. Sprinkle cashews over the top and garnish with the sprigs of mint. Serve at once.

Variation

1. Fry 1 minced serrano pepper in 1 tablespoon ghee (page 191) for 1 minute. Add 1 1/2 tablespoons brown mustard seeds and continue to cook until the seeds pop. Immediately pour this mixture into the cooked tofu, then mix. Serve.

Anasazi Refried Beans with Whole Grain Tortillas

Yield: 4 servings • Prep Time: 30 minutes • Cooking Time: 35 minutes

This is among the simplest recipes in this book, yet it is one that can be used in a number of different ways for strikingly different effects. Refried beans are traditionally very humble fare—mashed cooked beans that are fried in lard and often lightly seasoned with peppers and one or two other flavorings. This recipe uses canola oil in place of the lard and sweet anasazi beans instead of the familiar pinto beans.

3 cups cooked anasazi or
   pinto beans
2 tablespoons canola oil
1 1/2 cups chopped white onion
4 cups bean cooking liquid
   (supplement cooking liquid
   with water if necessary)
1 cup chopped tomato
2 jalapeño peppers, seeds
   removed and minced
2 teaspoons minced garlic
1 teaspoon ground cumin
3/4 teaspoon salt
1/2 teaspoon dried oregano,
   crushed
1/2 teaspoon cumin seeds, toasted
8 whole grain tortillas
2 tablespoons butter (optional)
1 cup fresh tomato salsa
   (page 182)
1 avocado, sliced
1/4 cup black olives, sliced
4 sprigs cilantro
6 tablespoons sour cream or
   soy cream (page 171) (optional)

1. Mash the beans with a potato masher or fork, leaving about half of them whole. In a 10-inch skillet, heat the oil over high heat until hot, but not smoking. Add the onion and toss. Reduce the heat to medium and continue to cook until the onions soften, about 8 minutes.

2. Add the beans, cooking liquid, tomato, jalapeños, garlic, ground cumin, salt and oregano. Cook, stirring occasionally, until most of the cooking liquid has evaporated, about 15 minutes. Stir in the cumin seeds, then taste and adjust the seasonings. The refried beans may be prepared up to 3 days in advance if refrigerated in an airtight container.

3. Preheat the oven to 325°F. Place the tortillas in a covered shallow baking dish with pieces of butter (optional) sandwiched between, then warm for 10 minutes, or until soft. Place each tortilla on the work surface. Spread a 1/4-inch-thick layer of the bean mixture evenly on the tortilla. Fold the tortilla in half and then in half again to form a rounded triangle. Fill the remaining tortillas, then arrange them in a single layer in the baking dish. Cover and warm briefly until piping hot.

4. Warm the salsa briefly in a small saucepan. On one large platter or 4 individual serving plates, arrange a layer of salsa with a filled tortilla on top. Garnish each with avocado, a sprig of cilantro, sliced olives, and sour cream. Serve.

Variation

1. Use the same filling to stuff hollowed-out tomatoes. Sprinkle grated Monterey Jack cheese on top and bake at 375°F. until the cheese melts, about 10 minutes. Serve warm.

Anasazi Beans with Ginger and Cauliflower

Yield: 6 servings • Prep Time: 15 minutes • Cooking Time: 3 hours

1 1/4 cups dry anasazi beans
1 tablespoon peanut oil
1 bay leaf
1 2-inch piece kombu, rinsed
    (page 192) (optional)
6 1/2 cups water
1 cup diced onion
1 tablespoon minced garlic
1 1/2 teaspoons minced ginger-
    root
1 dried red pepper (optional)
2 teaspoons ground cumin
1 teaspoon salt
1 teaspoon blackstrap molasses
3/4 pound butternut squash
1 small head cauliflower
1/2 cup fresh or frozen peas
2 teaspoons cumin seeds, toasted

Excellent served over Braised Greens (page 157), garnished with croutons or used as a filling for tortillas or crêpes (page 170). Anasazi beans need no presoaking, but if you use a different type of bean, allow appropriate soaking time.

1. Pick over the beans to remove all dirt and debris. Place them in a strainer and rinse well. In a 2-quart saucepan, combine the beans, the peanut oil, bay leaf, kombu, and 5 cups of water. Bring to a boil, stirring occasionally. Skim all foam that rises to the surface as the beans begin to boil. Reduce heat to a simmer, cover and cook, stirring occasionally, until the beans are tender, about 2 1/2 hours. If necessary, add more water, 1/4 cup at a time, to prevent the beans from burning. Once the beans are tender, remove them from the heat and set aside. The beans can be prepared up to 5 days in advance if refrigerated in an airtight container. They can be frozen for up to 2 months. Thaw before continuing with the recipe.

2. Transfer the beans to a 4-quart saucepan. Add the remaining 1 1/2 cups water, the onion, garlic, ginger, dried red pepper, cumin, salt, and molasses. Stir to combine, then cook at a simmer, stirring occasionally as you prepare the vegetables, about 15 minutes.

3. Peel and seed the squash, then cut it into small, 1/2-inch dice. Add the squash to the beans and cook until it is very tender, about 20 minutes. Meanwhile, trim the cauliflower into small florets and place it in a steamer rack, set in a 2-quart saucepan over rapidly boiling water. Cover and cook until tender, about 10 minutes. Drain immediately.

4. When the squash is tender, stir in the peas and continue to cook for 5 minutes. Remove the beans from the heat, then stir in the toasted cumin seeds. Taste and adjust the seasonings. Serve the beans surrounded with the steamed cauliflower, or mix the cauliflower into the beans if they are to be used as a filling. The dish can be prepared up to 3 days in advance if refrigerated in an airtight container. Warm before serving.

Cook's Note: By using cooked or canned anasazi, kidney or pinto beans, you can reduce cooking time to 30 minutes.

Tempeh with Macadamia Nuts and Lemon Grass

Yield: 4 servings • Prep Time: 40 minutes • Cooking Time: 15 minutes

The alluring scent of lemon grass penetrates the air as this light curry simmers. Serve it with sweet rice and a carrot salad (page 155).

1. Cut the tempeh into 3/4-inch cubes and place them in a steamer rack over rapidly boiling water. Cover and steam for 10 minutes.

2. Meanwhile, trim the stalks of lemon grass to about 3 inches, discarding the tough top part of each stem. Peel and discard all tough outer layers from each stalk, leaving only the cream-colored aromatic core. With the broad side of a cleaver or heavy knife, smash each stalk of lemon grass, turning it several times to flatten it from a number of directions. Then cut the stalks into 2-inch pieces and place them in a shallow baking dish. Add the shallots, soy sauce, orange juice, lime juice, rice syrup, ginger, garlic, cinnamon, coriander, and turmeric. Mix well, then add the tempeh to the dish. Turn the pieces of tempeh to coat with this marinade, then cover and refrigerate for at least 2 hours, turning several times. The tempeh may be marinated for up to 36 hours.

3. In a wok or 12-inch skillet, heat the oil over a medium high flame until hot, but not smoking. Add the dried peppers and cook, stirring constantly, until the peppers turn a dark red-brown color. Immediately add the green pepper and carrot along with the stock. Cook, stirring often, until the carrot just begins to soften, about 4 minutes.

4. Remove the lemon grass from the tempeh mixture. Add the tempeh with its marinade to the wok. Continue to cook, stirring frequently, until the flavors merge, about 3 minutes. Add the broccoli and continue to cook until it is just tender, about 8 minutes, then stir in the red pepper, mango, and corn. Cook just to warm through, then stir in the dissolved cornstarch and bring the sauce to a boil to thicken.

5. Turn the tempeh out onto a large serving platter and top it with the macadamia nuts. Surround the tempeh with sweet or basmati rice.

1/2 pound tempeh, cubed
6 stalks lemon grass
1/3 cup minced shallots
1/3 cup soy sauce
1/4 cup orange juice
2 tablespoons lime juice
3 tablespoons rice syrup (page 193)
2 teaspoons minced gingerroot
1 teaspoon minced garlic
1 teaspoon cinnamon
1 teaspoon ground coriander
1/8 teaspoon turmeric
2 tablespoons vegetable oil
2 dried red chili peppers
1/2 green bell pepper, cut into 1-inch pieces
1 carrot, roll cut (page 189)
1/2 cup light vegetable stock (page 162)
1 1/2 cups broccoli, cut in florets
1/2 red bell pepper, cut in tiny dice
1 medium mango, cut in small dice
1/3 cup baby corn
1 tablespoon cornstarch, dissolved in 2 tablespoons cold water
1/3 cup macadamia nuts, toasted (page 35)

Variation

1. Substitute pecans for the macadamia nuts and replace the mango with 1 cup diced apple.

Cook's Note: The tempeh is best if allowed to marinate for at least 2 hours.

Rolled Sweet Potato Soufflé
with Mellow Garlic Sauce

Yield: 6 servings • Prep Time: 35 minutes • Cooking Time: 2 hours

2 yams or sweet potatoes (about
   1 1/2 pounds)
1 bulb garlic
1 tablespoon olive oil
2 tablespoons flour
1/2 cup milk or plain soy milk
2 tablespoons almond butter
   (optional)
1/2 teaspoon salt
1/8 teaspoon black pepper
3 tablespoons minced scallions
6 egg whites, at room temperature
1/4 teaspoon cream of tartar
6 cups chopped kale
1/4 pound mushrooms, sliced
1 clove garlic, minced
1/2 cup crumbled tofu "feta"
   (page 173) or true feta, drained
   and crumbled
1/8 teaspoon nutmeg
1 tablespoon butter
2 tablespoons mellow barley miso
1/2 teaspoon Dijon-style mustard
1 cup light vegetable stock
   (page 162)
1/4 cup minced fresh parsley

In what many consider the cook's Bible, Mastering the Art of French Cooking, *a soufflé is described as "a sauce containing a flavoring or purée into which stiffly beaten egg whites are incorporated." This description (as are many in the book) is enlightening when contemplating variations on classics. A "sauce" or soufflé base must be stable enough to hold liquid in suspension when egg whites are added and it is baked, but it need not be overly thick or rich. This melt-in-the-mouth soufflé is a case in point.*

1. Preheat the oven to 350°F. Under cold running water, scrub the yams well to remove all dirt and the top layer of skin. Place them on a baking sheet. Alongside, place the bulb of garlic and drizzle about 1 teaspoon of oil over it. Bake the yams and garlic until they are very soft when squeezed, turning once or twice to allow them to cook evenly. The garlic will be ready in about 45 minutes, the yams in about 1 1/2 hours. Remove each to a cake rack to cool. The yams and garlic may be baked up to 5 days in advance if refrigerated, loosely wrapped in a plastic bag.

2. Slice the yams in half. Scrape their meat into a food processor and purée until absolutely smooth, about 2 minutes. You should have about 2 cups of purée.

3. In a 2-quart saucepan, whisk the milk into the flour. Place this over medium heat and cook, whisking constantly, until the mixture boils. Whisk in the yam purée, blending until smooth. Stir in the almond butter and season with 1/4 teaspoon salt, the pepper, and scallions. This soufflé base can be prepared up to 2 days in advance if refrigerated in an airtight container. Return the base to room temperature and whisk vigorously before continuing with the recipe.

4. Rinse the kale under cold water, then leave it in a strainer to drain as you cook the mushrooms. In a skillet, heat the remaining 2 teaspoons of oil over medium high heat. Add the mushrooms and cook, tossing often, for 1 minute. Reduce the heat slightly and continue to cook, stirring often, until the mushrooms are all beginning to soften, about 5 minutes. Add the kale and minced garlic, then continue to cook, tossing frequently, for about 8 minutes, or until the kale is just tender. Stir in the "feta" and season to taste with the remaining 1/4 teaspoon salt and the nutmeg, then set aside. This filling may be prepared up to 2 days in advance if refrigerated in an airtight container. Bring to room temperature before cooking the soufflé.

5. Cut the top off the bulb of baked garlic, then squeeze each clove into a clean processor bowl. Process until finely mashed, then add the miso and mustard, and continue to blend until smooth. In a 1-quart saucepan, boil the stock until it is reduced to 1/2 cup. Remove it from the heat and whisk in the miso mixture and the parsley. Allow the sauce to rewarm just before serving.

6. Preheat the oven to 400°F. Butter a 9- by 12-inch baking sheet, then line it with parchment or waxed paper (page 6). Place the egg whites in a large and spotlessly clean copper or plastic bowl. With a balloon hand whisk or an electric mixer, beat the egg whites until just frothy. Sprinkle the cream of tartar over them and continue to beat until they hold a stiff peak, but not so much that they break apart. Spoon about 1/5 of the egg whites into the yam mixture and gently fold it in to lighten the yams. Now, in about 3 installments, fold the lightened soufflé base back into the remaining egg whites. Work quickly, but very gently, so as to deflate the egg whites as little as possible. Pour the soufflé into the prepared baking sheet and smooth it out so that it is even. Place it in the center of the preheated oven and bake until puffed and lightly browned on top, about 20 minutes. The soufflé will have begun to pull away from the sides of the pan.

7. Dampen a clean kitchen towel and have it laid out on a flat work surface. When the soufflé is cooked, immediately invert it onto the towel. Quickly arrange the filling over the soufflé, leaving only about 1 inch of of uncovered surface along one of the long sides. Using the towel as a guide, lift the soufflé and roll it widthwise, as tightly as possible without cracking, into a long cylinder. Still using the towel as a guide, transfer the soufflé to a narrow serving platter. Drizzle with sauce and serve immediately.

Cook's Note: The sweet potatoes and base, as well as the filling for the soufflé, may be cooked up to 24 hours in advance to save on last-minute prep time. Bring the base to room temperature before proceeding with the recipe.

Spicy Stuffed Cornbread Pie

Yield: 6 servings • Prep Time: 45 minutes • Cooking Time: 20 minutes

An elaborate version of a recipe I once developed while working for Delicious! *magazine, this skillet dinner is tasty and filling, good for brunch or supper. Leftover pie can be wrapped in plastic and refrigerated for several days. To serve leftover pie, reheat it, uncovered, in a 350ºF oven for 10 minutes.*

2 tablespoons canola oil
1 cup diced white onion
1/2 cup diced red bell pepper
1/2 cup diced green bell pepper
2 cups peeled, seeded and diced
   fresh tomatoes (page 35) or one
   28-ounce can tomatoes,
   drained
1 serrano pepper, seeded
   and minced
1 tablespoon minced garlic
2 tablespoons balsamic vinegar
1 teaspoon fresh oregano or
   1/4 teaspoon dried
1 teaspoon ground cumin
   (optional)
1 1/2 cups cooked pinto beans
1/2 cup minced cilantro
1/2 teaspoon salt
Pinch of black pepper
1 1/4 cups yellow cornmeal
1/2 cup whole wheat flour
1/2 cup unbleached white flour
1 1/2 teaspoons non-aluminum
   baking powder
1 teaspoon salt
1/2 cup corn kernels
1 cup buttermilk
2 eggs or 8 ounces silken tofu,
   puréed
3 tablespoons honey
3 tablespoons melted butter or
   vegetable oil
1 cup grated Monterey Jack or soy
   mozzarella cheese

1. Preheat the oven to 425ºF. Heat the canola oil in a 10-inch cast-iron skillet. Add the onions and bell peppers and cook, stirring constantly, for 2 minutes. Reduce the heat to medium and continue to cook, stirring often, until the onion is very soft, about 10 minutes. Add the tomatoes, serrano pepper, garlic, vinegar, oregano, and cumin. Reduce the heat to low and cook until peppers are soft, about 10 minutes more. Remove from the heat. Mash about half of the pinto beans and leave the rest whole. Stir all of the beans into the tomato mixture along with the cilantro, salt and pepper. This filling may be prepared up to 3 days in advance if refrigerated in an airtight container.

2. In a large mixing bowl, combine the cornmeal, flours, baking powder, and salt. Add the corn kernels and toss. In a separate bowl, whisk together the buttermilk, eggs, honey, and remaining melted butter. Stir this mixture into the dry ingredients until just combined.

3. Transfer the vegetable mixture to a bowl. Pour half of the cornbread mixture into the skillet, spreading it out evenly. Arrange the vegetable-bean mixture over this in an even layer, then top with the remaining cornbread. Sprinkle the grated cheese on top and bake until the bread is done and the cheese is lightly browned, about 20 minutes. Serve hot.

Variations

1. Layer Gina Marie cheese or natural cream cheese on top of filling before adding second layer of cornbread.

2. For a nondairy version, replace the buttermilk with salsa and replace the eggs with 6 ounces puréed tofu.

Pizza

While living in India, I once had a dream of a piping hot pizza being delivered to our veranda. Swooning from the alluring aroma, I reached to lift the lid of the box, but to my dismay, found only a few old bits of crust and hard, melted cheese inside. I awoke with a very heavy heart, but the scent was still lingering in my awareness.

Though the dream and craving for pizza were, no doubt, caused by my long separation from Western flavors, pizza is a food that, for many of us, holds intense appeal. We may usually rely on a local pizza joint (or stylish restaurant complete with a wood-burning pizza oven) to satisfy the urge, but when the mood strikes, homemade pizza is delightful. Below you will find three crusts, one which can be prepared without wheat, and suggestions for toppings. All recipe variations yield 4 servings.

Potato Crust

Prep Time: 15 minutes • Cooking Time: 50 minutes

3/4 pound russet potatoes
1 cup whole wheat flour
1/2 teaspoon non-aluminum baking powder
1 teaspoon salt
1 teaspoon minced fresh oregano or 1/4 teaspoon dry, crumbled
3 tablespoons grated Parmesan (optional)

This flavorful home-style crust is crisp on the outside, soft and moist on the inside. It can be prepared wheat-free by using barley or rye flour (see variations).

1. Peel the potatoes, and cut them into 2-inch cubes. Steam the potatoes until completely tender, about 10 minutes. While still hot, transfer them to a food processor fitted with a metal cutting blade and purée the potatoes until smooth. Quickly add the flour, baking powder, salt, oregano, and Parmesan.

2. Lightly oil the center of a cookie sheet. Line the sheet with plastic wrap, then turn the dough out onto the prepared pan. Using your fingertips, press the dough out to form an 11-inch circle that is about 1 inch thick. Leave the dough to dry out at room temperature, for 2 to 4 hours. After 1 hour, place a second oiled baking sheet over the crust. Hold both sheets together and flip them over to invert the crust. Peel off the plastic wrap, then continue to dry the crust for 1 to 2 hours.

3. Preheat the oven to 400°F. Bake the untopped crust for 15 minutes. Top with desired fillings then sprinkle oil over and bake again for 20 minutes.

Cook's Note: This crust becomes crisper if allowed to dry at room temperature for at least 2 hours before baking.

Whole Wheat Crust

Prep Time: 15 minutes • Cooking Time: 20 minutes

1 1/2 cups warm water (115°F.)
2 packages dry yeast
2 teaspoons honey
1 3/4 cups whole wheat flour
1 1/2 cups unbleached white flour

This flavorful rosemary-scented dough produces a chewy, crisp-bottomed crust. It is more workable rolled slightly thick and serves well as an all-purpose crust. For variety, try other seasonings, such as caraway seeds, anise seeds or thyme, worked into the dough before rising.

1. Place the water in a small bowl or 2-cup measure. Add the yeast and honey, then stir to dissolve. Set this aside until bubbles form, about 10 minutes.

2. In a medium-sized mixing bowl, combine the flours with the salt and rosemary. Make a well in the center, then pour the yeast mixture and olive oil into it. Gradually incorporate flour from around the edge of the well into the liquid. Once a paste is formed, work more quickly until all flour is incorporated and the mixture has formed a ball. Place the dough on a lightly floured work surface and knead until it is smooth and elastic and no longer sticky, about 8 minutes.

3. Clean the mixing bowl, and lightly oil it. Place the dough in the bowl and turn it so that all surfaces are oiled. Cover the bowl loosely with a damp kitchen towel, and place it in a warm spot in the kitchen until doubled in volume, about 1 hour. Punch the dough down and allow it to rise again until doubled, about 45 minutes. (The dough can be refrigerated, tightly covered, for up to 15 hours before the second rising.)

4. Once the dough has risen a second time, punch it down again and shape it into one large or two smaller pizzas. To shape a pizza, form the dough into a ball and place it on a lightly floured work surface. Using a rolling pin, roll the dough from the center towards the edge in several directions, then flip the dough over and roll again. Repeat this process as necessary until the pizza is the desired size and thickness. (The dough will rise slightly, become thicker, and shrink in diameter as it bakes.) Top with desired toppings, then bake in a preheated 450° F. oven for about 20 minutes.

Cook's Note: Allow at least 1 3/4 hours rising time for the dough before shaping (or allow to rise then refrigerate the dough before shaping).

1 teaspoon salt
1 teaspoon rosemary
3 tablespoons olive oil
Additional oil for brushing bowl

Semolina Crust

Prep Time: 10 minutes • Cooking Time: 25 minutes

Semolina, or durum wheat flour, produces a crisp, light crust, best rolled thin and cooked on a pizza stone.

1. Combine the semolina, unbleached flour, and salt in a food processor fitted with the metal chopping blade.

2. Dissolve the yeast with the sugar in the warm water and allow to rest until bubbles form, about 8 minutes. Stir the oil into the yeast mixture.

3. With the motor running, slowly add the yeast mixture to the processor. Continue processing until the mixture forms a ball. Immediately remove the dough from the bowl and knead it on a lightly floured work surface until it is very smooth and elastic, about 10 minutes.

4. Brush a large bowl with additional olive oil and place the dough in the bowl. Turn it to coat all sides with oil. Cover the bowl with a damp kitchen towel and allow it to rise in a warm place until doubled in size, about 2 1/2 hours.

5. Punch the dough down and shape it into a ball on a lightly floured work surface. (The dough may also be punched down then refrigerated, tightly covered, for up to 12 hours.) Roll the dough into a circle or oval that is about 1/4 inch thick. Top with desired toppings then bake in a preheated 450°F. oven for 25 minutes.

Cook's Note: Allow at least 2 1/2 hours rising time for the dough before shaping (or allow the dough to rise then refrigerate before shaping).

2 cups semolina flour
1 cup unbleached white flour
1 1/2 teaspoons salt
1 package dry yeast
1 1/2 cups warm water (115°F.)
1 tablespoon maple sugar
2 tablespoons olive oil
Additional oil for brushing

How to Top a Pizza

When selecting ingredients to go on a pizza, keep in mind the balance of flavors, textures, colors, and shapes that the ingredients will bring to the pizza. Any of the toppings below may be used with any of the crusts on the preceding pages.

Some general guidelines for successful pizzas are as follows: First, have your oven heated to a very high setting, 450° to 500°F. is preferable. Also, a pizza stone or pizza tiles to line the oven are helpful in obtaining a crisp bottom crust. Second, have all topping ingredients assembled before you roll the crust to the desired thickness. Third, consider cooking or marinating ingredients before you add them to the pizza. Sautéed mushrooms, grilled eggplant, or oven-baked or caramelized onion, for example, are all far more interesting than those same ingredients raw. Fourth, you may drizzle olive oil over the crust and/or over the topped pizza before baking for a slightly richer-tasting pizza. This will increase the percentage of fat substantially. Finally, all pizzas need not have tomato sauce as their first layer. Other sauces or sliced tomatoes may provide the unifying base that tomato sauce provides in a standard pizza. The toppings suggested below are not given in amounts because that will vary depending on the size to which you roll your dough. All toppings are intended to be in one plentiful layer each and the ingredients are listed in the order in which they are to be layered.

Triple Tomato Pizza
Hearty tomato sauce (page 174)
Caramelized onion
Fresh tomato slices (yellow if available)
Sliced garlic (a thin sprinkling
    over the tomatoes)
Feta cheese, crumbled or tofu "feta" (page 173)
Black olives (whole, without pits)
Mozzarella (or soy mozzarella)
Fresh basil (for the last 5 minutes of cooking)

Pesto Pizza
Miso pesto (page 176) or classic pesto (page 176)
    (over the entire surface of the dough)
Sautéed onion slices
Sliced provolone
Roasted red peppers
Mozzarella

Caramelized Shallot and "Sausage" Pizza
Sliced Italian plum tomatoes
Caramelized shallots (page 188)
Rosemary
Tofu "sausage" (page 166)
Parmesan and/or mozzarella (optional)

Grilled Vegetable Pizza
Raw tomato slices
Thinly sliced garlic
Assorted grilled vegetables,
    each lightly brushed with olive oil
    or a mixture of olive oil, lemon juice,
    minced garlic and minced thyme:
    for example, eggplant, zucchini, onions,
    bell peppers, or mushrooms
Gruyère or mozzarella

Wild Mushroom Pizza
Madeira sauce (page 177)
Sautéed button mushrooms
Sautéed morel mushrooms
Sautéed tree oyster mushrooms
Fresh mozzarella (optional)
Grated Parmesan

Mixed Vegetable with Tempeh Pizza
Light tomato sauce (page 175)
Sliced green or red bell peppers
Sautéed onion slices
Crumbled baked tempeh (page 110)
Mozzarella

Three Cheese Pizza
Sliced Italian plum tomatoes
Caramelized onion
Chopped steamed spinach
    (squeezed dry)
Minced garlic
Mild goat cheese
Sautéed mushrooms
Mozzarella
Parmesan

Mexican Pizza
Ancho pepper sauce (page 181)
Sliced Italian plum tomatoes
Sautéed onions
Scallions
Sliced roasted bell peppers
Green olives
Capers
Chopped cilantro
Monterey Jack cheese

4 • Light and Simple

Tofu "Scallops"

Yield: 4 servings • Prep Time: 25 minutes • Cooking Time: 20 minutes

This playful presentation of marinated broiled tofu bares a striking resemblance to sea scallops. The rice vinegar and rice syrup mimic the rich sweet flavor of shellfish, and arame, a sea vegetable, adds a touch of authentic aroma.

1 1/2 pounds firm tofu
1/4 cup sweet rice vinegar
1 tablespoon rice syrup (page 193)
2 cloves garlic, minced
3/4 teaspoon salt
1/4 cup arame (page 190), rinsed
1 cup thinly sliced white onion
2 tablespoons butter or olive oil
1 red bell pepper, thinly sliced
1 yellow bell paper, thinly sliced
3 tablespoons minced fresh
   chervil

1. Drain the tofu and cut it into 1-inch-thick pieces. Arrange these slices on a clean kitchen towel. Fold the towel over the tofu and place a cutting board on top. Weight the tofu by placing a heavy skillet or several 1-pound cans on the board. Allow the tofu to rest at room temperature for 30 minutes. (If time is short, this step may be eliminated; however, the texture of pressed tofu is preferable.)

2. Transfer the tofu to a cutting board. Using a 1-inch circular cutter, cut scallop-shaped rounds from the tofu. (You may also use a small bottle cap as a guide and cut the rounds using the tip of a paring knife.) In a 9-inch square baking dish, combine the vinegar, rice syrup, garlic, and salt. Mix well, then add the tofu and turn to coat. Set aside for at least 20 minutes to marinate. The tofu improves with flavor if marinated overnight.

3. Place the arame in a small bowl and cover with boiling water. Set aside while you complete the recipe. Preheat the broiler to high. Transfer the tofu to a cutting board. Add the onion and butter to the baking dish and place the dish about 6 inches from the broiler. Broil, stirring twice, for 5 minutes. Sprinkle the peppers over the onion and arrange the tofu on top. Continue to broil, stirring frequently so that the vegetables and tofu cook evenly, until the peppers are soft, about 10 minutes.

4. Remove the tofu from the broiler. Drain the arame, squeezing as much water from it as possible. Stir it and the chervil into the tofu. Toss to mix evenly. Serve the tofu in individual scallop shells or small gratin dishes.

Variations

1. For a stronger sea-like flavor to the tofu itself, marinate the tofu overnight in the above marinade, but add the rinsed arame to it as well.

2. For a vegetarian version of trout with almonds, slice the tofu into 3- by 5-inch slabs that are 3/4 inches thick. Press them to remove excess liquid, then marinate as above. Dust lightly with flour, then pan-fry in butter or oil until lightly browned. For the last 2 minutes of cooking, add 1/2 cup sliced almonds to the pan. Cook, turning occasionally, until the nuts are lightly browned. You may serve these with lemon wedges, or prepare a light sauce by simmering together the remaining marinade and 1/2 cup vegetable stock. Once this liquid has reduced to 1/4 cup, whisk in butter or cream as an enrichment. Whether served with or without sauce, sprinkle the cooked tofu with minced parsley.

Steamed Ginger Scallion Tofu

Yield: 4 servings • Prep Time: 10 minutes • Cooking Time: 20 minutes

1 1/4 pounds soft tofu
2 cloves garlic, sliced thin
1/2 teaspoon salt
1/4 cup dry white wine
2 tablespoons rice syrup
    (page 193)
1 tablespoon minced garlic
6 scallions, shredded
2 tablespoons shredded ginger-
    root
1/4 cup soy sauce
2 tablespoons raspberry vinegar
1 teaspoon toasted sesame oil
Sprigs of cilantro

Six steps below street level in Boston's Chinatown was a small restaurant that in the late 70s served a shimmering dish of steamed sea bass. That preparation gave inspiration to this simple but elegant dish.

1. Drain the tofu and cut it into 1-inch-thick slabs. Place the tofu on a clean kitchen towel, and place another towel on top. Place a small cutting board on top of the towel and gently press down, being careful not to push so hard that the tofu crumbles. Allow the tofu to drain for about 30 minutes.

2. Remove the tofu from the towels and place it in a heatproof plate large enough to hold the tofu comfortably, but small enough to fit in the top of a bamboo steamer. (If you do not have a bamboo steamer, see page 6 for directions on how to construct a makeshift steamer.) With the tip of a paring knife, make several shallow slashes in the tofu and insert a slice of garlic in each slash. Sprinkle the salt over the tofu and gently rub it in.

3. Push the tofu to the side of the dish, then pour in the wine, rice syrup, minced garlic, half of the scallions, and half of the ginger. Stir in the soy sauce and vinegar. Arrange the tofu on top of this liquid, baste it with this marinade, then set it aside, covered, for at least 30 minutes.

4. Sprinkle the remaining scallions and ginger over the tofu and place the dish in the top of a flat steamer over rapidly boiling water. Cover and cook, basting several times, for 20 minutes. Sprinkle sesame oil over the tofu and scatter sprigs of cilantro on top. Serve immediately.

Cook's Note: The tofu is best pressed for 30 minutes before proceeding with the recipe.

Black Bean Banana Enchilada Pie

Yield: 6 servings • Prep Time: 25 minutes • Cooking Time: 30 minutes

1 cup diced white onion
1 tablespoon canola oil
4 cups chopped fresh tomatoes
    or 2 16-ounce cans chopped
    tomatoes, drained
2 teaspoons fresh oregano,
    chopped, or 1/2 teaspoon dried
    oregano, crumbled
1 tablespoon minced garlic
2 teaspoons salt
4 cups cooked black beans
2 tablespoons dry sherry
    (optional)
2 tablespoons red wine vinegar
5 teaspoons chopped green
    chilies
2 teaspoons ground cumin
1/3 cup minced cilantro

Don't be alarmed! This unusual combination of flavors and textures is extraordinary. To reduce the fat in this recipe, omit the oil and simply simmer the onion with the tomatoes and spices. Sautéed onions add depth and sweetness to the dish, but also contribute fat.

1. In a skillet, sauté the onion in the canola oil, stirring often, until it is translucent, about 8 minutes. Add the tomatoes, oregano, garlic, and 1 teaspoon of salt. Simmer, stirring occasionally, for 10 minutes. Remove from the heat and set aside. This sauce may be prepared up to 3 days in advance if refrigerated in an airtight container.

2. In a mixing bowl, combine the beans, remaining salt, sherry, vinegar, green chilies, cumin and cilantro. Set aside. Slice the bananas into 1/2-inch rounds. Heat the butter in a skillet over medium high heat. When it bubbles, add the bananas and cook until softened slightly, about 2 minutes. Shake the pan as the bananas cook so that they cook evenly.

3. Preheat the oven to 350ºF. Into a shallow, 8-cup baking dish, spoon a thin layer of tomato sauce. On top of this, place a layer of tortillas and top with the beans. Spoon half of the remaining tomato sauce over this and top with a layer of tortillas. Arrange the bananas in one layer over this and top with the remaining tortillas. Spoon the remaining tomato sauce over the tortillas and sprinkle with cheese. Bake in the center of the oven until the cheese is melted and the beans are piping hot, about 20 minutes. Cool briefly before serving.

3 ripe bananas
2 tablespoons butter or olive oil
12 6-inch yellow cornmeal
    tortillas
6 ounces mozzarella-style soy
    cheese or Monterey Jack
    cheese, grated

Spinach Mushroom Burritos
with Spicy Red Pepper Sauce

Yield: 4 servings • Prep Time: 45 minutes • Cooking Time: 10 minutes

It's a toss-up as to whether the filling is better served rolled in flour tortillas or layered with corn tortillas, then baked. Either way the recipe is delicious.

1. In a 9-inch skillet, heat the oil over medium high heat until hot, but not smoking. Add the onions and cook, stirring constantly, for 1 minute. Reduce the heat to medium low and continue to cook, stirring often, until the onions are translucent, about 10 minutes. Do not allow them to brown.

2. Return the heat to medium high and add the mushrooms. Cook, stirring constantly, until the mushrooms have all begun to soften, about 2 minutes. Add the lemon juice and garlic, then reduce the heat to low, and continue to cook, stirring often, until the mushrooms are very tender, about 8 minutes.

3. Place the thawed spinach in a strainer and quickly run cold water over it to rinse. Remove as much liquid as you can from the spinach by separating it into 2 or 3 balls and squeezing them firmly between your hands. Add the spinach to the skillet and cook just long enough to break it apart. Stir in the chopped yellow pepper, "feta," olives, and the cilantro. Season the mixture with salt and pepper. Taste and adjust the seasonings. This filling may be prepared up to 3 days in advance if refrigerated in an airtight container.

4. Preheat the oven to 375ºF. Divide the filling evenly among the tortillas, placing a strip of filling in the center of each and rolling the tortillas to enclose the spinach, forming a burrito. Place the burritos, seam side down, in a shallow baking pan and top with grated cheese. Cover the pan and bake until piping hot, about 10 minutes.

5. Meanwhile, warm the pepper sauce to a boil. On a large serving platter, spread a thin layer of sauce. Line the burritos side by side on the sauce and pour the remaining sauce over the center of the burritos. Sprinkle with the minced scallions and serve immediately.

2 teaspoons canola oil
1 cup diced white onion
1/2 pound mushrooms, sliced
1 tablespoon lemon juice
2 cloves garlic, minced
1 10-ounce package frozen
    chopped spinach, thawed
1 small yellow bell pepper, diced
1 cup tofu "feta" (page 173) or true
    feta
1/3 cup sliced green olives
    (optional)
1/3 cup chopped cilantro
1/4 teaspoon salt
Pinch of black pepper
6 whole wheat tortillas
1/2 cup mozzarella-style soy
    cheese or Monterey Jack
    cheese, grated
3 tablespoons minced scallions
1 recipe ancho pepper sauce
    (page 181)

Variation

1. Prepare the same recipe, but use 8 corn tortillas and bake as a pie, layering in sauce, tortillas, filling, tortillas, sauce and topping with cheese. Bake in a pre-heated 375ºF. oven until piping hot, about 30 minutes.

Cook's Note: The sauce may be prepared several days in advance, and the dish may be assembled up to 24 hours before baking.

Simmered Shiitake Tofu

Yield: 4 servings • Prep Time: 20 minutes • Cooking Time: 18 minutes

1 pound soft tofu
1/2 pound fresh shiitake
   mushrooms
3 tablespoons rice vinegar
2 tablespoons honey
4 1/2 tablespoons soy sauce
1 cup light vegetable stock
   (page 162)
3 teaspoons mirin (page 193)
1 tablespoon minced gingerroot
1 tablespoon minced garlic
1 red bell pepper, cut in small dice
1/2 cup sliced water chestnuts
2 1/2 tablespoons minced tarragon
1/4 cup minced scallions
2 tablespoons toasted pine nuts
   (page 35)

Serve this flavorful tofu dish alone or over a bed of sesame-flavored arame salad (page 156). You may use dried shiitakes if fresh are unavailable, but you must increase the amount of stock by 1/4 cup and simmer the mushrooms for 10 minutes before adding them to the tofu.

1. Drain the tofu and slice it into 3/4-inch slabs. Place them on a clean kitchen towel with a second towel on top. Put a light cutting board over the top towel, press the tofu very gently, and leave it to drain for 30 minutes. Cube the drained tofu.

2. Slice the mushrooms into 1/4-inch-thick strips. In a 10-inch skillet, combine the mushrooms, vinegar, honey, soy sauce, stock, mirin, ginger and garlic. Bring this to a boil, and cook, stirring occasionally, for about 5 minutes, or until the mushrooms are soft. Add the tofu and cook, stirring frequently and carefully so as not to cause the tofu to break apart. Once the cooking liquid has reduced to about 3 tablespoons, after about 5 minutes, stir in the red pepper and continue to cook until the peppers are warm through, about 2 minutes. Remove from the heat and toss in the water chestnuts, tarragon, and scallions. Serve immediately sprinkled with toasted pine nuts.

Cook's Note: The tofu is best if pressed for 30 minutes before cooking. If using dried shiitakes reduce the amount to 1 1/2 ounces.

Sesame Ginger Beans with Orzo

Yield: 8 servings • Prep Time: 25 minutes • Cooking Time: 20 minutes

3 cups cooked red or black beans
2 1/2 tablespoons minced pickled
   ginger
2 red bell peppers, diced
1 yellow bell pepper, diced
1/2 cup minced cilantro
1/4 cup tamari
1/4 cup toasted sesame oil
4 1/2 tablespoons rice vinegar
2 cloves garlic, minced
1/4 cup minced scallions
1/2 teaspoon salt
1 1/2 cups uncooked orzo
1 tablespoon rice syrup (page 193)
2 cilantro sprigs

Bean and pasta salads serve well as lunch or dinner entrées. An orzo-shaped pasta made from kamut flour has recently become available in many natural foods stores. It works well with this recipe. For a brighter look, select light-colored traditional Greek orzo.

1. If the beans have been stored in cooking liquid, drain them, then place them in a large mixing bowl. Add the pickled ginger, diced peppers, 3 tablespoons cilantro, the tamari, 1 tablespoon sesame oil, 1 tablespoon rice vinegar, the garlic, and scallions. Toss to combine well, then cover and refrigerate, stirring occasionally, for 24 to 36 hours. Bring the beans to room temperature before continuing with the recipe.

2. In a large saucepan, bring 2 quarts of water to a boil. Add 1/2 teaspoon of salt, then stir in the orzo. Stir the pasta once or twice to prevent it from sticking, then bring it to a boil. Reduce the heat slightly then cook until al dente, about 12 minutes. Immediately drain the orzo, then place the strainer it is in under cold running water to stop the cooking immediately. As soon as the pasta is cool to the touch, stop the water and shake the strainer vigorously to remove as much water as possible.

3. Transfer the orzo to a second mixing bowl. Stir in the remaining 3 tablespoons sesame oil, 3 1/2 tablespoons of rice vinegar, 5 tablespoons cilantro, and the rice syrup. Toss well. The pasta may be prepared to this point up to 24 hours in advance if refrigerated in an airtight container. Bring the orzo to room temperature before serving.

4. To serve, arrange a ring of the pasta on a large serving platter, then mound the beans in the center. Garnish with the sprigs of cilantro. Serve at room temperature.

Cook's Note: The beans are best marinated for at least a day, so if possible begin the preparation of this dish with ample resting time.

Bulgur Pilaf with Scallions and Azuki Beans

Yield: 6 servings • Prep Time: 15 minutes • Cooking Time: 40 minutes

1. Rinse the bulgur with cold water until the water runs clear. Set it aside to dry for 20 minutes.

2. Meanwhile, heat the oil over medium high flame until hot, but not smoking. Add the chili peppers and cook briefly, tossing them constantly in the pan, until they turn dark, about 1 minute. Remove the peppers from the pan and add the carrot and celery. Quickly cook them, stirring often, until they begin to soften, about 4 minutes. Reduce the heat slightly, add the ginger and garlic and cook for 1 minute. Stir in the anise seeds, turmeric, and mace, then cook, stirring constantly, until their aroma is released, about 1 more minute.

3. Return the peppers to the pan, then stir in the bulgur and stock. Stir well and reduce to a simmer. Combine the tamari, rice syrup, and sherry and add them to the bulgur. Drain the shiitake mushrooms and slice them into thin strips. Stir them into the pilaf. Cook, stirring occasionally, until almost all liquid is absorbed and the bulgur is tender, about 25 minutes.

4. Stir the azuki beans into the pilaf and continue to cook for 5 minutes. Add the mint. Stir then taste and adjust the seasonings. Mound the pilaf onto individual plates or one large serving plate. Surround the bulgur with cucumber and tomato and sprinkle peanuts over the center of the pilaf. Serve at once.

1 1/2 cups bulgur
2 tablespoons olive oil
2 dried red chili peppers
1 cup diced carrot
3/4 cup diced celery
1 tablespoon minced gingerroot
2 teaspoons minced garlic
1 1/2 teaspoons anise seeds, crushed
1/4 teaspoon turmeric
Pinch of mace
2 1/2 cups light vegetable stock (page 162)
3 tablespoons tamari
1 tablespoon rice syrup (page 193)
2 tablespoons dry sherry
4 dried shiitake mushrooms, softened in hot water
1/2 cup minced scallions
1 cup cooked azuki beans
1/4 cup minced fresh mint
1 cucumber, peeled, seeded, and diced
1 cup chopped tomato
3 tablespoons chopped roasted peanuts (page 35)

Spicy Bean Pilaf

Yield: 6 servings • Prep Time: 20 minutes • Cooking Time: 1 hour

Fresh soy beans, sugar snaps, and pearl barley team up beautifully in this unusual pilaf. Serve it with steamed kale sprinkled with tamari and soy mozzarella, for a warming winter meal.

1/4 cup pearl barley
1/2 teaspoon saffron
1/3 cup sweet rice vinegar
3 tablespoons rice syrup
  (page 193)
1/2 teaspoon cinnamon
1/2 teaspoon ground cardamom
1/8 teaspoon ground allspice
1/4 teaspoon ground cloves
1/4 cup unsulphured apricots,
  chopped
4 tablespoons olive oil
2 1/2 cups basmati rice
1 cup diced red onion
6 1/4 cups light vegetable stock
  (page 162) or water
2 teaspoons minced garlic
1/2 teaspoon minced gingerroot
1 1/4 teaspoons salt
1/8 teaspoon white pepper
1/4 cup raw almonds, toasted
  and chopped (page 35)
1/2 cup raisins
1 cup cooked soybeans (available
  frozen) or kidney beans
1 cup sugar snaps or snow peas,
  strings removed

1. Place the barley in a saucepan with enough water to cover by 2 inches. Bring to a boil, stirring occasionally. Reduce to a simmer and cook, stirring occasionally, until tender, about 25 minutes. Transfer the barley to a strainer and run cold water over it to stop its cooking. Set this aside.

2. In a small mixing bowl, combine the saffron with the vinegar and rice syrup. Stir to blend, then set aside for 20 minutes. In another small bowl, combine the cinnamon, cardamom, allspice, and cloves. If the apricots are hard, place them in a separate bowl and cover with boiling water, to soften.

3. Heat 2 1/2 tablespoons of oil in a 3-quart Dutch oven or heavy-bottomed saucepan over medium high heat until hot, but not smoking. Add the rice. Cook, stirring constantly until about half of the grains of rice have turned a milky white color, about 4 minutes. Do not allow the rice to brown.

4. Immediately add the vinegar and cook, stirring constantly, until the intense vinegar smell subsides, about 1 minute. Stir in the onion, spice blend, 6 cups of stock, garlic, ginger, salt, and pepper. Bring this to a boil, then stir once, cover, and reduce to a simmer. Cook until the rice is tender, about 30 minutes.

5. Meanwhile, in a skillet, heat the remaining oil over a medium flame until hot, but not smoking. Add the almonds, raisins, and apricots. Cook, stirring constantly, for 5 minutes. Add the remaining 1/4 cup stock, the soybeans, and sugar snaps. Heat just long enough to soften the sugar snaps and evaporate the stock, about 3 minutes. Add this to the cooked rice mixture along with the barley, toss, and serve immediately.

Crusty Lemon Tofu with Wild Mushrooms

Yield: 4 servings • Prep Time: 25 minutes • Cooking Time: 20 minutes

This is a simple preparation based on the classic French "Anglaise" method for breading foods. If you do not include eggs in your diet, you may substitute egg replacer (available at natural foods stores) for the egg whites. For a more succulent dish (which is slightly higher in fat), you can brown both tofu and mushrooms in butter or oil. If you prefer a lighter taste and wish to save on fat calories, broil the tofu and cook the mushrooms in stock.

1 pound firm tofu
2 tablespoons olive oil
1 1/2 tablespoons rice vinegar
1 tablespoon water
2 teaspoons honey
2 lemons
1 cup dry bread crumbs
2 tablespoons dried beefsteak leaves (page 190) or finely minced dulse (page 190)
1/2 teaspoon nutmeg
6 ounces chanterelle mushrooms
6 ounces tree oyster mushrooms
6 ounces button mushrooms
3 to 4 tablespoons butter or oil
1/4 teaspoon salt
2 egg whites, lightly beaten, or 1 1/2 tablespoons egg replacer mixed with 1 tablespoon olive oil and 4 tablespoons cold water
1/4 cup finely diced red pepper

1. Drain the tofu and cut it into 3/4-inch-thick pieces. Place them on a clean kitchen towel, cover with a second towel and place a cutting board on top of this. Allow the tofu to drain for 30 minutes. (This step may be skipped, although without pressing, the tofu is more fragile and may begin to fall apart as it is cooked.)

2. In a 9-inch square baking dish, combine the 2 tablespoons olive oil, rice vinegar, water, and honey and stir to mix. Quarter each slice of tofu into triangles, place them in the dish with this olive oil marinade, turn and set aside for at least 1 hour. The tofu may marinate, covered and refrigerated, for up to 3 days before proceeding with the recipe.

3. Grate the zest from one of the lemons and place it in a small mixing bowl. Add the bread crumbs to the lemon zest, then stir in the beefsteak leaves and 1/4 teaspoon nutmeg, then set this aside. Squeeze the juice from the now zestless lemon into a small bowl, then cut the second lemon into wedges. Set these aside.

4. Clean the mushrooms well, according to directions on page 35. Leave small chanterelles whole, slice larger ones. Break the tree oysters into small clusters, or if they are large, slice them. Slice the button mushrooms into 1/4-inch-thick slices.

5. In a 10-inch skillet, heat 1 tablespoon of butter over medium heat until hot, but not smoking. Add the mushrooms and cook, tossing and stirring constantly, until they have all just begun to soften on the exterior, about 1 1/2 minutes. Pour the lemon juice over them. Season with the remaining 1/4 teaspoon nutmeg and the salt. Reduce the heat to medium and continue to cook, stirring often, until the mushrooms are soft and their juices have just evaporated, about 10 minutes.

6. Meanwhile, dip the tofu first in the egg white or egg replacer, then coat each piece with the bread crumb mixture. Heat the remaining butter in a separate skillet over medium heat. Cook the tofu, turning once, until it is lightly browned on both sides, about 6 minutes.

7. Transfer the mushrooms to individual plates or one large serving plate. Arrange the tofu on top of the mushrooms and sprinkle the red pepper over this. Garnish the dish with lemon wedges.

Tofu with Broccoli and Ginger-Orange Sauce

Yield: 6 servings • Prep Time: 25 minutes • Cooking Time: 30 minutes

1 1/2 pounds soft tofu
1/4 cup tamari
2 tablespoons ume vinegar
   (page 196)
2 teaspoons minced garlic
1 orange
3 tablespoons shredded gingerroot
2 cups mushroom stock (page 163)
   or light vegetable stock
   (page 162)
3 tablespoons honey
1/4 teaspoon salt
4 cups broccoli florets
6 dried shiitake mushrooms,
   softened in hot water
3/4 cup julienne-sliced carrots
2 tablespoons fermented black
   beans (page 191)
1 1/2 tablespoons kuzu
   (page 192)+ 2 tablespoons
   cold water
2 tablespoons minced scallions

Tender, slightly sweet strips of ginger and orange add an extraordinary accent of color and taste to this delectable combination of tofu, broccoli, carrots, and shiitake mushrooms.

1. Drain the tofu and slice it into 3/4-inch-thick slabs. Place them on a clean kitchen towel and cover with a second towel. Place a light cutting board on top of this and allow the tofu to drain for 20 minutes. Meanwhile, in a shallow baking dish, combine the tamari, vinegar, and garlic. Cut the tofu into cubes and add it to the marinade. Turn to coat, then set aside for 20 minutes.

2. Rinse the orange well, then dry it and, using a swivel-bladed vegetable peeler, cut thin strips from the orange until all of the orange-colored skin is removed. Stack these strips on top of each other, shiny side up, and shred them into long, thin strips. Place the strips in a small saucepan. Squeeze the juice from the orange and set it aside. Add the shredded ginger and stock to the saucepan, cover, and bring to a boil. Reduce to a simmer and cook for 5 minutes.

3. Ladle 3/4 cup of the simmered stock into a 12-inch skillet or wok, leaving the remainder in the saucepan with the ginger and orange peel. Stir the honey and salt into the saucepan, then continue to simmer, uncovered, until the orange peel is very tender, about 15 minutes. By this time the liquid around the orange and ginger should be thick and syrupy. Stir this mixture into the skillet with the reserved stock.

4. Preheat the broiler to high. Place the tofu about 4 inches from the heat and broil, turning once, until it is lightly browned, about 10 minutes total.

5. Meanwhile, heat the orange-flavored stock over a high flame until it boils. Add the broccoli and shiitake mushrooms. Cover and cook, stirring occasionally, until the broccoli is a vibrant green, but still quite crisp, about 6 minutes. Add the carrots and black beans, then cover and continue to cook until the broccoli is just tender, about 3 more minutes. Mix together the kuzu and water until the kuzu is dissolved. Stir this into the broccoli mixture and cook briefly, just to thicken. Add the cooked tofu and any remaining marinade to the broccoli and toss gently to combine. (Do not overmix or the tofu will fall apart.) Serve on individual serving plates or one large platter, sprinkled with scallions.

Cook's Note: As the tofu must be pressed and marinated—each for at least 20 minutes—allow yourself ample time.

Curried Greens with Winter Squash and Garbanzos

Yield: 6 servings • Prep Time: 15 minutes • Cooking Time: 1 1/2 hours

I have served this as both a main course and—omitting the garbanzos—as a side dish. Leftovers keep well for up to 4 days and are equally good served rewarmed. If the cider you find is exceptionally sweet, add 1 tablespoon lime juice to the dish along with the cider. As a side dish it goes very nicely with Stuffed Tofu Roll (page 134) or Barbecued Seitan Roast (page 55).

1 small butternut squash
  (about 1 1/2 pounds)
4 cups kale leaves
4 cups chard leaves
Stems from chard (optional)
1 tablespoon peanut oil
2 teaspoons minced garlic
1 teaspoon minced gingerroot
2 tablespoons medium curry
  powder
3/4 cup unfiltered apple cider
2 tablespoons soy sauce
1 to 1 1/2 cups cooked garbanzo
  beans
2 Granny Smith apples, peeled
  and diced

1. Preheat the oven to 375°F. Place the squash on a baking sheet and bake until it just gives when squeezed, about 50 minutes. Remove it from the oven and, when cool enough to handle, slice it open, then scrape out and discard the seeds. Peel the squash halves and cut them into 1 1/4-inch cubes. The squash may be cooked and/or cut, up to 3 days in advance, if refrigerated in an airtight container.

2. Rinse the kale and chard, then chop them into rough pieces. Using a paring knife as a guide, peel the outer layer of sheath from the chard stems of the chard (as you would peel strings from a stalk of celery) and cut the stalks into 1/2-inch pieces.

3. Place the greens in a strainer and rinse, then leave them to drain, but allow some water to remain on the leaves. In a 10-inch skillet, heat the oil over medium high setting until it is hot, but not smoking. Add the garlic and ginger and cook briefly, stirring constantly, to infuse the oil with their scents, about 1 minute. (Do not allow the garlic to brown or it will give the dish a bitter taste.) Add as much of the greens as will fit into the skillet. Cook, stirring and turning to allow them to wilt and diminish in volume. Add more greens and continue to cook until they are all in. Immediately sprinkle the curry powder over and stir well.

4. Reduce the heat to low and continue to cook, stirring often, until the smell of curry penetrates the air, about 2 minutes. Add the cubed squash, apple cider, soy sauce, and garbanzos. Cook, stirring often until the squash is completely tender, about 5 minutes. Stir in the apples and warm through. Taste and adjust the seasonings. Serve hot or at room temperature.

Simmered Tofu Curry

Yield: 8 servings • Prep Time: 25 minutes • Cooking Time: 40 minutes

2 pounds extra-firm tofu
1 1-inch piece tamarind
2 1/2 tablespoons ground
   coriander
1 teaspoon cinnamon
1/2 teaspoon turmeric
1/2 teaspoon ground cardamom
1/4 teaspoon ground cloves
1/4 teaspoon nutmeg
1/2 teaspoon salt
1 tablespoon peanut oil
3 dried red chilies (or to taste)
2 cups diced red onion
1 tablespoon minced garlic
1 tablespoon minced gingerroot
2 teaspoons cumin seeds, toasted
1/4 cup molasses
1 cup hearty vegetable stock
   (page 162)
4 lime leaves or 1 tablespoon
   lime juice
1/2 cup fresh mint

A gentleman in India once described the quality of a restaurant's entrée as being based on how long after a meal its scent lingered on his fingertips. With this criterion, the penetrating aromas of this dish would make it among the best a restaurant could offer. Serve it with Masala Rice (page 159) and steamed broccoli with a squeeze of lemon juice.

1. Cut the tofu into 1/2-inch-thick slabs and place them on a clean kitchen towel. Cover with a second clean towel and place a cutting board on top. Press the board down, then place a heavy skillet or several 1-pound cans on top of the board. Allow the tofu to drain for 30 minutes.

2. Place the tamarind in a small bowl and cover with boiling water. Allow it to soften for at least 15 minutes, then rub the tamarind with your fingers to separate the pulp and seeds. Strain the juice through a tea strainer and set it aside. In a second mixing bowl, combine the coriander, cinnamon, turmeric, cardamom, cloves, nutmeg, and salt. Mix well. Once the tofu has drained, coat it with this spice mixture, then set it aside, covered, on a plate for 30 minutes at room temperature or refrigerated for up to 4 hours.

3. In a 12-inch skillet, heat the peanut oil over medium high flame until hot, but not smoking. Add the peppers and cook, stirring constantly, until they darken, about 45 seconds. Stir in the onions and cook, stirring constantly, for 1 minute. Reduce the heat to medium and continue to cook, stirring often, for 5 minutes. Add the garlic and ginger and continue to cook, stirring frequently, until the onions are very soft, about 10 minutes. Do not allow the garlic to brown or it will give the dish a bitter flavor.

4. Add the seasoned tofu to the onions and continue to cook for about 5 minutes. Reduce the heat slightly, then stir in the cumin seeds, molasses, stock, and lime leaves or juice. Cover and simmer for 15 minutes. Transfer the tofu to a serving dish and sprinkle with the mint. Serve at once.

Cook's Note: The tofu is best if it is pressed for 30 minutes before proceeding with the recipe and then marinated for at least 30 minutes.

Sweet and Sour Baked Beans

Yield: 4 servings • Prep Time: 25 minutes • Cooking Time: 4 hours

1 1/2 cups dried cannellini beans
   or baby lima beans
3 cups diced leek
1 bay leaf
1 tablespoon olive oil
2 tablespoons minced garlic
6 cups water
1 green bell pepper, diced

Served over orzo and garnished with radicchio leaves, the presentation of this simple bean dish is elegant.

1. Pick over the beans to remove all stones and debris. Rinse the beans well, then soak them overnight in cold water. Drain and add the beans to a 4-quart saucepan with 1 cup of the leeks, the bay leaf, olive oil, and 2 teaspoons garlic. Add the water and stir. Bring the beans to a boil, stir, then cover and simmer, stirring occasionally, until the beans are tender, about 1 1/2 hours. (The beans may also be cooked in a pressure cooker with or without presoaking. See page 9 for cooking time.)

2. Drain the beans, reserving their cooking liquid and removing the bay leaf from the beans. Preheat the oven to 300°F. Place the beans in a Dutch oven or heavy baking pan and add the remaining 2 cups leek and 4 teaspoons garlic. Stir in the bell peppers, dill seeds, caraway seeds, sage, 1 teaspoon salt, rosemary, cinnamon, thyme, coriander, molasses and vinegar. Place the reserved cooking liquid in a small saucepan and reduce it to 3 cups. Stir this into the beans, then cover and bake until the liquid has evaporated and the beans are extremely plump and tender, about 2 1/2 hours. Remove the beans from the oven and stir in the fresh dill. Taste and adjust the seasonings.

3. Bring 6 cups of water to a rolling boil. Stir in the remaining 1/2 teaspoon salt and the orzo, then cook, stirring occasionally, until it is just tender, about 10 minutes. Drain immediately and place it on a serving platter. Toss the orzo with the parsley to mix, then arrange the pasta in a ring around the circumference of the platter. Lay the radicchio leaves in the center of the ring so that their leaves overlap the orzo by about 1/2 inch. Place the beans in the center, then sprinkle the olives and goat cheese over the beans. Serve at once.

1 red bell pepper, diced
1 tablespoon dill seeds
1 tablespoon caraway seeds
2 teaspoons dried sage
1 1/2 teaspoons salt
1 teaspoon dried rosemary
1 teaspoon cinnamon
1 teaspoon dried thyme or
   3 sprigs fresh
1 teaspoon ground coriander
1 tablespoon blackstrap molasses
1/4 cup white wine vinegar
2 tablespoons chopped fresh dill
1/4 cup minced parsley
1 1/2 cups uncooked orzo (pasta)
8 radicchio leaves
10 Niçoise olives
3 ounces mild goat cheese,
   crumbled (optional)

Fluffy Bean Cakes

Yield: 4 servings • Prep Time: 20 minutes • Cooking Time: 10 minutes

Modeled after a bean dish I was served at a friend's house in Evergreen, Colorado, these cakes may also be served wrapped in corn husks and steamed as tamales.

1. Place the quinoa in a blender or coffee grinder and grind to a fine powder. Drain the beans thoroughly. In a mixing bowl, stir together the cornmeal, ground quinoa, salt, cumin, cinnamon, and sesame seeds. Mix well. Add the onion and beans, then stir in the buttermilk.

2. In a separate bowl, beat the egg whites until just frothy. Add the cream of tartar and continue to beat until they hold firm peaks. Fold this into the bean mixture.

3. Heat the oil in a skillet over medium high heat until hot, but not smoking. Ladle the bean mixture into the skillet, forming 6 cakes. Reduce heat to medium and allow the cakes to cook, undisturbed, until the edges have begun to firm, about 3 minutes. Carefully flip each cake and continue to cook on the second side until cooked through, about 2 minutes. Transfer to a serving platter and accompany with tomatillo salsa (page 182) or ancho pepper sauce (page 181).

3/4 cup uncooked quinoa, rinsed
   and dried
2 cups cooked anasazi beans or
   pinto beans
1 cup yellow cornmeal
1 teaspoon salt
2 teaspoons ground cumin
1/2 teaspoon cinnamon
2 tablespoons sesame seeds
1/2 cup diced sweet onion
1/2 to 2/3 cup buttermilk
3 egg whites, at room temperature
Pinch of cream of tartar
2 tablespoons corn oil

Black Bean Corn Cakes

Yield: 6 servings • Prep Time: 15 minutes • Cooking Time: 10 minutes

3 cups masa harina
1 teaspoon salt
2 teaspoons ground cumin
1 1/2 cups light vegetable stock
   (page 162)
1 1/2 cups cooked black beans
1 teaspoon minced garlic
2 tablespoons corn oil

The cumin-scented black bean cakes are a cross between a Mexican bean cake called bocoles *and a Native American cornmeal bean cake. Serve these with crostini (page 167) and a corn salad, or use the bean mixture as a filling for tamales and serve them with tomatillo salsa.*

1. In a bowl, mix together the masa harina, salt, and 2 teaspoons cumin. Gradually stir in the stock until the mixture is evenly combined.

2. Place half of the beans in a separate mixing bowl and mash them until quite smooth. Stir in the remaining beans, garlic, and the masa harina mixture. Stir to combine. Divide the bean mixture into 6 equal portions and shape each into a round "patty," about 1 inch thick. These bean cakes can be prepared up to 2 days in advance if refrigerated in one layer in an airtight container. They can also be frozen, tightly wrapped, for up to 3 months. Thaw before proceeding with the recipe.

3. Heat the oil in a heavy skillet over medium high heat. Cook the bean cakes, turning once, until warmed through and lightly browned, about 4 minutes per side. Serve immediately with tomatillo sauce (page 182).

Black Beans and Rice with Ginger

Yield: 4 servings • Prep Time: 30 minutes • Cooking Time: 40 minutes

3/4 cup brown basmati rice
2 teaspoons peanut oil
1 1/2 cups light vegetable stock
   (page 162) or water
2 teaspoons minced gingerroot
1 teaspoon minced garlic
2 tablespoons wasabi powder
   (page 196) (optional)
1 serrano pepper, seeded and
   minced (optional)
2 cups cooked black beans
3 tablespoons tamari
18 snow peas, strings removed
10 baby corn, halved lengthwise
2 large tomatoes, peeled, seeded,
   and chopped (page 35)
3 tablespoons minced cilantro
2 tablespoons pickled ginger,
   minced
1/2 teaspoon toasted sesame oil
4 scallions, minced

The classic combination of black beans and rice is punctuated with a spike of Japanese wasabi.

1. In a 2-quart, heavy-bottomed saucepan, sauté the rice in the peanut oil over medium heat until the grains of rice begin to appear milky in color, about 5 minutes. Stir constantly as the rice cooks to prevent burning. Stir in the stock, then add the gingerroot and garlic. Bring to a boil, cover, and simmer until all of the stock is absorbed and the rice is just tender, about 35 minutes. The rice can be prepared up to an hour ahead and left, covered, at room temperature. It may also be refrigerated in an airtight container for 2 days, but should be steamed briefly before continuing with the recipe.

2. Place the wasabi in a small bowl and combine it with enough hot water (about 1 teaspoon) to make a thick paste. Cover and set aside. When the rice is cooked, stir in the serrano pepper, beans, tamari, snow peas, baby corn, tomato, cilantro, and pickled ginger. Toss gently to combine, then warm thoroughly over medium heat. Turn the beans and rice out onto a warm serving platter. Sprinkle the sesame oil over the dish and top with minced scallions. Serve immediately, with the wasabi paste alongside for guests to dab into their servings as desired.

Variation

1. Use white basmati rice instead of brown and cook it in 1 1/2 cups light coconut milk (page 190) instead of the stock. Substitute cooked red beans for the black beans and omit the sesame oil.

Tofu Vera Cruz

Yield: 4 servings • Prep Time: 30 minutes • Cooking Time: 30 minutes

This simple-to-prepare dish has a fresh and memorable blending of flavors. Bell peppers, lime juice, garlic, and green olives serve as the base behind the contrasting textures of tofu and tempeh.

1 pound firm tofu
1/4 cup lime juice
1/2 teaspoon salt
2 tablespoons honey
1/4 pound tempeh, crumbled
2 tablespoons tamari
1 tablespoon balsamic vinegar
2 tablespoons canola oil
1 cup chopped white onion
3/4 cup chopped green bell pepper
3/4 cup chopped red bell pepper
1 serrano pepper, seeded and minced
1/2 cup diced carrot
1/4 cup diced celery
2 large tomatoes, chopped, or 1 1-pound can tomatoes, drained
3 cloves garlic, sliced
2 1/4 teaspoons ground cumin
1/2 teaspoon crushed dried oregano
Pinch of black pepper
3 tablespoons minced cilantro
10 green olives, pitted and sliced
6 cilantro sprigs

1. Drain the tofu, then slice it into 1/2-inch-thick pieces. Place these on a clean kitchen towel with a second towel on top. Put a light cutting board on this and allow the tofu to drain for 30 minutes. In a shallow baking dish, combine the lime juice, salt, and honey. Add the slices of tofu to this marinade. Turn to coat and marinate for at least 20 minutes or up to 24 hours. In a separate small dish, combine the tempeh with the tamari and balsamic vinegar. Stir well and set this aside to marinate as well.

2. In a 1-inch skillet, heat the oil over medium heat until hot but not smoking. Add the onion, peppers, carrot, and celery. Cook, stirring often, until they are well softened, about 10 minutes. Add the tempeh and tomatoes along with the marinade from the tofu. Stir in the garlic, salt, cumin, oregano, and pepper. Cook, stirring often, for 5 minutes. Stir in the minced cilantro.

3. Carefully place the tofu on top of this vegetable-tempeh mixture. Cover and cook at a simmer for 15 minutes. Transfer the tofu to one large plate or four individual dinner plates. Stir the olives into the skillet, then pour this around the tofu. Garnish with cilantro sprigs. Serve at once.

Cook's Note: The tofu is best if pressed for 30 minutes before proceeding with the recipe.

Miso-Marinated Tofu with Roasted Red Pepper Sauce

Yield: 4 servings • Prep Time: 30 minutes • Cooking Time: 30 minutes

4 medium red bell peppers, roasted (page 35)
1 pound firm tofu
1/4 cup white miso
3/4 cup light vegetable stock (page 162)
1/2 teaspoon minced gingerroot
1/2 teaspoon minced garlic
2 tablespoons mirin (page 193)
2 teaspoons honey
2 tablespoons lemon juice
2 sheets nori (page 193)
10 snow peas, strings removed
2 cups mung bean sprouts
2 teaspoons soy sauce
1 teaspoon toasted sesame oil (optional)
1/2 cup slivered almonds, toasted (page 35)
1/4 cup minced scallions

This versatile recipe can be served as is, or the components may be used as parts of other recipes. For example, the tofu is terrific grilled as a brochette and the sauce can be served with pasta.

1. Using a paring knife and your fingers, remove and discard the stems, seeds, and all of the skin from the peppers. Hold the peppers over a bowl as you work to allow all juices to drip into the bowl. Place the peeled peppers in a food processor or blender. Strain the pepper juice from the bowl onto the peppers. Purée until very smooth. Set this aside as you continue with the dish. This pepper purée may be prepared up to 3 days in advance if refrigerated in an airtight container.

2. Drain the tofu and slice it into 1/2-inch-thick pieces. Place the slices on a clean kitchen towel and place a second towel on top, with a cutting board on top of this. Weight the board down with a heavy skillet or several 1-pound cans. Allow the tofu to drain for 30 minutes. Cut each slice crosswise into 2 triangles.

3. In a shallow baking dish, combine the miso, 1/2 cup stock, the ginger, garlic, mirin, honey, and lemon juice. Stir until smooth. Place the tofu in this marinade, turning to coat both sides. Set aside for at least 1 hour. The tofu can marinate in this mixture for up to 24 hours.

4. Toast the nori by quickly waving it over the open flame of a gas burner, or near a hot electric burner. The nori will shrink slightly and change colors as it is toasted. Cut a 6-inch square out of one of the pieces of nori and set this aside. Cut the remains of this piece and all of the other sheet into 1/4-inch-wide strips and then into small squares or triangles. Set these aside to garnish the final dish.

5. Preheat the broiler to high. Place the pan of tofu about 6 inches from the heat and broil until the top is beginning to brown and most of the marinade has evaporated. This should take 12 to 15 minutes.

6. Meanwhile, finish preparing the other elements of the dish. Stack the snow peas and shred them lengthwise into matchstick-sized slices. Place the bean sprouts in a strainer and rinse under cold water. Heat a 9-inch skillet over medium high heat. Add the wet bean sprouts and the snow peas. Cook, shaking the pan and tossing often, until the peas are just tender, about 2 minutes. Add the soy sauce and toss again. Stir in the sesame oil, almonds, and scallions, then transfer the sprouts to the center of a serving platter.

7. Combine the red pepper purée and the remaining 1/4 cup stock in a small saucepan. Bring to a boil and season to taste with salt. Hollow out a well in the center of the bean sprouts and place the 6-inch square of nori in the hole, so that it forms a cup. Arrange the cooked triangles of tofu over the bean sprouts with tips pointing up to the nori. Fill the nori with pepper sauce and sprinkle additional nori around the edges of the platter. Serve immediately.

Cook's Note: The tofu is best if pressed for 30 minutes.

Singapore Curry

Yield: 6 servings • Prep Time: 30 minutes • Cooking Time: 20 minutes

The flavors of Singapore's cuisine are magical, blending the seasonings from neighboring cuisines that have influenced this tiny haven.

1 pound firm tofu
1 1/2-inch ball tamarind, softened in 1/4 cup hot water
4 stalks lemon grass
2 cups broccoli florets
1 cup shredded carrots
1 red bell pepper, cut into triangles
1 cup sugar snaps or snow peas
1 cup diced onion
2 teaspoons minced gingerroot
3 cloves garlic
1 to 2 serrano peppers, seeded and chopped
1 1/2 cups light coconut milk (page 190)
1 teaspoon toasted anise seeds
1 tablespoon ground coriander
2 teaspoons ground cumin
1/4 teaspoon turmeric
Pinch cayenne (optional)
1/2 teaspoon dried fenugreek leaves (page 191) (optional)
1 teaspoon salt
6 sprigs fresh cilantro
1/4 cup shredded basil

1. Drain the tofu and slice it into 3/4-inch-thick pieces. Place them on a clean kitchen towel with a second towel on top. Put a cutting board on top of this and weight it down with a heavy skillet or several 1-pound cans. Allow the tofu to drain for 30 minutes.

2. Rub the tamarind between your fingers to separate the pulp and seeds. Strain the juice through a tea strainer, discard the pulp and set the liquid aside. Trim the lemon grass stalks to about 3 inches.

3. Remove and discard all tough outer layers of each stalk. With the flat side of a cleaver or large kitchen knife, smash the stalks of lemon grass, turning them several times so that they are flattened open and the fibrous interior is visible. Set these aside.

4. Place the broccoli in a steamer rack over rapidly boiling water. Cover and steam until it has turned a vibrant green and is just beginning to soften, about 5 minutes. Add the carrots and continue to cook until both vegetables are just tender, about 3 minutes. Immediately transfer them to a strainer and run cold water over them to stop their cooking. Turn them out onto a clean kitchen towel to drain. Place the sugar snaps and peppers in the steamer rack over rapidly boiling water and steam until they are just softened slightly, about 2 minutes. Transfer them to the strainer and place under cold water to stop their cooking. Turn them out on the towel to drain, but keep them separate from the broccoli. The vegetables can be steamed up to a day in advance if refrigerated in an airtight container.

5. In a blender or food processor, combine the onion, ginger, garlic, and serrano peppers with 3 to 4 tablespoons coconut milk. Purée until smooth, scraping down the sides of the beaker as necessary. Transfer this mixture to a 12-inch wok or skillet. In a coffee mill or mortar and pestle, grind the anise seeds to a fine powder. Add them to the pan, then stir in the remaining coconut milk. Mix in the coriander, cumin, turmeric, cayenne, fenugreek leaves, salt, and lemon grass stalks. Bring this mixture to a simmer and cook, stirring occasionally, for 10 minutes.

6. Meanwhile, cut the tofu into small cubes. Add it to the cooked sauce along with the tamarind juice and return the mixture to a simmer. Cook, partially covered, for 10 minutes.

7. As the tofu cooks, quickly warm the two groups of vegetables over steaming water, keeping them separate. Arrange the peppers and peas in a mound in the center of a serving dish. Remove the lemon grass from the tofu, stir in the basil, and ladle the curry around the peppers. Place the broccoli and carrots around the edge of the dish, garnish with additional cilantro and basil leaves and serve immediately.

Cook's Note: The tofu is best if pressed for 30 minutes before cooking.

Tangy Tempeh Stew with Garden Vegetables

Yield: 4 servings • Prep Time: 40 minutes • Cooking Time: 25 minutes

1/2 pound tempeh (do not use a crumbly tempeh, such as sea vegetable)
2 tablespoons flour
1 teaspoon salt
1/4 teaspoon black pepper
1/8 teaspoon nutmeg
Pinch of cayenne
1 tablespoon canola oil
2 1/4 cups hearty vegetable stock (page 162)
1 1/4 cups fresh or frozen cranberries
1/2 cup finely grated horseradish root
3 tablespoons fruit juice sweetener or honey
1/4 teaspoon ground allspice
1/8 teaspoon ground cloves
4 cloves garlic, sliced
25 pearl onions
1/2 pound mushrooms
1 small butternut squash (1 to 1 1/2 pounds)
3 tablespoons minced fresh parsley
1 lemon, cut in wedges

While catering in Tennessee, I often got requests for dishes I had little experience with, given that I was fresh out of cooking school in France. One interesting combination of flavors that I discovered during this period was cranberry mixed with horseradish, which I have applied to this tempeh stew.

1. Cut the tempeh into 3/4-inch cubes. Place the flour in a shallow bowl, then stir in 1/4 teaspoon salt, the pepper, nutmeg, and cayenne. Roll the tempeh in the seasoned flour. In a small Dutch oven, heat the oil over medium high heat until hot, but not smoking. Add the tempeh and cook, stirring often, until it begins to brown, about 5 minutes. Drain off any oil that has not been absorbed.

2. Gradually stir the stock into the pan, scraping the bottom as you add it so that lumps do not form. Stir in the cranberries, 1/3 cup horseradish, the fruit juice sweetener, cinnamon, allspice, cloves, garlic, and remaining 3/4 teaspoon salt. Bring the stew to a boil, then cover and immediately reduce to a simmer. Cook, stirring occasionally, for 25 minutes.

3. As the stew cooks, prepare the vegetables. Peel the onions and, using the tip of a paring knife, make a small cross mark in the root end of each so that the onion will cook more evenly. Clean the mushrooms and trim woody parts from their stems. Halve the squash, then remove and discard the seeds. Peel the squash halves and cut them into 1-inch cubes. Steam each of these vegetables separately over rapidly boiling water until they are just tender. The onions will take about 15 minutes, the squash about 10, and the mushrooms about 5. Stir the vegetables and remaining horseradish into the stew for the last 10 minutes of cooking. Turn the stew out into individual serving dishes. Sprinkle with parsley and serve a lemon wedge alongside each dish.

Tempeh and Broccoli with Hot Almond Raisin Sauce

Yield: 4 servings • Prep Time: 20 minutes • Cooking Time: 25 minutes

Almonds, raisins, and orange juice combine to produce a lovely sweet and sour sauce for the tempeh and broccoli.

1 orange
1 tablespoon cornstarch
3 tablespoons red wine vinegar
1 tablespoon maple sugar or 3/4 tablespoon sugar
1/2 cup blanched almonds, toasted
1 cup mushroom stock (page 163) or light vegetable stock (page 162)
1/4 cup raisins
1 teaspoon minced garlic
1/2 teaspoon salt
1/4 teaspoon cayenne
12 ounces tempeh
1 cup diced carrot
1 1/2 pounds broccoli, cut into florets
1 cup straw mushrooms
1/3 cup grated daikon (Japanese radish)
2 tablespoons minced scallions

1. Zest the orange and set this aside. Squeeze the juice from the orange, then measure it. You should have about 1/3 cup. If you do not, add enough water to equal 1/3 cup. Set aside. In a small bowl, combine the cornstarch and vinegar. Mix well and set aside.

2. Combine the maple sugar and almonds in a blender or coffee grinder and pulverize. Turn this out into a small saucepan, then add the stock, raisins, garlic, salt, and cayenne. Bring this to a boil, then reduce to a simmer and cook, whisking occasionally, for 5 minutes. Add the orange juice and cornstarch mixture. Return this sauce mixture to a boil, whisking constantly. When the sauce has thickened, remove it from the heat, but keep it warm until the tempeh is ready.

3. Meanwhile, cut the tempeh into small cubes and place them in the top rack of a steamer. Place over rapidly boiling water, cover, and steam for 15 minutes. Add the carrot and cook until it just begins to soften when pierced with the tip of a sharp knife, about 4 minutes. Add the broccoli and continue to steam, covered, until it is a vibrant green and is just barely tender, about 5 minutes. Add the straw mushrooms and continue to steam, covered, for 1 minute. Stir in the orange zest and immediately turn the tempeh mixture out onto individual dinner plates or one large platter. Pour the sauce in an irregular pattern over the tempeh and vegetables, leaving at least half of the pieces of broccoli without sauce. Sprinkle the daikon and scallions on top. Serve at once.

Variations

1. Replace the orange with 2 lemons so that you have 1/4 cup lemon juice and zest from 1 lemon. Replace maple sugar with 2 tablespoons honey and almonds with pistachios.

2. Use either the original orange-flavored sauce or the lemon sauce above. Substitute 1/2 pound of cauliflower for the 1/2 pound of broccoli. Add 1 red pepper, minced, instead of the daikon.

Spaghetti Squash with Parmesan and Peas

Yield: 6 servings • Prep Time: 50 minutes • Cooking Time: 20 minutes

1 medium-size spaghetti squash
(about 2 pounds)
3 tablespoons butter
or olive oil
2 teaspoons minced garlic
1/2 cup minced shallots
1 cup diced red bell pepper
1/2 cup mushroom stock
(page 163)
1/2 cup fresh or frozen peas
1/4 teaspoon dried red pepper
flakes
1/2 cup chopped walnuts, toasted
(page 35)
1/2 cup freshly grated Parmesan
1/3 cup minced fresh Italian
parsley

Spaghetti squash gets its name from the fact that when it is cooked, the meat scraped out from the shell resembles spaghetti and can be used in many recipes that call for true spaghetti. One of spaghetti squash's attributes is that it's very low in calories. The only problem with this is that when even a small amount of fat is added to a spaghetti squash recipe, the percentage of fat calories skyrockets. Do not be alarmed! Simply work it into an otherwise low-fat menu.

1. Place the squash in the top rack of a steamer over rapidly boiling water. Cover and cook until it is easily pierced with a fork, about 45 minutes. If your steamer will not accommodate the squash, you can boil it instead. To do so, plunge the whole squash into a 6-quart saucepan which is 2/3 full of rapidly boiling water. Cover and cook at a slow boil for about 30 minutes, or until you can pierce it with a fork. In either case, immediately remove the squash from the pan and cool on a cake rack. When the squash is cool enough to handle (or when it has cooled completely), cut it in half. Scrape out and discard the seeds. Using the tines of a fork, scrape the squash from the shell into a bowl. It should separate into spaghetti-like strands. The squash may be prepared up to 3 days in advance if refrigerated in an airtight container.

2. In a 12-inch skillet, heat the butter over medium high heat until hot, but not smoking. Add the garlic and shallots and cook, stirring constantly, for about 30 seconds, in order to release the flavor of the garlic. Reduce the heat slightly and continue to cook, stirring constantly, until the shallots are soft and beginning to look translucent, about 6 minutes. Do not allow the garlic to brown or it will impregnate the dish with a bitter flavor.

3. Add the squash, red pepper, and stock to the skillet. Continue to cook, stirring often, until the squash just begins to soften and the stock has cooked down to a thin layer in the bottom of the pan, about 8 minutes. Stir in the peas and pepper flakes, then continue to cook, stirring often, until the peas are plump and bright green, about 4 minutes for fresh, 2 minutes for frozen. Add the walnuts, Parmesan, and parsley, then toss to blend thoroughly. Taste and adjust the seasonings.

Variation

1. Serve as is with slices of fresh goat cheese (Montrachet, for example).

Linguine with Capers and Black Olives

Yield: 4 servings • Prep Time: 10 minutes • Cooking Time: 20 minutes

3 yellow bell peppers, roasted
(page 35)
1 recipe light tomato sauce
(page 175)
4 cloves garlic, sliced thin
2 cups cubed Japanese eggplant

Complement the intense flavors of this simple pasta with braised greens or a green salad and crusty French bread.

1. Peel the skin from each, then tear them in half and scrape out and discard the seeds and white membrane. Cut the peppers into small pieces.

2. Meanwhile, in a 10-inch nonreactive skillet, heat the tomato sauce with the garlic and eggplant. Bring this to a boil, then reduce the heat to low and cook, stirring occasionally, until the eggplant is tender, about 10 minutes.

3. At the same time, bring 4 quarts of water to a boil. Add the linguine and cook, stirring occasionally, until it is al dente: about 2 minutes for fresh, 10 for dried. Drain the pasta and turn it into a large serving platter.

4. Stir the peeled peppers, olives, capers, Gruyère, and basil into the hot sauce. Season to taste with black pepper. Pour the sauce over the linguine, then toss and serve. Pass Parmesan cheese at the table.

10 black olives (preferably calamata with pits)
1 1/2 tablespoons capers
4 ounces Gruyère, cut in tiny cubes, or cubed tofu "cottage cheese" (page 172)
1/4 cup shredded basil leaves
Freshly ground black pepper
8 ounces uncooked linguine
Freshly grated Parmesan (optional)

Penne with Carrots, Black Olives and Fennel

Yield: 6 servings • Prep Time: 1 1/4 hours • Cooking Time: 25 minutes

The unusual, protein-rich sauce for this pasta dish is made from split peas. To enrich this dish, top each serving with thin slices of mild goat cheese or crumbled feta.

1. Pick over the split peas to remove all rocks and debris. Rinse the peas well, then place them in a small bowl and cover with cold water. Set them aside to soak for 8 hours. Drain the peas and place them in a 1 1/2-quart saucepan with 1 tablespoon minced garlic, 1 1/2 tablespoons oil, the bay leaf, and water. Bring this to a boil, stirring occasionally to prevent the peas from sticking. Cover halfway, reduce the heat to a simmer, and cook, stirring occasionally, until the peas are so soft that they have virtually puréed themselves, 45 to 60 minutes. Remove the bay leaf and transfer the peas to a food processor or blender. Cool briefly, then add 1/2 teaspoon of salt, the mirin, pepper, nutmeg, and cream. Purée this sauce mixture until very smooth, then set it aside.

2. Peel the carrots and cut them into 1/4-inch-thick rounds. (You may also cut them into decorative flower shapes with the aid of a zester, for a more festive look.) Place the carrots in the top rack of a steamer over rapidly boiling water. Cover and steam until just tender, about 8 minutes. Immediately transfer the carrots to a strainer and run cold water over them to stop their cooking. Set them aside.

3. Bring 2 quarts of water to a boil. Add the remaining 1/2 teaspoon of salt, then stir in the noodles. Cover, reduce the heat slightly and cook, stirring occasionally, until the noodles are al dente, about 12 minutes.

4. Meanwhile, in a 12-inch skillet, heat the remaining 1 1/2 tablespoons of oil over medium high heat until hot, but not smoking. Add the onion and cook, stirring constantly, until it is coated with oil, about 1 minute. Reduce the heat to medium and continue to cook, stirring often, until the onion is translucent, about 10 minutes. Add the remaining 1/2 tablespoon of garlic and the fennel. Toss to coat with oil. Stir in the cooked carrots, olives, capers, and the peas.

5. Gently warm the split pea sauce, then pour it into the center of individual plates or one large serving platter. When the noodles are cooked, drain them, then transfer them to a large mixing bowl. Add the fresh basil and cooked carrot mixture. Toss well and arrange this over the pea sauce. Sprinkle with Parmesan and serve.

Cook's Note: The split peas must soak for at least 8 hours.

1 cup dried green split peas
1 1/2 tablespoons minced garlic
3 tablespoons olive oil
1 bay leaf
3 cups water
1 teaspoon salt
2 tablespoons mirin (page 193)
1/8 teaspoon black pepper
1/8 teaspoon nutmeg
1 cup soy cream (page 171), or crème fraîche (page 172) or yogurt
1/4 pound carrots
8 ounces penne noodles (or other small noodle)
1/2 cup thinly sliced fennel bulb
1/2 cup thinly sliced red onion
18 Niçoise olives
1 tablespoon capers
1/3 cup fresh or frozen peas
1/4 cup grated Parmesan (optional)
1/3 cup shredded basil leaves

Rotini Primavera

Yield: 6 servings • Prep Time: 30 minutes • Cooking Time: 1 1/2 hours

1 garnet yam
1 small red onion
1 small bulb garlic
1 tablespoon olive oil
2 cups uncooked rotini noodles
2 carrots, sliced into 1/4-inch-thick
    rounds
2 cups broccoli florets
1 cup sliced zucchini
1/4 cup dry white wine
3/4 cup porcini vegetable stock
    (page 163)
3 cups chopped chard leaves
1/2 teaspoon salt
1/8 teaspoon black pepper
1/8 teaspoon dried red pepper
    flakes
1 small yellow bell pepper,
    seeded and sliced
1 small red bell pepper, seeded
    and sliced
18 sugar snaps or snow peas,
    strings removed
1 fennel bulb, sliced thin
1/3 cup minced fresh Italian
    parsley
1/4 cup grated Parmesan
    (optional)

Any curly shaped pasta works well for this dish because the rich-tasting sauce becomes caught in the folds of the noodle. The flavors are distinctive and light and the dish has a very festive appearance. You may vary the vegetables used, simply balance for color, taste, and texture.

1. Preheat the oven to 350°F. Wash the yam, onion, and garlic, then place them on a baking sheet. Brush the onion and garlic with about 1 teaspoon of oil, then place the baking sheet on the center rack in the oven. Bake, turning the vegetables occasionally, until each is very soft when squeezed. The garlic should be ready after about 50 minutes, the onion after about 1 1/4 hours and the yam after about 1 1/2 hours. As each is done, transfer it to a cake rack to cool.

2. Peel the yam and place the meat in a food processor fitted with the metal chopping blade or a blender. Cut off the top of the garlic, exposing the center of all cloves. Carefully squeeze the garlic to extract the cooked clove from the skin, and place this in the processor with the squash. Purée this mixture, scraping down the sides of the bowl as necessary, until it is absolutely smooth and creamy. Set aside.

3. In a 3-quart saucepan, bring 6 cups of water to a rolling boil. Stir in the noodles and cook until al dente according to package directions. Drain immediately.

4. Meanwhile, peel the onion and cut it into small pieces. In a 12-inch skillet, heat the remaining 2 teaspoons of oil over medium high heat until hot, but not smoking. Add the onion, carrots, and broccoli and toss to coat with oil. Reduce the heat slightly, then cover the pan and cook, tossing often, until the broccoli is a vibrant green, about 5 minutes. Add the zucchini and cook, tossing constantly until it is coated with pan juices, about 1 minute. Turn the heat to high and add the wine. Cook, tossing frequently, until the smell of alcohol evaporates, then reduce the heat slightly and stir in the stock. Cook over medium high heat, stirring often, until the broccoli is almost tender, about 6 minutes. By this time the stock should have reduced to about 1/4 cup.

5. Add the chard, salt, black pepper, and pepper flakes and continue to cook, stirring constantly, until the chard is tender, about 3 minutes. Stir in the bell peppers and snow peas and fennel. Cook for another minute until the peas have just begun to puff. Remove the pan from the heat and very gradually whisk in the puréed squash. Stir in the parsley, then taste and adjust the seasonings. Stir the cooked noodles into the vegetables and mix, then turn the pasta out onto a large serving platter. Top with the grated Parmesan.

Cook's Note: Once the yam, onion, and garlic are baked (which can be done up to 4 days in advance), the actual cooking time of this dish is reduced to 20 minutes.

Linguine with Spinach and Goat Cheese

Yield: 4 servings • Prep Time: 30 minutes • Cooking Time: 18 minutes

The secret ingredient that makes this dish a success is fresh pear. The combination of flavors, textures, and aromas gives the dish extraordinary depth.

1 pound fresh spinach
4 ounces creamy goat cheese
10 sun-dried tomatoes,
   softened in hot water
1 tablespoon olive oil
1 medium leek, cut in small dice
2 cloves garlic, sliced thin
1 cup porcini stock (page 163)
2 tablespoons fresh tarragon,
   chopped
1/4 teaspoon salt
8 ounces uncooked linguine
1 ripe Anjou pear, peeled and
   diced
2 tablespoons toasted pine nuts
   (page 35)

1. Clean the spinach thoroughly, discarding stems (page 34). Place the leaves in a strainer to drain briefly.

2. Remove and discard any rind that is attached to the goat cheese. Cut the remaining cheese into tiny (1/4-inch) dice. Set this aside. Drain the sun-dried tomatoes and cut them into thin strips, then set aside.

3. In a 12-inch skillet, heat the oil over medium high heat until hot, but not smoking. Add the leek and garlic and cook, stirring constantly, until they are glistening, about 1 minute. Reduce the heat slightly, then continue to cook, stirring often, until the leek begins to soften, about 5 minutes.

4. As the leeks cook, roughly chop the spinach into 1- to 2-inch pieces. When the leeks are ready, add the spinach to the skillet and continue to cook, stirring and tossing constantly until all spinach leaves are just wilted, about 3 minutes. Add the stock and increase the heat to medium high. When the liquid begins to bubble, stir in about 2/3 of the goat cheese and the tarragon. Use a wooden mixing spoon to smooth the cheese into the stock.

5. Meanwhile, bring 3 quarts of water to a boil. Stir in the salt and then the linguine and cook, stirring occasionally, until it is just al dente. Immediately drain the linguine and transfer it to a large serving platter. Pour the hot sauce over the pasta and toss to combine. (The sauce may be reheated if it has cooled off as the pasta cooks.) Sprinkle the pear and pine nuts on top of the pasta and serve at once.

Variation

1. Use fettuccine instead of linguine. Omit sun-dried tomatoes and substitute 1/4 cup basil for the tarragon. Serve with a garnish of slices of ripe Italian tomatoes (you will need about 2 pounds of tomatoes) outlining the individual serving plates.

Cinnamon Lentils with Angel Hair

Yield: 4 servings • Prep Time: 20 minutes • Cooking Time: 25 minutes

1 1/2 cups diced white onion
1 1/2 tablespoons olive oil
1/2 pound mushrooms
5 tablespoons orange juice
3 cloves garlic
1 teaspoon salt
1 teaspoon cinnamon
1/4 teaspoon pepper
1/8 teaspoon nutmeg
2 cups cooked lentils
5 tablespoons minced fresh
   parsley
1 cup peeled and diced orange
   bell pepper
6 ounces uncooked angel hair
   pasta
1 1/2 cups chopped tomatoes
2 tablespoons capers
1/4 cup finely chopped toasted
   walnuts

This unusual combination of flavors is light and inviting. The lentil mixture can be served, as suggested below, tossed with pasta or it can be served over rice.

1. In a 9-inch skillet, sauté the onion in the olive oil over medium heat until very soft, but not brown, about 15 minutes. Meanwhile, mince the mushrooms. When the onions are soft, add the mushrooms and orange juice and cook briefly, stirring constantly. Press the garlic through a garlic press into the pan and stir in 1/2 teaspoon of salt, the cinnamon, pepper, and nutmeg. Cook this mixture, stirring often, until all of the juices from the mushrooms have evaporated, about 15 minutes.

2. Stir the lentils into the skillet and cook just long enough to warm through. Stir in 3 tablespoons of the minced parsley and the bell pepper. Taste and adjust the seasonings. Toss well, cover, and set aside while preparing the noodles.

3. Bring 2 quarts of water to a rolling boil. Add the remaining salt and when the water settles down, stir in the angel hair. Reduce the heat slightly, to avoid having the water overflow, and cook, stirring once or twice, until the noodles are al dente. Immediately drain the pasta and transfer it to a mixing bowl. Toss in the remaining parsley, tomatoes, capers, and walnuts.

4. To serve the lentils, arrange a ring of noodles on individual serving dishes. Mound the lentils in the center of each nest and serve immediately. Toss together before eating.

Variation

1. Toss the noodles with 1 1/2 cups chopped tomatoes, 2 tablespoons of capers or 1/4 cup black olives, and 3 tablespoons olive oil before serving.

5 • New Classics

Black-Eyed Peas with Lemon Grass and Yard-Long Beans

Yield: 6 servings • Prep Time: 30 minutes • Cooking Time: 1 hour

Yard-long beans are available year-round in most Asian markets. Their delicate taste and rich green color make them excellent companions to black-eyed peas. Though the ingredients list is long, this recipe is actually very simple to prepare. Serve it as part of a mixed curry supper or alone with Masala Rice (page 159) and a salad of jicama and tomato.

1. In a 10-inch skillet, combine the black-eyed peas, coconut milk, stock, 1 tablespoon ginger, the coriander seeds, peppercorns, and 2 teaspoons garlic. Bring to a boil, stirring occasionally, then reduce to a simmer, cover, and cook until the peas are just tender, about 45 minutes. (If you are using fresh black-eyed peas, they need cook only about 25 minutes.)

2. As the black-eyed peas cook, prepare the lemon grass. Trim the tough tops from each stalk, so that the stalks are about 3 inches long. Peel off tough outer layers from the stalks, leaving only the fragrant, slightly supple, light-colored interior. Using a cleaver or chef's knife, slice the stalks into paper-thin rounds. You should have about 1/3 cup. Place these in a mortar or electric coffee grinder with the dried red peppers, and pound or grind to a smooth paste. When the black-eyed peas are tender, stir the lemon grass mixture, lime leaves, and 2 tablespoons tamari into the skillet. The black-eyed peas may be prepared up to 3 days in advance, if refrigerated in an airtight container. They may be frozen for up to 2 months.

3. Trim tough ends from the string beans and cut them into 3- to 4-inch lengths. Place them in a steamer rack over rapidly boiling water, cover and cook until just tender, about 8 minutes. Immediately turn them out into a strainer and place under cold running water, tossing them, to stop their cooking and seal their color. Transfer the string beans to a clean kitchen towel and pat dry. They may be steamed, then dried and refrigerated in an airtight container for 24 hours before continuing with the recipe.

4. In a second skillet, heat the peanut oil over high heat until hot, but not smoking. Add the remaining ginger and garlic and stir quickly. Reduce the heat to medium, then add the string beans and toss well. Cook, tossing often, for about 5 minutes, or until the beans have begun to brown. Add the mushrooms and continue to cook, stirring often, until the button mushrooms are soft, about 8 minutes. In a small bowl, combine the remaining 2 tablespoons tamari, the umeboshi paste, rice vinegar, and honey. Stir this into the string beans and cook for about 5 minutes to blend flavors.

5. Turn the string beans out onto a serving platter so that they form a ring. Arrange the warm black-eyed peas in the center and sprinkle with minced scallions. Serve at once.

2 cups fresh or frozen black-eyed peas
1 1/2 cups light coconut milk (page 190)
1 1/2 cups light vegetable stock (page 162)
6 1/2 teaspoons minced ginger-root
1/2 teaspoon coriander seeds
5 black peppercorns
1 tablespoon minced garlic
5 stalks lemon grass
2 dried red chili peppers (optional)
3 lime leaves (page 192) or 1 tablespoon lime juice
1/4 cup tamari
12 ounces green string beans (preferably yard-long)
1 tablespoon peanut oil
8 ounces button mushrooms, sliced
4 ounces fresh shiitake mushrooms, sliced, or 6 dried shiitake mushrooms soaked, drained, and sliced
1 teaspoon umeboshi paste (page 196)
2 tablespoons rice vinegar
1 tablespoon honey
2 tablespoons minced scallions

Broccoli and Black Beans with Cashew Sauce

Yield: 4 servings • Prep Time: 15 minutes • Cooking Time: 10 minutes

1 1/2 pounds broccoli
2 lemons
1/3 cup cashew butter (page 167)
1/4 cup boiling water
2 tablespoons soy sauce
1 tablespoon rice syrup (page 193)
1 tablespoon peanut oil
4 teaspoons minced gingerroot
1 tablespoon minced garlic
3/4 cup light vegetable stock
   (page 162)
1/8 teaspoon salt
1/2 cup cooked black beans
1/4 cup sliced water chestnuts
2 tablespoons chopped cashews,
   toasted

The sweet undertone of cashews coupled with the bite of ginger complements the crisp, sweet taste of broccoli in this light entrée. Serve over rice or rice noodles.

1. Trim the broccoli into florets. Peel and discard the tough outer layer from both the stem and the florets. Cut the stems into 1-inch pieces, then set the broccoli aside. Rinse and dry the lemon thoroughly. Grate the zest from one of the lemons, then squeeze and strain the juice from both lemons. Set the juice and zest aside.

2. In a small mixing bowl, combine the cashew butter, boiling water, soy sauce, rice syrup, and 2 tablespoons lemon juice. Mix well and set this sauce aside. This may be prepared up to 3 days in advance if refrigerated in an airtight container. Bring the sauce to room temperature before cooking the broccoli.

3. In a 10-inch skillet, heat the oil over high heat until hot, but not smoking. Add the ginger and reduce the heat to medium. Cook for about 30 seconds to release the flavor, then add the garlic and continue to cook, stirring constantly for 1 minute. Do not allow the garlic to brown or it will become bitter. Return the heat to high and add the broccoli. Toss to coat with the oil, then add the stock and salt. Stir, then cover and cook, tossing occasionally, until the broccoli is just beginning to soften and is still a vibrant green and all of the stock has evaporated, about 8 minutes. (If all liquid is not gone when the broccoli is tender, remove the lid for the last minute of cooking to expedite evaporation.)

4. Stir the beans and water chestnuts into the broccoli and warm through. Remove from the heat and toss in the lemon zest. Pour the sauce onto a medium-sized serving platter (or divide it evenly among 4 individual plates). Arrange the broccoli mixture on top of the sauce and sprinkle chopped nuts on top. Serve immediately.

Baked Barbecued Beans

Yield: 6 servings • Prep Time: 10 minutes • Cooking Time: 3 1/2 hours

These beans have just a hint of the sweetness that sometimes overpowers baked bean recipes. Red beans need no presoaking, though the time required to cook them can be reduced if they are soaked in cold water overnight.

1. Pick over the beans to remove all stones and debris. Rinse the beans well, then place them in a pressure cooker with the onion, bay leaf, oil, and 2 teaspoons of garlic. Add the water, lock the lid in place and bring to high steam. Cook undisturbed for 12 minutes. Place the pressure cooker in the sink and release the steam by running cold tap water over it. Open the cooker and check for doneness—the beans should be just tender when pressed between the fingers. If you are not using a pressure cooker, bring the 6 cups of water to a boil in a 3-quart saucepan. Add the beans and boil for 2 minutes. Turn off the heat and allow the beans to soak for 1 hour. Add the onion, bay leaf, oil, and garlic, then simmer until tender, about 1 hour. Stir the beans several times as they cook and add more water if the cooking liquid evaporates to less than 1 inch above the level of the beans.

2. Drain the beans, reserving their cooking liquid. Preheat the oven to 300°F. Place the beans in a Dutch oven or heavy baking pan and add the remaining garlic, molasses, fennel seeds, tomato paste, vinegar, soy sauce, thyme, and mustard. Place the reserved liquid in a small saucepan and reduce to 2 cups. Stir this into the beans, then cover and bake until the liquid has evaporated and the beans are extremely plump and tender, at least 2 hours. Serve with tortillas or rice and a salad.

1 1/2 cups uncooked red beans
1 cup diced onion
1 bay leaf
1 tablespoon canola oil
2 tablespoons minced garlic
6 cups water
2 tablespoons blackstrap
   molasses
1/2 teaspoon crushed fennel seeds
2 tablespoons tomato paste
3 tablespoons cider vinegar
1/4 cup soy sauce
1/4 teaspoon dried thyme
1 teaspoon Dijon-style mustard

Fava Beans in Parchment

Yield: 6 servings • Prep Time: 30 minutes • Cooking Time: 15 minutes

3 cups shelled fresh fava beans
  or cooked kidney or anasazi
  beans
1 1/2 cups light vegetable stock
  (page 162)
1 cup shredded leek, white part
  only
4 cloves garlic, sliced thin
1 cup julienne carrot strips
1 cup haricots verts (tiny string
  beans) or 1 cup French-cut
  string beans
1/4 teaspoon salt
Pinch of cayenne
Pinch of black pepper
Pinch of nutmeg
3 tablespoons fresh tarragon or 1/4
  cup fresh mint leaves, minced
1 tablespoon butter or olive oil
  (optional)
3 tablespoons milk, cream, or soy
  cream (page 171)
Baking parchment paper
  (page 6)
1 tablespoon vegetable oil
1 1/2 teaspoons lemon zest

If you are fortunate enough to find fresh fava beans in your market, buy them. Even if you do no more than steam them and eat them straight from the pods, you will be in for a treat. Their flavor and succulence are unparalleled, barely comparable to those that have been dried or bottled. If fava beans are unavailable, substitute kidney or anasazi beans.

1. Place the fava beans in a steamer rack over, not touching, rapidly boiling water. Cover and steam just long enough to loosen the skin from the beans, about 4 minutes. Immediately place them in a strainer under cold running water to stop their cooking. When they are cool enough to handle, peel the beans by slicing through the top of the skin and slipping the bean out into a bowl.

2. Place the stock, leek, and garlic in a 9-inch skillet and bring to a boil. Cover and cook, stirring occasionally, until the leeks begin to soften, about 6 minutes. Add the carrots and haricot verts, salt, cayenne, pepper, and nutmeg and cook, uncovered, until the beans are just tender, about 8 minutes. Remove the skillet from the heat and stir the tarragon, butter, and milk or cream into the vegetables. Mix in the fava beans. Taste and adjust the seasonings.

3. Preheat the oven to 400°F. Cut 6 heart-shaped pieces of parchment (by folding the parchment in half) that measure 13 inches tall by 10 inches at the widest part of the heart. Place one heart open on the work surface, point facing you. Arrange about 1/6 of the fava bean mixture in the center of the right half of the heart. Fold the parchment over the filling and crimp the edges to seal the package shut. (To crimp, hold the pouch with one hand on the edge of the heart at the top of the folded edge. Make a small fold—inward towards the filling. The fold should angle slightly towards the sealed edge of the pouch so that the fold appears triangular in shape. Move the securing hand to hold the pouch in place at the new fold, then make a second angled fold, beginning in the center of the first fold. Repeat this half-layered folding around the entire edge of the heart to the tip, then twist to seal the tip.) Place the parchment pouches on a baking sheet and brush each with oil. The pouches can be prepared up to 8 hours in advance if refrigerated.

4. Bake the fava bean pouches until puffed and lightly browned, about 15 minutes.

5. To serve, place pouches on individual serving plates and bring to the table. Snip open in the puffed center of each, or make a cross cut with the tip of a very sharp knife. Sprinkle lemon zest into each pouch.

Variations

1. Substitute Tempeh Fajita mixture (page 99) for the filling and bake as directed in parchment.

2. Replace the beans with 12 ounces of diced tofu and add 2 teaspoons minced gingerroot to the filling along with the garlic. Replace the haricot verts with sliced red pepper and the milk with soy sauce. Substitute 2 teaspoons anise seeds for the lemon zest.

Sliced Seitan with Wild Mushrooms

Yield: 6 servings • Prep Time: 45 minutes • Cooking Time: 2 hours

This is one of the most elegant and simple entrées in the book. The combination of seitan, lightly scented with red wine and rosemary, and succulent wild mushrooms makes for a truly memorable meal. Serve this with a simple sauce made by reducing the simmering liquid or by adding butter to the reduced liquid to make a mounted butter sauce (below) or with Béarnaise sauce (page 180).

1. Form the seitan into a large log shape, then tie kitchen twine around it at 2-inch intervals, as a means of helping it keep its shape. In a large Dutch oven, combine the water, red wine, soy sauce, vinegar, rice syrup, peppercorns, yellow onion, carrot, 2 cloves garlic, the bay leaf, thyme, sage, and rosemary. Bring this to a boil, then reduce to a simmer, and add the seitan. Gently simmer, basting the seitan occasionally, for 1 1/2 hours. Do not boil the liquid as the seitan cooks or it will develop an unpleasant spongy consistency. Remove the pan from the heat and cool the seitan in the liquid, then transfer the seitan to a storage container and strain the cooking liquid over it. Refrigerate overnight. The seitan may be prepared up to 4 days in advance if refrigerated in its liquid and stored in an airtight container. It can be frozen, in its liquid, for up to 2 months. Thaw before proceeding with the recipe.

2. In a 10-inch skillet, heat the olive oil over medium heat until hot, but not smoking. Add the shallots and cook, stirring constantly, until they are coated with oil. Reduce the heat slightly and continue to cook, stirring often until they are soft, but not browned, about 8 minutes. Return the heat to medium and add the mushrooms. Cook, stirring constantly, for about 2 minutes or until they are beginning to soften, then stir in the orange juice and remaining garlic. Continue to cook for about 1 minute, then reduce the heat slightly, season the mushrooms with salt and pepper and continue to cook, stirring often, until they are very soft and juicy, about 8 minutes. Transfer to a serving platter and keep warm as you finish cooking the seitan.

3. In the skillet, bring to a boil 1 cup of the simmering liquid and reduce the liquid to about 1/3 cup. Meanwhile, slice the seitan into 1/4-inch-thick slices. Place them in the liquid and warm through, then lift them out and place them on top of the mushrooms. Remove the cooking juices from the heat and whisk in the softened butter if desired. Whether or not you add the butter, swirl the parsley into the pan juices and drizzle this over the seitan. Serve at once.

Ingredients

2 1/2 cups uncooked seitan
5 cups water
1 cup dry red wine
1/3 cup soy sauce
1 tablespoon ume vinegar (page 196)
2 tablespoons rice syrup (page 193)
6 black peppercorns
1 yellow onion, quartered
1 carrot, sliced
4 cloves garlic, sliced
1 bay leaf
1/2 teaspoon dried thyme
1/2 teaspoon dried sage
1/4 teaspoon dried rosemary
1 tablespoon olive oil
1/2 cup minced shallots
1/2 pound morel mushrooms
1/2 pound button mushrooms, sliced
1/2 pound fresh shiitake mushrooms, sliced
2 tablespoons orange juice
Salt and pepper to taste
6 tablespoons softened butter (optional)
2 tablespoons minced fresh parsley

Variation

1. Prepare a filling of 1/2 cup prunes, 1/4 cup chopped walnuts, and 1 chopped oven-baked onion. Stuff this into the seitan before shaping (following the directions on page 148 for curried stuffed seitan). Proceed with the recipe as above, except heat the seitan, whole, in the oven before slicing and serving. For a sauce, reduce 1 cup of the liquid as above, adding 1 1/2 teaspoons Dijon-style mustard to it when you place it in the skillet. Enrich the sauce with butter or 2 tablespoons coconut milk. Serve as described above.

Cook's Note: The seitan must be prepared, simmered for 1 1/2 hours, then chilled overnight before proceeding with the recipe.

Twice-Baked White Bean Soufflé

Yield: 6 servings • Prep Time: 30 minutes • Cooking Time: 1 1/4 hours

3 red bell peppers, roasted and
    peeled (page 35)
1 cup cooked canellini beans
1 tablespoon cider vinegar
1 teaspoon honey
1/2 cup light vegetable stock
    (page 162) or water
2 tablespoons minced fresh
    parsley
1/8 teaspoon dried thyme
2 tablespoons minced shallots
1 teaspoon salt
1 teaspoon olive oil
1 bulb garlic
1 white onion
3/4 cup milk or plain soy milk
2 1/2 tablespoons flour
3 tablespoons minced fresh
    tarragon
6 egg whites
1/4 teaspoon cream of tartar
2 teaspoons butter
2 tablespoons grated Parmesan
    (optional)

Puréed beans replace egg yolks as a binder in the base of this light and tasty soufflé. For a nondairy version, combine egg replacer with tofu (see variation below) and serve the "soufflés" unmolded.

1. Remove the stems, seeds, and any stringy membrane from the peppers. Place the peppers in a food processor fitted with the metal chopping blade, or in a blender and purée until very smooth, scraping down the sides of the bowl as necessary. Set this purée aside for the sauce.

2. Preheat the oven to 325°F. In a small baking dish or 1 1/2-quart ovenproof casserole, combine the beans with the vinegar, honey, stock, parsley, thyme, shallots, and 1/4 teaspoon salt. Cover and bake for 1 1/2 hours, stirring occasionally. Place the onion and garlic in a shallow baking pan and brush them with oil. Bake, along with the beans, until they are tender when squeezed, about 50 minutes. Remove the onion and garlic, when they are soft, to a cake rack to cool.

3. Place the baked beans in a processor fitted with the metal chopping blade. Remove the skin from the onion and chop it roughly. Add it to the processor, then squeeze each clove of garlic into the bowl and purée the mixture until smooth.

4. In a small saucepan, whisk together the milk and the flour. Place over medium heat and whisk constantly until the mixture boils and thickens. Add this to the beans with the tarragon and 1/2 teaspoon of salt. This soufflé base can be prepared up to 2 days in advance if refrigerated in an airtight container. Warm the soufflé base in a double boiler before proceeding with the recipe.

5. Preheat the oven to 375°F. Brush one 1 1/2-quart or four 8-ounce soufflé molds with butter. In a copper bowl, or a large nonglass bowl, beat the egg whites with the cream of tartar until they hold stiff peaks. Fold about 1/2 cup of the egg whites into the bean base to lighten it. Fold this base back into the egg whites, working quickly and gently. Pour the soufflé mixture into the prepared mold(s) and sprinkle with Parmesan. Bake in the center of the oven until puffed and lightly browned on top, about 35 minutes for a large soufflé, 20 minutes for the small.

6. Meanwhile, warm the pepper purée in a small saucepan and season to taste with salt and pepper. When the soufflés are ready, bring them to the table with the sauce alongside.

Variation

1. For a nondairy pudding, use soy milk in place of milk and omit the egg whites and butter. Purée 10 ounces of drained silken tofu with 1 1/2 tablespoons egg replacer until smooth. Add this mixture to the soufflé base just before pouring it into the prepared baking pan. Prepare the rest of the recipe as above.

Cook's Note: This recipe requires that the already cooked beans be baked for 1 1/2 hours before preparing the soufflé base. This step may be done several days in advance or just before preparing the soufflé.

Tempeh Fajitas

Yield: 4 servings • Prep Time: 10 minutes • Cooking Time: 20 minutes

A light and highly flavorful fajita mix—my family's favorite tempeh marinade. The intensity of flavor requires marinating the tempeh for at least 24 hours before serving.

1 pound tempeh
3/4 cup fresh orange juice
1/4 cup fresh lime juice
1 teaspoon lime zest
3 tablespoons honey (orange blossom, if possible)
1/4 cup red wine vinegar
2 teaspoons minced garlic
2 1/2 teaspoons ground cumin
1/4 teaspoon cinnamon
1 teaspoon salt
1 tablespoon olive oil
1/2 teaspoon dried thyme, crushed
1/2 teaspoon dried oregano, crushed
1 bay leaf
5 black peppercorns, crushed
1/3 cup minced cilantro
1 1/2 cups thinly sliced sweet onion (Vidalia, if possible)
1 red pepper, seeded and sliced thin
1 green pepper, seeded and sliced thin
1 jalapeño pepper, seeded and minced
1 avocado, sliced
8 whole wheat tortillas

1. Cut the tempeh into thin strips. It may be necessary to first cut the tempeh in half widthwise. To do so, lay the tempeh flat on the cutting surface and place one hand on top, then with a large chef's knife or thin cleaver carefully saw the tempeh in half so that you have two thin slabs. Next, cut these pieces into 3-inch strips. Transfer the strips to a steamer and place over rapidly boiling water. Cover and steam for 10 minutes.

2. Meanwhile, prepare the marinade. In a shallow baking dish, combine the orange and lime juice. Mix in the lime zest, honey, vinegar, garlic, cumin, cinnamon, salt, oil, thyme, oregano, bay leaf, peppercorns, and cilantro. Stir well, then add the onion and red, green, and jalapeño peppers. Mix thoroughly. Place the warm tempeh in the marinade and carefully turn to coat. Cover and refrigerate for 24 to 48 hours, turning several times.

3. Preheat the broiler to high. Transfer the tempeh, onions, and peppers from the marinade to a broiling pan. Baste with the marinade, then place the pan about 8 inches from the heat. Broil, turning and basting twice, until the tempeh is warmed through and has begun to crisp along the edges. Turn the tempeh out onto a serving platter and drizzle some of the remaining marinade over the fajita mixture. Arrange sliced avocado around the edge.

4. As the tempeh cooks, warm the tortillas, covered, in the oven. Serve them warm alongside the tempeh. For best results keep them covered so they remain soft. Allow guests to fill their own tortilla, garnished with the fajita mixture and avocado.

Variation

1. Wrap the fajita mixture in parchment (see Fava Beans in Parchment, page 96) and bake as directed in the fava bean recipe. Serve warmed or toasted tortillas, rice, and sliced avocados alongside.

Curried Pea- and Potato-Stuffed Tofu

Yield: 6 servings • Prep Time 35 minutes • Cooking Time: 40 minutes

2 pounds firm tofu
1 1/2 pounds tomatoes
10 sun-dried tomatoes, softened
    in 1/3 cup hot water
4 cloves garlic
1 pound red potatoes
4 teaspoons minced gingerroot
2 1/2 teaspoons ground coriander
1/2 teaspoon salt
1/4 teaspoon turmeric
1/4 teaspoon cayenne
1/2 cup water
1 tablespoon ghee (page 191) or
    vegetable oil
1 1/2 cups diced white onion
1/4 teaspoon cumin seed
1 serrano pepper, seeded and
    minced
1/2 teaspoon brown mustard
    seeds
2 tablespoons dried coconut
1 teaspoon ground cumin
2 cups fresh or frozen peas
1/4 cup almond butter (page 167)

This modern interpretation of the classic Indian dish of curried peas and potatoes is perfect as a stuffing for tofu.

1. Drain the tofu and cut it into pieces that are the thickness of the blocks (1 1/2 to 2 inches) and measure about 2 x 1 1/2 inches. Place these on a clean kitchen towel with a second towel on top. Weight this down with a cutting board and allow the tofu to drain for 30 minutes. Take each small block of tofu and, with a paring knife and spoon, hollow out a rectangular cavity in the center, leaving a 1/4-inch border around the edges of the top and about 1/3-inch thickness on the bottom of the block. Use the hollowed-out tofu for a scrambled tofu dish.

2. Preheat the broiler to high. Place the tomatoes in a shallow baking pan about 4 inches from the heat and broil, turning several times, until they are charred on all sides. Immediately remove them from the oven. When they are cool enough to handle, peel the skin from the tomatoes, holding them over the pan to catch all juices. Discard the skins and stem ends, then roughly chop the tomato meat and add it to the pan.

3. Place the sun-dried tomatoes and their soaking liquid in a blender or food processor. Add 2 cloves garlic and purée until smooth. Add the broiled tomatoes and continue to process until evenly ground. Transfer this sauce to a small bowl.

4. Peel the potatoes and cut them into small, bite-sized pieces. Place these in the top rack of a steamer over rapidly boiling water. Cover and steam until tender, about 8 minutes. Immediately transfer the potatoes to a strainer and place them under cold running water to stop their cooking. Once cooled, turn the potatoes out onto a clean kitchen towel to drain.

5. Combine the ginger, remaining 2 cloves garlic, coriander, salt, turmeric, and cayenne in the blender. Purée for about 30 seconds, then drizzle in the 1/2 cup of water and continue to blend until the mixture forms a paste. Transfer this to a measuring cup.

6. In a small skillet, heat the ghee over medium high heat until hot, but not smoking. Add the onion and cook, stirring constantly, until it glistens, about 1 minute. Reduce the heat slightly and continue to cook, stirring often, until the onion begins to brown, about 12 minutes. Stir half of the ginger-spice paste into the onions and cook, stirring occasionally, until most of the liquid has evaporated, about 8 minutes. Add the cumin seed, serrano pepper, mustard seeds, coconut, cumin, potatoes, and peas. Stir well, then cook just until the peas are tender, about 4 minutes for fresh peas, 2 minutes for frozen. This filling can be prepared up to 2 days in advance if refrigerated in an airtight container.

7. Preheat the oven to 350°F. Stir the remaining ginger-spice paste into the puréed tomatoes, then slowly whisk the tomato sauce into the almond butter. Place this sauce in a shallow 8-cup baking dish. Divide the pea filling evenly among the blocks of tofu, pressing it firmly in place. Arrange the tofu in one layer on top of the tomato sauce. Cover the dish and bake for 20 minutes.

Variation

1. Prepare the dish through step 6 as described above. Stir 1/2 pound panir (page 174) or tofu, cut into tiny dice, then broiled, into the pea mixture. Warm briefly on top of the stove. Serve with chapatis or rice.

Vegetable Chole

Yield: 6 servings • Prep Time: 20 minutes • Cooking Time: 3 1/2 hours

If you have access to an Indian market, you will be able to find "channa dal" which is a small, slightly darker version of the familiar garbanzo bean. If you are unable to find channa dal, you may substitute garbanzos. In this recipe, I have added carrots for sweetness and cabbage for texture. Serve Chole over sweet brown rice or Masala Rice (page 159). Aromatic Spinach (page 102), without the panir, makes a great vegetable side dish.

1 1/2 cups dried channa dal or garbanzos
10 to 12 cups water
3 tablespoons peanut oil
2 bay leaves
2 dried red chilies
1 walnut-sized ball tamarind (page 195), softened in boiling water
1 cup diced red onion
3 cloves garlic, halved
1 tablespoon minced gingerroot
1 tablespoon molasses
2 1/4 teaspoons cinnamon
1 3/4 teaspoons salt
1 1/2 teaspoons ground coriander
1 1/4 teaspoons ground cumin
1 teaspoon paprika
8 black peppercorns
1/2 teaspoon turmeric
1/2 teaspoon ground cardamom
1 1/2 cups chopped tomatoes
1 cup diced boiling potatoes
1 cup chopped cabbage
1 cup carrots, cut in very small dice
2 to 3 serrano peppers, seeded and chopped
2 tablespoons chopped fresh mint or cilantro
2 teaspoons cumin seeds

1. Pick over the channa dal to remove all stones and debris. Rinse the dal well, then place it in in a large bowl and cover with cold water. Soak for 8 to 10 hours. Drain the beans, then place them in a 2-quart saucepan with 6 cups of water, 1 tablespoon oil, the bay leaves, and dried chilies. Bring this to a boil, then skim and discard any foam that rises to the surface. Cover and simmer, adding water and stirring as necessary to keep the beans from burning, until the dal is tender, about 3 hours.

2. Meanwhile, rub the tamarind between your fingers in its soaking water, until all seeds and stringy bits have separated from the pulp. Strain the liquid through a tea strainer into a blender. Add the onion, garlic, and ginger. Purée the mixture until the onions are finely ground. Add the molasses, cinnamon, salt, coriander, ground cumin, paprika, peppercorns, turmeric, and cardamom. Continue to purée until evenly blended.

3. When the channa dal is cooked, drain it, reserving the liquid. Add about 1/4 of the dal to the blender and purée again until smooth. Set the remaining dal and onion-dal purée aside.

4. In the 2-quart saucepan, heat 1 tablespoon oil over medium high heat until hot, but not smoking. Add the onion mixture and continue to cook, stirring constantly, for 3 minutes. Reduce the heat to medium and add the cooked dal and 3 cups bean cooking liquid (or additional water to equal 3 cups). Stir in the tomatoes, potatoes, and cabbage. Bring the mixture to a boil, then reduce to a simmer and cook, stirring occasionally, until the potatoes are almost tender, about 20 minutes. Stir in the carrots and continue to cook until the potatoes are very tender, about 6 more minutes. Remove from the heat and stir in the cilantro and serrano peppers.

5. In a small skillet, heat the remaining 1/2 tablespoon oil over high heat until hot, but not smoking. Add the cumin seeds and cook, stirring constantly, until they brown slightly, about 1 minute. Turn them out onto a paper towel to drain, then stir them into the finished chole. Serve at once. The chole can be prepared up to 4 days in advance if refrigerated in an airtight container. It can be frozen for up to 3 months. In either case, if you intend to prepare it ahead for later use, stop the preparation of the recipe part way through step 4, just before adding the potatoes, cabbage, carrots, and cilantro. When you are ready to serve the chole, add the vegetables in the order listed above and allow them to cook thoroughly. Again, add the cumin seeds at the last minute.

Aromatic Spinach Purée with Panir

Yield: 4 servings • Prep Time: 30 minutes • Cooking Time: 25 minutes

8 ounces panir cheese (page 174)
   or 8 ounces firm tofu
4 teaspoons minced gingerroot
1 teaspoon salt
1 walnut-sized ball tamarind
   pulp (page 195), softened in
   1/3 cup hot water
2 teaspoons oil
3 pounds fresh spinach
   or 2 10-ounce packages
   chopped frozen spinach
1 cup light vegetable stock
   (page 162)
1 tablespoon mirin (page 193)
2 teaspoon cumin seeds
1 teaspoons fennel seeds
4 teaspoons dried fenugreek
   leaves (page 191)
2 tablespoons ghee (page 191) or
   vegetable oil
1 cup diced onion
2 to 4 serrano or Thai chili peppers, seeded and minced
2 large tomatoes, peeled and
   chopped
2 teaspoons shredded gingerroot
Pinch of hing (asafoetida)
   (page 192)
2 teaspoons garam masala
   (page 191)
3 tablespoons minced fresh mint
1/2 cup diced red bell pepper
1/4 cup grated daikon (Japanese
   radish)

Saag—an aromatic spinach purée laced with fresh cheese—is a standard on menus at In-dian restaurants throughout the world. The Lalitha Mahal Palace in Mysore, South India, serves a delicate, gingery version from which I took inspiration for this recipe. Sweet red peppers and Japanese radish (daikon) add interesting texture and contrasting taste to the standard Indian fare. Although frozen spinach may be used, the quality derived from using fresh is far superior in this dish, and well worth the extra effort of removing the stems and cleaning the leaves.

1. Drain the block of panir and place it on a clean kitchen towel with a second towel on top. Press it gently with the palm of your hand, then leave it to drain for about 15 minutes. Cut the panir into 1/2-inch cubes. If you are using tofu, slice it into 1/2-inch-thick slabs, then drain them on paper towels for 20 minutes before cutting into cubes.

2. In a shallow dish, combine the minced gingerroot and 1/2 teaspoon salt. Strain the tamarind and its soaking liquid through a tea strainer, squeezing and rubbing the pulp with your fingertips to extract as much flavor as possible. Add this liquid to the ginger and discard the tamarind pulp. Add the panir or tofu to the dish, turn to coat and set aside to marinate for 30 minutes.

3. Preheat the broiler to high. Lightly brush a broiling pan with oil, then place the cubes of panir or tofu on the pan, reserving their marinade. Broil, about 5 to 6 inches from the heat, turning once, until they are lightly browned on 2 oppo-site sides. Remove them from the oven and set aside.

4. Remove the stems from the spinach (page 34) and clean the leaves in sev-eral changes of cold water. Place the leaves in the top rack of a steamer over rapidly boiling water. Cover and steam, stirring once, until the leaves are tender, but still a vibrant green color, about 10 minutes. Immediately transfer the spin-ach to a strainer and place it in the sink under cold running water to stop its cooking. Squeeze as much liquid from the spinach as possible by wrapping it in a clean kitchen towel, twisting the towel around the spinach to form a ball, and squeezing the ball. Place the spinach in a blender or food processor fitted with the metal chopping blade and purée until very smooth with 1/2 cup stock and the mirin.

5. Place the cumin and fennel seeds in a small dry skillet. Cook over medium high heat, stirring constantly, until the seeds have begun to release their aroma and appear slightly toasted. Transfer them immediately to a coffee grinder or mortar. Add the fenugreek and grind to a powder.

6. In a 10-inch skillet, heat the ghee over medium high heat until hot, but not smoking. Add the onion and cook, stirring constantly, until it just begins to soften, about 1 minute. Reduce the heat to low and continue to cook, stirring occasion-ally, until the onion is wilted, about 10 minutes. Increase the heat to medium and add the cumin seed mixture. Cook briefly so that they may release their flavors into the oil. Add the serrano peppers and ginger, then stir in the spinach mixture and the tomato. Stir to combine, then add the shredded ginger, hing, and garam masala. Gently add the remaining 1/2 cup stock and reserved marinade. Cover and simmer, stirring occasionally, for 5 minutes. Add the panir or tofu and cook, uncovered, until most of the liquid has evaporated and the panir is heated through. Be careful not to break the panir apart during this final step of cooking.

7. Stir the mint and bell pepper into the spinach purée. Taste and adjust the seasonings, then turn the spinach out onto a serving platter and sprinkle daikon in the center.

Cook's Note: If fenugreek leaves are unavailable, substitute 1/2 teaspoon crushed fenugreek seeds.

Idlis

Yield: 6 servings • Prep Time: 20 minutes • Cooking Time: 20 minutes

After months in India of palate-challenging meals—in which heat sometimes seems like the only recognizable taste—idlis (pronounced id-lees) are a haven for the taste buds. The mild-tasting, flying-saucer-shaped steamed cakes, made from rice and dal, are served at brunch time or for a late afternoon snack with chutney. Given that they are a complete protein source and are actually quite filling on their own, I include them as an entrée.

2 cups uncooked basmati rice
2/3 cup moong dal (skinned and split mung beans)
1/4 teaspoon non-aluminum baking powder
3 tablespoons ghee (page 191) or peanut oil

1. Pick over the rice and dal to remove all foreign matter, then rinse each separately and place each in separate bowls with enough cold water to cover. Allow them to soak for at least 8 hours.

2. Drain the rice, saving its liquid, and place the rice in a food processor fitted with the metal chopping blade. Begin to process, then gradually add 1/2 cup of the reserved water and continue to purée until very smooth. Transfer this to a large mixing bowl. Drain the dal and place it in the processor or blender. Again purée until very smooth, adding up to 1/4 cup of the reserved rice water, so that you obtain a very smooth consistency. Mix this into the puréed rice with the salt and stir well. Cover with plastic wrap and set aside in a warm place until the mixture has fermented, 24 to 36 hours. (Time will vary depending on heat and humidity.) Once fermented, the idli mixture will have doubled in volume and it will appear light and bubbly. At this point the batter is ready to use, but it can be refrigerated, tightly covered, for up to 8 hours.

3. Once the idli mixture has fermented, it is ready to steam. Brush the idli molds or 4-inch tart pans with melted ghee or oil. Stir the baking powder into the idli batter, then ladle it into the molds, filling them to about 1/4 inch of their top rim. Place the molds over, not touching, rapidly boiling water. Cover tightly and steam for 20 minutes. When cooked the idlis should be light and fluffy, firm and not sticky to the touch. Molds of different sizes will require slightly different cooking times. Once cooked, turn the idlis out onto one large platter or 8 individual serving plates. Serve chutney alongside for dipping.

Variations

1. Add minced scallions or chopped cashews to the batter just before ladling into the molds.

2. Steam the batter in bite-sized smooth-edged tart shells for an hors d'oeuvre.

3. Add 2 tablespoons brown mustard seeds and 1 tablespoon minced serrano pepper to the batter before filling the molds.

Cook's Note: The idli batter must ferment for 24 to 36 hours—the warmer and more humid the day, the faster the fermentation.

Couscous and Garbanzo Idlis

Yield: 6 servings • Prep Time: 10 minutes • Cooking Time: 20 minutes

2 cups uncooked whole wheat
  couscous
1/2 cup cooked garbanzo beans
1/2 teaspoon salt
2 tablespoons ghee (page 191)
  or peanut oil

This variation on the classic Indian idli (steamed cake) is delightfully simple. Unlike the classic version which is made with raw rice and dal and must ferment overnight, these tasty cakes can be whipped up in less than 30 minutes from start to finish if you use canned or your own stock of precooked garbanzos. As with traditional idlis, serve these with chutney , or dip them in a quick curry-flavored yogurt sauce (page 184). I often serve them with at least two dipping sauces.

1. Place the raw couscous in a food processor fitted with the metal chopping blade, or in a blender. Process until very fine. Transfer the couscous to a mixing bowl, then place the garbanzos in the processor and purée until they are as finely ground as possible. Add them to the couscous, then stir in the salt.

2. Brush 24 idli molds or 6 pot-pie pans with ghee. Divide the couscous mixture evenly among the molds. Place the idli maker in a large pot with just enough water so that it comes to about 1/4 inch of the bottom of the mold. Bring the water to a boil, then insert the idli maker. Cover the pan tightly and steam for 20 minutes. If you are using pot-pie molds, arrange them in a Chinese bamboo steamer or a makeshift steamer (page 6) and place them over rapidly boiling water. Cook these larger pot-pie molds for 30 minutes. In either case, check the level of the water in the bottom of the steamer to be certain that it does not boil away before the idlis are cooked.

3. Once cooked, the idlis will have puffed slightly and will be firm and not at all sticky to the touch. Loosen the idlis from their mold by running the tip of a paring knife around the edge, then turn the idlis out, upside down onto a serving platter. Serve with the yogurt curry sauce alongside for dipping. These idlis also go very nicely with any of the chutney recipes found in Chapter 7.

Moussaka

Yield: 8 servings • Prep Time: 45 minutes • Cooking Time: 1 1/2 hours

1 cup dried lentils
4 cups water
1 1/2 cups chopped red onion
1 bay leaf
4 cloves garlic, sliced thin
4 Japanese eggplants
  or 1 small standard eggplant
2 small zucchini
1 1/2 teaspoons salt
3 tablespoons olive oil
1/2 pound button mushrooms,
  minced
1 ounce porcini mushrooms,
  softened in hot water

Classic Greek moussaka is rich and robust, often containing both white and tomato sauces and several kinds of meat. This vegetarian version is lighter than the traditional with lentils serving as the protein source. It is formed in a ring mold, then served with a light tomato sauce and crostini in the center. You will need parchment or waxed paper for lining the mold.

1. Pick over the lentils to remove all stones and debris. Rinse the beans in several changes of clean water until the water runs clear. Bring the 4 cups of water to a boil in a 2-quart saucepan. Add the lentils, 1/2 cup of the onion, the bay leaf, and 1 clove of garlic. Bring the lentils to a boil, stirring occasionally, then reduce to a simmer. Cover and cook, stirring from time to time, until they are just tender, about 45 minutes. As the lentils cook, add additional water if necessary to prevent burning. Immediately drain the lentils to stop their cooking. Remove and discard the bay leaf. The lentils can be cooked up to 3 days in advance, if refrigerated in an airtight container.

2. Trim and discard the stem and blossom ends from the eggplants and zucchini. Slice each lengthwise into 1/4-inch-wide strips. (If you are using standard eggplants, cut them into 1/4-inch rounds.) Lay them out in a single layer on clean kitchen towels. Sprinkle with about 3/4 teaspoon of salt, turning the slices to salt both sides. Allow the sliced vegetables to "sweat" for 20 minutes.

3. Preheat the broiler to high. Pat the slices of vegetable dry, then brush them lightly on one side with olive oil. Lightly oil a baking sheet and place as many of the sliced eggplant and zucchini on the sheet as you can fit in one layer. Place the baking sheet 6 inches from the heat and broil the vegetables until they are lightly browned, about 5 minutes. Return the broiled slices to the kitchen towel and repeat the process until all slices are broiled.

4. In a skillet, heat the remaining 1 1/2 tablespoons oil over a high flame until hot, but not smoking. Add the remaining cup of onions and cook briefly, stirring constantly so that all pieces of onion are coated with oil. Reduce the heat to medium and cook, stirring often, until the onions are translucent, about 10 minutes. Add the remaining 3 cloves of garlic and the button mushrooms. Continue to cook, stirring frequently, until the mushrooms have given off all of their juices and the juices have then evaporated. Drain the porcini mushrooms, chop them finely, and add them to the skillet. Stir in the cooked and drained lentils, the remaining teaspoon of salt, parsley, black pepper, and cayenne. Cook for 5 minutes to marry the flavors, then stir in the bread crumbs, pistachios, and 1/4 cup of the tomato sauce. Taste and adjust the seasonings. Remove this filling from the heat and stir in the puréed tofu or egg. The filling can be prepared up to 24 hours in advance if refrigerated in an airtight container.

5. Line an 8-cup ring mold, or eight 1-cup ramekins with parchment or waxed paper (page 6). Drape one slice of cooked eggplant into the mold so that it is at a slight angle to the center hole, and lines the bottom and sides of the mold. Its ends should hang out about an inch on either side of the top lip of the mold. Arrange overlapping strips of eggplant and zucchini over the entire surface of the mold. Pour the filling into the mold and smooth it into place. Fold the overhanging ends of eggplant and zucchini over the filling, and press them down firmly. The moussaka can be assembled up to 24 hours in advance if refrigerated, tightly covered.

6. Preheat the oven to 375°F. Cover the moussaka with a piece of parchment or waxed paper and place the mold in a shallow baking dish. Pour boiling water into the baking dish, around the mold, so that it comes about 1/4 of the way up the side of the mold. Bake the moussaka in this "bain marie" for 45 minutes. Remove it from the oven and allow it to cool out of the bain marie for 5 minutes before unmolding.

7. Warm the sauce until piping hot. Preheat the broiler to high. Remove the top piece of parchment from the moussaka mold and place a heatproof serving platter over the moussaka. Invert the plate, holding the mold in place, and give both the plate and mold a firm shake to dislodge the ring. It should drop down easily onto the plate. Carefully peel off any parchment that sticks. Sprinkle Parmesan over the moussaka and place it under the broiler briefly to melt the cheese. Pour half of the sauce over the ring, arrange the crostini in the center of the ring, and serve the remaining sauce alongside. Serve the moussaka in slices, cut with a wavy-edged knife.

3 tablespoons minced fresh
  parsley
1/8 teaspoon black pepper
1/8 teaspoon cayenne pepper
3/4 cup soft bread crumbs
1/4 cup pistachio nuts, chopped
2 1/2 to 3 cups light tomato sauce
  (page 175)
3 ounces soft tofu, puréed,
  or 1 egg, lightly beaten
1/4 cup freshly grated Parmesan
16 cinnamon crostini (page 167)

Panir Kabobs

Yield: 4 servings • Prep Time: 35 minutes • Cooking Time: 25 minutes

1 recipe panir (page 174)
2 medium yellow onions
1 small green bell pepper
1 small red bell pepper
1 small ripe pineapple
1 1/2 cups buttermilk
3 tablespoons lime juice
2 tablespoons honey
1 serrano pepper, seeded
   and minced
1 teaspoon salt
1 teaspoon ground cumin
1/4 teaspoon paprika
1/2 cup minced cilantro
Cilantro sprigs for garnish

While living in Mysore, South India, I became particularly fond of a tandoori oven kabob called a sashlik which was made with panir (homemade cheese). It was served at a restaurant named The Sarate, and it is after that dish that I modeled this recipe. For a dairy-free version of this recipe, you may substitute tofu for panir.

1. Cut the panir into 1 1/2-inch cubes. Cut the onions in half, leaving the root ends intact. Cut each half into 3 pieces with a bit of the root end holding each piece together. Quarter the peppers and remove and discard the seeds and white membrane. Cut each quarter into 2-inch pieces. Break off the top from the pineapple and trim about 1/2 inch from the bottom. Using a large kitchen knife, quarter the base. Remove the hard central core from each quarter, then, using a paring knife, cut the meat away from the skin of the fruit. Cut the meat into 1-inch wedges.

2. In a small bowl, combine the buttermilk, lime juice, honey, serrano pepper, salt, cumin, paprika, and minced cilantro. Skewer the onions through the center of each piece, leaving the root ends intact to keep the layers of the onion from falling apart. Make two skewers with the peppers and pineapple and skewer the panir separately. Brush all of the brochettes generously with the marinade. Begin by cooking the onions. Place them over hot coals or broil under a high setting, turning and brushing frequently with the marinade, until they are tender and beginning to brown, about 10 minutes. Start to cook the mixed vegetable/fruit skewers, again turning and brushing with marinade, and after about 7 minutes, add the panir brochettes. Cook until all of the ingredients are slightly browned.

3. Remove all of the skewers from the heat and arrange the cooked ingredients on one large plate or 6 individual serving plates. Drizzle remaining marinade over the brochettes and garnish with a few sprigs of cilantro.

Variation

1. For a nondairy version of the recipe, substitute 1 pound firm tofu, pressed and cut into large cubes, for the panir and replace the buttermilk with 1 1/2 cups plain soy milk mixed with 1 tablespoon tahini, 2 tablespoons lemon juice, and 2 teaspoons mirin.

Cook's Note: If you are using bamboo skewers, soak them in water for 30 minutes before threading and broiling.

Tamale Pot Pie

Yield: 6 servings • Prep Time: 45 minutes • Cooking Time: 20 minutes

This is a classic American pot pie with a Southwestern twist. A layer of cornmeal tops a spicy bean and ancho pepper filling. These pies may be prepared ahead and frozen, then baked just as you need them.

1 recipe all-purpose pie dough (page 168)
1 red bell pepper
1 green bell pepper
2 large tomatoes
1 ancho pepper, softened in hot water
1 cup diced white onion
2 cloves garlic, halved
1/2 teaspoon dried oregano
2 tablespoons dry sherry
2 teaspoons honey
1 1/2 teaspoons salt
1 teaspoon ground cumin
1/2 teaspoon black pepper
1 1/2 cups water
1/2 cup yellow cornmeal
2 cups cooked pinto beans
1 cup fresh corn kernels
2 tablespoons canned green chilies (optional)
6 black olives (optional)

1. On a lightly floured work surface, roll the pastry dough to 1/8-inch thickness. Line 6 pot-pie molds with the pastry (page 168), and chill for 20 minutes. Press the pastry up from the side of each mold, over the rim. Return to the refrigerator.

2. Preheat the broiler to high. Place the washed peppers and tomatoes on a baking sheet as close to the broiler as possible. Cook them, turning several times, until they are blistered on all sides. (The tomatoes will cook in about 6 minutes, the peppers in 8 to 10 minutes.) When the tomatoes are cooked, put them in a bowl to cool. Transfer the cooked peppers to a paper bag and fold the bag shut to catch the steam. When the tomatoes are cool enough to handle, hold them over the bowl, and scrape off most of their peel, then transfer them, and all juice that remains in the bowl, to a blender or food processor fitted with the metal chopping blade. Do the same to the peppers, discarding their stems, ribs, and seeds, but adding the peeled meat and juice to the blender.

3. Drain the ancho pepper. Pull off the stem and scrape out the seeds. Add the pepper to the blender along with the onion, garlic, oregano, sherry, honey, 1 teaspoon salt, cumin, and pepper. Purée until very smooth, scraping down the beaker as necessary. Transfer this mixture to a saucepan and simmer for 10 minutes. Remove the sauce from the heat, stir in the beans and corn, then cool. This filling can be prepared up to 3 days in advance if refrigerated in an airtight container.

4. Bring the water with 1/2 teaspoon of salt to a boil in a 2-quart saucepan. Pour the cornmeal into the water in a thin stream, stirring constantly as you pour. Once all cornmeal is in, reduce the heat to a simmer and cook, stirring frequently, until the mixture is thick, about 20 minutes.

5. Divide the bean filling evenly among the pie plates, then cover each with a layer of warm cornmeal. Preheat the oven to 350°F. Bake the pies for 45 minutes. After 20 minutes of baking, garnish the pies with sliced olives, if desired. Serve hot.

Cook's Note: The components of this pie (pastry dough, cornmeal topping, and filling) may be prepared over the course of 3 days, if desired.

Vegetable Pot Pie

Yield: 4 servings • Prep Time: 45 minutes • Cooking Time: 1 hour

1 recipe all-purpose pastry dough
   (page 168)
1 cup diced yellow onion
2 teaspoons olive oil
2 cloves garlic
1 cup diced leeks
3 tablespoons flour
2 cups hearty vegetable stock
   (page 162)
1/2 cup sliced celery
   (about 1 stalk)
1 cup diced carrot (about 2)
1 cup diced red or yellow potato
1/2 teaspoon dried thyme, crushed
1/2 teaspoon salt
1 1/4 teaspoons dried sage
2/3 cup fresh or frozen peas
8 ounces firm tofu
1 tablespoon minced fresh
   parsley

Tofu replaces chicken in this new twist on an old favorite.

1. Cut the pastry dough into 2 pieces, one that is about 1/3, the other that is about 2/3 of the dough. On a lightly floured work surface, roll the larger piece of dough out to about 1/4-inch thickness. Line 4 small (4-inch) pie pans with the dough (page 168), then place the pans on a cookie sheet and refrigerate. Again on a lightly floured surface, roll the remaining dough out to about 1/4-inch thickness and cut four 6-inch rounds from the dough (to use as tops). Transfer these to a cookie sheet and refrigerate them while preparing the filling. The pie pans can be lined up to a day before baking if wrapped in waxed paper and refrigerated.

2. In a 10-inch skillet, sauté the onion in the olive oil over medium low heat, until translucent, about 10 minutes. Press the garlic through a garlic press into the pan, then add the leeks and cook, stirring often, until the leek softens, about 10 minutes. Sprinkle the flour over the pan, increase the heat to medium and cook, stirring constantly, for 2 minutes. Gradually add the stock, stirring constantly to prevent lumps from forming. Add the celery, carrot, potato, thyme, salt, and sage. Cook, stirring often, until the potatoes are just beginning to soften, about 8 minutes. The potatoes should still be raw as they will continue to cook as the pies bake. Remove the skillet from the heat and stir in the peas. Drain the tofu and cut it into small cubes, then stir it along with the parsley into the pan. The filling can be prepared up to 3 days in advance if refrigerated in an airtight container.

3. Preheat the oven to 400°F. Remove the pot pies from the refrigerator and, in each, press the top edge of the pastry over the upper lip of the pan. Divide the filling evenly among the pies. Top each pie with one of the rounds of dough, and crimp the tops in place (page 168). Cut 4 slashes through the top crust of each pie to allow the steam to escape. (The pies can be wrapped tightly and frozen for up to 2 months. Thaw at room temperature for 30 minutes before baking according to the directions that follow.) Place the pot pies, on the baking sheet, in the center of the oven. After 10 minutes, reduce the heat to 350°F and continue to cook for 50 minutes, or until the top crust is lightly browned and the pies are bubbling hot. Cool briefly before serving.

Variation

1. For a chewier, more "meat-like" filling, use frozen tofu.

Cook's Note: Allow time for the pastry dough to chill and the filling to cool as you prepare this.

Farmer's Mushroom Pie

Yield: 6 servings • Prep Time: 30 minutes • Cooking Time: 20 minutes

Having English parents, and a mother who was a notoriously good cook, I was raised on the best of English cuisine. Delicacies such as standing rib roast, Yorkshire pudding, kippered herring, and shepherd's pie were family standbys. As luck would have it, I never liked meat. So, much to the dismay of my poor mother, I often found myself at mealtime rooting around in the kitchen for the freshest box of breakfast cereal as a substitute. Those anguished meals served the purpose, if nothing more, of inspiring me now to develop recipes, such as this, that are vegetarian versions of some of the world's classic meat dishes. This shepherd's pie variation and the one that follows use the classic idea of a tasty goulash baked under a crust of potatoes.

1 orange
1/2 cup bulgur wheat (fine-grain, if possible)
1/3 cup boiling water
1 1/2 cups cooked pinto beans or kidney beans
1/2 cup minced scallions
4 teaspoons minced garlic
1 1/2 teaspoons salt
1 1/2 teaspoons dried thyme
1 teaspoon dried sage
1/2 teaspoon crushed dried rosemary
1/4 teaspoon black pepper
1/8 teaspoon nutmeg
3 ounces firm silken tofu
1 tablespoon olive oil
1 pound mushrooms, sliced
2 tablespoons whole wheat flour
1 cup mushroom stock (page 163)
2 cups chopped tomatoes
1 cup cubed carrot
3/4 cup fresh or frozen peas
1 1/2 tablespoons balsamic vinegar
1 1/2 pounds russet potatoes
1 tablespoon butter
1/4 cup plain soy milk or milk
3 tablespoons snipped chives

1. Grate the zest from the orange and set it aside, covered. Squeeze the juice from the orange, then set it aside as well.

2. In a mixing bowl, combine the bulgur and water. Stir to mix, then cover and set aside for 30 minutes. Drain the beans and place them in a separate bowl. With the tines of a fork, mash about 1/3 of the beans into a paste, leaving the rest intact. Stir in the scallions, garlic, 1 teaspoon of salt, the thyme, sage, rosemary, pepper, and nutmeg.

3. Drain the tofu, then place it in a blender or food processor and purée until smooth. Stir this into the beans and mix well. Toss the bulgur into a strainer to drain any unabsorbed water, then stir the bulgur into the bean mixture as well. Set this aside.

4. In a 10-inch skillet, heat the oil over medium heat until hot, but not smoking. Add the mushrooms and toss to coat with oil. Strain the orange juice over the mushrooms and continue to cook, stirring often, until they are very soft. Sprinkle the flour over the mushrooms and cook, stirring constantly, for about 1 minute. Gradually add the stock, stirring constantly to avoid having lumps form. Stir in the tomatoes, carrot, peas, and vinegar, then bring the mixture to a boil. Immediately pour this into the bean mixture. The recipe can be prepared up to 2 days in advance to this point, if refrigerated in an airtight container.

5. Peel the potatoes and cut them into large pieces. Place them in a saucepan and cover with water. Bring this to a boil, stirring often. Reduce to a low boil and cook, stirring occasionally, until the potatoes are very tender, about 20 minutes. Immediately drain the potatoes, then return them to the saucepan. Add the butter and milk, then mash with a potato masher until they are smooth. (This step can also be done in a food processor, but be careful not to overprocess or the potatoes will become paste-like.) Stir in the remaining 1/2 teaspoon of salt, the orange zest, and chives.

6. Preheat the oven to 400°F. Turn the bean mixture into a deep 2-quart baking dish. Arrange the mashed potatoes on top, smoothing them out into an even layer. Bake, uncovered, for 5 minutes. Reduce the heat to 350°F. and continue to bake for 20 minutes or until the potatoes are lightly browned. Cool briefly before serving.

Layered Baked Tempeh

Yield: 8 servings • Prep Time: 30 minutes • Cooking Time: 30 minutes

This loaf may be baked in a loaf shape, but it is more elegant baked and served in individual ramekins or in a ring mold.

8 ounces tempeh
2 cups cubed eggplant
2 1/2 cups dried cubed bread
1 3/4 cups mushroom stock (page 163), hot
2 tablespoons olive oil
1/2 cup minced shallots
2 teaspoons minced garlic
1/2 pound sliced fresh shiitake mushrooms or use button mushrooms
2 tablespoons lemon juice
1 teaspoon dried oregano
1/4 teaspoon nutmeg
1/4 teaspoon salt
1/2 cup chopped pecans
2 tablespoons soy sauce
1/4 cup minced fresh parsley
1/2 teaspoon dried thyme
1/2 teaspoon dried marjoram
1/2 teaspoon crushed dried rosemary

1. Break the tempeh into several pieces, then place it in a steamer rack over rapidly boiling water. Cover and steam for 10 minutes. If you have a double-tiered steamer, place the eggplant in the second steaming rack and steam it at the same time, cooking it until it is tender, about 8 minutes. Otherwise, cook the 2 separately.

2. As the tempeh and eggplant steam, place the bread cubes in a mixing bowl. Pour 1 cup of hot stock over them and stir; then set aside while liquid is absorbed. When the tempeh and eggplant are cooked, remove them from the heat. Grate the tempeh over the bread cubes and stir it in. Place the eggplant in a separate mixing bowl.

3. In a 10-inch skillet, heat the oil over medium heat. Add the shallots and cook, stirring often, until they are soft, about 5 minutes. Add the garlic and continue to cook for 1 minute, then transfer half of this mixture to the bowl containing the tempeh. Add the mushrooms to the skillet with the remaining half of the shallots. Continue to cook, stirring often, until the mushrooms begin to soften, about 2 minutes. Stir in the lemon juice, oregano, nutmeg, and salt. Reduce the heat to low and cook, stirring occasionally, until the mushrooms are very soft, about 8 more minutes. Add the mushrooms to the eggplant and toss well.

4. As the mushrooms cook, stir the pecans, soy sauce, parsley, thyme, marjoram, and rosemary into the tempeh mixture. Stir to blend, then taste and adjust the seasonings. Lightly oil six 1-cup timbale molds or one 6-cup ring mold with the remaining oil. Press 3/4 of the tempeh into the molds, shaping it over the bottom and up the sides of the molds, and leaving a hollow space in the center of each mold. Fill the center of each mold with the eggplant mixture, then cover the eggplant with a layer of tempeh. Press this firmly into place. The molds can be prepared up to 24 hours in advance, if covered and refrigerated.

5. Preheat the oven to 375°F. Place the molds in a shallow baking dish and surround them with hot water. Cover each mold, then place this "bain marie" in the center of the oven. Bake until the tempeh has begun to pull away from the edges of the mold, about 30 minutes. Remove from the oven and cool for 5 minutes before unmolding.

6. To unmold, invert a plate over the mold. Holding the plate and mold together, invert the mold and shake it briskly once or twice to dislodge the tempeh. Serve with apple onion sauce (page 181) drizzled over and additional sauce alongside.

Variation

1. Steam 12 large Swiss chard leaves until wilted, about 4 minutes. Drain the leaves on a clean kitchen towel, then line the molds with these leaves before layering in the tempeh.

Eggplant Parmesan

Yield: 4 servings • Prep Time: 20 minutes • Cooking Time: 25 minutes

The harmonious aromas of fresh basil and garlic fill the air as this light version of the classic dish bakes. It is ideal prepared and served in individual baking dishes.

1 large eggplant
1 teaspoon salt
3/4 cup wheat germ or dry bread crumbs
1/2 teaspoon dried oregano, crumbled
1/8 teaspoon red pepper flakes
1/4 cup olive oil
2 pounds tomatoes, peeled, seeded, and chopped (page 35)
2 1/2 teaspoons minced garlic
6 ounces fresh mozzarella cheese
Freshly ground black pepper
1/2 cup chopped fresh basil
1/3 cup freshly grated Parmesan

1. Trim and discard the stem end and peel from the eggplant. Slice it crosswise into 3/4-inch-wide rounds and place these on a baking sheet lined with a clean kitchen towel. Sprinkle the slices with 1/2 teaspoon salt, turning to dust both sides, and set aside at room temperature to "sweat" for 30 minutes.

2. In a small mixing bowl, combine the wheat germ, oregano, pepper flakes and 1/4 teaspoon of salt. After the eggplant has rested, pat the slices dry with a clean kitchen towel. Preheat the broiler to high. Brush one side of each slice of eggplant with a light coating of olive oil, then gently press a thin coating of wheat germ onto the slice. Brush a broiling pan lightly with oil and place the eggplant on the pan. (If all of the slices do not fit, work in several batches.) Broil the slices, placing them about 6 inches from the heat, until they are lightly browned and have begun to soften, about 7 minutes. Transfer the slices to a plate with a pancake turner.

3. Combine the tomatoes and garlic, then slice the mozzarella into 1/4-inch-thick rounds. Have ready four 1-cup ramekins. In each, arrange a layer of tomatoes. Top this with a single layer of cooked eggplant slices, then a layer of mozzarella. Sprinkle with salt and pepper and top with basil. Repeat the layers in the same order, using all of the ingredients and ending with mozzarella, salt, pepper, and basil. Sprinkle about 2 tablespoons of Parmesan on top and, if desired, drizzle any remaining oil over this. (For one large serving dish, you may use a shallow 5-cup baking dish instead of the ramekins.) The dish can be prepared up to 24 hours in advance to this point, covered tightly and refrigerated. It does not freeze well.

4. Preheat the oven to 375°F. Place the ramekins in the center of the oven and bake until lightly browned and bubbly, about 25 minutes.

Variation

1. Replace 1/4 cup of the wheat germ with 1/4 cup finely ground almonds. This breading enhances the subtle nutty taste of eggplant.

Eggplant Roulades with Light Tomato Sauce

Yield: 4 servings • Prep Time: 30 minutes • Cooking Time: 25 minutes

1 large eggplant, about 1 1/4
    pounds
1 1/2 teaspoons salt
10 ounces tofu "cottage cheese"
    (page 172) or true ricotta
1/2 cup minced scallions
1 tablespoon minced garlic
1 teaspoon crushed dried oregano
1/8 teaspoon black pepper
1/8 teaspoon nutmeg
1 tablespoon olive oil
2 egg whites
    or 1/4 cup plain soy milk
1 cup toasted wheat germ
3 3/4 cups light tomato sauce
    (page 175)
1 1/2 teaspoons toasted fennel
    seeds, crushed
1/4 cup, each, grated provolone
    and mozzarella or 1/2 cup
    grated soy mozzarella

These eggplant roulades are broiled rather than fried to produce a light and delicate entrée. This dish may be made nondairy by using all soy alternatives listed below.

1. Wash the eggplant well, then dry it and trim off and discard the stem end. Slice the eggplant crosswise on the diagonal into 1/4-inch-thick ovals. Place the slices on a clean kitchen towel and sprinkle on both sides with 1 teaspoon of salt. Allow the eggplant to "sweat" for 30 minutes at room temperature.

2. In a small mixing bowl, combine the "cottage cheese," remaining 1/2 teaspoon salt, scallions, garlic, oregano, pepper, and nutmeg. Mix well and set aside.

3. Preheat the broiler to high. Lightly brush a baking sheet with oil. Beat the egg whites until frothy. Dip the eggplant slices in the egg whites, then in the wheat germ to coat. Pat the eggplant slices dry. Place on the baking sheet and broil, turning once, until the slices are soft and have begun to brown, about 8 minutes. (You may need to cook the eggplant in more than one batch, depending on the size of your pan and broiler.)

4. Cover the bottom of a 9- by 13-inch baking pan with a thin layer of tomato sauce. Sprinkle the fennel seeds on top of this. Place the eggplant slices on a work surface and fill each with a strip of the "cheese" filling. Roll the eggplant around the filling so that its edges overlap. Place each roulade in the casserole, seam side down, lining the roulades up so their edges touch. Pour the remaining sauce over the roulades and sprinkle the grated cheese on top. The dish may be prepared up to 24 hours in advance if refrigerated, tightly covered. It may be frozen, airtight, for up to a month.

5. Preheat the oven to 375ºF. Bake the roulades, covered, in the center of the oven until they are piping hot and the cheese has completely melted, about 25 minutes.

Eggplant Steaks with Madeira Sauce

Yield: 4 servings • Prep Time: 25 minutes • Cooking Time: 20 minutes

1 large eggplant (about 1 1/2
    pounds)
2 teaspoons salt
12 ounces mushrooms
3 tablespoons olive oil
3/4 cup minced shallots
2 teaspoons minced garlic
1 tablespoon lemon juice
8 ounces tempeh, finely chopped
3 tablespoons minced fresh
    tarragon or parsley
3 tablespoons cognac (optional)
1 1/4 cups mushroom stock
    (page 163)
1 teaspoon Dijon-style mustard

Thick slices of eggplant are stuffed, then "oven braised" and served with a full-bodied Madeira sauce. Select a firm, tight-skinned eggplant that tapers as little as possible at each end so that the slices can be equal in size.

1. Slice off and discard both ends of the eggplant, about 3/4 inch from each tip. Leaving the skin on the eggplant, quarter it widthwise so that you have four rounds. (This is most easily accomplished by piercing the eggplant with the tip of a sharp knife, then slicing the rounds using a sawing motion.) Slice a pocket-like opening in each round. The opening of the pocket should reach about half the circumference of the round, but the pocket itself should be deep, to 1/4 inch of the edge all round. Sprinkle the slices inside and out with 1 teaspoon of the salt. Set them aside on a clean kitchen towel to "sweat" for 20 minutes.

2. Slice half of the mushrooms into about 1/4-inch-thick slices. Set them aside. Mince the remaining mushrooms. To do this, trim stems from caps, even with the cap, and set them aside. Mince each cap by making thin, horizontal slices through it without allowing the slices to separate. Place the sliced cap, stem side down, on the cutting board and, again holding it so that its shape remains, slice it into thin matchstick shapes. Rotate the cap 180 degrees and slice again. This will produce tiny dice. This process may also be approximated very quickly (with a more rustic look) by processing quartered mushroom caps in the food processor fitted with the steel chopping blade and using an on-off pulse action until the mushrooms are finely chopped. Once all of the caps are minced, mince the stems in a similar manner and combine the two. Set aside.

1/4 cup Madeira
3 tablespoons minced fresh parsley
3 tablespoons butter or soy margarine (optional)
Salt and pepper to taste

3. Heat 1 tablespoon of olive oil in a medium-size skillet over high heat. Add half of the shallots and toss quickly for about 30 seconds. Reduce the heat to medium and continue to cook, stirring often, until the shallots are soft and translucent, but not brown, about 8 minutes. Increase the heat slightly. Add the garlic and mushrooms. Cook, stirring constantly, until the mushrooms are just beginning to cook, about 1 minute. Add the lemon juice. Reduce the heat to medium and continue to cook, stirring often, until the mushrooms are soft, about 8 minutes. Add the tempeh, tarragon, cognac, and remaining salt. Continue to cook, stirring often, for 5 minutes. This filling can be prepared up to 3 days in advance, if refrigerated in an airtight container.

4. Pat the eggplant dry, inside and out. Divide the mushroom and tempeh mixture into 4 equal portions and stuff each eggplant with this filling. The eggplant steaks can be prepared to this point up to 8 hours in advance if stored on a plate and refrigerated, loosely covered.

5. Preheat the oven to broil. Lightly coat a 9-inch square baking pan with about 2 teaspoons of the remaining olive oil. Place the stuffed eggplant in the pan, allowing at least 1 inch of space between them, then brush the steaks with the remaining oil. Broil them about 4 inches from the heat for 5 minutes, until the top of each eggplant is lightly browned. Remove from the oven and immediately add the cognac and 1/4 cup of the stock to the pan. Place this over a burner that is turned on high. Shake vigorously until the sizzling subsides. Remove the pan from the heat. Reduce the oven temperature to 375°F. and return the eggplant to the oven. Cook until the steaks are soft through, but still hold their shape, about 10 minutes. If the sauce is not completed when the steaks are cooked, remove them from the oven and cover to keep warm.

6. As the eggplant cooks, combine the reserved sliced mushrooms, shallots, remaining stock, mustard, and Madeira in a small saucepan. Cook over high until the liquid is reduced to about 1/4 cup, about 10 minutes. Set aside.

7. Using a pancake turner, place the cooked eggplant on a warm serving platter or individual plates. Drain the remaining cooking liquid from the eggplant and add it to the reduced sauce. Cook briskly for 1 minute. Remove from the heat and whisk in the parsley and, for a slightly thicker sauce, the butter or margarine. Taste and adjust the seasonings with salt and pepper. Pour a small amount of sauce on each eggplant and serve the remaining sauce at the table.

Variations

1. Prepare the eggplant in the same manner as described above, but fill it with the spinach filling for Spinach-Stuffed Polenta (page 45) and serve it with hearty tomato sauce (page 174).

2. Add 1/2 cup chopped pecans to the recipe above and replace the tarragon with mint. Serve with Orange "Hollandaise" (page 130).

Steamed Stuffed Eggplant with Tahini Lemon Sauce

Yield: 4 servings • Prep Time: 25 minutes • Cooking Time: 35 minutes

1 large eggplant (about 1 1/2
    pounds)
3/4 teaspoon salt
2 lemons
8 ounces mushrooms, finely
    minced (page 34)
1 tablespoon olive oil
1 cup diced red onion
1 teaspoon minced garlic
1 1/2 cups cooked garbanzo beans
1/8 teaspoon black pepper
Pinch of fresh nutmeg
1/2 cup tahini
1/4 cup soy sauce
3 tablespoons chopped fresh mint
2 Italian plum tomatoes, sliced

I once knew someone who described a blind date as having the personality of an eggplant. I don't think the description was actually meant as a compliment; however, eggplant, when steamed, takes on a rather sweet and satisfying character. This dish highlights that sweet quality and complements it with the meaty taste of garbanzo beans and a rich tahini-based sauce.

1. Slice the eggplant in half lengthwise. Using a paring knife, carve a boat shape into each half of the eggplant, leaving a layer of about 1/2 inch of shell around the edges and bottom of each half. Chop the eggplant that you have removed from the center into small pieces and place it on a kitchen towel. Sprinkle about 1/4 teaspoon of salt over this, toss, then allow it to "sweat" for about 20 minutes.

2. Grate the zest from 1 lemon and set it aside in a small covered bowl. Squeeze the juice from both lemons and measure it; you should have about 1/4 cup. Place the minced mushrooms in the center of a clean kitchen towel. Draw the corners of the towel together and twist the towel so that the mushrooms form a ball. Squeeze as much juice as possible from the mushrooms, then set them aside briefly.

3. In a 1-inch skillet, heat the oil over medium heat until hot. Add the onion and cook, stirring constantly, until it begins to soften, about 5 minutes. Add the garlic and continue to cook, stirring for about a minute. Add the mushrooms and cook, stirring constantly, until they just begin to soften, about 2 minutes. Stir in the lemon juice and eggplant. Continue to cook, stirring often, until the eggplant is just beginning to soften, about 4 minutes. Add the garbanzos, the remaining 1/2 teaspoon salt, the pepper, and nutmeg. Stir to combine and remove from the heat.

4. Divide the filling between the two eggplant halves, mounding it high. The eggplant can be prepared to this point up to 8 hours in advance, if covered and refrigerated. Place the eggplant halves on a steamer over rapidly boiling water and cover tightly. (A Chinese bamboo steamer is ideal.) Steam until the eggplant "boats" are just tender, about 25 minutes.

5. Meanwhile, in a small mixing bowl, whisk together the tahini, soy sauce, lemon juice, and mint. Warm gently, but do not allow the sauce to boil. When the eggplants are cooked, arrange the tomato slices on top and transfer the eggplants to a serving plate, then drizzle a small amount of sauce over the filling in each. Serve additional sauce alongside.

Variations

1. Sprinkle freshly grated Parmesan over each half and place under the broiler to brown before serving.

2. For an Oriental flavor, use peanut oil in place of the olive oil and add 2 teaspoons minced gingerroot with the garlic to the filling. Substitute 1 1/4 cups azuki beans for the garbanzos and stir in 1/2 cup minced scallions, 1/4 cup diced water chestnuts, and 1 teaspoon five-spice powder (page 191) at the end of cooking the filling. For the sauce, substitute 1/4 cup chopped pickled ginger and its juice for the lemon juice and add cilantro instead of mint.

Stuffed Cauliflower

Yield: 4 servings • Prep Time: 1 1/2 hours • Cooking Time: 25 minutes

The look of this outstanding entrée is beautiful and the taste is heavenly—the tang of raspberry vinegar balances the strong character of the cauliflower.

1. Rinse the cauliflower, then trim and discard all leaves that hold the head. With a paring knife, core out the center of the cauliflower, leaving the head intact, but removing as much tough stem from the center as possible. Place the cauliflower, stem side down, in a steaming rack over rapidly boiling water. Cover and steam until just tender, about 10 minutes. Immediately remove the cauliflower to a strainer and run cold water over it to stop its cooking. When cool, pull the florets apart, keeping them as even as possible in size. Place them on a clean kitchen towel to dry. The cauliflower can be prepared up to 2 days in advance, if refrigerated in an airtight container.

2. Drain and rinse the split peas, then place them in a 2-quart saucepan and cover with water. Bring to a boil, stirring occasionally to prevent sticking. Reduce to a simmer, cover, and continue to cook, stirring occasionally, until the peas are very tender, about 45 minutes. As the peas cook, add more water if necessary to prevent sticking. When done, they should have absorbed all of the liquid. Turn the heat off and allow the peas to cool to room temperature.

3. Transfer the cooled peas to a food processor fitted with the metal chopping blade or to a blender. Add the garlic, cheese, vinegar, 1/4 teaspoon salt, pepper, oregano, and 2 tablespoons parsley. Purée until very smooth, scraping down the sides of the bowl as necessary. Taste and adjust the seasonings.

4. Preheat the oven to 400°F. Brush the bread on both sides with olive oil, then place it on a baking sheet and bake until crisp and lightly browned, about 15 minutes. Transfer it to a cake rack to cool. This crouton may be prepared up to 5 days in advance if stored at room temperature in an airtight bag.

5. Preheat the oven to 350°F. Line the inside of a 6-cup ovenproof bowl with pieces of cauliflower (a stainless steel bowl with an 8-inch top lip opening is ideal). Arrange the cauliflower so that the florets fit snugly next to each other and the stems are facing in towards the center of the bowl. Pour the split pea mixture into the center of the cauliflower, filling it to just below the top edge. Place the crouton over the filling and press gently to secure in place. The mold may be filled up to 8 hours in advance, if covered and refrigerated. Remove the cover and bring to room temperature before proceeding with the recipe. Place the bowl in the center of the preheated oven and bake until warmed through, about 25 minutes.

6. Allow the mold to cool for 5 minutes, then place a 10-inch plate over the bowl. Invert the bowl and plate, then shake quickly downwards several times to release the cauliflower. Serve immediately, sprinkled with the remaining parsley and leek sauce (page 178).

Variations

1. Serve the same preparation with kale sauce (page 178).

2. Add 1 cup cooked puréed spinach and 4 chopped sun-dried tomatoes to the filling. Serve the cauliflower with roasted pepper sauce (page 84).

1 large head cauliflower
   (about 3 pounds)
3/4 cup split peas, soaked for
   3 hours in cold water
1 1/2 cups water
2 cloves garlic, minced
1/4 cup farmer's cheese, tofu
   "feta" (page 173) or mild goat
   cheese
3 tablespoons raspberry vinegar
1/4 teaspoon salt
1/8 teaspoon black pepper
2 teaspoons minced fresh oregano
   or 1/2 teaspoon dried
1/3 cup minced fresh parsley
1 7-inch round slice sourdough
   or whole grain bread (or cut
   several slices of bread so that
   they will fit together to form a
   circle)
1 tablespoon olive oil

Savory Jambalaya

Yield: 6 servings • Prep Time: 30 minutes • Cooking Time: 25 minutes

1 pound tofu "sausage" (page 166)
1/3 cup dry bread crumbs
3 tablespoons olive oil
2 cups diced red onion
2 cups basmati rice
3 1/2 cups hearty vegetable stock
   (page 162)
1 tablespoon minced garlic
1 cup green bell pepper
1/3 cup red bell pepper
1/2 cup sliced celery
1 28-ounce can whole tomatoes,
   drained and chopped
1 bay leaf
1 teaspoon salt
1 teaspoon dried thyme
   or 3 sprigs fresh thyme
1/4 teaspoon black pepper
1 chipotle pepper, softened in hot
   water
1 tablespoon butter
3/4 pound tree oyster mushrooms,
   sliced into 1-inch pieces
1/2 cup minced fresh parsley
1/3 cup minced scallions

Some speculate that the name jambalaya is derived from the French word for ham, jambon. A few traditional recipes are vegetarian, most contain at least one type of sausage or meat and many also contain seafood. In this recipe I replace the meat with homemade tofu "sausage" (page 166) and use tree oyster mushrooms to mimic the texture and appearance of oysters. If tree oysters are unavailable, substitute button mushrooms. If you haven't the time to make homemade tofu "sausage," there are several vegetarian "sausages" on the market that could be substituted quite well.

1. Form the sausage into 1-inch oval patties. Place the bread crumbs on a piece of wax paper and roll the patties in the crumbs so that they are lightly coated. In a 10-inch skillet, heat 2 tablespoons of the oil over medium heat until hot, but not smoking. Add the sausage ovals and cook, turning once or twice, until they are lightly browned, about 5 minutes. Turn them out of the pan onto a paper towel to drain.

2. Heat the remaining oil in the same skillet over medium heat. Add the onions and sauté, stirring constantly, until all pieces are coated with oil, about 1 minute. Reduce the heat to low and continue to cook, stirring often, until the onion is wilted, but not browned, about 5 minutes. Add the rice and continue to cook, stirring constantly, until all grains of rice are coated with oil and about 1/4 of them have begun to turn opaque, about 3 minutes. Do not let the rice burn. Add the stock and stir briskly. Stir in the garlic, peppers, celery, and tomatoes along with the bay leaf, salt, thyme, and black pepper. Bring this mixture to a boil, then cover and reduce to a simmer.

3. Meanwhile, drain the chipotle. Remove the tough stem end, slice the pepper in half and scrape out the seeds. Chop the pepper and stir it into the jambalaya. Add the bay leaf, salt, thyme, and pepper. Stir once, then allow the jambalaya to cook undisturbed until the rice is tender, about 25 minutes.

4. As the jambalaya cooks, heat the butter in a small skillet over medium heat. Add the mushrooms and sauté, stirring constantly, until they are softened, about 5 minutes. Set them aside. When the jambalaya is cooked, stir in the tofu "sausages," mushrooms, parsley, and scallions. Serve immediately with crostini (page 167) or crusty French-style bread.

Spinach Mushroom Lasagna
with Feta and Sun-Dried Tomatoes

Yield: 6 servings • Prep Time: 30 Minutes • Cooking Time: 1 1/4 hours

While working on recipe development for a large natural foods store in Colorado I developed a simpler version of this recipe. It was so popular that a restaurant in Aspen added it to their menu.

12 ounces lasagna noodles
1 tablespoon olive oil
3/4 cup chopped red onion
8 ounces button mushrooms, sliced
4 cloves garlic, sliced thin
1 ounce porcini mushrooms, softened in hot water
2 pounds fresh spinach
8 ounces cow's milk feta, crumbled, or use tofu "feta" (page 173)
1/4 teaspoon black pepper
1/8 teaspoon cayenne pepper
1/8 teaspoon nutmeg
10 ounces soft tofu, drained and crumbled
15 sun-dried tomatoes, softened in hot water, then drained and chopped
1 cup fresh basil, chopped
3 1/2 to 4 cups hearty tomato sauce (page 174)
1/4 cup grated Parmesan

1. In a large stockpot, bring 3 quarts of water to a boil. Lower the noodles into the water and stir gently until they have begun to soften and have dropped into the water. Reduce the heat so the water does not boil over, then cook, stirring occasionally, until the noodles are just beginning to get tender. (The noodles will finish cooking in the oven.) Immediately drain them, then carefully transfer the noodles to a bowl of cold water to rest as you prepare the rest of the ingredients.

2. In a 10-inch skillet, heat the oil over medium high heat until very hot. Add the onion and cook, stirring constantly, until the onion is coated with oil. Reduce the heat slightly and continue to cook, stirring often, until the onions are translucent, about 10 minutes.

3. Turn the heat to medium high again and add the button mushrooms. Cook, stirring often, until the mushrooms begin to wilt, about 3 minutes. Reduce the heat again, stir in the garlic and continue to cook, stirring often, until the mushrooms are very soft, about 10 minutes. Drain the porcini mushrooms and stir them into the pan.

4. Meanwhile, clean the spinach, removing the stems and rinsing the leaves. Chop the leaves roughly. When the mushrooms are soft, stir in the spinach and cook, stirring and tossing, until the spinach is wilted and has released its juice. Remove the mushroom-spinach mixture from the heat and drain off any liquid that has accumulated in the pan. Stir in the feta and season with 1/8 teaspoon black pepper, all of the cayenne pepper, and the nutmeg. Mix well, then set aside. In a small bowl, combine the tofu, sun-dried tomatoes, basil, and remaining pepper. Set this aside as well.

5. Preheat the oven to 350°F. Remove the noodles from the water and dry on kitchen towels. In the bottom of a 9- by 13-inch baking pan, spread a thin layer of the tomato sauce. Cover this with a layer of noodles, then half of the spinach mixture, another layer of noodles and a thick layer of sauce. Top this with half of the tofu mixture, then a layer of noodles. Repeat the layering until all ingredients are used, ending with the sauce. Sprinkle the Parmesan on top. The lasagna may be assembled up to 24 hours in advance if refrigerated tightly covered. It may be frozen, tightly covered, for up to 3 months, but should be thawed in the refrigerator overnight before baking.

6. Bake the lasagna, covered, for 30 minutes. Remove the cover and continue to bake for 45 minutes. Cool briefly before serving.

Variation

1. Substitute 10 ounces tofu "sausage" (page 166) for the crumbled tofu, above, then proceed with the recipe.

Grilled Vegetable Lasagna

Yield: 4 servings • Prep Time: 30 minutes • Cooking Time: 30 minutes

4 cups hearty tomato sauce
   (page 174)
1 pound dried lasagna noodles
2 medium eggplants
2 zucchini
1/4 teaspoon salt
4 cups packed Swiss chard leaves
12 ounces tree oyster mushrooms
   or button mushrooms
3 tablespoons olive oil
1/2 cup shredded basil leaves
2 cups low-fat ricotta cheese
   or tofu "cottage cheese"
   (page 172)
6 ounces mild goat cheese,
   crumbled
2 cups grated mozzarella
   or soy Monterey Jack

This elegant grilled-vegetable lasagna is served free-form, so assemble and bake it just before serving. For a nondairy version, omit the goat cheese, then use tofu "cottage cheese" (page 172) and soy Monterey Jack cheese.

1. Prepare the tomato sauce according to directions on page 174. In the final step, cook the sauce for 2 1/2 hours so that it is quite thick. The sauce may be prepared up to 5 days in advance if refrigerated in an airtight container. It can be frozen for up to 3 months.

2. Bring 4 quarts of water to a rolling boil. Add the pasta quickly, but very carefully, so that the pieces do not stick to the bottom or sides of the pan. Cook, stirring very gently once or twice, until the pasta is just beginning to get tender (it finishes cooking in the oven). Immediately drain the noodles, transferring them carefully into the strainer to avoid breaking them. Immediately plunge the noodles into a bowl of cold water and allow them to rest until you are ready to assemble the lasagna.

3. Peel and discard the stem ends and skin from the eggplants. Slice the eggplant into 1-inch rounds, then place these on a clean kitchen towel. Slice the zucchini into 1/2-inch rounds and place them on another towel. Sprinkle these vegetables with salt and allow them to "sweat" for 20 minutes. Meanwhile, place the chard in the top of a steamer over rapidly boiling water and cook until soft, about 5 minutes. Transfer immediately to a strainer and run cold water over the chard to stop its cooking. When it is cool enough to handle, squeeze as much excess water out of it as you can, then chop it roughly.

4. Cut the tree oyster mushrooms into 1-inch pieces. (If using button mushrooms, slice them into 1/2-inch-thick pieces.) Preheat the broiler to high. Brush the eggplant, zucchini, and mushrooms with oil and place them in a single layer on a lightly oiled baking sheet about 3 inches from the heat. Cook, turning once and brushing again with oil, until lightly browned and softened, about 5 minutes. You will probably need to cook the vegetables in several batches, unless you have an exceptionally large broiler. As each vegetable is cooked, remove it to the work surface.

5. To assemble the lasagna, lift the noodles from their soaking water and place them on a clean kitchen towel, then pat dry. Place a thin layer of sauce in four 3-by 5-inch areas on a shallow baking sheet. Cut each noodle in half so that it is a short rectangle. Lay two pieces of lasagna, slightly overlapping, to form a square on each pool of sauce. Spoon about 3 tablespoons of sauce onto each set of noodles, then divide the zucchini and mushrooms among the 4 pieces of pasta, arranging them in an even layer on each. Top this with another 2 tablespoons of sauce and divide the ricotta among the stacks. Place a second piece of pasta over this and repeat the layers, using the eggplant and chard instead of the zucchini and mushrooms. In this layer replace the ricotta with the goat cheese and 1/2 cup of the mozzarella. Top each lasagna with a third piece of pasta, spoon 1/4 cup of sauce over each, and top with the remaining mozzarella.

6. Preheat the oven to 450°F. Place the lasagna on the center rack and bake until the edges of the pasta are just beginning to crisp and the cheese is fully melted, about 12 minutes. Meanwhile, heat the remaining sauce until piping hot. Ladle about 1/3 cup of sauce on 4 individual serving plates. Using 2 metal spatulas or palette knives, transfer the cooked lasagna squares to the plates. Sprinkle with basil and serve immediately.

Variation

1. Replace the zucchini with 1/4 pound fresh morel mushrooms (broil them with the button mushrooms). Sprinkle 1/4 cup toasted pine nuts over the mushrooms when layering them into the lasagna.

Piccadillo

Yield: 4 servings • Prep Time: 30 minutes • Cooking Time: 20 minutes

Growing up in Florida, I was privileged to get an authentic sampling of fine Caribbean cuisines. The tastes of Cuba are the most memorable to me and Piccadillo is a dish I recall well. The principle of Piccadillo—traditionally made with beef—is to combine the sweet taste of raisins with the salty bite of capers, and it works delightfully well with tempeh. Serve with long-grain brown or white rice and a jicama salad.

2 large fresh tomatoes
  or use 3 cups canned
  tomatoes, drained and chopped
1 tablespoon olive oil
1 1/2 cup diced red onion
4 cloves garlic, sliced
1 pound tempeh, broken into
  small pieces
1 teaspoon salt
1 bay leaf
1/4 teaspoon black pepper
1 tablespoon balsamic vinegar
1 teaspoon ground cumin
1/4 teaspoon cinnamon
1/8 teaspoon ground cloves
1 cup diced green bell pepper
1/2 cup raisins
2 tablespoons capers, drained
3 tablespoons minced scallions
3 tablespoons slivered almonds
  (optional)

1. With a paring knife, cut out and discard a cone-shaped piece from the stem end of each tomato. Make a cross mark just through the skin of each tomato at the blossom end. Bring 3 quarts of water to a boil, then drop the tomatoes into the water. Allow them to cook, stirring them often, for about 30 seconds or until the sliced skin begins to peel back. Immediately transfer the tomatoes to a strainer in the sink and run cold water over them to stop their cooking. When they are cool enough to handle, stop the water and peel the tomatoes, then chop them into rough pieces.

2. In a 12-inch skillet, heat the oil over medium high until hot, but not smoking. Add the onion and cook, stirring constantly, until they are all lightly coated with oil, about 1 minute. Reduce the heat slightly and continue to cook, stirring often, until the onions are soft, about 8 minutes. Stir in the tomatoes, garlic, tempeh, salt, bay leaf, and pepper. Add the vinegar, cumin, cinnamon, and cloves. Bring this to a simmer and cook, partially covered and stirring occasionally, for 20 minutes. Add the green pepper, raisins, and capers. Stir well and continue to cook for 10 minutes. Taste and adjust the seasonings. Serve over millet which has been cooked like Fluffy Millet with Marinated Tempeh (page 59), or mint-flavored basmati rice topped with scallions and almonds.

Variation

1. Serve wrapped in corn tortillas then warmed briefly in the oven.

Mandala of Crêpes with Garbanzo Sauce

Yield: 6 servings • Prep Time: 1 hour • Cooking Time: 12 minutes

15 almond crêpes (page 171)
1 Japanese eggplant
  or 4 ounces large eggplant
2 tablespoons olive oil
1 cup diced red onion
1 cup diced red bell pepper
1/2 cup diced green bell pepper
2 tomatoes, peeled, seeded, and
  chopped (page 35)
5 teaspoons minced garlic
1/2 cup diced zucchini
1/4 teaspoon dried thyme
1/4 teaspoon salt
1/4 teaspoon black pepper
1/4 teaspoon nutmeg
3/4 cup light vegetable stock
  (page 162)
1 cup diced fennel bulb
1/4 cup minced fresh basil
1 1/2 cups cooked garbanzo beans
2 tablespoons mellow white miso
2 tablespoons almond butter
  (page 167)
1/3 cup lemon juice
Basil leaves for garnish

A blending of flavors and aesthetics from East and West, these French-style crêpes with flavors of the Mediterranean are assembled to look like an Indian Mandala. This recipe is actually very simple to prepare and various components can be prepared in advance, leaving you with only a small amount of last-minute preparation.

1. Have the crêpes ready and at room temperature. If they have been frozen, be certain that they are thoroughly thawed before beginning the recipe.

2. Trim and discard the stem and blossom ends from the eggplant, then slice it into 1/2-inch-thick rounds. Place these in the steaming rack of a steamer over rapidly boiling water. Cover and steam until tender, about 8 minutes. Remove from the heat and set aside.

3. In a 10-inch skillet, heat the oil over medium high heat until hot, but not smoking. Add the onion and cook, stirring often, until soft and translucent, about 8 minutes. Do not allow the onions to burn. Add the red and green peppers and continue to cook, stirring frequently, until soft, about 6 minutes. Stir in 1 cup of tomato and 1 teaspoon of garlic. Cook this until the tomatoes begin to give off their juices, about 2 minutes. Add the zucchini, thyme, salt, 1/8 teaspoon pepper, 1/8 teaspoon nutmeg, and 1/4 cup of stock. Stir to combine, then reduce the heat to medium and continue to cook, stirring occasionally, for 10 minutes. Remove from the heat, stir in the fennel and basil. Taste and adjust the seasonings. This filling may be prepared up to 4 days in advance if refrigerated in an airtight container.

4. Meanwhile, prepare the sauce. In a food processor fitted with the metal chopping blade or blender, combine the garbanzos, remaining tablespoon of garlic, 1/8 teaspoon black pepper, and 1/8 teaspoon nutmeg, the miso, almond butter, and lemon juice. Process until very finely ground, scraping down the sides of the bowl as necessary. With the motor running, pour the remaining 1/4 cup of stock into the beans. Blend well until the sauce is as smooth as possible. For a smoother sauce, press the mixture through a fine-mesh strainer. Taste and adjust the seasonings.

5. Preheat the oven to 400°F. Spread about 1/4 cup of the sauce over the surface of a 10-inch heatproof serving platter. (A stainless steel Indian Thali plate is ideal.) Place a crêpe on the counter and visually divide it into pie-shaped quarters. Place 3 tablespoons of the filling in the center of the lower left quadrant of the crêpe. Fold the crêpe in half, then in half again to form a rounded triangular shape. Repeat this with the remaining crêpes and filling. Arrange 6 crêpes, evenly spaced and points facing out, around the perimeter of the platter. Arrange 6 more crêpes in a smaller circle, with points overlapping the gaps between the crêpes in the outer circle. (The bottom edge of the crêpes in this second circle should touch in the center.) Finally arrange the last 4 crêpes, points out, in the very center of the platter. Cover the platter with foil or another platter. Place in the center of the oven and bake for 10 to 12 minutes, or until piping hot.

6. As the crêpes bake, heat the remaining sauce until piping hot. Remove the platter from the oven and remove the cover immediately. Arrange the remaining 1/2 cup of chopped tomatoes in the center of the platter and garnish the rest of the crêpes with basil leaves. Serve at once with additional sauce on the side.

Seitan Bourguignon

Yield: 6 servings • Prep Time: 30 minutes • Cooking Time: 4 hours

Use a full-bodied cabernet for this vegetarian variation of the French classic. The recipe is more complex than most in this book but well worth the effort for a special occasion. Porcini stock is essential to the success of this dish by deepening the flavor which is traditionally developed by the addition of rich meat stock.

1. Prepare the seitan according to directions on page 184. Cut it into 1-inch cubes and set them aside. In a 2-quart saucepan, combine the ingredients for the marinade. Bring this to a boil, then reduce to a very slow simmer. Gently add the pieces of seitan to the simmering broth. Simmer gently, partially covered, for 2 hours. Do not allow the broth to boil rapidly as this will cause the seitan to be spongy in texture. Stir the broth and turn the pieces of seitan occasionally as they cook so they are evenly bathed in the liquid. After about 2 hours the seitan will be firm, but tender. Remove the pan from the heat and allow the seitan to cool in the remaining broth. The seitan can be cooked to this point up to 4 days in advance if stored in an airtight container in its cooking marinade. It can also be frozen for up to 2 months.

2. In a 3-quart Dutch oven or heavy-bottomed pan, heat 1 tablespoon of oil over high heat until hot, but not smoking. Add the sliced onion and carrot and cook, stirring constantly, for 2 minutes. Reduce the heat to low and continue to cook, stirring often, until the onion is translucent, about 8 minutes. Remove the vegetables and set them aside.

3. Preheat the oven to 375°F. Again, heat the Dutch oven over medium high heat, with the remaining tablespoon of oil. Add the flour and stir to mix well. Reduce the heat to low and cook, stirring constantly, until this roux has turned a dark nutty brown, about 20 minutes. Whisk in the wine and cook until the smell of alcohol has evaporated. Add the stock, cooked vegetables, seitan, tomato paste, thyme, garlic, bay leaf, salt, peppercorns, and parsley. Bring this to a slow boil, stirring occasionally, then cover and place the pan in the middle of the pre-heated oven. Cook for 1 hour, stirring 2 or 3 times. Remove the lid from the pan and continue to cook until the liquid has reduced to about 1/4 the height of the seitan. Remove the stew from the oven.

4. As the stew cooks, prepare the garnish. Peel the pearl onions and in the root end of each, make a 1/4-inch-deep cross mark with the tip of a paring knife. Heat 2 teaspoons of oil and 2 teaspoons of butter in a small skillet over medium heat. Sauté the onions, shaking the pan often to allow them to begin to brown. Reduce the heat to low. Season with salt and pepper, then cover and cook, shaking the pan occasionally, until the onions are soft, about 20 minutes. Meanwhile, heat the remaining butter and oil in a separate skillet and sauté the mushroom caps over medium heat, tossing often, until they are just soft, about 12 minutes. Set both onions and mushrooms aside.

5. To serve the dish, remove the seitan from the cooking liquid and arrange it on a warm serving platter or individual plates. Arrange cooked pearl onions and mushroom caps around the seitan. Strain the sauce from the stew through a fine mesh strainer and drizzle it over the seitan. Sprinkle with minced parsley.

2 cups uncooked seitan (page 184)

MARINADE:
1/2 cup dry red wine
3 1/2 cups water
1 tablespoon olive oil
2 cloves garlic, sliced
1 yellow onion, sliced
1 large sprig fresh thyme or 1/4 teaspoon dried
1 bay leaf
1 teaspoon salt
4 peppercorns
4 sprigs parsley

2 tablespoons olive oil
1 cup cubed carrot (1 large carrot)
1 cup thickly sliced onion
3 tablespoons flour
1 1/4 cups dry red wine
1 3/4 cups porcini stock (page 163) or hearty vegetable stock (page 162)
2 teaspoons tomato paste
1 large sprig thyme (or 1/4 teaspoon dried)
1 1/2 tablespoons minced garlic
1 bay leaf
1 teaspoon salt
5 peppercorns
3 sprigs parsley

GARNISH:
20 pearl onions
1 tablespoon olive oil
1 tablespoon butter
1 pound small mushroom caps
3 tablespoons minced fresh parsley

Potato Layer Cake

Yield: 4 servings • Prep Time: 30 minutes • Cooking Time: 45 minutes

Pommes Anna is a classic French potato cake served as a side dish. Here I reduce the amount of butter usually called for in the traditional version and fill the cake with a slightly sweet tempeh stuffing. It may be prepared as one large cake or in individual pot-pie pans for individual servings.

3/4 cup cooked diced butternut squash
1 cup minced shallots
1/4 cup finely diced celery
1/2 cup finely diced carrot
1 tablespoon olive oil
8 ounces tempeh, crumbled
8 cloves garlic, sliced paper-thin
1/4 cup light vegetable stock (page 162)
1/4 cup minced fresh tarragon
1 1/4 teaspoons salt
2 1/2 pounds russet potatoes
3 tablespoons melted butter or oil

1. Purée the squash in a food processor fitted with the metal chopping blade or a blender, then set this aside. In a skillet over medium heat, sauté the shallots, celery, and carrot in the olive oil, stirring often, until the shallots are soft, about 8 minutes. Stir in the tempeh, 1 tablespoon of the sliced garlic, and the vegetable stock. Reduce to a simmer and cook for 15 minutes or until the stock has reduced to a glaze. Remove the skillet from the heat and stir in 3/4 teaspoon salt and 2 tablespoons of tarragon, then blend in the puréed squash. This filling may be prepared up to 2 days in advance, if refrigerated in an airtight container.

2. Peel the russet potatoes and slice them into 1/4-inch-thick rounds. Place the slices in a bowl of cold water as you work to prevent them from discoloring. The potatoes can be sliced and refrigerated in water for up to 8 hours before proceeding with the recipe.

3. Preheat the oven to 375°F. Generously butter the bottom and sides of a 9-inch pie plate or 4 pot-pie pans. Drain the potatoes and place them, in a single layer, on one or more clean kitchen towels. Pat the slices of potato to dry them as thoroughly as possible. Transfer the potatoes to a large mixing bowl and mix in the remaining garlic, 2 tablespoons tarragon, and 1/4 teaspoon salt. Toss to combine. Arrange a layer of potato slices in the bottom of the pie pan so that they form an overlapping, flower-like pattern. Top this with half of the remaining potato mixture. These slices need not be arranged neatly, but should be pressed firmly down once they are in place. Arrange an even layer of the tempeh filling over the potatoes, then add the remaining potatoes. Again, press the potatoes down firmly into the pie pan. Drizzle any remaining butter over the potatoes.

4. Heat a burner to medium-high and place the pan directly over the heat. Cook, turning the pan often, for about 4 minutes, to brown the potatoes. Place the pie pan on the bottom rack of the preheated oven and bake, covered, for 45 minutes, or until a knife inserted in the center feels no resistance. Remove the cake from the oven and allow to cool for 5 minutes. Run the blade of a metal spatula or a thin paring knife around the edge of the potato cake. Place a 10-inch serving plate over the pie pan and, holding the rim of the pan to the plate, invert the cake onto the plate. Briskly shake the pie pan several times to be certain that the cake has unmolded properly. Remove the pie pan and serve.

6 • Celebrations

Orange Hazelnut Tofu

Yield: 4 servings • Prep Time: 20 minutes • Cooking Time: 15 minutes

Slices of tofu are bathed in a light orange sauce and accented by the lingering taste of hazelnuts. This dish—inspired by a bluefish recipe in the Four Seasons' Cookbook—*is ideal on a hot summer's evening. Serve it with a mixed green salad and cornbread.*

1/3 cup hazelnuts
1 pound firm tofu
1/2 teaspoon minced garlic
3 tablespoons butter or olive oil
3 tablespoons rice vinegar
1 tablespoon honey
1/2 teaspoon salt
1 sweet navel orange
1/4 cup flour
1/8 teaspoon black pepper
1/8 teaspoon paprika
3 tablespoons capers
2 tablespoons chopped cilantro

1. Preheat the oven to 375°F. Place the hazelnuts on a baking sheet and toast, stirring a few times, until they are browned to the core, about 12 minutes. Immediately transfer them to a clean kitchen towel and rub them vigorously to remove their skins. (If the skins are particularly resistant to being removed, place the nuts in a strainer and rub them against the wire mesh. This will make them less attractive, but will remove the bitter skin. Since the hazelnuts for this recipe are chopped, they need not look perfect.) Discard the skins and chop the nuts into rough pieces.

2. Drain the tofu and cut it into 1/2-inch-thick slices. Place these on a clean kitchen towel with a second towel on top, then put a cutting board on top of this and press firmly. Allow the tofu to drain at room temperature for 30 minutes. Cut the pressed tofu into 1/2-inch-wide strips.

3. In a shallow baking pan, combine the minced garlic, 2 tablespoons butter, the rice vinegar, honey, and 1/4 teaspoon salt. Mix well, then place the tofu in this marinade. Turn to coat. Marinate, covered, for 1 hour (or refrigerate for up to a day).

4. Zest the orange, then add the flour, 1/4 teaspoon salt, the pepper, and paprika to the zest and mix well. Peel the orange, being careful to remove the skin through just the outer layer of membrane. Section the orange, removing all inner membrane, and place the sections in a bowl. Set aside.

5. Dust the strips of tofu with the flour mixture and set aside. Heat 2 tablespoons butter in a heavy skillet over medium high heat. Add the tofu and cook, turning once, until lightly browned on both sides, about 8 minutes. Transfer the tofu to a serving platter and cover it to keep it warm as you prepare the sauce.

6. Heat the remaining 1 tablespoon butter in the same skillet over medium high heat until just warmed. Stir in the orange pieces and capers. Cook, stirring constantly, until the orange juice just begins to thicken, about 5 minutes. Remove from the heat and swirl in the cilantro. Pour this sauce over the tofu and sprinkle hazelnuts on top as a garnish.

Lettuce-Wrapped Tofu

Yield: 6 servings • Prep Time: 30 minutes • Cooking Time: 20 minutes

1 1/2 pounds firm tofu
3 lemons
3 tablespoons maple sugar
1/4 cup hatcho miso
1/4 cup minced scallions
1 1/2 tablespoons minced garlic
10 to 12 outer leaves romaine
    lettuce
1/2 pound chard leaves
1/2 teaspoon salt
1/4 teaspoon pepper
1/4 teaspoon nutmeg
Pinch of cayenne pepper
1/2 cup minced shallots
1 small fennel bulb, sliced paper-
    thin
1/4 cup dry white wine or
    vermouth (optional)
1 cup light vegetable stock
    (page 162)
1 red pepper, sliced into rings
    (optional)
10 black olives (optional)
Pan juices (from tofu, above)
1 teaspoon Dijon-style mustard
6 to 8 tablespoons softened
    butter
Freshly ground black pepper
2 tablespoons minced tarragon
    leaves

Lettuce leaves turn a vibrant green when steamed, and they present a striking contrast in color to the tofu stuffing. The dish can be served with a reduction sauce enriched with butter—which is divine, but high in fat—or you may opt for the lower-fat tahini fennel sauce. Either way, the dish is fit for a banquet.

1. Drain the tofu and slice it into 3/4-inch-thick slabs. Set them aside on a clean kitchen towel, with the towel folded over the tofu, but no weight put on top, so that the tofu can drain for 20 minutes. Grate the zest from 1 of the lemons and set it aside. Squeeze and strain the juice from all 3 lemons; you should have about 6 tablespoons. Set this aside as well.

2. In a shallow baking dish, combine 1/4 cup of the lemon juice, 2 tablespoons maple sugar, the hatcho miso, scallions, and 2 teaspoons garlic. Mix well, then add the tofu. Turn to coat with this marinade, then refrigerate, covered, for at least 5 hours, turning several times as it rests. The tofu may be marinated for up to a day.

3. Fill the bottom of a steamer with 1/2 inch of water and bring this to a boil. Arrange the lettuce leaves in the steaming rack so that they are in as even a layer as possible. Steam the leaves until they are tender, but still a vibrant green, about 6 minutes. Immediately transfer them to a strainer and run cold water over them to stop their cooking. Once they are cold to the touch, place them in a single layer on a clean kitchen towel to drain.

4. Place the chard in the top of the strainer and, in the same manner as the lettuce, steam it until it is tender, about 7 minutes. Place under cold running water to stop its cooking. When cool, place the chard in the center of a clean kitchen towel. Draw the corners together, forming a ball out of the chard. Twist the towel and squeeze the chard to extract as much liquid as possible. Transfer the chard to a chopping board and chop roughly. Place it in a small bowl and season with the remaining 2 1/2 teaspoons garlic, salt, pepper, nutmeg, cayenne, and 2 tablespoons minced shallots.

5. Preheat the oven to 375°F. Brush the bottom and sides of a shallow baking dish with olive oil, then sprinkle the remaining shallots over the pan. Arrange 5 of the lettuce leaves lengthwise across the pan, so that they overlap each other on the edges and the ends of the leaves hang out over the sides of the dish. Place half of the slices of tofu in the center of the pan, on top of the lettuce leaves. Arrange the tofu so that the slices touch, end to end. Cover the tofu with the chard mixture, then top this with the remaining slices of tofu. Drizzle any remaining marinade over the tofu and place the fennel slices over this. Fold the lettuce leaves from one side over the tofu, tucking them under the tofu if they are long enough. Fold the leaves from the other side, wrapping the tofu snugly. Pour the wine and stock into the baking dish and place, covered, in the center of the oven. Bake for 20 minutes.

6. Remove the pan from the oven. Drain the juices from the pan into a 1 1/2-quart saucepan, holding the tofu in place with a spatula as you pour. Set the tofu aside, but cover it to keep it warm as you prepare the sauce.

7. With the aid of 2 long metal palette knives or two metal spatulas, carefully lift the tofu from the baking dish by sliding the utensils under at opposite ends of the lettuce-wrapped package. Transfer the tofu to a long and narrow serving platter and surround it with the sauce. Garnish the platter, if desired, with red pepper rings and black olives.

8. In a small saucepan, combine the vegetable stock and pan juices from cooking the tofu with the mustard. Whisk well, then bring to a boil and cook quickly to reduce, whisking occasionally. When the liquid has reduced to about 3 to 4 tablespoons, remove the pan from the heat and gradually whisk in the softened butter. Season to taste with black pepper and stir in the tarragon. Serve immediately. The sauce will not hold and cannot be reheated without having the butter separate.

Variation

1. Serve this dish with a sauce made from 1 cup light vegetable stock (page 162), pan juices (from tofu), 3 tablespoons tahini, 2 tablespoons mellow white miso, 2 tablespoons lemon juice, 1 1/2 teaspoons toasted fennel seeds, crushed, and 2 tablespoons minced tarragon. To prepare the sauce, in a small saucepan combine the vegetable stock and pan juices. Bring this to a boil and reduce to 1/4 cup. Remove from the heat and whisk in the tahini, miso, lemon juice, fennel seeds, and tarragon. Whisk vigorously, then serve immediately.

Soba Noodles with Wild Mushrooms in Parchment

Yield: 4 servings • Prep Time: 40 minutes • Cooking Time: 15 minutes

1 lemon
1 tablespoon olive oil
2 teaspoons butter
2 cups sliced onion
1/2 pound button mushrooms, sliced
1/4 pound tree oyster mushrooms, quartered
1/4 pound fresh shiitake mushrooms, quartered
1/2 ounce dried porcini mushrooms, softened, then drained
3/4 teaspoon salt
1/8 teaspoon black pepper
1/8 teaspoon nutmeg
Pinch dried red pepper flakes
1 pound garnet yam, peeled and cut in julienne strips
1 red bell pepper, cut in small dice
1/2 cup porcini stock (page 163)
3 large cloves garlic
6 ounces soba noodles (page 194)
3/4 cup cooked garbanzo beans
10 black olives pitted and sliced (preferably calamata)
1/2 cup fresh basil, shredded
1/2 cup grated Parmesan or Gruyère (optional)

In Giuliano Bugialli's book, Foods of Italy, *he includes a mouthwatering photograph of his recipe for "Pasta al Cartoccio," which served as inspiration for this dish. Porcini bouillon is essential to give the dish its rich flavor. If you do not have it, add 1 tablespoon almond butter to the stock. Though the parchment presentation is certainly more elegant, this recipe works very well when prepared ahead and baked in a casserole dish.*

1. Grate the zest and squeeze the juice from the lemon and set both aside. In a 12-inch skillet, heat the oil and butter over medium high heat until the butter begins to bubble. Add the onion and cook, stirring constantly, until it glistens, about 1 minute. Reduce the heat to medium low and continue to cook, stirring often, until the onions have caramelized, about 15 minutes. The onions should turn a light brown and be sweet; they should not burn.

2. Increase the heat to medium and add the mushrooms. Cook, stirring constantly, for about a minute, then pour the lemon juice over them. Add the salt, pepper, nutmeg, and pepper flakes, then continue to cook, stirring frequently, until the mushrooms soften, about 10 minutes. Stir in the yam, bell pepper, and stock and continue to cook for 5 minutes. Remove from the heat and squeeze in the garlic through a garlic press. Stir in the lemon zest and set aside.

3. Bring 2 quarts of water to a rolling boil. Stir in the noodles and cook, stirring occasionally, until they are almost al dente, about 8 minutes. (The noodles will continue to cook in the oven, so do not overcook them at this stage.) Immediately drain the noodles and stir them into the mushroom mixture. Add the garbanzos, black olives, and basil. Taste and adjust the seasonings.

4. Preheat the oven to 400°F. Cut 4 heart-shaped pieces of parchment (by folding the parchment in half) that measure 13 inches tall by 10 inches at the widest part of the heart. Place one heart open on the work surface, point facing you. Arrange 1/4 of the noodle mixture evenly in the center of the right half of the heart. Fold the parchment over the filling and crimp the edges to seal the package shut. (To crimp, hold the pouch with one hand on the edge of the heart at the top of the folded edge. Make a small fold—inward towards the filling. The fold should angle slightly towards the sealed edge of the pouch so that the fold appears triangular in shape. Move the securing hand to hold the pouch in place at the new fold, then make a second angled fold, beginning in the center of the first fold. Repeat this half-layered folding around the entire edge of the heart to the tip, then twist to seal the tip.) Fold the paper over the noodles and pinch the edges to seal. Place the parchment packets on a baking sheet and bake until puffed and lightly browned, about 15 minutes. The parchment pouches can be prepared and refrigerated up to 8 hours in advance. Serve each parchment on an individual plate and provide a knife or scissors for cutting open the paper at the table. Serve the grated cheese alongside.

Variations

1. If you wish to serve this in a more casual manner, instead of using parchment, simply transfer the noodle mixture to a lightly oiled casserole. Cover and bake at 350°F. for 25 minutes. Serve at once.

2. For a more refined taste, peel the garbanzos by squeezing them between your fingertips until the bean pops out. Discard the skins.

3. Combine 1/3 cup pesto (page 176) with 3 tablespoons water, mixing until smooth. Omit the olives and fresh basil from the recipe above, then mix the pesto paste into the noodles just before arranging them in the parchment. Bake as directed above.

Tandoori-Style Mixed Grill

Yield: 6 servings • Prep Time: 25 minutes • Cooking Time: 15 minutes

The first time I saw a tandoori oven was at the outdoor garden restaurant at the Metropol hotel in Mysore, South India. In the shadow of a bougainvillea bush that separated the hotel grounds from one of the city's busiest intersections stood a chef making naan (bread) by slapping raw pieces of dough against the side of the adobe-style oven. He also hung brochettes basted in a flavorful yogurt-based sauce. This mixed kabob was inspired by that memory. It may be prepared on an outdoor grill or under the broiler. If you are using wooden skewers, soak them for at least 30 minutes to prevent burning.

8 ounces extra-firm tofu
1 lemon
4 ounces seitan (page 184)
1 1/2 teaspoons salt
8 ounces tempeh
2 cups plain yogurt
4 teaspoons paprika
1 tablespoon ground coriander
4 teaspoons ground cumin
1 teaspoon cinnamon
2 teaspoons minced gingerroot
2 teaspoons minced garlic (optional)
2 green or red bell peppers
2 medium carrots, cut in 1 1/2-inch roll cuts (page 189)
2 medium red potatoes, cut in 1 1/2-inch cubes
1 1/2 teaspoons cumin seeds, toasted
1 pound fresh tomatoes, sliced
1/4 cup chopped fresh mint leaves

1. Cut the tofu into 1-inch-thick slabs and place them on a clean kitchen towel. Fold the towel over the tofu and place a cutting board on top. Weight this down with an iron skillet or several 1-pound cans, then allow the tofu to drain at room temperature for 30 minutes.

2. Grate the zest from the lemon, cover it, and set aside until ready to finish the recipe. Squeeze the juice from the lemon onto the seitan, then sprinkle it with 1/4 teaspoon salt. If using uncooked seitan, knead and work in these two flavorings. Cut the seitan into 1/2-inch pieces. If using uncooked seitan, roll each piece into a neat ball. Place in a small mixing bowl and set aside.

3. Cut the tempeh into 1-inch cubes and place them in a shallow 9-inch baking pan. Place the tofu in a separate pan. Combine the yogurt, paprika, coriander, cumin, cinnamon, ginger, garlic, and remaining salt. Mix well, then pour about 1/3 of this marinade over the seitan, tempeh, and the tofu. Gently stir each to coat with this marinade. Cover and refrigerate, turning once or twice, for 24 to 36 hours.

4. Quarter the peppers lengthwise, then remove and discard their stems, white membrane and seeds. Cut the peppers into 1 1/2-inch squares and set them aside. Steam the carrots and potatoes over rapidly boiling water until they are just beginning to become tender, about 8 minutes. Immediately place them in a strainer and run cold water over them to stop their cooking. Transfer them to a clean kitchen towel and pat dry.

5. Preheat a grill or the broiler to high. Thread the skewers with alternating pieces of seitan, tofu, tempeh, and vegetables. Place them on a lightly oiled rack. Baste with the yogurt mixture, then broil, turning and basting once or twice, until the tofu is lightly browned, about 10 minutes. Just before serving, brush the mixed grill with all remaining marinade and sprinkle with the reserved lemon zest and cumin seeds.

6. To serve, arrange the sliced tomatoes on one large serving platter. Sprinkle the mint over the tomatoes and arrange the skewers on top.

Cook's Note: Allow time for the tofu to press as you prepare the sauce and other ingredients. You may use either cooked or uncooked seitan for the skewers—the latter has a chewier, less meat-like quality.

Spinach Sorrel Pie with Fava Beans

Yield: 4 servings • Prep Time: 1 hour • Cooking Time: 30 minutes

This may be prepared in individual pot-pie molds or ramekins for an elegant service, or for more casual fare, it may be presented as one large casserole.

1 cup sorrel leaves
4 cups spinach leaves
4 cups kale leaves
1 1/2 tablespoons olive oil
1/2 cup minced shallots
1/4 cup dry white wine
2 cups chopped tomatoes
1 teaspoon minced garlic
1 teaspoon dried oregano, crushed
1/2 teaspoon ground coriander
1/4 teaspoon salt
1/8 teaspoon black pepper
1 tablespoon flour
1 cup cooked fava beans (page 96)
   or kidney beans
1/4 cup fresh mint leaves
3 tablespoons ghee (page 191)
   or butter, melted
1 teaspoon cinnamon
1/2 pound filo dough, thawed
4 ounces cow's milk feta, strong
   goat cheese, or tofu "feta"
2 tablespoons chopped walnuts
   (optional)

1. Stack the sorrel leaves, then slice them lengthwise into fine strips. Set these aside. Roughly chop the other greens and place them in a large colander. Rinse under cold running water and allow them to drain as you prepare the rest of the ingredients.

2. In a 12-inch skillet, heat the oil over medium high heat until hot, but not smoking. Add the shallots and toss to coat with oil. Reduce the heat slightly and continue to cook, stirring often, until the shallots begin to soften, about 8 minutes. Add the chopped kale, turning the leaves as you add them so that they wilt and allow space for the remaining leaves to be added. When it is possible to add more leaves, do so and continue to cook, stirring constantly, until they, too, begin to wilt. Add the spinach and continue to cook, stirring often, until it is wilted, about 3 minutes.

3. Once all leaves have begun to wilt, increase the heat to high and add the wine. Cook, stirring constantly, until the smell of alcohol evaporates, about 1 minute. Stir in the tomatoes, garlic, oregano, coriander, salt, pepper, and flour. Reduce the heat to medium and simmer, stirring often, until the liquid has reduced and thickened, about 10 minutes. Remove the pan from the heat, then stir in the sorrel, fava beans, and mint. Taste and adjust the seasonings. The filling can be prepared up to 3 days in advance if refrigerated in an airtight container.

4. Preheat the oven to 400°F. Stir the cinnamon into the melted ghee, then lightly brush 4 pot-pan tins with the ghee mixture. Lay the filo sheets out flat on a clean, dry work surface. Cover them with a very lightly dampened dish towel to prevent them from drying out as you work. Cut 4 circles (through the 6 layers of dough) that measure 2 inches more in diameter than the top diameter of the pans. (For the average pot-pie pan, this is 7 inches). Line the bottom and sides of each pan with a round of dough, then brush the dough with butter and cover with a second sheet. Continue to brush butter and layer rounds in each pan until each mold contains 6 layers of pastry.

5. Stack the remaining filo dough and cut it into thin shreds. (The thinner the shreds, the lighter the effect of the top crust.) With your fingertips, carefully separate and "feather" the strips of pastry by picking them up, then allowing them to gently drop to the counter. Divide the spinach filling evenly among the pie pans. Cover the filling with a layer of cheese, then cover each pan with a 1/4-inch layer of pastry strips. Brush these with ghee, then cover with the remaining pastry strips and brush again with ghee. The pies can be prepared ahead and refrigerated, loosely covered, for up to 24 hours. They can also be frozen for up to 1 month, but should be thawed before baking.

6. Place the pies on a baking sheet and bake in the center of the oven for 10 minutes. Reduce the heat to 350°F. and continue to bake until the top crust is crisp and golden, about 18 minutes. Sprinkle with walnuts and serve at once.

Variation

1. The pie can be baked in a 9-inch pie plate and served family style. To do so, cut a circle 3 inches bigger in diameter than that of the pie pan and cover it with 8, rather than 6 layers.

Peanut-Broiled Tofu over Rice Noodles

Yield: 6 servings • Prep Time: 25 minutes • Cooking Time: 15 minutes

Various cuisines throughout Southeast Asia feature recipes for peanut-based dishes. They vary distinctly, depending on region and cook, from sauces rich with coconut milk to thin marinades used for meats or tempeh. A common element in many is the taste combination of peanuts and soy sauce. This simple marinade and sauce is an example of a moderately light peanut dish.

1 pound firm tofu
1 lemon
3/4 cup minced scallions
1 tablespoon minced garlic
2 teaspoons minced gingerroot
2 teaspoons ground cumin
1 teaspoon ground coriander
1/4 teaspoon turmeric
1/8 teaspoon black pepper
1 1/2 tablespoons blackstrap molasses
1/3 cup + 1 teaspoon soy sauce
6 tablespoons smooth natural peanut butter
2 tablespoons honey
1 tablespoon rice vinegar
1/4 teaspoon red pepper flakes (optional)
1 teaspoon mirin (193)
1 cup water
2 tablespoons minced cilantro
2 cups broccoli florets
6 ounces flat rice noodles or egg-less spaghetti noodles
1 cup mung bean sprouts
1/2 cup shredded carrot
1/2 cucumber, peeled, seeded, and sliced
6 cilantro sprigs

1. Drain the tofu and cut it into 1-inch-thick slices. Place them on a clean kitchen towel with a second towel on top. Put a light cutting board on the towel and press gently. Allow the tofu to drain for 30 minutes.

2. Zest the lemon and set this aside, covered, in a small bowl. Squeeze the juice from the lemon into a shallow baking dish. Add to this 1/4 cup of scallions, the garlic, ginger, cumin, coriander, turmeric, pepper, molasses, and 1/4 cup soy sauce. Mix well. When the tofu has drained, place it in the dish with the lemon juice mixture. Turn the pieces of tofu to coat, then cover and allow them to marinate in the refrigerator for at least 2 hours or up to a day.

3. In a small mixing bowl, combine the remaining 1/2 cup scallions, soy sauce, 2 tablespoons peanut butter, honey, vinegar, red pepper flakes, mirin, water, and minced cilantro. Mix well and set aside.

4. Place the broccoli in the top rack of a steamer over rapidly boiling water. Cook, covered, until it is a vibrant green and just tender, 5 minutes. Transfer immediately to a strainer and place under cold running water to stop its cooking. Allow it to drain once cold.

5. Preheat the broiler to high. Place the tofu about 6 inches from the heat and broil, turning once and brushing with the marinade, until it is lightly browned on both sides, about 10 minutes.

6. Meanwhile, cook the noodles in 3 quarts of rapidly boiling water until they are al dente. (Depending on the type of noodle the time will vary.) Drain the noodles immediately, then transfer them to a large serving platter. Add the broccoli and pour the peanut butter sauce over the noodles. Toss thoroughly. Place the bean sprouts in the center of the noodles with the cooked tofu on top. Garnish with carrots and cucumber slices, then place the cilantro sprigs on top. Serve at once.

Cook's Note: It is not essential to press the tofu here, but if time allows it, do so as the texture is improved.

Couscous-Stuffed Artichokes with Orange "Hollandaise"

Yield: 4 servings • Prep Time: 1 hour • Cooking Time: 15 minutes

1 1/2 cups whole wheat couscous
2 1/4 cups light vegetable stock
    (page 162) or water
6 ounces mushrooms
2 tablespoons olive oil
3 tablespoons orange juice
2 teaspoons minced garlic
3 tablespoons minced fresh
    tarragon or 1 1/2 teaspoons
    dried
2 cups chopped tomatoes
6 oil-packed sun-dried tomatoes,
    chopped
1/2 cup pistachio nuts
1 1/2 teaspoons cinnamon
1/2 teaspoon salt
1/8 teaspoon red pepper flakes
    (optional)
4 artichokes
5 ounces soft silken tofu
3/4 cup orange juice
1/4 teaspoon salt
1 clove garlic
    or 1/8 teaspoon garlic powder
Pinch nutmeg

Elegant and inviting, this light entrée is wonderful. The filling is also excellent as a stuffing for tofu, replacing the mushroom mixture in Pecan-Mushroom-Stuffed Tofu (page 140).

1. Place the couscous in a large mixing bowl. Bring the stock to a boil, and pour it over the couscous. Stir to mix evenly, then cover it with a lid or plate and set aside until all of the liquid is absorbed, about 30 minutes.

2. Clean and dry the mushrooms, then chop them into 1/2-inch pieces. In a 10-inch skillet over medium flame, heat 1 tablespoon of oil until hot, but not smoking. Add the mushrooms and cook, stirring constantly, until about 1/4 of them have begun to change color, for 1 to 2 minutes. Add 2 tablespoons orange juice and toss. Add the garlic, then reduce the heat to medium low and continue to cook, stirring frequently, until the mushrooms are soft and most of their liquid has evaporated, about 8 minutes. Remove from the heat and set aside.

3. Once the couscous has absorbed all of the liquid, fluff it with a fork, then add it to the cooked mushrooms. Stir in the tarragon, tomatoes, sun-dried tomatoes, nuts, cinnamon, salt, and red pepper flakes. Mix well. Taste and adjust the seasonings. This filling can be prepared up to 3 days in advance if refrigerated in an airtight container.

4. Rinse the artichokes well. Using a wavy-edged knife, saw off the stem even with the bottom of each artichoke. Cut off the top of each artichoke about 1 1/2 inches from the tip. With scissors, trim the sharp point from all remaining leaves. Rub each artichoke all over with the remaining lemon half, being especially careful to apply juice to all cut surfaces. This will prevent some discoloration. Place the artichokes in the top of a steamer over rapidly boiling water. Cover tightly and cook, turning occasionally to insure that they cook evenly, until their bottoms are just beginning to soften, about 25 minutes. Immediately remove the artichokes from the steamer rack and rinse under cold water to stop their cooking.

5. When the artichokes are cool enough to handle, stop rinsing them and carefully pull the center leaves out of each. Using a sharp-edged spoon (a grapefruit spoon works well) scrape out and discard the chokes. Place the artichokes upside down on a clean kitchen towel to drain. They can be prepared to this point up to 24 hours in advance if refrigerated in a loosely folded plastic bag.

6. Stuff each artichoke with as much couscous mixture as possible, mounding it up high. Return the artichokes to the steamer rack and steam over rapidly boiling water until the filling is warmed through, about 10 minutes. Place remaining couscous mixture in a small heatproof bowl and steam alongside the artichokes until just warmed through, about 8 minutes.

7. Meanwhile, prepare the sauce. Drain the tofu and place it in a blender, then blend briefly. With the motor running, add the orange juice in a thin stream and blend until smooth, scraping down the sides of the beaker several times. Add the salt, garlic, and nutmeg through a garlic press. Blend again, then transfer to the top of a double boiler and warm over hot water as the artichokes finish cooking. To serve, place a small mound of couscous on each plate, place an artichoke in the center of the filling, and pour a small amount of sauce over it.

Cook's Note: This recipe works very well cooked in stages over the course of a day or so. The artichokes should not be stuffed more than 6 hours in advance, however.

Black-Eyed Pea and Rice Timbales

Yield: 6 servings • Prep Time: 15 minutes • Cooking Time: 1 1/4 hours

Aromatic basmati rice surrounds a delicately flavored black-eyed pea mixture in these delightful timbales.

1. Rinse the black-eyed peas and place them in a 3-quart saucepan. Add enough water to cover them by 1 inch. Bring to a boil, stir, and reduce to a simmer. Cover and cook until just tender, about 20 minutes.

2. As the peas cook, combine the sesame oil, molasses, vinegar, soy sauce, 6 tablespoons water, ginger, garlic, and salt. When the peas are cooked, drain them and immediately transfer them to a mixing bowl. Pour half of the sesame oil mixture over them and add the red pepper. Toss well, cover, and refrigerate for at least 4 hours or up to 2 days. Turn the black-eyed peas several times as they marinate. Reserve the remaining sesame oil mixture for the sauce.

3. Rinse the rice and drain it thoroughly. In a 2-quart saucepan, combine 3 cups of stock with 2 teaspoons of butter. Bring this to a boil and stir in the rice. Reduce the heat to a simmer and cook, covered, until the rice is just tender, about 20 minutes. Set the rice aside until it is lukewarm.

4. Rinse the arame and place it in a small bowl. Cover with boiling water and set aside until soft, about 10 minutes. When the rice is lukewarm, drain the arame, squeezing out as much water as possible. Stir the arame and 1/3 cup mint into the rice.

5. Line four 1 1/2-cup ramekins or an 8-cup charlotte mold with waxed paper. To do this, place each mold on a piece of waxed paper and outline the bottom circumference with the tip of a sharp paring knife. Remove the mold and cut out the circle. Cut a strip of waxed paper as wide as the mold is deep, and long enough to encircle the mold. Use the reserved butter to grease the mold, then place the circle of paper in the bottom of the mold and wrap the strip around the inside edge. Smooth the paper onto the surface of the mold. Pat the rice into the mold(s) to form a 1/2-inch layer on the bottom and sides of the mold. You may find it helpful to dip your fingertips in a small amount of water as you work to prevent the rice from sticking to your hands. The rice should be packed firmly in place.

6. Drain the marinade from the black-eyed peas back into the reserved sesame oil mixture. Fill the mold(s) with peas and cover with a layer of rice. The mold(s) can be prepared up to 24 hours in advance to this point if refrigerated, tightly covered. Preheat the oven to 425°F. Bake the timbales, covered, in the center of the oven until warmed through, about 30 minutes. Remove from the oven and allow to rest at room temperature while you finish the sauce.

7. In a 1-quart saucepan, combine the reserved sesame oil mixture with the remaining stock and wine. Bring to a boil and cook for 5 minutes. Stir in the dissolved kuzu and whisk until the sauce boils. Remove from the heat and stir in the remaining mint. Arrange the lettuce leaves on one large platter if you are using the charlotte mold, or individual serving dishes if you used ramekins. Invert the platter or plates over the mold(s), then re-invert and shake briskly once or twice. The rice should drop out onto the lettuce. Remove the mold and peel off the paper. Serve with sauce alongside.

Cook's Note: The cooked beans must marinate for at least 4 hours.

3 cups fresh or frozen black-eyed peas
5 teaspoons toasted sesame oil
1 tablespoon blackstrap molasses
2 tablespoons rice vinegar
1/4 cup soy sauce
6 tablespoons water
1 1/2 teaspoons minced garlic
1 teaspoon minced gingerroot
1 teaspoon salt
1/2 cup diced red pepper
1 1/2 cups uncooked basmati rice
5 cups light vegetable stock (page 162)
2 tablespoons butter or vegetable oil
1/2 cup arame (page 190)
1/2 cup minced fresh mint
1/4 cup dry white wine
1 tablespoon kuzu (page 192)
4 to 6 large lettuce leaves

Spicy Sliced Seitan with Garlic Noodles

Yield: 6 servings • Prep Time: 30 minutes • Cooking Time: 2 hours

2 1/2 cups uncooked seitan (page 184)
3 cups water
1/2 cup dry white wine
2 whole star anise
1/4 cup sake
8 tablespoons tamari
2 stalks lemon grass, completely flattened and cut in 2-inch pieces, or 2 teaspoons lime juice
4 smashed rounds gingerroot
1/4 cup minced garlic
1/4 teaspoon dried red pepper flakes
2 tablespoons rice syrup (page 193)
2 tablespoons mirin (page 193)
1/2 cup minced scallions
6 ounces rice stick noodles (page 193)
1 teaspoon salt
1/2 cup hearty vegetable stock (page 162)
1 teaspoon toasted sesame oil
2 tablespoons sesame seeds
3 tablespoons minced fresh mint

This dish can be prepared well in advance and is lovely served either warm or cold. It is an unusual and inviting addition to any picnic or potluck. Don't be put off by the long list of ingredients. The recipe is actually simple to make and absolutely mouthwatering.

1. Prepare the seitan according to directions on page 184. Shape it into 2 ovals, each about 8 inches long. Tie 4 or 5 pieces of twine snugly around each roll so that it will retain its shape as it cooks. Repeat this wrapping with the second piece of seitan.

2. In a 3-quart, heavy-bottomed saucepan, combine the water, wine, star anise, sake, tamari, lemon grass, ginger, 2 tablespoons garlic, pepper flakes, rice syrup, mirin, and 1/4 cup of scallions. Bring this to a boil, then remove from the heat and carefully place the seitan rolls in the broth. Cover and simmer gently for 2 hours. Move and rotate the seitan several times as it cooks to prevent it from sticking. Do not allow the liquid to boil, otherwise the seitan develops an unpleasant, spongy texture.

3. After 2 hours, remove the pan from the heat and cool the seitan in the broth. Remove the seitan from the broth, then strain and reserve the liquid. The seitan can be used immediately or it can be prepared ahead and refrigerated in the broth, if stored in an airtight container.

4. Before serving, remove the seitan from the broth and slice it on the diagonal into 1/4-inch-thick pieces. Place the sliced seitan and remaining broth in a saucepan and warm briefly as you prepare the noodles.

5. Cook the rice stick noodles in 3 quarts of rapidly boiling water until just tender. Drain immediately. Meanwhile, in a large skillet, combine the remaining 2 tablespoons garlic, salt, and stock. Cook rapidly, stirring occasionally, for 5 minutes. Remove from the heat and add the cooked noodles, sesame oil, sesame seeds, and mint. Toss to coat and turn out onto a large serving platter. Arrange the sliced seitan over this and sprinkle with remaining minced scallions.

Cook's Note: You may make seitan from scratch (page 184) which is a lengthy but satisfying process. If you choose to do so, allow yourself the extra prep time required. Alternatively, use the Arrowhead Mills Seitan Mix (page 185) and prepare the seitan in 5 minutes.

Tempeh with Lemon Grass and Coriander

Yield: 4 servings • Prep Time: 35 minutes • Cooking Time: 45 minutes

Here tempeh is bathed in a delicately scented coconut sauce and served with millet.

1. Preheat the oven to 375°F. Place the almonds on a baking sheet in the oven and toast them, stirring several times, until they are lightly browned to the core, about 12 minutes. Immediately pour the nuts onto a cold counter or plate so that they do not burn. Allow them to cool for 5 minutes, then place them in a blender or food processor fitted with the metal chopping blade. Add 1/2 cup water and purée until very smooth, scraping the sides of the beaker as necessary. Set this aside.

2. In a 3-quart saucepan, heat the oil over medium high heat until hot, but not smoking. Add the onion and cook, stirring constantly, for about 1 minute, or until the onion is completely coated with oil. Reduce the heat to medium and continue to cook, stirring frequently, until the onion just begins to brown, about 5 minutes. (Do not let the onion burn.) Add the garlic and galangal and reduce the heat to low. Continue to cook, stirring often, for 5 minutes.

3. Meanwhile, trim the tough tops from the lemon grass so that the stalks are about 4 inches long. Remove and discard all tough outer layers of each stalk. Place a stalk on the work surface and place the flat side of a cleaver over it. Firmly smash the cleaver with the side of your fist so that the lemon grass is flattened. Turn the stalk and flatten it in this manner on 2 other sides. Repeat this with the remaining lemon grass, then add them to the pan. Stir in the coconut milk and simmer for about 2 minutes.

4. Using your fingertips, rub the tamarind pulp and seeds to loosen them and mix them into their soaking water. Strain the water through a tea strainer into the coconut milk mixture. Add the coriander, cumin, ume paste, cinnamon, cayenne, cloves, and tempeh. Stir in the ground almond mixture. Cover and simmer for 30 minutes.

5. As the tempeh cooks, prepare the millet. Rinse the millet quickly, then turn it out onto a clean kitchen towel and rub it until mostly dry. Heat a skillet over medium high heat, then toast the millet, tossing it frequently, until it just begins to give off a slightly toasty aroma and begins to darken slightly. Do not let the millet burn. Immediately transfer it to the strainer. In a 2-quart saucepan, bring the remaining 3 cups of water to a boil. Stir in the millet and the salt. Bring to a boil, then reduce to a simmer and cook, stirring occasionally, until the millet is light and fluffy, about 30 minutes. Watch the water level as the millet cooks. If the water evaporates before the millet is cooked, stir in more water, 1/4 cup at a time. Once cooked, add the raisins, scallions, and cilantro to the millet; toss to mix evenly. Cover and set aside.

6. To serve, arrange the millet on a serving platter, leaving room in the center for the tempeh. Before serving the tempeh, remove the lemon grass, then taste the tempeh and adjust the seasonings. Pour the tempeh into the center of the millet nest and serve.

1/3 cup blanched almonds
3 1/2 cups water
2 tablespoons vegetable oil
1 cup diced onion
2 teaspoons minced garlic
1 1-inch piece galangal (page 191), sliced and smashed (or 1 teaspoon minced ginger-root)
4 stalks lemon grass
1 cup coconut milk
1 walnut-sized ball tamarind (page 195), softened in 3 table spoons boiling water
1 tablespoon ground coriander
2 teaspoons ground cumin
1 1/2 teaspoons umeboshi paste (page 196)
1 teaspoon cinnamon
1/4 teaspoon cayenne pepper
1/8 teaspoon ground cloves
1 pound tempeh, cubed
3/4 cup millet
1/4 teaspoon salt
1/2 cup raisins
1/4 cup minced scallions
1/4 cup minced cilantro

Stuffed Tofu Roll

Yield: 6 servings • Prep Time: 1 1/4 hours • Cooking Time: 35 minutes

This is our family's Thanksgiving "turkey," a recipe that is a favorite at our table among vegetarians and nonvegetarians alike. It is filled with a classic bread stuffing, and rice sheets, available at Asian markets, serve as an incredibly realistic skin for this vegetarian "bird." The recipe, therefore, is actually three in one:; the roll itself, the stuffing, and the sauce—a standard gravy.

The stuffing has the reminiscent flavor of a traditional bread stuffing. In this version, however, contrasting color of the spinach next to the tofu is lovely. You will have about 3 times as much as you need to fill one roll, but it seems you can never have too much stuffing at a Thanksgiving feast. You can vary the stuffing using rice or a pilaf, or you can add chestnuts or cranberries to the recipe that follows (see variations). As I worked to develop this recipe I came across a similar notion of a tofu roll recipe in the delightful Shoshoni Cookbook by Anne Sacks and Faith Stone. In it they used egg replacer as a stabilizer in a tofu roll. This inspired me to try potato flour here.

Stuffing

Yield: About 5 1/2 cups

BREAD STUFFING:
3 cups dried bread cubes
1 1/2 cups dried corn bread
1/4 to 1/2 cup mushroom stock
   (page 163)
3 tablespoons butter
1 onion, diced
2 stalks celery, sliced
8 ounces mushrooms, sliced
1 tablespoon lemon juice
2 teaspoons minced garlic
1 teaspoon salt
1 1/2 teaspoons dried thyme
1 teaspoon celery seeds
1/4 cup minced fresh parsley
1 cup steamed spinach,
   chopped and squeezed dry
1/2 cup chopped pecans or
   walnuts (optional)

1. In a large mixing bowl, combine the two types of bread and enough stock to begin to soften. Set this aside as you cook the vegetables.

2. In a 10-inch skillet, heat the butter over medium until bubbly. Add the onion and celery and cook, stirring often, until the onions are soft, about 8 minutes. Add the mushrooms and toss to coat with butter. Cook for 1 minute, then add the lemon juice. Continue to cook, stirring often, until the mushrooms are soft, about 8 minutes.

3. Add the onion mixture to the bread cubes. Stir in the garlic, salt, thyme, celery seeds, parsley, spinach, and nuts. Mix well. Add more stock if the bread is still very hard. Taste and adjust the seasonings. The stuffing can be prepared up to 3 days in advance if refrigerated in an airtight container.

Tofu Roll

TOFU ROLL:
1 pound firm tofu
3 tablespoons soy sauce
1 tablespoon umeboshi paste
   (page 196)
3 tablespoons minced fresh
   parsley
1 tablespoon dried sage, crushed
2 teaspoons dried thyme
1 teaspoon dried oregano, crushed
1/2 teaspoon dried marjoram,
   crushed
1/8 teaspoon nutmeg
1/8 teaspoon white pepper
2 garlic cloves, pressed

1. Drain the tofu and slice it into 1/2-inch slices. Place these on a clean kitchen towel with a second towel on top. Place a heavy cutting board on top of this and press gently. Allow the tofu to drain for 30 minutes.

2. In a blender or food processor fitted with the metal chopping blade, combine the pressed tofu with the soy sauce, ume paste, parsley, sage, thyme, oregano, marjoram, nutmeg, white pepper, garlic, tahini, potato flour, baking powder, and scallions. Blend, scraping down the sides of the beaker as necessary, until the mixture is absolutely smooth, about 3 to 4 minutes.

3. Fill a large bowl with cold water. Carefully sink the rice sheets into the water and allow them to soften completely. Lay a clean kitchen towel on a work surface. Remove two of the sheets from the water and gently squeeze most of the water from them, being careful not to tear the sheets. Place one on the kitchen

towel and the second, overlapping it halfway, next to it. They should form a rough rectangle. Remove the remaining two rice sheets from the water, squeeze them and lay them on top of the first for a double thickness.

4. With a palette knife or spatula, spread the puréed tofu mixture out evenly over the rice sheets to about 3/4 inch of the edge on three sides and 1 inch of the edge on one of the long sides. Spread 2 cups of the bread stuffing with spinach over the tofu in an even layer. Brush the edge of the rice sheet that has a 1-inch border with water, then using the towel as a guide, roll the rice sheets into a long cylinder towards that edge. Allow the roll to rest on its seam so that it will seal shut. Tuck the ends of the rice sheets under and transfer the roll to a lightly buttered baking sheet. Brush with melted butter and refrigerate, covered, for 2 to 8 hours.

5. Preheat the oven to 375°F. Bake the roll, uncovered, until it is lightly browned and slightly firm to the touch. Remove from the oven and cool briefly, then transfer to a cutting board and slice into rings. Arrange the rings on serving plates or a platter, drizzle a small amount of mushroom sauce over the rings and serve immediately.

1 tablespoon tahini (optional)
3 tablespoons potato flour
1 teaspoon non-aluminum baking powder
1/2 cup minced scallions
4 large (12-inch) rice sheets

Mushroom Gravy

Yield: About 3 cups

1. In a 2-quart saucepan, heat the butter over medium flame, until completely melted and beginning to bubble. Add the flour and cook, stirring constantly for 2 minutes. Whisk in the wine and continue to cook until the smell of alcohol is nonexistent. Whisk in the stock and mushrooms, then reduce to a simmer. Cook, stirring often, until the sauce has a creamy texture and is smooth in taste. Remove from the heat. Stir in the parsley and milk and season with salt and pepper to taste.

MUSHROOM GRAVY:
2 tablespoons butter
3 1/2 tablespoons flour
1/2 cup dry white wine (optional)
2 1/2 cups mushroom stock (page 163)
1 cup quartered mushrooms, steamed or sautéed until soft
Salt and pepper to taste
2 tablespoons minced fresh parsley
3 tablespoons milk or cream (optional)

Variation

1. Prepare the tofu as described above. Mix 1/3 cup pesto (page 176) or miso pesto (page 176) into the spinach stuffing, then fill and shape the tofu roll as directed above. Serve with leek sauce (page 178).

Vegetarian B'Stilla

Yield: 6 servings • Prep Time: 45 minutes • Cooking Time: 40 minutes

1 1/2 pounds tempeh
2 cups light vegetable stock (page 162) or water
1 tablespoon honey
1 tablespoon olive oil
1 cup diced red onion
1 tablespoon minced gingerroot
8 cloves garlic, sliced thin
1/4 cup minced fresh parsley
3/4 teaspoon crushed saffron
1 1/2 teaspoons salt
1 teaspoon ground cumin
1/4 teaspoon cayenne
1/4 teaspoon ground allspice
1/2 pound soft tofu
1/4 cup minced fresh cilantro
1 orange
1 cup blanched almonds
3 tablespoons maple sugar
1 pound filo dough, thawed
5 tablespoons melted butter
3 tablespoons orange flower water
1 1/2 teaspoons cinnamon
3 tablespoons confectioner's sugar (optional)

This is a delectable vegetarian version of a Moroccan specialty (also spelled bastila or b'steeya) that is traditionally made with either pigeon or chicken and wrapped in a crisp dough, called warkha (similar to filo).

1. Cut slabs of tempeh in half widthwise, to produce thinner slabs. Cut these into thin strips that are about 3 inches long. Put the tempeh in a 2-quart saucepan with the stock, honey, oil, red onion, ginger, garlic, parsley, saffron, half the salt, cumin, cayenne pepper, and allspice. Place this over a medium flame and bring to a slow boil, stirring occasionally. Reduce to a simmer, cover, and cook, stirring often, for 20 minutes.

2. Drain the tofu, place it in a bowl and mash it into small pieces with a fork. Stir in the cilantro and remaining salt. Grate 1 1/2 teaspoons of zest from the orange and set it aside in a small mixing bowl. Then squeeze and strain the juice from the orange into the tofu.

3. In a food processor fitted with the metal chopping blade or a blender, combine the almonds and maple sugar. Process until the nuts are fine and evenly ground, scraping down the sides of the bowl as necessary. Add this mixture to the grated orange zest and mix well.

4. Unwrap the filo dough and lay it out flat on a clean work space. Using a paring knife and a round 12-inch platter or cake pan as your guide, cut through all layers of the dough to form a stack of 12-inch circles. Cover the circles with a very lightly dampened kitchen towel so that the pastry does not dry out and crack. Save the trimmings to use for another use.

5. Lightly brush a pizza pan or cookie sheet with butter. Stir the orange flower water and 1/2 teaspoon cinnamon into the remaining butter. Lay one round of filo in the middle of the pizza pan. Arrange 4 more circles of dough on top of the first piece, so that the new circles form an overlapping petal-like design. Repeat this pattern again with 5 new pieces of pastry, then brush with melted butter and repeat with 2 new layers, fashioned in the same manner. Brush once more, and repeat again with 2 new layers of filo. Arrange 2/3 of the nut mixture so that it forms a 9-inch circle in the center of the filo, thus leaving about a 2 1/2-inch border of uncovered dough around the edge. Place the tofu on top of this and the tempeh as a third layer. Top all of this with the remaining nut mixture. Carefully bring the uncovered edges of the filo up over the top of the mound of filling, and press it gently to shape the pastry into a neat round. Now repeat the pastry layering on top of this, again forming 6 layers of the flower-like pattern and brushing with butter between layers. This time, tuck the edges of the pastry under the b'stilla. Brush the entire surface with butter and prick it several times in the center with the tines of a fork. The b'stilla may be prepared up to 24 hours in advance to this point if covered and refrigerated. (Pricking the pastry is easier after the pie has chilled for at least 20 minutes.) It can be frozen, tightly covered, for up to 2 months.

6. Preheat the oven to 450ºF. Bake the b'stilla in the center of the oven for 10 minutes. Reduce the heat to 350ºF. and continue to bake until the pie is lightly browned and puffed, about 30 minutes. Remove the b'stilla from the oven and allow it to cool for 5 minutes.

7. Cut four 2-inch-long strips of waxed paper, the width of the roll. Place them on a serving plate so that they form a square and cover the edges of the plate. Transfer the b'stilla to the center of the plate, allowing the waxed paper to hang out around its borders. Sift the confectioner's sugar through a tea strainer over the top of the b'stilla to form an even layer. Gently place additional strips of waxed paper on top of the confectioner's sugar so that they leave only 3 or 4 strips of sugar, like spokes in a wheel. Sift the cinnamon over these exposed strips, then carefully remove all pieces of wax paper. (The bottom strips will have protected the plate from the sprinklings and top pieces will have acted like a stencil for the cinnamon.) Serve at once.

Cook's Note: Give yourself ample time to let this chill for at least 20 minutes before baking.

Wild Mushroom B'Stilla

Yield: 6 servings • Prep Time: 40 minutes • Cooking Time: 40 minutes

1/4 pound fresh morel
   mushrooms
1/2 pound fresh tree oyster
   mushrooms
1 pound button mushrooms
2 teaspoons olive oil
2 teaspoons butter
1 cup chopped leeks
2 lemons
4 cloves garlic, sliced thin
3 tablespoons fresh tarragon
1 teaspoons salt
1/8 teaspoon black pepper
Pinch of cayenne pepper
3/4 pound soft tofu
2 cups cooked spinach
   or 2 packages frozen chopped
   spinach, thawed
2 tablespoons tamari
2 tablespoons rice vinegar
1/4 cup fresh parsley
1 cup blanched almonds
3 tablespoons maple sugar
1 pound filo dough, thawed
5 tablespoons melted butter
1 teaspoon cinnamon
3 tablespoons confectioner's sugar
   (optional)

This is a sumptuous variation on the traditional B'Stilla. If you are feeling extravagant with time and ingredients, prepare fillings for both recipes, then assemble two B'Stillas with alternating layers of both fillings. Freeze one B'Stilla for up to 2 months.

1. Clean the mushrooms (page 35) and place them on clean kitchen towels to dry for at least 20 minutes. Slice large morels in half lengthwise and cut the tree oysters into 1-inch pieces. Slice the button mushrooms into 1/4-inch-thick slices.

2. In a 12-inch skillet, heat the oil and butter over medium heat until the butter is melted. Add the leeks and cook, stirring frequently, until they are soft, about 8 minutes. Add the mushrooms and toss to mix well. Squeeze the juice from one lemon over the mushrooms, add the garlic and continue to cook until they are very soft, about 12 minutes. Mix in the tarragon, salt, pepper, and cayenne. Set this aside to cool. This filling can be prepared up to 3 days in advance if refrigerated in an airtight container.

3. Drain the tofu, place it in a bowl and mash it into small pieces with a fork. Chop the spinach finely, then stir it into the tofu. Add the tamari, rice vinegar, and parsley, and set this aside. This filling can be prepared up to 3 days in advance if refrigerated in an airtight container.

4. In a food processor fitted with the metal chopping blade or a blender, combine the almonds and maple sugar. Process until the nuts are evenly ground, scraping down the sides of the bowl as necessary.

5. Unwrap the filo dough and lay it out flat on a clean work space. Using a paring knife and a round 12-inch platter or cake pan as your guide, cut through all layers of the dough to form a stack of 12-inch circles. Cover the circles with a very lightly dampened kitchen towel so that the pastry does not dry out and crack. Save the trimmings to use for another use (see Vegetable Pot Pie, page 108; or Featherlight Croutons, page 167).

6. Lightly brush a pizza pan or cookie sheet with melted butter, then stir 1/4 teaspoon cinnamon and the juice from the second lemon into the remaining butter. Lay one round of filo in the middle of the pizza pan. Lightly brush this with butter, then arrange 4 more circles of dough on top of the first piece, so that the new circles form an overlapping petal-like design. Butter all layers where they overlap the original 12-inch circle Repeat this pattern again with 5 new pieces of pastry. Brush with melted butter and repeat with 2 new layers, fashioned in the same manner. Arrange 2/3 of the nut mixture so that it forms a 10-inch circle in the center of the filo, thus leaving about a 2-inch border of uncovered dough around the edge. Place the tofu mixture on top of this and the mushrooms as a third layer. Top all of this with the remaining nut mixture. Carefully bring the uncovered edges of the filo up over the top of the mound of filling, folding them one by one and brushing with butter as you fold so that the layers stick to each other. Press the "pie" gently to shape the pastry into a neat round. Now layer the remaining 3 rounds of pastry over the top of the pie, brushing with butter between layers. Tuck the edges of the pastry under the b'stilla. Brush the entire surface with butter and prick it several times in the center with the tines of a fork. The b'stilla may be prepared up to 24 hours in advance to this point if covered and refrigerated. (Pricking the pastry is easier after the pie has chilled for at least 20 minutes.) It can be frozen, tightly covered, for up to 2 months.

7. Preheat the oven to 450°F. Bake the b'stilla in the center of the oven for 10 minutes. Reduce the heat to 350°F. and continue to bake until the pie is lightly browned and puffed, about 30 minutes. Remove the b'stilla from the oven and allow it to cool for 5 minutes. Cook frozen b'stilla an extra 20 minutes.

8. Cut four 2-inch long strips of waxed paper, the width of the roll of paper. Place them on a serving plate so that they form a square and cover the edges of the plate. Transfer the b'stilla to the center of the plate, allowing the waxed paper to hang out around its borders. Sift the confectioner's sugar through a tea strainer, over the top of the b'stilla to form an even layer. Gently place additional strips of waxed paper on top of the confectioner's sugar so that they leave only 3 or 4 strips of sugar showing, like spokes in a wheel. Sift the cinnamon over these exposed strips, then carefully remove all pieces of waxed paper. (The bottom strips will protect the plate from the sprinklings and top pieces will act like a stencil for the cinnamon.) Serve at once.

Cook's Note: Leave yourself ample time to chill this dish at least 20 minutes before baking.

Crispy Soba Noodles with Tempeh and Garlic Sauce

Yield: 4 servings • Prep Time: 20 minutes • Cooking Time: 20 minutes

The contrast in textures and interplay of tastes make this tempeh dish memorable. Serve it with baked yams and steamed broccoli.

1. Crumble the tempeh and place it in a shallow baking dish. Combine the miso, ginger, mirin, cumin, and apple juice. Pour this over the tempeh and mix well. Marinate this for at least 2 hours. The tempeh can marinate, covered and refrigerated, for up to 24 hours.

2. Place the carrots and celery in the top rack of a steamer over rapidly boiling water. Cover and steam for 3 minutes. Add the squash and bell pepper, then continue to steam for 3 minutes. Immediately transfer to a strainer to prevent overcooking.

3. Preheat the oven to 450°F. In a 3-quart saucepan, bring 2 quarts of water to a rolling boil. Add the noodles and cook, stirring occasionally, until they are almost al dente, about 6 minutes. Drain the noodles. Immediately brush a pizza pan with sesame oil, then shape the cooked noodles into an 8-inch round on the oiled sheet. Sprinkle the remaining oil over the noodles, then place them in the oven and allow them to crisp while finishing the dish.

4. In a blender, combine the scallions and garlic. Blend briefly, then add the stock, maple sugar, and salt. Blend until evenly ground. Transfer this mixture to a wok and cook over medium high heat for 2 minutes. Add the tempeh with its marinade and cook for another 5 minutes. Add the cooked vegetables and toss.

5. Slide the noodles off the pizza pan onto a platter. Pour the tempeh mixture over the noodles. Sprinkle the sesame seeds on top and scatter the cilantro around the platter. Serve at once.

Cook's Note: Allow two hours marinating time for the tempeh.

8 ounces tempeh
1/4 cup red miso
1 tablespoon minced gingerroot
3 tablespoons mirin (page 193)
2 teaspoons ground cumin
1/3 cup unfiltered apple juice
1 cup julienne-sliced carrots
3/4 cup sliced celery
1 cup julienne-sliced yellow
  summer squash
1 small red bell pepper, sliced
6 ounces soba noodles (page 194)
1 tablespoon toasted sesame oil
1/2 cup minced scallions
6 cloves garlic
1/2 cup light vegetable stock
  (page 162)
1 1/2 tablespoons maple sugar
1/4 teaspoon salt
2 tablespoons sesame seeds
Sprigs fresh cilantro

Pecan-Mushroom-Stuffed Tofu
with Chard and Saga Cheese

Yield: 4 servings • Prep Time: 55 minutes • Cooking Time: 20 minutes

2 pounds firm or extra-firm tofu
3 tablespoons tamari
1/2 cup tawny port
5 cloves garlic, sliced thin
1 cup pecans
1/2 pound mushrooms
3 tablespoons olive oil
1/4 cup minced shallots
1 tablespoon orange juice
1/4 teaspoon salt
1/8 teaspoon nutmeg
Pinch of black pepper
Pinch of cayenne pepper
6 ounces saga blue cheese
   or tofu "feta" (page 173)
8 cups chard leaves, chopped
   (about 8 ounces chard)
2 small beets, peeled and grated

With a few last-minute cooking steps, this elegant dish can be prepared ahead. The tofu may be stuffed and made ready to steam up to 24 hours in advance and you can prep all the vegetables. To put it together, simply steam the chard and tofu just before serving.

1. Drain the tofu and cut it into 1 1/2-inch cubes. Place these on a clean kitchen towel with a second towel on top. Weight this down with a cutting board and allow the tofu to drain for 30 minutes. Take each small block of tofu and, with a paring knife and spoon, hollow out a rectangular cavity in the center, leaving a 1/4-inch border around the edges of the top and about 1/3-inch thickness on the bottom of the block. Use the hollowed-out tofu for one of the scrambled tofu dishes (see recipe index) or to make tofu "feta" for this recipe.

2. In a shallow baking dish, combine the tamari, 2 tablespoons of port and 1 clove of garlic. Place the blocks of tofu in this marinade and spoon the marinade over. Allow them to rest at room temperature as you prepare the stuffing.

3. Preheat the oven to 375°F. Place the pecans on a baking sheet in the center of the oven and bake, stirring once or twice, until they are brown to the core, about 12 minutes. Immediately turn them out onto a clean kitchen towel to cool. Finely chop 2/3 cup of the nuts and place them in a small bowl to use for for the filling. Set the remaining nuts aside to garnish the finished dish.

4. Meanwhile, slice the mushrooms, then finely mince them. Place the mushrooms in the center of a clean kitchen towel. Draw the edges of the towel together and twist the towel so that the mushrooms form a ball. Hold the towel over the sink, then twist and squeeze the ball tightly to extract as much mushroom liquid as possible.

5. In a 10-inch skillet, heat 1 1/2 tablespoons oil over high heat until hot, but not smoking. Add the shallots and cook, stirring constantly, until they are all coated with oil, about 1 minute. Reduce the heat to medium, add the remaining sliced garlic and continue to cook, stirring often, until the shallots are soft, about 8 minutes. Add the mushrooms, orange juice, salt, nutmeg, pepper, and cayenne. Cook, stirring frequently, until the liquid from the mushroom is released and then cooks off, about 10 minutes. Stir the chopped nuts and 1/4 of the cheese into this filling and set aside. The filling can be prepared up to 4 days in advance if refrigerated in an airtight container.

6. Remove the tofu from the marinade. Divide the filling evenly among the blocks of tofu, pressing it firmly in place. Arrange the tofu in one layer on 1 or 2 flat steaming racks. Place the steaming racks over, not touching, rapidly boiling water. Cover tightly and steam for 20 minutes.

7. As the tofu steams, heat the remaining 1 1/2 tablespoons oil in a 10- to 12-inch skillet over medium high heat. When it is hot, but not smoking, add the remaining 4 cloves of garlic and toss briefly to impregnate the oil with their scent. Add as much of the chard as possible and cook, stirring often, until the leaves wilt and more can be added. Again, add as much of the remaining chard as possible. Stir in the remaining port and any marinade that remains from the tofu. Continue to cook the chard, adding more as you can and stirring often,

Seitan Bourguignon
(page 121)

Cinnamon-Pumpkin-Stuffed Tofu
(page 141)

Polenta "Salmon" with Greens and Mustard Sauce
(page 44)

Barbecued Seitan Salad
(page 56)

Lettuce-Wrapped Tofu
(page 124)

Crusty Lemon Tofu with Wild Mushrooms
(page 77)

Fava Beans in Parchment
(page 96)

Stuffed Shells with Asparagus Sauce
(page 152)

until all of the leaves are in the skillet and the chard is tender. Remove the chard from the heat, add the remaining cheese and pecans. Toss well.

8. Turn the chard mixture out onto one large or 6 individual serving plates. Arrange nests of grated beet on top of the chard and place the steamed tofu in these nests. Sprinkle the remaining nuts over the nests and serve immediately.

Variations

1. To reduce the fat, use only 1/3 cup pecans, putting them all into the filling. Also eliminate the saga from the filling and use only 3 ounces to sprinkle over the cooked greens.

2. For a cinnamon-pumpkin-stuffed tofu, replace the mushroom filling with a purée made from 3 cups cooked pumpkin flavored with 1 teaspoon cinnamon, 1 teaspoon curry powder, and 1/4 teaspoon salt.

3. For a Thanksgiving-style dish, shape and marinate the tofu as described above. Stuff each piece of tofu with bread stuffing (page 134), then bake the tofu packages in their marinade at 375°F. for 20 minutes. Serve on a bed of steamed chard, if desired.

Cook's Note: Be certain to use firm tofu as the boxes must be handled several times during the preparation, and soft or, worse yet, silken tofu will break apart. Allow time for the tofu to be pressed for at least 30 minutes.

Steamed Stuffed Tofu with Cauliflower

Yield: 6 servings • Prep Time: 45 minutes • Cooking Time: 15 minutes

1 1/2 pounds firm or extra-firm
    tofu
1/4 cup blanched almonds, toasted
    (page 35)
1/4 cup dried currants
1 serrano pepper, minced
1 teaspoon garlic, minced
1/4 cup minced scallions
1 cup nonfat plain yogurt
1 tablespoon honey
1 tablespoon curry powder
1/8 teaspoon salt
1/4 cup water
1/4 cup chopped mint
1 small head cauliflower, cut in
    florets
1 small yam, peeled and cut in
    1/4-inch cubes
4 cups chopped kale leaves
2 tablespoons orange juice
4 teaspoons soy sauce

Flavors of the Far East and India are combined in this magnificent dish. Serve it with rice.

1. Drain the tofu and cut it into 1 1/4-inch-thick slabs. Place them on a clean kitchen towel and cover with a second towel. Put a heavy cutting board on top of this and press it down firmly, but not so much that the tofu cracks. Allow the tofu to drain as you prepare the rest of the dish for steaming.

2. Place the almonds in a food processor fitted with the metal chopping blade or a blender. Process for about 30 seconds in order to break the almonds into small pieces. Add the currants, serrano pepper, garlic, and scallions, then continue to process, scraping down the sides of the bowl as necessary, until the mixture forms a rough paste. Set this filling aside.

3. In a small mixing bowl, combine the yogurt, honey, curry powder, and salt. Mix well, then whisk in the water. Beat briefly so that the mixture becomes slightly frothy. Stir in the mint and set this sauce aside.

4. Cut the tofu into 1 1/2-inch cubes. Using a paring knife, hollow out a rectangular cup in each piece of tofu, leaving about 1/4 inch of tofu as a rim around the top of the hole and 1/3 inch on the bottom. Divide the filling evenly among the pieces of tofu, stuffing it into the hollowed-out space and mounding it up on top. The tofu can be stuffed up to 24 hours in advance if refrigerated, tightly covered.

5. Place the cauliflower in one tier of a steamer over rapidly boiling water. Cover tightly and steam until it begins to look as if it is made of porcelain, about 3 minutes. Add the yam and continue to steam, tightly covered and stirring once or twice, until both are just tender, about 8 minutes. When they are cooked, toss them to combine evenly, then turn the vegetables out onto a serving platter, arranging them in a circle around the edge.

6. Meanwhile, place the kale in the second tier of the same steamer. After the kale has been in for 1 minute, remove the lid and sprinkle it with the orange juice. Arrange the tofu on top of the kale, filling side up. Cover and continue to steam for 12 minutes. Transfer the kale and tofu to the center of the platter, then sprinkle the soy sauce over the kale. Serve immediately with the curry sauce alongside.

Cook's Note: Be certain to use firm tofu for the boxes since soft or, worse yet, silken tofu will break with the amount of handling required.

Layered Crêpe Cake with Leek and Watercress Sauce

Yield: 6 servings • Prep Time: 45 minutes • Cooking Time: 35 minutes

This classic method for serving crêpes—layering them with various stuffings—gives latitude in serving time. Both cake and sauce can be prepared ahead, then baked before serving.

1. Have crêpes prepared ahead. If they have been frozen, have them thoroughly thawed before proceeding with the recipe.

2. In a 12-inch skillet, heat the oil over medium high heat until hot, but not smoking. Add the button mushrooms and toss to coat with oil. Squeeze the lemon juice over the mushrooms and toss again. Reduce the heat slightly and cook, stirring constantly, until the mushrooms begin to soften, about 5 minutes. Add the porcini mushrooms and their soaking liquid. Stir in the shallots, 1 teaspoon garlic, the tomatoes, cinnamon, thyme, 1/4 teaspoon salt, the black pepper, and saffron. Cook, stirring often, until most of the liquid has evaporated, about 10 minutes. Mix in the bread crumbs, then taste and adjust the seasonings. Set aside.

3. Remove and discard the spinach stems. Wash the leaves in several changes of cold water. Place the spinach in the top of a steamer rack over rapidly boiling water. Cook, covered, until soft, about 6 minutes. Immediately transfer the spinach to a strainer and place it in the sink under cold running water to stop its cooking. Once cool to the touch, place the spinach in the center of a clean kitchen towel. Draw the corners of the towel together and twist it to form a ball of spinach. Twist and squeeze the spinach to extract as much liquid as possible, then place it on a cutting board and chop finely. Place the chopped spinach in a mixing bowl. Add the remaining teaspoon garlic and 1/4 teaspoon salt, then stir in the tofu "feta" and the dill. Taste and adjust the seasonings. Set this filling aside.

4. Lightly butter a cookie sheet. Preheat the oven to 375°F. Place 2 crêpes on the cookie sheet about 4 inches apart. Place a thin layer of mushroom filling on each, then top with a crêpe. Top these with a layer of the spinach filling and another crêpe. Repeat these layers until all crêpes and the fillings have been used. Top each cake with Parmesan. These cakes can be prepared up to 4 hours in advance if refrigerated, tightly covered. (Bring to room temperature before baking.) Place the cookie sheet in the center of the oven and bake until the crêpe cakes are piping hot, about 20 minutes.

5. To prepare the sauce, in a 2-quart saucepan combine the leeks, eggplant, stock, and sliced garlic. Bring this to a boil, then reduce to a simmer and cook, covered, until the eggplant is tender, about 20 minutes. Transfer the sauce to a food processor fitted with the metal chopping blade or a blender and purée, scraping down the sides of the bowl as necessary, until the sauce is very smooth. Return the sauce to the clean saucepan and stir in the watercress. Season to taste with salt and pepper.

6. To serve, place 2 small pools of sauce on an oval serving platter. With the aid of a long metal palette knife or spatula, transfer the cooked crêpe cakes to the platter, placing one in the center of each pool of sauce. Garnish with additional watercress and serve the remaining sauce on the side. At the table, slice wedges from the cakes with a sharp, thin-bladed knife.

Cook's Note: The components of this dish (crêpes, filling, and sauce) may be prepared in advance, and the cake itself can be assembled well ahead. Warm before serving.

12 herb crêpes (page 171)
1 tablespoon olive oil
12 ounces button mushrooms, sliced
1 tablespoon lemon juice
1 ounce dried porcini mushrooms, softened in 1/4 cup hot water
1/2 cup minced shallots or scallions
2 teaspoons minced garlic
1 pound fresh tomatoes, chopped, or 1 16-ounce can chopped tomatoes, drained
1/2 teaspoon cinnamon
1/2 teaspoon dried thyme
1/2 teaspoon salt
1/4 teaspoon black pepper
1/8 teaspoon ground saffron
1/2 cup dry bread crumbs
2 pounds fresh spinach
6 ounces tofu "feta" (page 173) or mild goat cheese
2 tablespoons snipped fresh dill
2 teaspoons butter
2 tablespoons grated Parmesan
2 leeks, chopped
1/2 pound peeled and cubed eggplant
1 cup mushroom stock (page 163) or light vegetable stock (page 162)
4 cloves garlic, sliced
3/4 cup chopped watercress
Salt and pepper to taste
Additional watercress leaves as garnish

Double Artichoke Soufflé

Yield: 4 servings • Prep Time: 1 3/4 hours • Cooking Time: 30 minutes

1 pound Jerusalem artichokes
1 tablespoon olive oil
1 small bulb garlic
1 orange
1 lemon
8 fresh baby artichokes or substitute frozen artichoke hearts
2 tablespoons butter, melted
1/2 cup minced shallots
2 tablespoons flour
1 1/2 cups porcini mushroom
   stock (page 163)
1/2 teaspoon salt
1/4 teaspoon white pepper
1/8 teaspoon nutmeg
Pinch cayenne
2 egg yolks
3 tablespoons minced fresh
   tarragon or 1/2 tablespoon
   dried
6 egg whites
1/4 teaspoon cream of tartar
3 tablespoons grated Parmesan

Jerusalem artichokes, which are actually the root of a sunflower native to North America, are coupled here with true baby artichokes for a flavorful soufflé. Serve it with Orange "Hollandaise" (page 130) or garlicky kale sauce (page 178).

1. Preheat the oven to 350°F. Wash the Jerusalem artichokes well, scrubbing them carefully over all the nooks and crannies to remove all dirt. Your scrubbing should leave only a thin, delicate layer of skin over the entire surface of each Jerusalem artichoke. Coat a 2-quart baking dish with a layer of oil. Place the artichokes and garlic (whole) in the dish, then drizzle the remaining oil and butter over them. Cover tightly and bake, turning occasionally, until both the garlic and artichokes are soft when squeezed. The garlic will be ready after about 1 hour, the artichokes after about 1 1/2 hours. Remove each from the oven when soft and allow it to cool on a cake rack.

2. As the Jerusalem artichokes cook, grate the zest from the orange and set it aside. Squeeze the juice from the orange into a small bowl, then squeeze juice from half of the lemon into this. Trim tough outer leaves from the artichokes and cut off the sharp tips of each, then rub them with the second lemon half so that the juice will retard discoloration. Place the baby artichokes in the top rack of a steamer over rapidly boiling water and steam until they are very tender, about 20 minutes. Immediately transfer them to a strainer and place under cold running water to stop their cooking. Drain on a clean kitchen towel as you finish preparing the recipe. (The artichokes can be cooked up to 3 days in advance if refrigerated in an airtight container.)

3. Remove the Jerusalem artichokes and garlic from the oven when they are soft. Cut the artichokes into small pieces and place them in a food processor fitted with the metal chopping blade. Trim the top from the garlic and squeeze the meat from the head of each clove, then place it in the food processor. Purée until very smooth, scraping down the sides of the bowl.

4. In a 2-quart saucepan, heat 1 1/2 tablespoons of the butter over medium heat until hot, but not smoking. Add the shallots and cook, stirring constantly, until they are coated with butter, about 1 minute. Reduce the heat to medium low and continue to cook, stirring often, until they are translucent, about 8 minutes. Raise the heat slightly and add the flour. Stir constantly for about 1 1/2 minutes to begin cooking the flour, then whisk in the stock. Add the salt, pepper, nutmeg, and cayenne. Mix well and continue to cook, stirring constantly, for 2 minutes. Remove this soufflé base from the heat and whisk in the Jerusalem artichoke purée, egg yolks, and tarragon. This base can be prepared up to 2 days in advance if refrigerated in an airtight container. Bring it to room temperature before proceeding with the recipe.

5. Preheat the oven to 375°F. With the remaining 1/2 tablespoon of butter, grease one 8-cup or six 1 1/2-cup soufflé dishes. You may fit them with a paper collar to give more rise to the soufflés. To do this, cut pieces of parchment that are long enough to wrap around the circumference of the mold. Fold the parchment so that it is about 3 1/2 inches wide. Wrap this strip around the mold and tie it securely beneath the rim of the mold. Butter both the parchment and the mold.

6. In a copper or stainless steel mixing bowl, beat the egg whites with a balloon whisk or electric mixer until they become frothy. Add the cream of tartar and continue to beat until the whites form stiff peaks. Gently fold about 1/2 cup of the whites into the soufflé base to lighten it, then fold the lightened base gradually back into the whites. Fill the mold(s) half full with the soufflé mixture, then arrange a layer of the cooked artichokes on this. Top with the remaining soufflé mixture and sprinkle with grated Parmesan if desired. Immediately place the soufflé in the center of the preheated oven and bake for 30 minutes. When ready, it will have puffed up above the top of the mold and will be lightly browned. Serve immediately.

Variation

1. You may omit the egg yolks—saving on fat and cholesterol—but increase the flour to 3 tablespoons and expect the soufflé to be more delicate.

Cook's Note: The prep time includes 1 1/2 hours for baking the Jerusalem artichokes.

Shiitake Eggplant Rolls

Yield: 4 servings • Prep Time: 30 minutes • Cooking Time: 20 minutes

This delightful variation on the classic eggplant roulade is festive and satisfying.

1. Wash the eggplant well, then dry it and trim off and discard the stem end. Slice the eggplant crosswise into 1/4-inch-wide rounds. Place the rounds on a clean kitchen towel and sprinkle on both sides with 1 teaspoon of salt. Allow the eggplant to "sweat" for 30 minutes at room temperature.

2. Preheat the broiler to high. Pat the eggplant dry. Lightly brush a baking sheet with light sesame oil, then brush the eggplant slices with the remaining oil. Place the slices on the baking sheet and broil, turning once, until the slices are soft and have begun to brown, about 8 minutes. As the slices are cooked, remove them to a plate.

3. Drain the tofu and place it in a bowl with the rice vinegar, rice syrup, 2 1/4 teaspoons garlic, the tamari, and scallions. Mix well with a fork, breaking the tofu into small pieces so that it resembles large-curd cottage cheese. This filling may be prepared up to 24 hours in advance.

4. In a wok or 12-inch skillet, heat the peanut oil over high heat until hot, but not smoking. Add the cabbage and toss well. Cook, stirring constantly, until the cabbage softens. Add the bell pepper, lily buds, mushrooms, and carrot. Cook, stirring constantly, until all the vegetables begin to soften, about 2 minutes. Remove them from the heat, stir in the sesame oil, and set aside.

5. In a 2-quart saucepan, combine the stock, wine vinegar, remaining 2 1/2 teaspoons garlic, and ginger. Bring to a boil, then reduce the heat slightly and cook, stirring occasionally, for 5 minutes. Stir in the chili paste with garlic. Combine the kuzu with water and stir it into the stock. Bring to a boil, just to thicken.

6. Preheat the oven to 375°F. Cover the bottom of a 9- by 13-inch baking pan with a thin layer of sauce. Place the eggplant slices on a work surface and fill each with a strip of the tofu filling. Cover with a thin layer of the cabbage mixture. Roll the slice of eggplant around the filling so that its edges overlap. Place each roulade in the casserole, seam side down, lining the roulades up so their edges touch. Pour the remaining sauce over the roulades. Bake the roulades, covered, in the center of the oven until they are piping hot, about 25 minutes.

1 large eggplant, about 1 1/2 pounds
1 1/2 teaspoons salt
1 tablespoon light sesame oil
1/2 pound soft tofu
2 tablespoons sweet rice vinegar
1 tablespoon rice syrup (page 193)
5 teaspoons minced garlic
1/4 cup tamari
1/4 cup minced scallions
2 tablespoons peanut or corn oil
4 cups shredded napa cabbage
1 1/2 cups shredded red bell pepper
1/4 cup dried lily buds, softened in hot water, then drained and shredded
6 shiitake mushrooms, softened in hot water, then drained and shredded
1 1/2 cups grated carrot
1/2 teaspoon toasted sesame oil
2 1/2 cups light vegetable stock (page 162)
1 1/2 tablespoons red wine vinegar
2 teaspoons minced gingerroot
1/2 to 1 teaspoon chili paste with garlic (page 190)
2 tablespoons kuzu (page 192) + 1 tablespoon cold water

Spicy Baked Beans with Posole

Yield: 6 servings • Prep Time: 25 minutes • Cooking Time: 2 1/2 hours

1 ancho chili, softened in hot
water
1 chipotle chili, softened in hot
water
1 tablespoon olive oil
1 cup diced white onion
2 teaspoons minced garlic
1 1/2 cup diced green bell pepper
1 cup diced red bell pepper
3 cups cooked pinto beans
2 teaspoons ground cumin
1 teaspoon dried oregano
1 teaspoon cinnamon
1/4 teaspoon dried thyme
1 bay leaf
2 cups chopped fresh tomatoes
or 1 16-ounce can whole
tomatoes, drained
3 tablespoons balsamic vinegar
2 tablespoons currants
1 1/2 teaspoons salt
5 1/2 cups water
1 cup frozen or dried posole
3 tablespoons minced cilantro
3 cups shredded lettuce
1 cup grated carrots (optional)
8 whole grain or corn tortillas
1 cup grated Monterey Jack
or soy mozzarella (optional)
2 avocados, sliced
10 black olives, sliced
1/4 cup low-fat sour cream
(optional)

Chipotle and ancho chilies give this dish its smoky hot flavor. The beans are slow-cooked to fully merge all flavors, then they are served wrapped in tortillas with posole (hominy) and grated fresh vegetables. It is a meal in itself.

1. Drain the ancho and chipotle chilies. Remove their stems, then scrape out and discard their seeds. Chop the chilies finely and set aside.

2. Preheat the oven to 300°F. In a 3-quart Dutch oven, heat the oil over medium heat until hot. Add the onion and cook quickly, stirring constantly, until the onion begins to soften, about 8 minutes. Add the garlic and bell peppers and cook for another 3 minutes. Stir in the beans, cumin, oregano, cinnamon, thyme, and bay leaf. Add the tomato, vinegar, currants, 1/2 teaspoon salt, and 1 1/2 cups water. Mix well, then cover and place in the oven. Bake the beans, stirring occasionally, until all liquid has evaporated, about 2 hours. (The beans can be cooked longer; simply add additional water to prevent burning.)

3. As the beans cook, prepare the posole. Place it in a 2-quart saucepan with 4 cups of water and 1 teaspoon of salt. Bring the posole to a boil, stir, and reduce the heat to a simmer. Cover and cook, stirring occasionally, until the beans are tender, about 1 1/2 hours. Add more water as necessary to prevent burning. When cooked, remove the posole from the heat and stir in the cilantro. Both the beans and posole can be prepared up to 3 days in advance if refrigerated in an airtight container. Rewarm before serving.

4. To serve, warm the tortillas, then fill each with a layer of posole topped with beans, lettuce, and carrots. Roll and place on serving plates, seam side down. Garnish the top of each with slices of grated cheese, avocado, black olives, and sour cream.

Variation

1. To reduce fat in the recipe, omit the sautéing. Simply combine the onion, garlic, and peppers with the beans and spices and bake. Serve with chopped tomatoes or fresh salsa (page 182).

Soba Noodles with Dipping Sauce

Yield: 6 servings • Prep Time: 20 minutes • Cooking Time: 20 minutes

3 tablespoons tamari
1 tablespoon rice vinegar
1 tablespoon smooth peanut
butter
1 tablespoon honey
1 tablespoon minced garlic
1 cup cooked azuki beans
1/4 cup mirin (page 193)
1/4 cup soy sauce
1 cup mushroom stock (page 163)
2 tablespoons chopped dulse
(page 190)

This traditional method for serving soba noodles is light and refreshing. The noodles are topped with a few delicate garnishes, then dipped in a dashi-based sauce. Marinated azuki beans and a peanut butter-flavored sauce give this recipe an unconventional twist.

1. In a medium-size mixing bowl, combine the tamari, vinegar, peanut butter, honey, and garlic. Stir to blend, then add the beans. Toss well and allow to marinate for at least 2 hours. The beans can be marinated for up to 2 days if refrigerated in an airtight container.

2. In a small saucepan, combine the mirin, soy sauce, and stock. Heat just to the boil, then pour into a small bowl. Stir in the dulse and set this dipping sauce

r about 1 tablespoon of hot water into the
　to make a paste thick enough to retain its

quarts of water to a boil. Stir in the noodles,
til they are just tender, about 9 minutes.
t, heat the peanut oil over medium high heat.
dd the mushrooms. Cook, tossing often, for
　to soften. Reduce the heat slightly and con-
they are very soft, about 8 minutes. Add the
　remove from the heat.
them to the skillet. Turn this out onto indi-
　the top of each with minced scallions and
-shaped heap of wasabi paste on the side of
ce in shallow individual bowls alongside.

2 tablespoons wasabi powder
　(page 196)
8 ounces soba noodles (page 194)
2 teaspoons peanut oil
8 fresh shiitake mushrooms,
　sliced
1/2 pound tree oyster mushrooms,
　quartered
1/4 cup minced scallions
3 tablespoons crumbled nori
　(page 193)

s and Lemon Grass

utes • Cooking Time: 25 minutes

penetrates this simple, succulent dish.

it into 1-inch slabs. Place these on a clean kitchen
towel. Place a cutting board on top of this and
avy skillet or several 1-pound cans on the board.
Allow the tofu to　　　　minutes.

2. Cut the tough top stems from the lemon grass so that each stalk measures about 3 inches. Place the stalks on a cutting board and, using the flat side of a cleaver, smash and flatten the stalks. Cut them into 1/4-inch pieces and place them in a shallow baking dish. Stir in the scallions, lime juice, rice syrup, tamari, water, and black pepper. Cut the tofu into 1-inch square pieces and place these in this lemon grass marinade. Turn once to coat, then cover and refrigerate for 24 to 48 hours. Turn the tofu several times as it marinates.

3. Preheat the broiler to high. Remove the tofu from the marinade and place it on a broiling rack about 6 inches from the heat. Broil, turning once, until the tofu is lightly crisped on each side, about 12 minutes. Remove the tofu from the broiler and cover to keep warm until the dish is completed.

4. Meanwhile, heat the oil in a 10-inch skillet or wok over high heat until it is hot, but not smoking. Add the chili and garlic. Cook, stirring constantly, until the chili darkens, abut 1 minute. Drain off the oil, then add the marinade to the pan. Stir in the stock and broccoli, then cook, covered and stirring often, until the broccoli is just crisp, about 6 minutes. Stir in the arrowroot and bring the sauce to a boil so that it thickens. Add the tofu and warm for about 15 seconds. Transfer to a serving platter and top with the chopped nuts. Serve at once with steamed rice or pan- fried noodles (page 139).

Cook's Note: The tofu is best pressed for 20 minutes and should marinate overnight.

1 pound firm tofu
4 stalks lemon grass
1/4 cup minced scallions
1/4 cup lime juice
1/4 cup rice syrup (page 193)
1/4 cup tamari
2 tablespoons water
1/4 teaspoon black pepper
2 tablespoons peanut oil
1 dried red chili
2 teaspoons minced garlic
1/2 cup light vegetable stock
　(page 162)
1 1/2 cups broccoli florets
1 tablespoon arrowroot + 2 table-
　spoons cold water
1/4 cup chopped macadamia nuts
2 tablespoons chopped peanuts
2 tablespoons chopped almonds

Apple-Stuffed Curried Seitan

Yield: 6 servings • Prep Time: 40 minutes • Cooking Time: 1 1/2 hours

2 1/2 cups uncooked seitan
   (page 184) prepared with
   1 tablespoon tamari and
   1 teaspoon ground cumin
3 tablespoons canola oil
2 cups diced onion
2 1/2 tablespoons curry powder
2 Granny Smith apples, peeled
   and cut in 1/4-inch cubes
1 tablespoon minced garlic
1/2 cup light vegetable stock
   (page 162)
1/4 cup unfiltered apple juice
6 dried apricots, soaked and
   chopped
1/4 cup dried currants
1/4 cup chopped almonds
1/2 teaspoon salt
1/8 teaspoon black pepper
4 cups water
1/4 cup tamari
3/4 cup diced carrot
1/2 cup puréed butternut squash
2 tablespoons butter or almond
   butter (optional)
4 cups mixed greens (kale,
   collards etc.), steamed
1 cup sliced carrots, steamed

Choose unsulphured apricots—preferably Turkish—for the stuffing. If the apricots you find are very dry and hard, soak them in hot water for 10 minutes before adding to the recipe.

1. Prepare the seitan, including in the mixture 1 tablespoon tamari and 1 teaspoon cumin, according to directions on page 184. Set this aside, covered with a damp kitchen towel as you prepare the stuffing.

2. In a medium-size saucepan, heat 1 tablespoon of oil over medium high heat until hot, but not smoking. Add 1 cup onion and cook, stirring constantly, until it is coated with oil, about 1 minute. Reduce the heat to medium and continue to cook, stirring frequently, until the onions are translucent, about 10 minutes. Increase the heat to medium high and add 1 tablespoon curry powder. Cook, stirring constantly, until the smell of curry fills the air, about 1 minute. Add the apples and toss to combine. Stir in 1 teaspoon garlic, the stock, and apple juice. Bring the mixture to a simmer and continue to cook, stirring often until the liquid has evaporated and the apples are very soft. Remove this stuffing from the heat and, with the back of a spoon, mash the apples to a rough purée. Stir in the currants, apricots, and nuts. Season with salt and pepper. The stuffing may be prepared up to 3 days in advance if refrigerated in an airtight container.

3. Place the seitan on a clean work surface. Stretch and flatten it out to a rough rectangular shape that measures about 8 inches by 10 inches and is as even a thickness as possible. (Seitan by nature is extremely elastic. Work patiently. You may find it helpful to shape it, then place a cutting board on top to hold it in place.) Spread the filling on the seitan, leaving a 3/4-inch border on each 8-inch side and a 1-inch border on the two 10-inch sides. Fold about 1 1/2 inches of each of the two short sides over the filling. Carefully roll the seitan, from the other direction, to form a log. Seal the edges together by pinching the seitan in place. Tie pieces of kitchen twine at 2-inch intervals around the roll to secure its round shape, from one end of the roll to the other.

4. In a large saucepan, combine the water, tamari, 1 tablespoon oil, remaining cup of onion, 1 1/2 tablespoons curry powder, and 2 teaspoons garlic with the diced carrot. Bring this to a simmer. Gently lower the seitan roll into this poaching liquid and cook it, partially covered, for 1 1/4 hours. Do not allow the liquid to boil at any point or the seitan will have an unpleasant, spongy texture when cooked. As the seitan cooks, baste it often with cooking liquid. When cooked, remove the pan from the heat and allow the seitan to cool in the liquid.

5. Remove the seitan from the poaching liquid. Snip and discard the strings that tied it together. Preheat the broiler to high. Brush the outside of the seitan with the remaining tablespoon of oil and place it about 6 inches from the heat. Broil it quickly to just begin to crisp the outside. You should cook it about 8 minutes, turning it once so that it browns evenly. Remove the seitan from the oven and cool for 3 minutes.

6. Meanwhile, strain the poaching liquid into a small saucepan. Place it over high heat and bring it to a boil. Reduce the liquid to about 1/2 cup, then remove it from the heat and whisk in the squash. For a richer sauce, also whisk in butter or almond butter. Taste and adjust the seasonings.

7. Toss together the greens and carrots, then arrange them on individual serving plates. Slice the seitan into pieces and arrange it over the greens. Pour the sauce over and serve at once.

Cook's Note: Allow ample time to prepare the seitan before beginning the recipe.

Sweet and Sour Tempeh over Quinoa

Yield: 4 servings • Prep Time: 35 minutes • Cooking Time: 25 minutes

Raisins and anise seed add a subtle sweetness to balance the earthy quality of the tempeh. There are several last-minute steps to this recipe that must be carried out simultaneously, but because none require constant attention, it is actually quite a simple recipe to execute, provided you don't expect lots of distractions to be at hand.

3 tablespoons raisins
4 tablespoons boiling water
8 ounces tempeh, grated
2 ounces soft silken tofu
1 teaspoon minced garlic
1 teaspoon minced gingerroot
1 tablespoon sesame seeds
1 cup broccoli florets
2 cups carrots, sliced 1/4 inch thick
1 cup snow peas, strings removed
1/2 cup sliced celery
1/4 cup minced scallions
1 cup light vegetable stock (page 162)
2 tablespoons red wine vinegar
2 tablespoons soy sauce
1 teaspoon honey
1 teaspoon anise seeds
1/4 teaspoon dried chili flakes
1 cup uncooked quinoa
3 cups water
1/4 teaspoon salt
3 tablespoons minced cilantro

1. Place the raisins in a small mixing bowl and cover with the boiling water. Set this aside for 20 minutes, then transfer raisins and soaking water to a food processor fitted with the metal chopping blade or to a blender. Add the tempeh, tofu, garlic, and ginger. Blend briefly to combine. Add the sesame seeds and continue to blend until the mixture is stiff and evenly mixed. Shape the tempeh mixture into 1-inch balls and set them aside. These can be prepared up to 2 days in advance if refrigerated, tightly covered.

2. Place the broccoli and carrots in the top rack of a steamer over rapidly boiling water. Cover and steam until just tender, about 5 minutes. Add the snow peas and celery and continue to cook, covered, for 1 minute. Immediately remove the vegetables from the steamer. Leave them uncovered at room temperature until the rest of the dish is prepared.

3. Meanwhile, in a 12-inch wok or skillet, combine the scallions, stock, vinegar, soy sauce, honey, anise seeds, and chili flakes. Bring this mixture to a boil, then reduce to a simmer. Gently lower the tempeh into the sauce and cook, covered, for 10 minutes. Remove from the heat and stir in the vegetables.

4. At the same time, place the quinoa in a fine-mesh strainer and rinse it thoroughly, until the water runs absolutely clear. (If it is not rinsed well it will have a strong, earthy taste.) Combine the water and salt in a 1 1/2-quart saucepan and bring it to a boil. Stir in the quinoa, then cover and reduce to a simmer. Cook until all water is absorbed and/or all of the grains of quinoa have popped open and are just tender, about 15 minutes. Immediately transfer the quinoa to a strainer and shake several times to remove all excess water. Place the quinoa on a serving platter and toss with the cilantro. Pour the tempeh and vegetable mixture over. Serve at once.

Quick-Simmered Bean Curry

Yield: 6 servings • Prep Time: 20 minutes • Cooking Time: 35 minutes

1/4 cup uncooked moong dal
(split mung beans, available
where Indian foods are sold)
1 lemon
2 1/2 cups water
2 tablespoons maple sugar
or 2 1/2 tablespoons maple
syrup
1 1/2 teaspoons salt
2 tablespoons ghee or
vegetable oil
1 cup diced onion
1 tablespoon minced garlic
1 tablespoon minced gingerroot
1 serrano pepper, seeded and
minced
3 tablespoons slivered almonds
1 tablespoon white poppy seeds
(optional)
1 teaspoon fennel seeds
2 teaspoons ground cumin
1 teaspoon ground coriander
1/4 teaspoon ground cardamom
1/4 teaspoon turmeric
1/2 teaspoon cinnamon
1/8 teaspoon ground cloves
1/8 teaspoon ground saffron
1/4 teaspoon black pepper
1 tablespoon blackstrap molasses
2/3 cup buttermilk or soy milk
2 cups cooked black-eyed peas
1 cup cooked azuki beans
1/4 cup minced fresh mint
1 teaspoon brown mustard seeds
2 dried red chilies

Sweet azuki beans team up with the more robust flavor of black-eyed peas in this simple curry. The list of ingredients is long, typical of many curries, but once you have assembled all of the spices, you will find that the bulk of the prep work for this recipe is completed. Serve this curry with chapatis or tortillas, a tomato-cucumber salad, and steamed kale.

1. Pick over the moong dal to remove all rocks and debris. Rinse the dal, then place it in a bowl, cover with cold water, and soak for 2 to 5 hours.

2. With a swivel-bladed vegetable peeler, peel wide strips from the lemon until all skin is removed. Avoid as much of the white pith as possible. Stack the strips of skin, then slice them into long 1/8-inch-wide strips. In a very small saucepan, combine the lemon peel strips, 3/4 cup water, maple sugar, and 1 teaspoon of salt. Bring this to a boil, then cook about 20 minutes, stirring often until the lemon strips are soft and most of the liquid has evaporated. Transfer the lemon strips to a small bowl, cover and set aside. The lemon can be prepared 3 days in advance if refrigerated in an airtight container.

3. In a large saucepan or Dutch oven, heat 1 1/2 tablespoons ghee over medium high heat until hot, but not smoking. Add the onion and cook, stirring constantly, until it is evenly coated with ghee. Reduce the heat to medium and continue to cook, stirring often, until the onion is wilted, about 8 minutes. Add the garlic, ginger, and serrano pepper, then turn off the heat as you prepare the spice mix.

4. In a blender, combine the almonds, poppy seeds, and fennel seeds with 2 tablespoons of water. Grind until even, then add the cumin, coriander, cardamom, turmeric, cinnamon, cloves, saffron, and black pepper. Blend again, then transfer this into the onion mixture and turn the heat to medium.

5. Drain the moong dal and add it to the pan with the remaining 1 3/4 cups water. Stir in the molasses and buttermilk until blended. Simmer, stirring occasionally, for 25 minutes. Add the black-eyed peas and azuki beans, and continue to cook for 10 minutes. Stir in the minced mint, lemon juice, and remaining 1/2 teaspoon of salt. The curry can be prepared up to 5 days in advance if refrigerated in an airtight container. It can be frozen for up to 3 months.

6. In a small skillet, heat the remaining ghee until very hot. Add the mustard seeds and red chilies. Cook, stirring constantly, until the seeds pop and the chilies blacken, about 1 minute. Immediately pour these over the beans and serve.

Cook's Note: Allow 2 to 5 hours soaking time for the dal.

Bean Medley with Port

Yield: 6 servings • Prep Time: 30 minutes • Cooking Time: 20 minutes

This unusual treatment of beans—bathing them in a reduction sauce—is highly success-ful. The creamy sauce, sweetened with port, complements the smooth consistency of fava beans. Serve this with fluffy millet or rice.

1 pound fresh fava beans
  or 1 cup shelled fresh lima or
  butter beans
2 teaspoons olive oil
1/3 cup minced shallots
  or 1/4 cup minced onion
2 teaspoons minced garlic
8 ounces mushrooms, sliced
1/4 cup cognac
3 tablespoons tawny port
1 cup hearty vegetable stock
  (page 162)
1/2 teaspoon salt
1/8 teaspoon black pepper
Pinch of nutmeg
1 cup cooked kidney beans
2 cups snow peas, strings
  removed
1/4 cup crème fraîche (page 172)
  or milk or use soy cream
  (page 171)
2 teaspoons Dijon-style mustard
1 teaspoon tomato paste
1/4 cup minced fresh parsley

1. Remove the fresh favas from their pods, then place the beans (in their inner husks) in the top rack of a steamer over rapidly boiling water. Cook, tightly covered, for 4 minutes. Immediately transfer the beans to a strainer and run cold water over them to stop their cooking. When they are cool enough to handle, carefully slice open the thick skin and slide the beans out into a bowl. Set the shelled beans aside.

2. In a 12-inch skillet, heat the olive oil over medium high heat until hot, but not smoking. Add the shallots and toss to coat with the oil. Cook, stirring often, for about 2 minutes, then add the garlic and mushrooms. Continue to cook, stir-ring often, until the mushrooms begin to soften, about 3 minutes.

3. Turn the heat to high. Add the cognac and, if you are cooking on a gas burner, tilt the pan to the side so that the cognac will ignite. (If you are using an electric cook top, light the cognac with a match or lighter immediately after add-ing it to the pan.) Shake the pan, tossing the mushrooms, until the flame dies down.

4. Stir the port, stock, salt, pepper, and nutmeg into the saucepan and bring this to a boil. Reduce to a simmer and cook, stirring occasionally, until the mush-rooms are very soft and the stock has reduced slightly, about 8 minutes.

5. Stir the cooked fava beans, kidney beans, and snow peas into the skillet. Cook, covered, until the snow peas are puffed and vibrant green, about 1 minute. In a small bowl, combine the crème fraîche, mustard, tomato paste, and parsley. Remove the skillet from the heat and whisk the crème fraîche mixture into the sauce. Taste and adjust the seasonings. Serve over millet or rice.

Variations

1. Double the sauce ingredients (port, stock, salt, pepper, nutmeg, crème fraîche, mustard, and tomato paste). Otherwise, prepare the recipe as above, and serve it over soba or udon noodles.

2. Substitute 1 pound cubed, pressed frozen tofu for both types of beans. Increase the stock to 2 cups. Prepare the recipe as above through step 4, then simmer the tofu for 30 minutes before adding snow peas, cream, mustard, and tomato paste. Stir in 3 tablespoons snipped chives.

Stuffed Shells with Asparagus Sauce

Yield: 6 servings • Prep Time: 50 minutes • Cooking Time: 20 minutes

1 pound jumbo shells
8 ounces mushrooms
1 tablespoon olive oil
2 teaspoons butter
1/2 cup minced shallots
2 teaspoons minced garlic
8 ounces tempeh, crumbled
1/4 cup cognac
3 1/2 cups mushroom stock
  (page 163)
1 teaspoon dried thyme
1 1/2 teaspoons salt
1 teaspoon quatre épices
2 tablespoons minced fresh
  parsley
1/4 cup grated Parmesan
  (optional) or use grated soy
  mozzarella
1 small russet potato, peeled and
  cubed
2 leeks, chopped
1 pound asparagus
2 teaspoons lemon zest
3 tablespoons minced tarragon
  leaves
1/4 to 1/3 cup additional stock
  or milk
10 romaine lettuce leaves

The fresh bite of lemon zest and sweetness from tarragon combine with asparagus to give an interesting undertone to the dish. You may use jumbo shells or manicotti.

1. In a large saucepan, bring 4 quarts of water to a rolling boil. Stir in the shells. Cook, stirring gently and frequently to prevent sticking, until they are almost al dente, about 8 minutes (they will cook more after being stuffed). Once cooked, gently pour the shells into a colander and carefully run cold water over them to stop their cooking. Place them open side down on a clean kitchen towel to drain.

2. Mince the mushrooms into tiny dice (see page 35). Place them in the center of a clean kitchen towel. Draw the corners of the towel together, then twist it to form a ball of mushrooms. Hold the towel over the sink and continue to twist and squeeze the towel to extract as much liquid from the mushrooms as possible.

3. In a 10-inch skillet, heat the oil and butter over medium high heat until the butter melts. Add the shallots and cook, stirring constantly, until they glisten, about 1 minute. Reduce the heat to medium and continue to cook, stirring frequently, until they are very soft, but have not browned, about 8 minutes. Add the mushrooms and garlic, then cook, stirring often, until the mushrooms have softened and most of the liquid they release has evaporated, about 8 minutes.

4. Stir the tempeh into the mushroom mixture. Increase the heat to high and, after the tempeh is sizzling, add the cognac. Cook, stirring constantly until the smell of alcohol has evaporated, about 1 minute. Reduce the heat and stir in 1/2 cup stock, the thyme, 1 teaspoon salt, and the quatre epice. Cook, stirring occasionally until all liquid has cooked off, about 5 minutes. Remove the tempeh from the heat and mix in the parsley and Parmesan. Taste and adjust the seasonings. This filling can be prepared up to 3 days in advance if refrigerated in an airtight container.

5. In a 2-quart saucepan, combine the remaining 3 cups of stock, potatoes, and leeks. Bring to a boil, then reduce to a simmer and cook, covered and stirring occasionally, until the potatoes are easily mashed when pressed against the side of the pan, about 15 minutes. Meanwhile, break off and discard the woody part of each stalk of asparagus. Chop the remaining asparagus into 1- to 2-inch pieces. Add them to the cooked potatoes and continue to cook, stirring occasionally, until they are tender, but still retain an attractive green color, about 12 minutes. Immediately transfer this sauce mixture to a food processor fitted with the metal chopping blade or to a stainless steel bowl and allow it to cool, uncovered, for at least 5 minutes. (It may cool completely, but in either case it must remain uncovered in order for the asparagus to retain its color.) Purée the sauce, scraping down the sides of the processor bowl as necessary, until it is absolutely smooth. Return the sauce to a saucepan and, if desired, thin with additional stock or milk. Whisk in the lemon zest and tarragon.

6. Line 2 layers of a bamboo steamer (or use a makeshift steamer, page 6) with lettuce leaves. Divide the filling evenly among the shells, piling it up high in each shell. Arrange the shells, filling side up, on the lettuce leaves. Place the steamer racks over rapidly boiling water and cook, covered, for 5 minutes. Meanwhile warm the sauce to piping hot. To serve, either spoon the sauce onto individual plates and arrange the shells on top of the sauce, or bring the shells in the bamboo steamer to the table and serve from the steamer with the sauce in a sauce boat.

Cook's Note: Quatre épices is a French seasoning often used in pâtés, sausages, and stuffings. It is sold commercially in most fine supermarkets.

Japanese Eggplant with Jeweled Yam Stuffing

Yield: 6 servings • Prep Time: 25 minutes • Cooking Time: 40 minutes

Japanese eggplant, filled with bright orange yam and mung bean stuffing, is an elegant alternative to a standard stuffed eggplant dish. Split mung beans are available at most Asian markets.

1/2 cup moong dal (split mung beans)
12 small Japanese eggplants (5 to 6 inches long)
1 tablespoon peanut oil
4 cloves garlic, sliced thin
1 teaspoon cumin seeds
1 jalapeño pepper, seeded and minced
1 1/2 tablespoons minced ginger-root
1 1/4 teaspoons garam masala (page 191)
1 teaspoon ground coriander
1 teaspoon salt
1/8 teaspoon cayenne (optional)
1/4 teaspoon turmeric
3 cups water
1 jewel yam (about 1 pound) cut into 1/2-inch cubes

1. Pick over the mung beans and rinse them well, then cover them with cold water and soak for 3 hours.

2. With the tip of a paring knife, cut a long oval shape, reaching to 1/2 inch of both stem and flower end of each eggplant. Hollow out the core of each eggplant, below the oval, creating a pouch that may be stuffed. Use this eggplant meat, steamed to thicken another sauce, or add it to a soup. Sprinkle the pouch of each eggplant with a small amount of salt, then turn them, pouch side down, onto a clean kitchen towel to sweat.

3. In a 9-inch nonstick skillet, heat the oil over medium heat until hot, but not smoking. Add the garlic, cumin seeds, jalapeño, and ginger. Cook quickly, stirring constantly for about 1 minute to allow the spices to release their flavor. Drain the beans and add them, then stir in the garam masala, coriander, salt, cayenne, and turmeric along with 1 cup of water. Bring this mixture to a boil, then stir in the yams and the remaining water. Cook, stirring occasionally, until the beans are tender, about 20 minutes. Remove this filling from the heat. It may be prepared up to 3 days in advance if refrigerated in an airtight container.

4. Stuff each eggplant with this filling, mounding it up over the top of the eggplant. The eggplants can be stuffed up to 8 hours in advance if covered tightly and refrigerated. Place the eggplants on a bamboo steamer rack (or a makeshift steamer, page 6) over rapidly boiling water. Cover and steam until the eggplants are tender, about 15 minutes. Serve immediately plain or accompanied by garlicky kale sauce (page 178).

Cook's Note: Allow 3 hours soaking time for the dal.

Saffron Sesame Tofu

Yield: 6 servings • Prep Time: 10 minutes • Cooking Time: 20 minutes

1 1/2 pounds firm tofu
2 lemons
3 tablespoons olive oil
2 teaspoons honey
1 teaspoon saffron threads, crushed
1/2 cup minced fresh parsley
1 tablespoon minced fresh thyme
1 tablespoon minced garlic
2 teaspoons salt
1/4 teaspoon ground coriander
1/4 teaspoon black pepper
1/2 cup finely minced onion
1 egg white, lightly beaten (optional)
1/2 cup hulled sesame seeds
1/3 cup light vegetable stock (page 162)
2 tablespoons tahini (page 195) or butter (optional)
6 sprigs fresh parsley

Allow the tofu to marinate overnight so that the subtle taste of saffron penetrates.

1. Drain the tofu and slice it into 3/4-inch-thick pieces. Set them on a clean kitchen towel, then cover with another towel and top with a cutting board. Weight the board down with a heavy iron skillet or several 1-pound cans. Allow the tofu to drain for 30 minutes. Cut each slice of tofu into quarters (either triangles or squares).

2. Rinse the lemons and dry them thoroughly. With the fine side of a grater, grate the zest from each and refrigerate it in an airtight container. Squeeze the juice from the lemons into a shallow, non-aluminum baking dish; you should have about 1/4 cup. Stir in 2 tablespoons of olive oil, the honey, saffron, parsley, thyme, garlic, salt, coriander, pepper, and onion. Mix well. Place the drained tofu in this marinade and turn to coat. Cover and refrigerate for 24 hours, turning several times.

4. Preheat the oven to 450°F. Lightly coat a shallow baking pan with the remaining 1 tablespoon of olive oil. Spread the sesame seeds out on a piece of waxed paper. Place the egg white in a small bowl and beat it until frothy. Remove each slice of tofu from the marinade and dip it in the egg white, then in the sesame seeds to coat. Place the tofu in the oiled pan and repeat the coating with the remaining tofu. If you choose not to use the egg white, simply remove the tofu from the marinade and coat with sesame seeds. Fewer seeds will stick and the end result is less crisp, but both methods are very nice.

5. Bake the tofu in the center of the preheated oven until the coating is golden brown, about 18 minutes. Meanwhile, pour the remaining marinade into a 1-quart saucepan. Add the stock and bring this mixture to a boil. Cook over high heat to reduce slightly, about 5 minutes. Remove from the heat and whisk in the tahini or butter (optional). Taste and adjust the seasonings. Pour about 3 tablespoons of sauce onto individual serving plates. Arrange triangles of tofu on top and drizzle a small amount of remaining sauce over the tofu. Garnish with a sprig of parsley and serve immediately.

Cook's Note: The tofu must marinate overnight.

7 • Extras

Salads

A well-rounded entrée needs only a salad as an accompaniment to make an absolutely satisfying, balanced meal, and virtually any food can be turned into a successful salad. Below I give some general pointers on making green and vegetable salads as well as dressings. Use these suggestions as inspiration to suit your tastes.

Composition

1. Choose one type of leafy green as the base of the salad, then select greens to combine with it for contrast in color, texture and bite. For example, if Boston lettuce is the base, choose other greens such as chard or red leaf lettuce, to complement it for the bulk of the salad. For an accent, toss in a small amount of radicchio, dandelion greens, or sorrel. Combine according to color, taste, and texture to achieve a visually attractive blend that tastes balanced.

2. Incorporate leaves from one or two complementary fresh herbs, such as fresh basil and mint or tarragon and parsley.

3. If you have access to edible flowers (nasturtiums, violets, daylilies, etc.) or flowers from herb plants, use them sparingly. Always be certain that the flowers you use in cooking have not been sprayed with insecticides or fertilizers.

4. Be certain to clean and dry whatever greens or fresh leaves you use.

5. One or more types of fresh vegetable can be added to any green salad. It is generally advisable to slice fresh vegetables thinly or steam them before mixing them into the salad.

6. It is often nice to incorporate a small number of olives, capers, pickled peppers or other strong, vinegared, salty ingredients.

7. Top the salad with toasted nuts, seeds, or croutons for balance in texture.

8. Salads made purely from sliced fresh vegetables tossed with fresh minced herbs and lemon or orange juice, balsamic vinegar and oil, or one of the salad dressings below, can make a delightful accompaniment to many of the entrées in this book. Jicama mixed with orange slices, orange juice, cumin and garlic is a light and refreshing salad. Grated carrots mixed with ginger, lemon juice, salt, raisins or soft dried apricots, a tiny amount of olive or toasted sesame oil (depending on the flavors of the rest of the meal), and minced mint can complete a curry or a pasta dish, and so on.

Salad Dressing Notes

1. A general rule for preparing salad dressing is that some form of acid (vinegar, citrus juice, tomato juice) in combination with strong flavors, such as garlic or mustard, is usually successful. A small amount of oil, yogurt, nut butter, or puréed tofu takes the "edge" off the taste of the acid ingredient and gives the salads a satisfying feel in the mouth.

2. A versatile light vinaigrette is made by whisking together 1 teaspoon Dijon-style mustard, 1 tablespoon honey (optional), 2 tablespoons vinegar, 3 tablespoons olive oil, and 1/3 cup warm water. The dressing may be flavored with one or two fresh herbs, salt, pepper, pepper flakes or other seasonings. This same notion in dressing can be modified with Oriental ingredients—rice vinegar, toasted sesame oil, and minced pickled ginger—or given a Mediterranean flavor with champagne vinegar, canola oil, roasted tomato, and roasted garlic. The variations are endless, and if you combine flavors typical of a specific region, you are likely to be successful.

3. For a thick nondairy dressing, tahini may be mixed with lemon juice, garlic, tamari, water, and whatever spices suit the meal.

4. For a thick dairy-based dressing, simply season and flavor plain yogurt. For example, you could season it with honey, mustard, poppy seeds, and minced parsley, or combine it with maple syrup, curry powder, minced ginger and cilantro.

Sesame Flavored Arame Salad

Yield: 4 servings • Prep Time: 10 minutes • Cooking Time: 10 minutes

1 cup, packed, arame
   (page 190)
1 3/4 cup boiling water
1 tablespoon canola oil
2 teaspoons minced garlic
1 teaspoon rice vinegar
1 tablespoon maple sugar
   or 2 teaspoons rice syrup
   (page 193)
3 1/2 tablespoons soy sauce
1/2 teaspoon toasted sesame oil
1/4 cup hulled sesame seeds

When I first began eating mostly vegetarian foods, it took me ages to work up enough courage to try eating sea vegetables. I regret waiting so long, because they can add a fabulous dimension to many foods. The first sea vegetable to appeal to most is either nori—used to wrap sushi rice—or arame.

This simple recipe for arame is excellent and it serves as an accompaniment to many dishes—in particular Simmered Shiitake Tofu (page 74)—or it may be used with leftover broiled tofu or panir (page 174) stirred in, as a main course salad.

1. Place the arame in a strainer in the sink and rinse it under cold running water. As you do so, gently rub the arame with your fingertips to remove all sand. Place the arame in a small bowl and cover it with boiling water. Set this aside for 15 minutes, then drain, squeezing excess water from the arame.

2. In an 8-inch skillet, heat the oil until hot, but not smoking. Add the garlic and toss to impregnate the oil with its flavor, for 1 minute. Do not allow the garlic to brown or it will have a bitter flavor. Add the vinegar, maple sugar, soy sauce, and arame. Cook, tossing often, until the arame is heated through, about 3 minutes. Remove from the heat and stir in the sesame oil and sesame seeds. Serve hot or at room temperature.

Variations

1. Add 1/3 cup sliced dried and steamed or fresh shiitake mushrooms to the garlic when sautéing. Cook these until just tender, about 5 minutes. Proceed with the recipe as directed above.

2. Stir 1/2 cup diced cucumber, 1/2 cup diced red pepper, and 1/3 cup diced jicama into the arame at the end of cooking. Serve as is or with 1/2 pound leftover broiled tofu, cut in cubes.

3. Stir in 1 cup diced tofu that has been marinated and broiled; Rosemary Orange Tofu (page 53) is particularly good.

Cook's Note: The most important step when preparing any sea vegetable (except nori) is to rinse it thoroughly so as to remove any sand or small shells that might have clung to it in the drying process.

Braised Greens

Yield: 4 servings • Prep Time: 15 minutes • Cooking Time: 15 minutes

Foods that are braised are first sautéed, then stock, wine or other liquid is added to the pan while it is very hot. Once the sizzling dies down, the food is basted with the pan juices, covered, and cooked slowly until done—in the oven (classically) or on top of the stove. Greens work especially well with this cooking treatment because the addition of wine or another acidic liquid helps to balance their flavor. Try mixing the type of greens included, having only one—like escarole—that is very pungent.

10 cups kale, chard, mustard turnip, beet greens, escarole
1 tablespoon olive oil
1/4 cup minced onion (optional)
1 1/2 teaspoons minced garlic
3/4 cup dry white wine
Salt and pepper to taste

1. Clean the greens well (page 34), then chop the leaves into rough pieces. Wash them in several changes of cold water, then leave them to dry in a strainer. Water that remains on the leaves will contribute to the pan juices when the leaves are cooked.

2. In a 12-inch skillet, heat the oil over medium-high flame until hot, but not smoking. Add the onion and cook briefly, tossing constantly. After about 3 minutes, add the garlic and gradually add the greens, adding as many as will fit into the pan, then turning the leaves as they wilt. As you can, add more greens until all are in. Season to taste with salt and pepper, then cover the pan and reduce the heat to medium low. Cook, stirring often, until they are tender. Serve at once.

Mixed Grilled Vegetable Kabobs

Yield: 4 servings • Prep Time: 25 minutes • Cooking Time: 15 minutes

Grilled vegetables add visual appeal and a deep, rich quality when served as a vegetable side dish or mixed in as part of a pasta or bean salad. All vegetables, except leafy greens, may be successfully grilled outdoors or under the broiler. Except for very soft and watery vegetables, cucumber and tomato, for example, most vegetables are best if lightly steamed before grilling. The precise length of steaming required will vary depending on the vegetable and its shape and thickness—each vegetable should be steamed until it is cooked about halfway to the center. Use the following list of vegetables as inspiration for kabobs to complement the entrée you are serving. When selecting vegetables for a mixed kabob, select for contrast in color, texture, and taste.

1 small eggplant, cut in 1-inch cubes
3 tablespoons olive oil
1 tablespoon lemon juice
1/2 teaspoon minced garlic
1/4 teaspoon crushed dried thyme
2 small sweet or Spanish onions, quartered (leaving the root end intact)
1 large sweet potato, cut in 1-inch cubes
1 red bell pepper, seeded and cut into squares
1 yellow squash, cut into 1/2-inch slices
1 cucumber, peeled, seeded and cut into 1/2-inch slices

1. Cut up the eggplant. Spread the eggplant out on a clean kitchen towel and sprinkle with salt. Allow it to "sweat" for about 10 minutes as you prepare the other vegetables.

2. Preheat the broiler to high, or ready the grill. In a small dish, combine the oil, lemon juice, garlic, and thyme. Skewer the onion quarters and brush them with the oil mixture. Place them on a baking sheet under the broiler or directly on the grill, about 6 inches from the heat.

3. Meanwhile, steam the vegetables separately, each until cooked almost to the center. Remove each vegetable immediately and when cool enough to handle, thread onto skewers. Brush each skewer with oil and broil or grill (turning the skewers several times and brushing with the oil mixture) until the vegetables are lightly crisped and cooked through. Serve immediately.

Puréed Vegetables

Yield: 4 servings • Prep Time: 20 minutes • Cooking Time: 10 minutes

1 pound small beets
1/2 pound russet potato
1/4 cup finely grated horseradish
1/4 teaspoon salt
2 teaspoons lemon juice
2 tablespoons butter (optional)

Puréed vegetables add an elegant touch to a simple broiled or grilled entrée, and they serve equally well as a garnish for more formal dishes such as the Tofu Roll (page 134) or B'Stilla (page 136). The most successful purées have a vibrant or distinctive color, and the texture is creamy and never watery. Potatoes and winter squash serve well to bind purées and are often successfully mixed with other ingredients of complementary flavor and color within a purée. Purées may be seasoned simply with salt and pepper, or they may be spiked with distinctive spicing, like a sprinkling of minced jalapeños, roasted garlic, or cinnamon.

1. Cut the tops from the beets, then scrub and rinse them well to remove all dirt. Place the beets in a steamer over rapidly boiling water and steam, covered, until tender. Young, tender beets will be ready in about 45 minutes, older and tough beets may require as long as 1 3/4 hours steaming before they are tender. Once tender, cool the beets, then slip off and discard the skin. Quarter the cooked beets and place them in a food processor.

2. Meanwhile, peel and quarter the potato, then steam it (separately, or in the same basket) until it is very tender, about 15 minutes. Place the cooked potato in the processor with the beet. Add the horseradish, salt, lemon juice, and butter. Purée until smooth, scraping down the sides of the bowl as necessary. Taste and adjust the seasonings. Serve at once or refrigerate in an airtight container for up to 3 days, then rewarm in the oven or in the top of a double boiler.

Variations

1. Steam until tender 1 pound peeled and sliced carrot, 1 small peeled parsnip, and 3/4 pound peeled russet potato. Purée the vegetables and season with salt, pepper, and a pinch of cinnamon.

2. Steam until tender a 1 1/2-pound celery root which has been peeled and cubed. Meanwhile, steam 1/2 pound spinach leaves (no stems) and 3/4 pound russet potato. Combine the vegetables in a food processor and purée until very smooth. Season to taste with salt and pepper. Serve the purée warmed, sprinkled with toasted fennel seeds.

Cook's Note: The purée may be prepared several days in advance, then reheated in a double boiler or oven as the main course is being cooked.

Masala Rice

Yield: 6 servings • Prep Time: 5 minutes • Cooking Time: 30 minutes

Seldom is a meal in India served without rice. Most often rice is served in its simplest form—boiled to be eaten with the assortment of curries, dal, and rasam that make up the meal. The versatile grain also serves as the base for a variety of dishes that may become the focal point of a family meal. Masala rice is just such a recipe. It can take the place of simple steamed rice or fried rice in a complex menu, or may be served as the base for a simple dal or bean dish in a less elaborate setting. The seasonings listed below as well as the suggested variations can add depth to any compatible menu.

2 1/4 cups basmati rice
2 tablespoons peanut oil
2 3-inch sticks cinnamon, broken in half
4 whole cloves
4 cardamom pods
1/3 cup raw cashew nuts
5 1/2 cups water
2 bay leaves
1 teaspoon salt
3 tablespoons minced mint

1. Rinse the rice in several changes of cold water, until the water runs clear, then allow it to drain in the strainer for at least 15 minutes before proceeding with the recipe.

2. In a 2-quart saucepan, heat the oil over medium high heat until hot, but not smoking. Add the cinnamon, cloves, cardamom, and 1/4 cup cashews. Cook, tossing frequently, until the cashews begin to brown, about 2 minutes. Immediately add the rice and continue to cook, stirring often, until about half of the rice begins to turn slightly opaque, about 3 minutes. Do not allow the rice to brown and burn. Add the water, bay leaves, and salt. Stir once, then cover and simmer until the rice is tender and all water is absorbed, about 25 minutes. Remove from the heat, add the mint, and fluff the rice with a fork. Serve with the remaining cashews sprinkled on top.

Variations

1. Add 1 tablespoon grated lemon zest to the rice along with the mint to the finished recipe.

2. For a simple lemon rice, omit the cinnamon sticks, cloves, cardamom, and cashews. Stir 1 tablespoon grated lemon zest into the rice and sprinkle 3 tablespoons minced cilantro or mint over the rice just before serving.

3. Sauté the rice with 1/4 cup minced shallots. Substitute mushroom stock (page 163) or hearty vegetable stock (page 162) for the water. Add 1/2 teaspoon dried thyme or 1/2 teaspoon dried rosemary to the rice with the stock, in addition to the bay leaves and salt. Sprinkle 3 tablespoons minced chervil or parsley over the finished rice. You may also stir 1/2 cup grated Gruyère, Parmesan or nondairy soy cheese into the warm rice just before serving.

4. Sauté the rice with 1/2 cup minced scallions and 2 tablespoons minced garlic. Substitute light coconut milk (page 190) for the water. Stir 3 tablespoons minced cilantro into the dish just before serving.

5. For a Spanish-style rice, sauté the rice with 1/2 cup diced onion and 2 teaspoons minced garlic. Add 1 bay leaf, 1/2 teaspoon saffron, and 1/4 teaspoon white pepper to the rice with the stock. You may stir sliced green olives, peeled and diced red bell peppers, and minced fresh parsley into the finished rice, if desired.

Sweet Brown Rice with Raisins and Cashews

Yield: 4 servings • Prep Time: 10 minutes • Cooking Time: 40 minutes

2 cups sweet brown rice
4 cups light vegetable stock
   (page 162) or water
1/4 teaspoon salt
3 tablespoons raisins
3 tablespoons chopped toasted
   cashews

Sweet brown rice is extremely sticky and sweet when cooked. It makes a delightful accompaniment to broiled marinated tofu and tempeh dishes as well as baked beans. Here cashews add mild flavor and a soft crunch to the rice.

1. Place the rice in a 2-quart saucepan and cover with cold water. Rub the rice with your fingertips to begin cleaning it, then drain it through a strainer. Return the rice to the saucepan and, again, cover with water and rinse. Repeat this process until the water runs clear.

2. In the saucepan, combine the rice with the stock and salt. Cover and bring to a boil, stirring once. Reduce the heat so that the rice is just simmering and cook, stirring occasionally, until the grains are tender, about 40 minutes. Remove from the heat and stir in the raisins. Transfer the rice to a serving bowl and top with the nuts. Serve at once.

Variations

1. Do not stir the rice as it cooks (this increases stickiness). Mix 1/3 cup minced onions, 2 teaspoons minced gingerroot, and 1 teaspoon minced garlic into the stock before adding the rice. Add 1/4 cup minced cilantro to the rice along with the raisins before serving.

2. Replace 1/2 cup of the stock with dry white wine. Add 3 tablespoons minced scallions, 1 teaspoon minced garlic, and 1 teaspoon anise seeds to the liquid before stirring in the rice. Omit the raisins, and stir 1/3 cup minced Italian parsley into the cooked rice. Top with chopped almonds instead of cashews.

Three-Grain Bake

Yield: 6 servings • Prep Time: 25 minutes • Cooking Time: 35 minutes

Combining the textures and flavors of more than one grain transforms a simple rice side dish into an interesting element within a meal. This rice works well served as is or topped with cheese. It may also be used as a filling for winter squash or tofu.

1/4 cup wild rice
1 1/2 cups water
1/2 cup millet
1 cup jasmine or long-grain rice
1 tablespoon olive oil
2 1/2 cups light vegetable stock (page 162) or water
1/4 teaspoon salt
1 cup grated carrot
3 tablespoons hulled sesame seeds
1 tablespoon chopped nori (page 193) or dulse (page 190)

1. Place the wild rice in a 1-quart saucepan and cover with cold water. Rinse the grain, rubbing it with your fingers, then drain it through a strainer. Repeat this rinsing 3 times. Combine the wild rice and water in the small saucepan. Bring it to a boil, stirring occasionally. Cover and reduce the heat so that the liquid simmers. Cook the wild rice, stirring occasionally, until all of the grains have popped open and are tender, about 45 minutes. As the wild rice cooks, add more water if necessary to prevent burning. Once cooked, set the wild rice aside. It may be cooked up to 24 hours in advance if refrigerated in an airtight container.

2. Meanwhile, rinse the millet briefly, then transfer it to a hot skillet. Cook over medium high heat, stirring often, until the millet begins to brown. Immediately transfer the millet to a bowl so that it does not continue to cook and burn. The millet can be toasted in this manner up to 48 hours in advance. Store at room temperature in an airtight container.

3. Preheat the oven to 375°F. Place the jasmine rice in a 2-quart saucepan and cover with water. Rinse the rice, rubbing it between your fingers, then drain it through a strainer. Repeat the rinsing and straining process several times, until the water runs clear. Strain the rice.

4. Dry the 2-quart saucepan and heat the oil in it over medium high heat. Add the rice and cook, stirring constantly, until about 1/4 of the grains have turned slightly milky. Immediately add the stock, salt, and carrot. Stir once to combine, then cover and bring to a boil. Transfer the pot to the oven and cook, covered, until all water is absorbed and the rice is tender, about 25 minutes.

5. Remove the pan from the oven and stir in the wild rice, millet, sesame seeds, and nori. Return to the oven to warm for 5 minutes. Serve at once.

Variations

1. Top the rice with 1/4 cup minced scallions, 1/4 cup grated daikon and 2 tablespoons toasted pine nuts. Omit the nori and sesame seeds.

2. Omit the nori and sesame seeds. Once the grains are combined, transfer them to an ovenproof serving dish. Sprinkle 1/3 cup grated Gruyère cheese over them and bake in a 350°F. oven until the cheese is melted.

Hearty Vegetable Stock

Yield: 2 1/2 quarts • Prep Time: 25 minutes • Cooking Time: 1 1/2 hours

1 large onion, quartered
4 whole cloves
2 tablespoons olive oil
2 carrots, cut into 1-inch pieces
1 turnip, cut into 1-inch pieces
1 parsnip, cut into 1/2-inch pieces
2 stalks celery, sliced
1 red potato, cubed
1 Granny Smith apple, cored and chopped
1 leek, chopped
1/2 cup brown lentils, picked over and rinsed
1 cup dry white wine
14 cups water
1 teaspoon salt
10 black peppercorns
2 cloves garlic, smashed
10 sprigs parsley
1 1/2 teaspoons dried thyme
1 bay leaf
2 sprigs winter savory
1/2 teaspoon marjoram

Lentils add depth and character to this hearty recipe. You may vary the type of bean used and/or other ingredients and spices to suit the taste of the dish for which the stock is intended.

1. Peel and quarter the onion, then stud 4 of the pieces with the cloves. Heat the oil in a heavy 6-quart saucepan over medium high heat until hot, but not smoking. Arrange the onion pieces, cut side down, in the oil and cook, turning occasionally, until they begin to brown, about 8 minutes. Reduce the heat to low and continue to cook, turning several times until the onions are evenly browned and quite soft. Remove them from the pan and set aside.

2. Return the pan to a medium heat and add the carrots, turnip, parsnip, celery, potato, apple, leek, and lentils. Cook, stirring constantly, until the vegetables are just beginning to brown, about 4 minutes.

3. Turn the heat to high and pour the wine over the vegetables. Cook, stirring constantly, for 1 minute, then add the remaining ingredients and bring to a boil. Reduce the heat to a simmer. Skim and discard any foam that rises to the surface. Cover and simmer, stirring occasionally, for 1 1/2 hours.

4. Remove the pan from the heat and strain into a large bowl. Use immediately or transfer to storage containers. Cool, then seal tightly and refrigerate for up to 3 days before using. Skim and discard all fat that rises to the surface as the stock cools. You may also freeze the stock for up to 3 months.

Variation

1. For a more strongly flavored stock, replace the white wine in the recipe above with dry red wine, then proceed with the recipe as directed.

Light Vegetable Stock

Yield: About 3 quarts • Prep Time: 20 minutes • Cooking Time: 1 1/2 hours

1 red onion, quartered
1 large yellow onion, quartered
3 leeks, chopped
3 large carrots, cut in 1-inch pieces
1 stalk celery
1 large potato, cubed
1 parsnip, peeled and sliced
3 cloves garlic, sliced
15 cups water
1 teaspoon dried thyme
2 bay leaves
6 sprigs parsley

This stock is light in taste and aroma, which makes it extremely versatile for use as a simmering liquid as well as a foundation for many sauces. The vegetables may be varied depending on what dish the stock is intended for and what is in season. If you do not know what you will be using the stock for, make it according to this recipe, then you may flavor it with additional ingredients, by simmering it with them just before it is added to the dish.

1. Combine the onions, leeks, carrots, celery, potato, parsnip, and garlic in a large stockpot. Add the water and bring to a boil, stirring occasionally. Skim and discard any scum that rises to the surface, then reduce to a simmer and stir in the thyme, bay leaves, parsley, sage, marjoram, salt, and peppercorns. Cover and simmer, stirring occasionally, for 1 1/2 hours.

2. Remove the stock from the heat and cool briefly. Strain the broth into a large bowl, then transfer it to storage containers and cover tightly. The stock may be refrigerated for up to 5 days or frozen for up to 3 months.

1/2 teaspoon dried sage
1/4 teaspoon dried marjoram, crushed
1 1/4 teaspoons salt
8 black peppercorns

Variations

1. For a mushroom stock, add 4 dried shiitake mushrooms and 1/2 pound button mushrooms to the original recipe. Increase the garlic to 6 cloves, the parsley to 10 sprigs, and the salt to 1 1/2 teaspoons. You may also substitute 1 cup dry white wine for 1 cup of the water.

2. For a kombu stock, add a 4-inch washed strip kombu to the original recipe. Increase the garlic to 6 cloves and, if the intended recipes are Oriental in flavor, add 1 tablespoon minced ginger.

Porcini Stock

Yield: About 10 cups • Prep Time: 15 minutes • Cooking Time: 1 1/2 hours

This deliciously rich mushroom-based stock serves beautifully as a replacement for rich meat stock in recipes that require a very strongly flavored base. If porcini stock is called for in a recipe in this book, the flavors are likely to be very unbalanced if you use another stock instead.

1 1/4 ounces dried porcini mushrooms (page 193), softened in 2 cups hot water
1/2 pound button mushrooms, sliced
2 carrots, peeled and sliced
1 small white onion, quartered
2 leeks, cleaned and chopped
1 stalk celery, sliced
3/4 cup diced turnip
3 cloves garlic, sliced
1 teaspoon dried thyme
1 bay leaf
12 cups water
1 1/2 teaspoons salt
10 black peppercorns
1/4 cup parsley sprigs

1. In a 3-quart saucepan, combine the porcini mushrooms with their soaking liquid, the button mushrooms, carrots, onion, leeks, celery, turnip, garlic, thyme, bay leaf, water, salt, peppercorns, and parsley. Bring to a boil, then reduce to a simmer and cook, covered and stirring occasionally, for 1 1/2 hours.

2. Remove the stock from the heat and allow it to cool with the ingredients in the liquid. Strain and use immediately or store in 1-cup airtight containers in the freezer for up to 3 months.

Tofu

Yield: About 1 pound • Prep Time: About 1 1/2 hours

1 cup dry organic soybeans
15 cups purified water
1 1/2 teaspoons nigari (or other coagulant) or 3 tablespoons undiluted vinegar

In Japan it is common practice to shop daily for fresh tofu, just as Parisians make a trip each day to the baker for bread. Once you have tasted fresh tofu, you will understand why. Its delicate, pure taste is so appealing that many enjoy fresh tofu served quite simply chilled with a light soba-style dipping sauce alongside. In addition to a better taste, making your own tofu allows you to control the texture of the tofu you make to fit precisely with the needs of particular recipes. The only drawback to making tofu from scratch is the time involved—count on at least 1 1/2 hours the first time you make it. If, however, you find yourself eating tofu on a regular basis, it is well worth the investment to experiment, at least once, with making your own; the process becomes demystified and less of a challenge once you know how it works.

Making tofu is similar to making dairy cheese. Just as rennet is used to curdle milk for cheese, a coagulant is added to soy milk which causes it to curdle. Nigari (or bittern), a salt evaporated from sea water, is the most traditional coagulant. Nigari, sold in most natural foods markets, has a pale, almost translucent quality with a pinkish tinge and, like many sea salts, it dries in small chunks. Nigari should be stored in an airtight container as even in the driest climates it will eventually begin to liquefy if exposed to moisture in the air. Epsom salt, calcium chloride, calcium sulfate, or magnesium chloride (all available at most pharmacies) may also be used as coagulants. The process also works with undiluted vinegar or lemon juice, though their flavor can be overly dominant and they may produce a tofu with a slightly grainy texture.

Besides the coagulant, the only unusual item needed to make tofu is a mold in which the tofu can drain (a "forming box"). You can easily make a satisfactory tofu mold out of a 1-quart, square- or rectangular-shaped plastic storage container. Punch or drill 1/4-inch holes spaced about 3/4 inch apart over the bottom and sides of the container. You must also fashion a flat lid to fit snugly inside the container to within 1/8 inch of the perimeter of the mold. Once the tofu is draining, the lid is weighted down as a means of achieving tofu of desired firmness. You will also need a blender, a 6- to 8-quart pot, and a second large pot or very large bowl, a large strainer, cheesecloth, and sufficient purified or clean spring water.

1. Pick over the beans to remove any debris, then rinse the beans and place them in a bowl with enough cold water to cover. Set aside to soak for at least 8 hours, preferably overnight. Drain and rinse the beans before proceeding.

2. The beans will have expanded to about 3 1/2 cups. Place about 1 cup of the soaked beans in the blender and add 1 1/2 cups water. Grind the beans until they are a very fine, even texture. Pour this mixture into a large pot and grind the remaining beans in the same way. Then rinse the blender bowl with an additional cup of water and add this to the pot as well. You will have used about 6 1/4 cups of purified water to this point.

3. Cook the beans over medium heat, stirring often, until the mixture reaches a boil. Reduce the heat and simmer the bean mixture for 20 minutes, stirring often. (This cooking step is essential as soybeans contain an enzyme called trypsin which, unless properly cooked, interferes with the body's assimilation of the protein contained in the beans.)

4. As the beans cook, wet a triple thickness of cheesecloth that is big enough to line your strainer and tofu mold. Place the cheesecloth in the strainer and set the strainer over the second pot or large bowl which should be placed in the sink.

5. Pour the cooked beans through the cheesecloth allowing the liquid to drain into the second pot. Rinse the emptied cooking pot out with an additional cup of water and pour this through the strainer.

6. Gradually pour the 5 1/2 cups cold water into the pot, through the ground soybean pulp that remains in the strainer. Once this pulp is cool enough to handle, twist the cheesecloth around it and begin squeezing to extract as much liquid as possible. The liquid that has been strained out of the pulp is soy milk. The pulp that remains in the cheesecloth is called "okara" (see note, below).

7. Heat the soy milk to a boil, stirring often. Meanwhile, dissolve the nigari in the remaining cup of water. (If using vinegar or lemon juice, do not dissolve it.) Once the soy milk boils, remove it from the heat and gently stir in about 1/3 of the nigari mixture. Allow the soy milk to rest for a minute, then gently stir in another 1/3 of the nigari. Cover the pot and allow it to rest, undisturbed, for 5 minutes. If, at this point, the soy milk appears curdled, with a clear and yellowish whey distinctly separated from the curds, no more coagulant is needed. If the soy milk still appears milky, gently add the remaining nigari so that the curds separate from the whey.

8. Transfer the okara from the cheesecloth to a storage container and rinse the cloth well. Line the tofu mold with the cheesecloth and place the mold over a large bowl in the sink. Ladle the curds gently into the mold, allowing the whey to drain into the bowl. Once all curds are in the mold, gently squeeze the cheesecloth to extract excess whey, then allow the curds to settle back into the shape of the mold. Fold a smooth layer of cheesecloth over the top of the curds and place the lid on top. Place a 2- to 3-pound weight on top of the lid and allow the curds—which are transforming into tofu—to drain for 30 minutes to 1 1/2 hours or until it is the desired firmness. For a slightly more even-textured tofu, carefully lift the cheesecloth from the mold partway through the pressing. Place the block of tofu on the work space and gently peel off the cheesecloth. Flip the tofu over and return it to the cheesecloth-lined mold to finish pressing. Use the tofu immediately, or refrigerate it, covered with purified water, in a plastic container for several days. Change the water daily.

Variation

1. You can prepare seasoned tofu by adding flavors to the curds before they are molded. If you wish to experiment with this, try the flavor combinations in the tofu "sausage" recipe (page 166).

Cook's Notes: The soybeans must soak at least 8 hours before beginning the procedure of preparing the tofu. Also, once prepared, the tofu must drain for at least 30 minutes, depending on the firmness desired, before being used in a recipe.

Okara is the pulp that is left once soy milk is strained from ground, cooked soybeans. It contains some of the soybean's protein and most of the fiber. Okara has a very mild, slightly beany flavor and can be used in a number of ways as you cook. Okara can be added to Seitan Cutlets (page 48) (add 1/2 cup) for added fiber, or it may be stirred into chili or soups along with the beans. It also holds moisture in baked goods, adding up to 1/2 cup to many standard muffin or fruit breads. You may also use okara as the base for a spread, adding ingredients such as miso, garlic, minced scallions, spices, and so on.

Tofu "Sausage"

Yield: 1 pound • Prep Time: 10 minutes

1 pound firm tofu
1/3 cup dry red wine
1/3 cup soy sauce
2 tablespoons minced fresh
　parsley
1 teaspoon dried thyme, crushed
1 teaspoon crushed fennel seeds
1/2 teaspoon dried oregano,
　crushed
1/2 teaspoon dried sage, crushed
1/8 teaspoon, each, nutmeg,
　cinnamon, cloves, and black
　pepper
2 cloves garlic, minced
2 teaspoons blackstrap molasses
1/4 cup minced scallions
2 tablespoons olive oil (optional)

Frozen tofu takes on an interesting, firm quality that, when thawed and crumbled, resembles ground meat. When flavored with traditional sausage flavorings, tofu can give the illusion of meat to many dishes. Use this "sausage" as a component of many recipes calling for ground meat or sausage which is either simmered in a dish (as in chili) or baked into a filling (as in lasagna).

1. Drain the tofu, then slice it into 1-inch-thick slabs. Wrap each slab separately in plastic and freeze until solid, at least 24 hours and no longer than 2 months.

2. Thaw the tofu, then unwrap it and place the slices on a clean kitchen towel with a second towel on top. Place a heavy cutting board on top of this and weight it down with an iron skillet or several 1-pound cans. Allow the tofu to drain for 30 minutes.

3. In a shallow baking pan, combine the red wine, soy sauce, parsley, thyme, fennel, oregano, sage, nutmeg, cinnamon, cloves, black pepper, garlic, molasses, and the scallions. For a slightly richer-tasting sausage, add 2 tablespoons olive oil to this mixture. Mix well, then crumble the tofu and stir it into this marinade. Toss to coat evenly, cover, and refrigerate. Allow this "sausage" mixture to marinate for 24 to 48 hours before using, turning it several times.

Variations

1. For a taste that resembles traditional farm sausage, season the tofu with 1/3 cup minced onions, 2 tablespoons dried sage, 3 tablespoons minced fresh parsley, 2 teaspoons dried thyme, 1 1/2 teaspoons dried marjoram, 2 tablespoons minced garlic, 1 1/2 teaspoons salt, 1/4 teaspoon cayenne, and 2 tablespoons olive oil.

2. For a French-style sausage, season the tofu with 1 teaspoon ground black pepper, 1/4 teaspoon whole peppercorns, 2 teaspoons salt, 1/4 teaspoon cayenne, 1/2 teaspoon dried thyme, 2 tablespoons minced garlic, 1/3 cup minced scallions, and 1/2 cup cognac.

3. For a spicy sausage mix, combine the tofu with 1/2 cup dry white wine, 2 minced jalapeño peppers, 1 tablespoon chili powder, 1 teaspoon mace, 1/4 teaspoon cloves, 1 tablespoon salt, 1 teaspoon anise seeds, 1 teaspoon black peppercorns, and 1 tablespoon minced garlic.

Cook's Note: The tofu must be frozen for at least 24 hours before seasoning in order to obtain the correct texture. It must then thaw and be pressed for 30 minutes.

Nut Butter

Yield: 1 cup • Prep Time: 10 minutes

Nut butter can be made from any type of nut and used as the base or an enrichment for sauces and salad dressings. It can also be used as a spread like peanut butter. Commercially produced pure nut butters (peanut, almond, and cashew) are readily available in most natural foods markets. With a food processor, you can easily make nut butter yourself.

2 cups nuts

1. Place the nuts in a food processor fitted with the metal chopping blade. Grind until the nuts become a creamy, evenly textured paste. As you work, scrape nuts that have stuck from the sides and corners of the bowl. When the nut butter reaches the desired texture, transfer it to a container and seal airtight. Store at room temperature for up to a week. Refrigerate if stored longer.

Cook's Note: Nut butters can be made from either raw or toasted nuts. As an enrichment, the flavor produced by toasted nuts is superior. For instructions on toasting nuts, see page 35.

Crostini

Yield: 16 crostini • Prep Time: 8 minutes • Cooking Time: 20 minutes

Crostini are, in effect, large croutons and, like croutons, they may be made with virtually any spice or flavoring added to the butter and/or oil crisping mixture. Below I give a few ideas for variations, but you could alter these to go with flavors in a particular dish. The main recipe below incorporates olive oil or butter as a means of crisping the crostini. To save on fat, you may reduce the amount and/or replace the fat with egg white.

8 slices sourdough, whole-grain
  or quality Italian bread
4 tablespoons olive oil or butter
2 cloves garlic
1 tablespoon dried rosemary,
  crushed
2 tablespoons fresh parsley
Pinch of salt

1. Preheat the oven to 375°F. Trim the crusts from the bread and cut each piece in half to form 2 triangles. Place these on a baking sheet. In a small saucepan over low heat, warm the oil or butter with the garlic (pressed through a garlic press), rosemary, parsley, and salt, until the flavors merge, about 4 minutes. Remove from the heat. With a pastry brush, coat each slice of bread on both sides. Bake, turning once, until the crostini are crisp and lightly browned, about 20 minutes. Do not allow them to burn. Cool the crostini on a cake rack, then store in an airtight container until ready to use. They may be stored, airtight, at room temperature for up to a week.

Variations

1. For cinnamon crostini, use butter and add to it 1 tablespoon cinnamon and a pinch of cloves. These may be served with Indian-flavored curries or with dishes including tomato sauces.

2. Replace the rosemary and parsley with 3 tablespoons minced basil.

3. For a "featherlight" crouton, replace the bread with raw, shredded filo dough (scraps from B'Stilla work well). Place the dough on a baking sheet, then brush with flavored butter and bake as directed above.

All-Purpose Pie Dough

Yield: 2 single-crust pie shells • Prep Time: 15 minutes

1 cup whole wheat pastry flour
1 cup unbleached white flour
1/4 teaspoon salt
8 tablespoons butter (1 stick)
About 10 tablespoons cold water

The following all-purpose pie dough is a pâte brisée *(a standard, all-purpose French pastry dough). In this recipe I substitute whole wheat flour for half of the white flour traditionally used, and the effect is still light and flaky. Using all whole wheat results in a crust that is too heavy for my taste. For alternative doughs (nondairy, nonwheat), see the variations below. As with all pastry doughs, the light and delicate quality of this is dependent on two factors. First, the fat is worked quickly into the flour before liquid is added. In this way it retards gluten bonding, which results in less elasticity. The type of fat used also contributes to flakiness, a solid fat being more effective than a liquid. In addition, the dough should not be overworked, again as a means of minimizing elasticity and toughness. Although it is easier to prepare the dough using a food processor, I recommend preparing the dough by hand, at least a few times, as a means of truly understanding the pastry dough.*

1. Combine the flours and salt in a mixing bowl. Drop the stick of butter into the flour and roll it to coat with flour. Pick it up, using only your fingertips, then quickly cut off 1/2-inch pieces from the stick, allowing them to drop into the flour. Toss the pieces in the flour, then using your fingertips, work the butter into the flour. This motion is a combination rubbing-gentle pressing motion. If you can imagine you are feeling the texture of a cloth between your fingertips, you will approximate the motion. Work only with your fingertips (avoiding contact with the palms of your hands keeps the butter the coolest possible and, therefore, avoids melting it). If you have particularly hot hands, use two knives or a pastry blender to work the butter into the flour. Once all of the flour has come in contact with the butter, the flour will look slightly darker in color and the mixture's texture will resemble a combination of coarse meal and various sorts of dried beans. At this point stop working the flour. It is important to have the mixture slightly uneven—with some large and some small pieces of butter— as a means of improving flakiness.

2. With a fork, make a well in the center of the flour. Pour the water into the well and, with the tines of the fork, begin to incorporate the flour mixture into the water, working quickly. Once all water is incorporated, quickly work the dough into a ball. Do not knead the dough, simply gather it together (avoiding contact with the palms of your hands) so that no flour looks dry and powdery. Divide the dough into two pieces and shape each into a round, then wrap them in lightly floured pieces of waxed paper and refrigerate for at least 2 hours before rolling. To freeze the dough, wrap the balls in a second layer of foil and freeze for up to 2 months. Thaw before rolling.

3. To roll the dough, lightly flour a clean, smooth work surface (a cool marble surface is ideal, but any smooth, cool surface works). Place one unwrapped half of the dough on the flour and press the rolling pin down on its surface, through the center axis, from several directions. This will begin to work the dough. Then roll the dough out from the center out to, but not over, the edge. Rotate the dough frequently, lightly dusting the work surface beneath and the top surface of the dough to prevent sticking. Once or twice you should flip the dough over completely. If the dough becomes overly soft and/or the butter seems to be turning slightly liquid, transfer the dough to a baking sheet and chill for about 20 minutes before continuing.

4. Once the dough is rolled to the desired thickness, wrap it around the rolling pin (rolling it over on itself, not pressing the layers together to seal), then unroll it as you place it where you want it. Trim to the desired shape and proceed with the recipe. Scraps of the pastry dough may be reformed into a ball, then chilled and used once again. Repeat with the second ball of dough.

Processor Method

Fit the processor with the metal chopping blade. In the bowl, combine the flours and salt; process to blend. Cut the butter into about 18 pieces and drop these around the bowl into the flour. With an on-off pulsing motion, combine the butter with the flour until it resembles mixed beans with a coarse grain. Turn the motor off momentarily as you position the water. With the motor running, quickly pour the water through the feed tube. Leave the motor running until the dough forms a ball, about 30 seconds. Stop processing immediately, then turn the dough out onto a lightly floured work surface and roll it around in the flour until it is not sticky. Divide it into two rounds and wrap in waxed paper as directed in step 2 above. Proceed with the recipe as above.

Using Alternatives in Pastry Dough

The gluten contained in wheat flour allows pastry dough to develop a smooth and flaky texture. You may substitute other flours for some or all of the wheat flour in the standard recipe, but without wheat, the texture will always be slightly (to very) crumbly, depending on the flour used. If you use alternative flours, it is always best to combine more than one—for example, rice flour mixed with spelt or wheat gives a very delicate crust. Rye flour can be mixed with barley flour or spelt for a tasty, but heavy crust. To fortify a pastry dough with protein you may replace 2 to 3 tablespoons of the wheat flour with soy or quinoa flour.

Butter or margarine is the best choice for fat in pastry doughs. Oils will never produce the same degree of flakiness as a solid fat. You can reduce the ratio of fat to flour, though the dough will become increasingly heavy.

Crêpes

Yield: 25 6-inch crêpes, 15 10-inch crêpes • Prep Time: 10 minutes • Cooking Time: 30 minutes

1 cup whole wheat flour
1 cup unbleached white flour
1/4 teaspoon salt
2 eggs
2 cups low-fat milk
3 tablespoons butter

Classic French crêpes are light and delicate, made with white flour, whole eggs, milk and a drizzling of butter. They may be eaten with just a squeeze of lemon and a sprinkling of sugar, or in a complex recipe such as a layered crêpe cake. Whatever the use, this versatile pancake reveals its adaptability in the recipes and variations below that incorporate a wide range of alternative ingredients.

1. Sift, into a medium-sized mixing bowl, both types of flour and the salt. Make a well in the center of the flour. In a smaller bowl, combine the eggs and milk, then whisk until frothy. Gradually pour the egg mixture into the well. As you do so, use a fork to incorporate the flour mixture smoothly into the liquid. Once all of the egg mixture has been added, whisk the batter until smooth, then cover the bowl with a damp cloth and set aside for at least 20 minutes. (The batter may be prepared up to 2 days in advance, if refrigerated in an airtight container. Bring it to room temperature and whisk well before using.)

2. Before you begin cooking the crêpes, have a plate big enough to hold the crêpes and twenty-five 7-inch or fifteen 11-inch squares of waxed paper next to the stove. Place one square of paper on the plate. Also have a small dish for the butter and the crêpe batter with a ladle and a rounded metal spatula (palette knife).

3. Place an iron crêpe pan over a medium high heat. Add the butter and allow it to melt, swirling the pan as it does. When all has melted, stir 1 tablespoon into the crêpe batter and pour the rest into a small dish. Wipe the pan with a paper towel so that just a thin film of butter remains. Now test the consistency of the batter. It should be just thick enough to form a thin coating with your fingers, pick some out of the batter and rub it as if feeling cloth. If the batter is too thick, add a small amount of water. If you are uncertain how to judge the consistency, it is best to cook one crêpe before adding water. If the batter is too thick to pour out into a paper-thin coating, finish cooking that crêpe, then thin the remaining batter slightly.

4. To begin cooking the crêpes, return the pan to the heat and allow it to warm briefly. Brush it with butter, then remove the pan from the heat, holding it in one hand with the front lip of the pan pointing slightly down and angled to the side. With the other hand, scoop a ladle full of batter. Immediately pour the batter into the pan, onto the point of the pan at the bottom edge of the lip that is pointed down. The batter should sizzle. Immediately rotate the pan in an angled circle to coat it with batter. Once the pan is coated, pour any batter that remains liquid back into the bowl of batter. Place the pan over the flame. (Though the description is long, once it is mastered, this entire action should take about 15 seconds so that the pan retains heat.)

4. Allow the crêpe to cook until it is lightly browned on the bottom, about 1 1/2 minutes. After about 30 seconds of cooking, when the edges of the crêpe have curled back slightly, shake the pan to loosen the crêpe. Rotate the crêpe in a clockwise manner once or twice in order to cook it evenly. When the first side is cooked, flip the crêpe by allowing it to hang out slightly over the edge of the pan, then flipping it into the air by briskly jerking the pan down, then up. (Or for a less flashy production, simply flip it with the palette knife.) Allow the crêpe to cook briefly, about 30 seconds, or until the second side has golden brown specks. Immediately slide the crêpe out of the pan onto the plate and cover with waxed paper. Continue to cook the crêpes until all batter is used up. As you do so, adjust the heat or allow the pan to cool briefly between crêpes if it overheats. The best indication that the pan is too hot is that the crêpes look lacy. If this happens, slow down the cooking process slightly by cooling the pan. If the pan is too cool, the batter will not sizzle very enthusiastically and the crêpes will be too thick.

5. Once all crêpes are prepared, cover the last with waxed paper. Use immediately or wrap the entire stack in waxed paper and then plastic wrap. They may be prepared up to 24 hours before using if wrapped airtight and refrigerated. They may also be frozen for up to 2 months.

Variations

1. Add 3 to 4 tablespoons snipped chives or other fresh, minced herbs to the batter just before cooking.

2. Use only egg whites and increase liquid by adding 1/3 cup water.

3. Use all whole wheat flour or 1 cup whole wheat flour and 1 cup cornmeal.

4. Use 1 cup rice flour and 1 cup whole wheat flour.

5. Use soy milk instead of milk.

6. To make almond crêpes, combine 3/4 cup ground almonds, 1/2 cup whole wheat flour, 1 cup unbleached white flour, and 1/4 teaspoon salt. In a second bowl, beat the 3 egg whites until frothy, then stir in the 1 cup milk. Whisk the liquid into the flour mixture and proceed as above.

7. To make dairy-free crêpes, combine 1 cup whole wheat flour, 1 cup white flour, 1 tablespoon egg replacer, 1/4 teaspoon salt. Purée 8 ounces silken tofu in a food processor, then add 1 1/2 cups plain soy milk or water and process to blend. With the motor running, add the flour mixture and process until smooth. Cook the crêpes as described above.

Soy Cream

Yield: 1 cup • Prep Time: 5 minutes

This nondairy "cream" may be whisked into sauces just before serving to add a creamy texture. It will not stand up to cooking.

10 ounces silken tofu, drained
1 3-inch piece kombu (page 192)
6 cups water
1/2 teaspoon salt
1 to 2 tablespoons tahini
  (page 195)
1 tablespoon lemon juice

1. Drain the tofu and rinse the kombu. Place the kombu in a 2-quart saucepan with the water. Bring this to a boil and add the tofu. Reduce to a simmer and cook for 5 minutes.

2. Drain the tofu and transfer it to a blender. Discard the kombu. Add the remaining ingredients to the blender and purée until very smooth, scraping the beaker as necessary. The cream can be prepared up to 2 days in advance if refrigerated in an airtight container.

Crème Fraîche

Yield: 2 cups • Prep Time: 5 minutes

1/2 cup low-fat ricotta
1/4 cup cream
1/2 cup plain nonfat yogurt
2 tablespoons cultured buttermilk

Crème Fraîche is thickened cream used in many classic French dishes, often to enrich a sauce. I use very little in my recipes (no more than a few tablespoons) and always offer low-fat and nondairy alternatives. For a simple low-fat alternative, you can often use low-fat or nonfat yogurt. Do not boil low-fat cream sauces as they will separate. The crème fraîche recipe below is a spin-off idea from Roy Andries de Groot's crème fraîche recipe in Revolutionizing French Cooking *.*

1. Place the ricotta in a blender or food processor and purée until very smooth. Add the remaining ingredients and purée for 30 seconds more. Transfer to a 6-cup glass jar and cover tightly. Set the jar aside in a warm, draft-free place to ripen. A gas-lit oven is ideal.

2. After 24 hours the cream should have thickened substantially. A layer of whey will have separated from the solid cream. Line a large strainer with two layers of cheesecloth and place it over the sink. Transfer the cream mixture into the strainer, being careful to disturb it as little as possible. Allow the whey to drain off for at least 30 minutes. Place the cream in a clean jar, cover tightly, and refrigerate until ready to use. Use within 5 days. The cream does not freeze.

Cook's Note: The crème fraîche must rest for 24 hours before it is ready for use.

Tofu "Cottage Cheese"

Yield: 2 3/4 cups • Prep Time: 5 minutes • Cooking Time: 7 minutes

1 pound firm tofu
10 ounces soft silken tofu
1 tablespoon lemon juice
1 teaspoon salt
1 teaspoon brewer's yeast
  (optional)

This cheese alternative is remarkably similar to true cottage cheese, especially after it has been left to mature overnight. It works well in lasagna and other baked dishes in which ricotta or cottage cheese is often used and is also quite nice as is.

1. Drain the firm tofu and place it in a mixing bowl. With the back of a fork, mash the tofu into small pearl-shaped pieces. Line the steaming rack of a steamer with cheesecloth or a loosely woven dish towel and place the tofu in the rack. Place it over, not touching, rapidly boiling water and steam for 7 minutes. Transfer the tofu to a clean kitchen towel, fold the towel over and press the tofu to extract as much liquid as possible, then return it to the mixing bowl.

2. Drain the silken tofu and place it in a blender or food processor fitted with the metal chopping blade. Purée this until absolutely smooth, scraping down the sides of the beaker as necessary. Pour the puréed silken tofu over the cooked tofu. Add the lemon juice, salt, and brewer's yeast. Mix well, then cover with plastic wrap and leave at room temperature overnight to ripen. The tofu mixture should sour slightly. Transfer to a storage container, cover tightly, and refrigerate for up to 5 days.

Tofu "Feta"

Yield: 1 pound • Prep Time: 5 minutes • Cooking Time: 15 minutes

Tofu is traditionally marinated with miso and other flavors in Japan and used as a condiment/appetizer. In China, forms of marinated tofu are sometimes used as a sort of cheese. In an attempt to find alternatives for cheese, I came across a recipe for tofu "feta" in Barbara and Leonard Jacobs' book Cooking with Seitan. *It served as inspiration for this tofu "feta" recipe.*

1 pound extra-firm tofu
5 teaspoons umeboshi paste
   (page 196)
1 tablespoon roasted tahini
   (page 195)
1 tablespoon rice vinegar
1 tablespoon mirin (page 193)

1. Slice the tofu into 1-inch slabs, then place them on a clean kitchen towel. Place a second clean towel on top and a cutting board over this. Press the board gently, then allow the tofu to drain for 30 minutes.

2. Place the tofu in a mixing bowl and mash it with a fork until it is evenly crumbled. Add the umeboshi paste, tahini, vinegar and mirin. Stir until evenly mixed. Transfer this mixture into a steamer tray and spread it out evenly, then place the tray in the top of a steamer over, but not touching, rapidly boiling water. If you do not have a steamer tray, place the tofu on a double layer of cheesecloth and tie the cloth around it to form a flat ball; then place the cheesecloth in the top of a steamer. Steam the tofu for 20 minutes.

3. Remove the tofu from the steamer and place it, still in the rack or cheesecloth, over a bowl allowing room below the rack for the tofu to drain. Place a plate on top of the tofu and press firmly. Place a 3-pound weight (or several cans) on top and drain for 30 minutes.

4. Transfer the "feta" to a container and refrigerate, tightly covered, until ready to use. It can be used immediately or prepared up to 4 days in advance. In a separate container, save the juices that were pressed from the tofu. These should also be stored in an airtight container in the refrigerator and may be added to dishes in which the "feta" is used in order to increase the flavor.

Cook's Note: The "feta" must drain 30 minutes before using it.

Tofu "Gorgonzola"

Yield: 1 cup • Prep Time: 5 minutes

This is a slightly more intense version of tofu "feta" (page 173).

10 ounces firm silken tofu
2 tablespoons mellow white miso
1 tablespoon tahini (page 195)
1 tablespoon raspberry vinegar
2 tablespoons brewer's yeast
2 tablespoons shredded dulse
   (page 190)

1. Drain the tofu, then place it in a food processor, fitted with the metal chopping blade, or a blender. Add the miso, tahini, vinegar, and yeast. Purée until smooth.

2. Transfer the tofu mixture to a shallow storage container (approximately 5 inches square). With the tip of a paring knife, slide the pieces of dulse into the tofu, somewhat perpendicular to the bottom of the container. Cover the tofu and refrigerate for at least 2 days. The tofu will keep for up to 7 days if refrigerated. Use to flavor, as you would a cheese. The tofu mixture does not have the same creamy quality as cheese and will not melt in the same way as true Gorgonzola.

Cook's Note: The "Gorgonzola" must rest for 2 days before being used.

Panir

Yield: 2 cups • Prep Time: 5 minutes • Cooking Time: 25 minutes

1 gallon whole milk
2 tablespoons lemon juice
1/2 teaspoon salt (optional)

Panir is an Indian-style fresh cheese. It can be used as you would fresh mozzarella in salads or on pizza for example. It is central to Aromatic Spinach (page 102) and Panir Kabobs (page 106).

1. Place the milk in a 6-quart saucepan over high heat and bring it to a boil, stirring occasionally. Remove it from the heat and allow it to cool for 2 minutes, then return the milk to a boil. Repeat this process again. The second time, remove the milk from the heat and allow it to cool for 5 minutes. Gradually pour the lemon juice and salt into the milk, stirring gently. The instant the milk starts to separate into curds stop adding lemon juice. (You might need only part of the lemon juice.) Also stop stirring the liquid and set it aside for 5 minutes.

2. Line a strainer with a triple layer of cheesecloth. Gently ladle the milk into the cheesecloth. If you wish to save the whey that will drain off, place the strainer over a large bowl. Once all the milk is poured into the strainer, pull the corners of the cheesecloth together and squeeze excess liquid out of the panir. Hang the bundle of cheese over the sink and allow it to drain for several hours. Remove the cheesecloth, place the panir in an airtight container, and refrigerate overnight.

Variations

1. Stir 1 tablespoon toasted cumin seeds into the milk mixture just before straining.

2. Flavor the milk with 1 tablespoon orange flower water when you add the lemon juice.

Cook's Note: The whey must drain from the panir overnight.

Hearty Tomato Sauce

Yield: 3 quarts • Prep Time: 20 minutes • Cooking Time: 3 to 4 hours

2 tablespoons olive oil
1 1/2 cups diced red onion
3/4 cup diced carrot
1/2 cup diced celery
3/4 cup diced green pepper
8 ounces mushrooms, chopped
3 tablespoons dry red wine
1 cup porcini stock (page 163)
   or water
2 20-ounce cans plum tomatoes
2 tablespoons tomato paste
4 cloves garlic, sliced
1/4 ounce dried porcini, softened
   in hot water

This thick and rich tomato sauce is ideal for lasagna (page 118). It also makes an excellent all-purpose sauce for simple pasta and cheese dishes. In addition, this sauce can be used as an accompaniment to broiled tofu or tempeh that has been marinated in a light marinade. As with many long-cooking tomato-based sauces, this one matures in flavor if it is simmered slowly, then left refrigerated for a day or so before being used.

1. In a large Dutch oven or stockpot, heat the oil over high heat until hot, but not smoking. Add the onion and cook, stirring constantly, until all pieces of onion glisten with a coating of oil. Reduce the heat to medium low and continue to cook, stirring often, until the onion is translucent, about 10 minutes. Add the carrot and celery and continue to cook, stirring frequently until the celery just begins to soften, about 10 minutes. Stir in the green pepper and continue to cook, stirring often, until it has released its fragrance and it too has begun to soften, about 8 minutes. Now add the mushrooms and cook, stirring very frequently, until the mushrooms are soft, about 8 minutes.

2. Increase the heat to high and, while stirring, add the wine. It will sizzle and release the aroma of alcohol, then the sizzling will subside. At this point, add the stock, tomatoes, tomato paste, garlic, thyme, oregano, parsley, marjoram, salt, pepper, honey, and 6 basil leaves. Break the tomatoes into small chunks as you stir and allow the sauce to come to a boil. Cook the sauce for 10 minutes on high, stirring often, then reduce to a simmer and cook, partially covered and stirring occasionally, for 3 to 4 hours.

3. Once the sauce has thickened to the desired consistency, remove it from the heat. Chop the remaining basil and stir it into the sauce. Allow it to cool, then refrigerate, in an airtight container, for at least 24 hours. The sauce can also be used immediately, though it improves in flavor when cooked ahead. It can be frozen, in an airtight container, for up to 3 months.

1/2 teaspoon dried thyme
1 1/4 teaspoons dried oregano
6 sprigs fresh parsley
1/4 teaspoon dried marjoram
1/2 teaspoon salt
1/4 teaspoon black pepper
1 tablespoon honey
1/2 cup (packed) fresh basil

Variations

1. Omit the basil and add 1 tablespoon dried rosemary along with the thyme.

2. Additional spices such as red pepper flakes, minced garlic (stirred at the end of cooking), lemon zest, or 1 teaspoon of cinnamon add interesting twists to the sauce.

3. Stir tofu "feta" (page 173) or tofu "sausage" (page 166) into the sauce for the last 30 minutes of simmering.

Light Tomato Sauce

Yield: 5 cups • Prep Time: 10 minutes • Cooking Time: 15 minutes

This delicate sauce can be used over pasta or with any light broiled main course dish.

1. With the tip of a paring knife, cut a cone shape from the stem end of each tomato. On the blossom end of each, cut a cross just through the skin. Bring 3 quarts of water to a rolling boil. Drop the tomatoes into the pot and, stirring often, allow them to cook until the skin at the blossom ends just begins to peel back, about 30 seconds. Immediately transfer the tomatoes to a strainer and run cold tap water over them just long enough to stop their cooking. When they are cool enough to handle, peel the skin from the tomatoes. Cut each in half and squeeze out all seeds, then chop them coarsely.

2. In a 2-quart saucepan, heat the butter over medium heat until large bubbles form. Stir in the tomatoes, garlic, red pepper flakes, rosemary, parsley, salt and pepper. Bring the sauce to a boil, then reduce to a simmer and cook, stirring often, until the flavors have merged, about 8 minutes. Remove the rosemary and parsley. Taste and adjust the seasonings, then serve immediately.

2 pounds fresh Italian plum
  tomatoes
1 tablespoon butter
2 cloves garlic, sliced thin
1/8 teaspoon dried red pepper
  flakes
1 sprig fresh rosemary
6 sprigs fresh parsley, preferably
  Italian
1/4 teaspoon salt
Pinch of black pepper

Pesto

Yield: About 1 cup • Prep Time: 20 minutes

8 cloves garlic
1/4 cup pine nuts
3 cups, packed fresh basil leaves
1/4 cup olive oil
2/3 cup grated Parmesan
1/4 cup grated Romano
2 tablespoons butter, softened to room temperature (optional)

Pesto, made from fresh garlic, basil, and Parmesan, is a classic concoction that captures the essence of Mediterranean flavors. It is traditionally made in a mortar and pestle but a food processor simplifies the work. Pesto is a high-fat condiment, but because it is so powerful in flavor, a small amount goes far.

1. Have all the cloves of garlic peeled and halved lengthwise. With the aid of a paring knife, remove and discard the center germinating section of each half (this will sometimes be green).

2. Fit a food processor with the metal chopping blade. Lock the lid in place and turn on the motor. With the motor running, drop the garlic, all at once, into the bowl. It will quickly be chopped fine and the pieces will, for the most part, stick to the sides of the bowl. Scrape down the bowl and add the pine nuts. With an on-off, pulse action, chop the nuts until the pieces of nut are about the same size as the garlic. Add the basil and, again with a pulse action, chop the leaves until they are all roughly chopped.

3. Leave the motor running and add the olive oil in a thin stream. When it is all in, scrape down the sides of the bowl and process for another 10 seconds. Add the grated cheeses and quickly process just to blend. For a richer paste, add the butter and process again, just to blend. Transfer the pesto to a glass jar or airtight storage container. The pesto can be prepared up to 2 weeks in advance if refrigerated in an airtight container. It can be frozen for up to 3 months.

Miso Pesto

Yield: About 1 cup • Prep Time: 20 minutes

10 cloves garlic
1/4 cup pine nuts or walnuts
3 1/2 cups packed fresh basil leaves
1/4 cup olive oil
3/4 cup mellow barley miso
1 tablespoon tahini (page 195)
2 teaspoons mirin (page 193)
2 tablespoons butter, softened to room temperature (optional)

For those wishing to eliminate or reduce fat in the diet, this dairy-free pesto can serve exceptionally well. It may be used in most recipes calling for a classic pesto. The one note of caution is that the miso may give some dishes the "natural foods brown hue," but this can usually be remedied by the addition of colorful vegetables or by layering the pesto beneath other brighter ingredients.

1. Have all the cloves of garlic peeled and halved lengthwise. With the aid of a paring knife, remove and discard the center germinating section of each half (this will sometimes be green).

2. Fit a food processor with the metal chopping blade. Lock the lid in place and turn on the motor. With the motor running, drop the garlic, all at once, into the bowl. It will quickly be chopped fine and the pieces will, for the most part, stick to the sides of the bowl. Scrape down the bowl and add the pine nuts. With an on-off, pulse action, chop the pine nuts until they are about the same size as the garlic. Add the basil and, again with a pulse action, chop the leaves until they are all roughly chopped.

3. Leave the motor running and add the olive oil in a thin stream. When it is all in, scrape down the sides of the bowl and process for another 10 seconds. Add the miso, tahini, and mirin. Quickly process just to blend. For a richer paste, add the butter and process again, just to blend. Transfer the pesto to a glass jar or airtight storage container. The pesto can be prepared up to 2 weeks in advance if refrigerated in an airtight container. It can be frozen for up to 3 months.

Variations

1. For a dairy-free, oil-free version, replace the oil with water.
2. Add 2 tablespoons of butter for a smoother, more mellow quality.
3. Replace the pine nuts with pecans and the basil with cilantro.

Madeira Sauce

Yield: 1 1/2 cups • Prep Time: 15 minutes • Cooking Time: 45 minutes

Use this sauce for Braised Eggplant (page 112) or to dress up simple grilled tofu dishes such as Crusty Lemon Tofu with Wild Mushrooms (page 77).

2 tablespoons olive oil
1/2 cup minced shallots
1 carrot, cut into tiny dice
8 ounces mushrooms, minced
3 tablespoons flour
2/3 cup Madeira
2 3/4 cups porcini stock (page 163) or other mushroom stock (page 163)
1 teaspoon tomato paste (optional)
Salt and pepper to taste
2 tablespoons minced chervil

1. In a 1 1/2-quart saucepan, heat the oil over medium heat until hot, but not smoking. Add the shallots and cook, stirring constantly, until they just begin to soften, about 2 minutes. Reduce the heat slightly, then add the carrots and mushrooms. Cook, stirring often, until the carrots are just tender, about 15 minutes.

2. Sprinkle the flour over the vegetables, then stir to coat evenly. Cook, stirring constantly, until the flour turns a light, nutty brown, about 18 minutes. Increase the heat to high and whisk in the Madeira. Cook, whisking constantly, until the intense smell of alcohol has evaporated, about 1 minute. Whisk in the stock, then add the tomato paste. Bring the sauce to a boil, then reduce to a simmer and cook, stirring occasionally, until the sauce is thick and rich, about 25 minutes. Taste and adjust the seasonings. Strain the sauce through a fine-mesh strainer and stir in the chervil. The sauce can be prepared ahead and refrigerated, in an airtight container, for up to 5 days. It can also be frozen for up to 2 months. Warm until piping hot before serving.

Variation

1. Add 8 ounces mushrooms, sliced and sautéed, to finished sauce.

Light Madeira Sauce

Yield: 2 cups • Prep Time: 5 minutes • Cooking Time: 20 minutes

This is a lighter version of the previous sauce that serves equally well with eggplant steaks as it does tossed in with pasta or as an accompaniment to Seitan Cutlets (page 48).

3 1/2 cups hearty vegetable stock (page 162)
1/2 cup Madeira
1 teaspoon Dijon-style mustard
1 teaspoon minced garlic
2 teaspoons arrowroot
1 tablespoon cold water
3 tablespoons minced fresh parsley
Salt and pepper to taste

1. In a 2-quart saucepan, combine the stock, Madeira, mustard, and garlic. Bring this to a boil, whisking occasionally. Reduce the heat slightly and allow the liquid to boil, uncovered, until it is reduced to 1 1/2 cups, about 20 minutes.

2. In a small bowl, combine the arrowroot and water. Stir this into the sauce and return to a boil. Remove from the heat and stir in the parsley, then season to taste with salt and pepper.

Leek Sauce

Yield: 2 1/2 cups • Prep Time: 10 minutes • Cooking Time: 20 minutes

1 1/4 pounds leeks (about 3), chopped
2 tablespoons butter or olive oil
1/4 cup minced shallots
1 cup dry white wine
1 cup light vegetable stock (page 162)
1/4 teaspoon salt
Pinch white pepper
1 bay leaf
Pinch cayenne
Pinch nutmeg
3 tablespoons minced chervil or 2 tablespoons minced fresh parsley

This is an example of a simple puréed sauce. The high proportion of solid to liquid ingredients gives the sauce a delicate, yet thick consistency without any additional thickener. This sauce is very versatile, suited for well-balanced dishes that simply need a cloak of slightly contrasting flavor, such as Stuffed Cauliflower (page 115), Layered Tempeh (page 110), or Twice-Baked White Bean Soufflé (page 98). You can vary the fresh herbs used in this sauce depending on the dish with which it is to be served.

1. Trim the tough tops and roots from the leeks, leaving their root ends intact. Place each leek on a cutting board and, with the tip of a paring knife, slice the leek lengthwise from about 1/2 inch above the root through the top. Rotate the leek 90 degrees and make a second cut in the same manner. Peel off and discard all tough outer layers, then rinse the leeks under cold running water, rubbing well to remove all dirt. Chop the leeks into 1/4-inch pieces.

2. Heat the butter over moderate heat until it is melted and hot, but not brown. Add the leek and shallots and cook, stirring constantly, until the leeks are very soft, about 12 minutes. If the leeks begin to brown before they are soft, reduce the heat immediately.

3. Turn the heat to high and stir in the wine. It should sizzle, then immediately boil. Continue to cook until the smell of alcohol is gone, about 2 minutes. Reduce the heat slightly and add the stock, salt, pepper, bay leaf, cayenne, and nutmeg. Continue to cook, stirring often, for 5 minutes. Remove from the heat and cool briefly, then purée in a blender or food processor, making the sauce as smooth as possible. Press the sauce through a fine-mesh strainer into a clean saucepan and stir in the chervil.

Variations

1. Stir 1/4 cup milk, cream, or soy milk into the sauce once it is passed through the strainer.

2. Replace the chervil with 1/4 cup fresh shredded basil. Stir 1/4 cup grated Gruyère into the sauce and warm briefly before serving.

Garlicky Kale Sauce

Yield: About 2 cups • Prep Time: 15 minutes • Cooking Time: 25 minutes

2 1/2 pounds kale
3/4 cup dry white wine
12 cloves garlic, peeled, halved, and germinating center removed
3 cups hearty vegetable stock (page 162)
1/2 cup minced shallots

Serve this scrumptious, calcium-rich sauce with marinated broiled tofu, steamed vegetables, soufflés, or other simple entrées.

1. Remove the stems from the kale and wash the leaves well in several changes of cold water. Transfer them to a strainer and leave them in the sink to drain as you prepare the rest of the sauce.

2. In a 2-quart saucepan, combine the wine and garlic. Bring this to a boil and cook, stirring often, until the smell of alcohol dissipates, about 1 minute. Add the stock and shallots and continue to boil, stirring often, for 15 minutes.

3. Meanwhile, chop the kale leaves into small pieces. You should have about 5 cups. After 15 minutes, add the kale, salt, pepper, and nutmeg to the stock and continue to cook, stirring frequently, until the kale is very tender, about 10 more minutes. Immediately drain the kale, reserving the cooking liquids. Place the kale in a blender or processor fitted with the metal chopping blade and purée until it becomes an even texture. Gradually mix in 1/2 cup of the cooking liquid and continue to process until the kale mixture is as fine as possible. Press this mixture through a fine-mesh strainer.

4. Place the remaining cooking liquid in a small saucepan and boil to reduce to about 3/4 cup. Mix in the kale and warm briefly, then stir in the parsley and milk or cream. Taste and adjust the seasonings.

1/4 teaspoon salt
1/8 teaspoon white pepper
1/8 teaspoon nutmeg
3 tablespoons finely minced fresh parsley
3 tablespoons milk, cream, or low-fat sour cream

Caper Sauce

Yield: 4 servings • Prep Time: 20 minutes • Cooking Time: 15 minutes

The intense flavor of capers serves as a piquant base for this flavorful sauce. Serve it with simple broiled tofu, stuffed pasta, or Idlis (page 103).

2 tablespoons olive oil
3/4 cup minced white onion
1/4 cup small capers, chopped
1 teaspoon minced garlic
1 cup hearty vegetable stock
2 teaspoons arrowroot or cornstarch
2 tablespoons cold water
1/4 cup minced fresh parsley

1. In a 1-quart saucepan, heat the olive oil over medium heat until hot, but not smoking. Add the onions and cook, stirring constantly, for 1 minute. Reduce the heat to low and continue to cook, stirring frequently, until the onions are completely soft, but not brown, about 10 minutes. Add the garlic and capers and cook for an additional 2 minutes.

2. Stir the stock and bring to a gentle boil. Place the arrowroot in a small mixing bowl, then stir in the cold water. Whisk the arrowroot paste into the sauce and boil just to thicken. Remove from the heat and stir in the parsley. Taste and adjust the seasonings. Serve drizzled over the Seitan Cutlets (page 48) or Crispy Lemon Tofu with Wild Mushrooms (page 77).

Variations

1. Make a paste out of 1 tablespoon tomato paste and 1 teaspoon Dijon mustard. Whisk a small amount of the finished sauce into this, then return the mixture to the sauce and heat through.

2. Prepare the sauce as above, adding 1/4 cup cognac with the garlic and cook for 2 minutes. Proceed from that point to the end as described above. You can enrich the sauce with 3 tablespoons milk or cream.

Watercress Sauce

Yield: 2 cups • Prep Time: 20 minutes • Cooking Time: 20 minutes

4 cups watercress
1 onion, oven-baked (page 36)
1 head garlic, oven-baked
   (page 36)
2 tomatoes, broiled
2 teaspoons crushed anise seeds
1/4 teaspoon salt
1/8 teaspoon black pepper
1/8 teaspoon nutmeg
1/2 cup orange juice
2 cups light vegetable stock
   (page 162)
1/4 cup diced russet potato
3 tablespoons minced fresh
   parsley or mint
2 tablespoons milk, soy cream
   (page 171), or crème fraîche
   (page 172)

This unusual sauce made from watercress and anise seeds has quite a bite. It can be served hot or at room temperature.

1. Clean the watercress, then remove 1 cup of leaves and set them aside. Place the remaining watercress stems and leaves in a 2-quart saucepan.

2. Remove and discard the skin from the onion, then quarter the onion and place it in a blender or food processor fitted with the metal chopping blade. Cut the top off the garlic and squeeze the cloves into the blender as well. Remove the skin from the tomatoes and add their meat to the blender along with the anise seeds, salt, pepper, and nutmeg. Purée until evenly ground, scraping down the sides of the beaker as necessary.

3. Add this purée, along with the stock and potato, to the saucepan containing the watercress. Simmer, stirring often, until the potato is tender, about 15 minutes. Return this sauce to the blender and purée until it is as fine as possible. Press it through a fine-mesh strainer into a clean saucepan.

4. Roughly chop the reserved watercress and add it to the sauce. Stir in the parsley or mint and enrich the sauce, if desired, with milk or cream. Taste and adjust the seasonings.

Béarnaise Sauce

Yield: 1 cup • Prep Time: 10 minutes • Cooking Time: 15 minutes

1/4 cup porcini stock (page 163)
2 tablespoons tarragon vinegar
Pinch of cayenne
1 tablespoon finely minced
   shallot
1 teaspoon minced garlic
3 egg yolks
8 tablespoons very cold butter
2 tablespoons crème fraîche
   (page 172)
1/2 teaspoon tomato paste
   (optional)
1 tablespoon chopped tarragon
   leaves
Salt to taste

A classic béarnaise sauce is simply a variation on the egg-based hollandaise sauce, but instead of lemon juice as a base flavor, béarnaise is made with vinegar and tarragon. Different chefs vary the precise mixture of flavorings; I find that the addition of a small amount of shallots is essential to the balance of the sauce. This recipe is a demonstration of the classic emulsification method. It is naturally high in fat and very unstable (the yolks can curdle if overheated). The variation listed below is much lower in fat and is appropriate for diets that do not include eggs.

1. In a 1 1/2-quart saucepan, combine the porcini stock with the vinegar, cayenne, shallot, and garlic. Bring the mixture to a boil and cook, swirling the pan often, until the liquid is reduced to about 2 tablespoons.

2. Meanwhile, in a small bowl, beat the yolks until creamy. When the liquid has reduced, add it to the yolks in a thin stream, whisking constantly, then return the mixture to the saucepan. Place this over boiling water (in a saucepan slightly larger than the first) and cook over medium heat, whisking constantly, until the mixture has thickened and turned a very pale yellow color. Immediately remove the saucepan from the heat and whisk in the butter, little by little.

3. Whisk in the crème fraîche, tomato paste, fresh tarragon, and salt. Taste and adjust the seasonings. Serve immediately.

Variation

1. Place 5 ounces drained silken tofu in a blender and purée until extremely smooth. Mix in 5 tablespoons porcini stock (page 163), the vinegar, shallots, garlic, and fresh tarragon. Season to taste with salt and warm briefly in the top of a double boiler. Serve at once.

Apple Onion Sauce

Yield: About 2 cups • Prep Time: 5 minutes • Cooking Time: 25 minutes

Pecans complement the taste of apple in this simple sauce. Serve it with Layered Tempeh (page 110) or Roasted Seitan (page 148).

2 Granny Smith apples
1 tablespoon lemon juice
3/4 cup minced onion
1 teaspoon garlic
1 cup light vegetable stock
(page 162)
2 tablespoons light miso
2 tablespoons pecan butter
(page 167)
3 tablespoons snipped chives

1. Quarter, core, and peel the apples, then cut them into small dice. Place them in a small saucepan with the lemon juice, onion, garlic, and stock. Bring this mixture to a boil, then reduce to a simmer and cook, covered and stirring often, until the apples are very tender, about 25 minutes.
2. Transfer the apple mixture to a food processor fitted with a metal chopping blade or a blender. Purée until very smooth, scraping down the sides of the bowl as necessary. Add the miso and pecan butter and blend. Mix in the chives and serve.

Ancho Pepper Sauce

Yield: 3 cups • Prep Time: 20 minutes • Cooking Time: 25 minutes

This simple yet rich-tasting sauce serves well with Spinach Mushroom Burritos (page 73), Steamed Vegetables (page 51), or Idlis (page 103).

1 pound red bell peppers, roasted
(page 35)
2 ancho peppers, softened in
warm water
1 1-pound can chopped tomatoes,
drained
1 1/2 tablespoons balsamic
vinegar
1 teaspoon honey
1/4 teaspoon salt
2 cloves garlic, minced

1. Peel the roasted peppers using a paring knife. Discard the skin, stems, and seeds, then cut the peppers into large pieces and place them in a blender or food processor fitted with a metal chopping blade.
2. Remove the ancho peppers from their soaking water, saving the water. Remove and discard the stems from the peppers, then split them open and scrape out and discard all seeds. Chop the anchos into large pieces and add them to the blender. Purée the pepper mixture until it is very smooth, scraping down the sides of the beaker as necessary. Add the drained tomatoes, vinegar, honey, salt, and garlic, then continue to purée until the mixture is smooth. Transfer this sauce to a small saucepan and cook over medium heat, stirring often, for 5 minutes. The sauce may be prepared up to 2 days in advance if refrigerated in an airtight container.

Cook's Note: I include roasting time for the bell peppers in the cooking time listed above. You may also use 1 1/2 cups bottled roasted peppers if you are short on time.

Creamy Tomatillo Sauce

Yield: About 2 cups • Prep Time: 15 minutes • Cooking Time: 10 minutes

1/2 pound fresh tomatillos
(page 196)
1/2 teaspoon salt
2 teaspoons ground cumin
1 cup diced white onion
3 cloves garlic, minced
1/2 cup cilantro, packed
1 large fresh tomato, chopped
1 serrano pepper, seeded and
minced
1 teaspoon tomato paste
2 teaspoons honey
1/4 cup orange juice
1/4 cup sour cream, plain yogurt,
or soy cream (page 171)

The pungent taste of tomatillos is softened by the addition of sour cream, yogurt, or soy cream (page 171). Serve with steamed vegetables and tempeh, tamales, or burritos.

1. Warm a heavy skillet over medium heat. Place the tomatillos in the pan and cook quickly, tossing frequently, until they begin to brown and sizzle, about 5 minutes. Immediately turn them out onto a clean kitchen towel to cool. When the tomatillos are cool enough to handle, remove and discard their husks, then quarter each tomatillo.

2. In a blender or food processor, combine the tomatillos, salt, cumin, onion, garlic, cilantro, tomato, serrano pepper, tomato paste, honey, and orange juice. Purée until smooth. Transfer this sauce to a small saucepan and heat for 5 minutes. Remove from the heat and whisk in the sour cream. Taste and adjust the seasonings. Serve at once.

Fresh Salsa

Yield: About 2 1/2 cups • Prep Time: 15 minutes

1 1/4 pounds fresh tomatoes
1/3 cup chopped cilantro
3 cloves garlic, peeled and halved
1 white onion, quartered
1/4 cup minced scallions
1 to 2 jalapeño peppers, seeded
and diced
2 tablespoons balsamic vinegar
1 teaspoon maple sugar
1/2 teaspoon salt

Use this all-purpose salsa as a sauce for dipping hors d'oeuvres or chips, for Steamed Vegetables (page 51), or as a flavoring in Mexican Rose Polenta (page 46).

1. Quarter the tomatoes. Remove and discard their stem ends, then set them aside. Fit a food processor with the metal chopping blade. Place the cilantro in the bowl and, using an on-off pulse action, chop it roughly. Transfer the cilantro to the work surface. Drop the garlic into the bowl through the feed tube and process. It will immediately become roughly chopped. Remove the lid and add the onion. Chop, using an on-off pulse action, scraping down the sides of the bowl as necessary.

2. Add the tomatoes to the bowl and continue to process to blend. Add the scallions, jalapeños, vinegar, maple sugar, and salt. Mix briefly, then add the cilantro and blend until combined. Transfer the salsa to a serving bowl. The salsa can be prepared up to 24 hours in advance if refrigerated in an airtight container.

Tomatillo Salsa

Yield: 2 cups • Prep Time: 10 minutes • Cooking Time: 10 minutes

1/2 pound fresh tomatillos
(page 196) or 1 8-ounce can
tomatillos
1 tablespoon minced garlic
1 teaspoon ground cumin

This green salsa serves well with Black Bean Corn Cakes (page 82), Tamales (page 48), and Idlis (page 103).

1. If you are using fresh tomatillos, warm a heavy skillet over medium heat. Place the tomatillos in the pan and cook quickly, tossing frequently, until they begin to brown and sizzle, about 5 minutes. Immediately turn them out onto a clean kitchen towel to cool. When the tomatillos are cool enough to handle, remove and discard their husks, then quarter each tomatillo. If you are using canned tomatillos, skip this browning and quartering step, but drain and rinse them.

2. In a blender or food processor, combine the tomatillos, garlic, cumin, and salt. Add the onion, cilantro, tomato, serrano pepper, honey, and lime juice. Purée until smooth. Transfer this sauce to a small saucepan and heat for 5 minutes. The sauce may be used immediately, or refrigerated in an airtight container for up to 3 days. Rewarm before serving.

1/2 teaspoon salt
1 cup diced red onion
1/2 cup cilantro, packed
1 large fresh tomato, chopped
1 serrano pepper, seeded and minced
2 teaspoons honey
2 teaspoons lime juice

Tomato Chutney

Yield: About 3 cups • Prep Time: 15 minutes • Cooking Time: 5 minutes

Serve this spicy chutney with Idlis (page 103), Couscous and Garbanzo Idlis (page 104), or as a sauce for one of the tamale recipes.

1. Place the tomatoes in a strainer over the sink and allow them to drain for 5 minutes as you prepare the other ingredients for the chutney. In a 1 1/2-quart saucepan, heat the oil over medium heat until hot, but not smoking. Add the onion and cook, stirring constantly until it becomes translucent, about 10 minutes. Add the garlic and ginger, then stir in the tomatoes, honey, garam masala, fenugreek leaves, and salt. Bring the mixture to a simmer and cook, stirring once or twice, for 5 minutes. Remove the salsa from the heat. Stir in the vinegar, minced pepper, and cilantro.

3 cups chopped fresh tomatoes
2 teaspoons canola oil
1/2 cup chopped white onion
1 teaspoon minced garlic
2 teaspoons minced gingerroot
3 tablespoons honey
1 teaspoon garam masala (page 191)
1 tablespoon fenugreek leaves (page 191)
1/4 teaspoon salt
2 tablespoons cider vinegar
1 serrano or habanero pepper, seeded and minced
1/4 cup minced cilantro

Cucumber Date Chutney

Yield: 2 1/2 cups • Prep Time: 15 minutes • Cooking Time: 8 minutes

Try this sweet chutney with Idlis (page 103) or as a sauce for spicy tamales.

1. Place the dates, water, ginger, and coconut in a small saucepan. Bring to a boil, stirring often, then reduce to a simmer and cook until the dates have fully softened and can be mashed against the side of the pan, about 8 minutes. Place this mixture in a food processor fitted with a metal chopping blade or a blender. Add the cucumber, cumin, salt, cinnamon, lime juice, almond butter, and Thai pepper. Purée until smooth, then add the cilantro or mint and continue to process until smooth. Taste and adjust the seasonings. The chutney may be prepared up to 3 days in advance if refrigerated in an airtight container.

1/4 cup dates
1 cup water
2 teaspoons minced gingerroot
2 tablespoons dissected coconut
1 cucumber, seeded and chopped
1 1/2 teaspoons ground cumin
1/2 teaspoon salt
1/4 teaspoon cinnamon
1/4 cup lime juice
2 tablespoons almond butter
1 Thai or serrano pepper, minced
1 cup, packed, cilantro or fresh mint leaves

Variation

1. Cook 1 minced serrano pepper and 2 teaspoons brown mustard seeds in 1 tablespoon ghee or vegetable oil until the seeds begin to pop. Immediately stir these into the chutney.

Yogurt Dipping Sauce

Yield: 1 1/4 cups • Prep Time: 5 minutes

1 cup nonfat yogurt
1 tablespoon honey
1 teaspoon minced gingerroot
   (optional)
2 tablespoons curry powder
2 tablespoons minced fresh mint
   or cilantro

Use this simple sauce for Idlis (page 103) as well as a salad dressing for fruit or vegetables.

1. In a small mixing bowl, combine the yogurt, honey, ginger, curry powder, and mint or cilantro. Mix well and transfer to a serving bowl. Cover and chill or serve at once.

Tamarind Chutney

Yield: About 2 cups • Prep Time: 25 minutes

1/4 pound tamarind
1 1/4 cups boiling water
2/3 cup raisins
1 teaspoon salt
2 teaspoons finely ground toasted
   cumin seeds or use 1 1/4
   teaspoons ground cumin
1 teaspoon grated gingerroot

Tamarind gives this incredible chutney a chocolate brown color and rich consistency. Its mellow, sour taste is accented by cumin, ginger, and sweetness from raisins. Serve this with Idlis (page 103), Couscous and Garbanzo Idlis (page 104), or Crusty Lemon Tofu with Wild Mushrooms (page 77).

1. Soak the tamarind in 1 cup boiling water for at least 30 minutes or until it is completely soft. In a separate bowl, soak the raisins in the remaining 1/4 cup water for 15 minutes.

2. When both tamarind and raisins are softened, place the raisins, with their soaking liquid, in a blender. Purée until very fine. Rub the tamarind to separate the pulp and seeds, then strain this through a tea strainer into the blender. Add the salt, cumin, and ginger and purée again, scraping the sides of the beaker down as necessary, until the chutney is very smooth. Press the chutney through a fine-mesh strainer. Serve cold.

Seitan

Yield: About 2 1/2 cups uncooked; 6 cups cooked • Prep Time: 1 hour

8 cups whole wheat flour
5 1/2 to 6 cups warm water

The first time I heard someone describing how to make seitan I was convinced I had suffered a momentary brain lapse midway through the description. Washing flour in order to get the gluten? It sounded impossible. But it works and the result is astonishing the first time you attempt it. Below I give a basic recipe for preparing uncooked seitan dough. You may vary the type of flour used for slightly different effects in texture (see variations), but all will be quite mild in flavor. You may knead seasonings such as minced garlic, dried herbs, or soy sauce directly into the dough for a more flavorful beginning.

1. Place the flour in a mixing bowl large enough to fill the bowl to only about 1/3 the bowl's height. Stir the flour to make sure there are no lumps. Gradually incorporate the water, beginning with about 1 1/2 cups and mixing constantly. Continue to stir in the water, turning the dough over as you add the water and mixing the liquid into the flour as evenly as possible. Once all the water has been incorporated, vigorously mix the dough with a flat spoon for about 1 minute. Cover the bowl with a damp kitchen towel and set aside for 45 minutes.

2. During this resting period the gluten in the flour will begin to develop elasticity and the dough will begin to take form. After allowing it to rest, gently pick as much of the dough up in your two hands as you can and, holding it over the bowl, squeeze it together. Place this back in the bowl and pick up more and squeeze/stretch it as well. Repeat this process for about 30 seconds.

3. Gradually begin to run a thin stream of lukewarm tap water into the bowl, aiming it down the inside of the bowl, not directly on the dough. As you add water, continue to knead and work the dough, gently lifting it out of the bowl and placing it back in. Continue to add water until the bowl is about 3/4 full and the water is very milky. Stop the water and pour most of the water out of the bowl, then continue to work the dough, adding more lukewarm water in a thin stream. As the bowl fills with water, allow some to drain out and continue to work the flour. After about 10 minutes the dough should have transformed into a very elastic ball of light brown gluten. Most of the bran and starch will have washed away. Work this dough briefly, then use in one of the recipes calling for uncooked seitan.

4. For recipes that call for cooked seitan, in a large stockpot combine 6 cups water, 1/3 cup soy sauce, 1 diced onion, 1 diced carrot, and any flavorings that will complement the dish for which the seitan is intended. (For Western-style dishes, try thyme, parsley, bay leaf, and garlic; for Asian-style dishes, use ginger, garlic, coriander seeds, and rice vinegar.)

5. Shape the seitan into balls or logs and place in the liquid. Bring just to a simmer and cook, never allowing the liquid to boil, for 1 1/2 to 2 hours. If the liquid boils, the seitan will have an unpleasant and spongy texture.

Variations

1. Use 4 cups whole wheat flour and 4 cups unbleached white flour for a more elastic, more durable dough. This mixture is good for stuffed seitan recipes such as curried seitan (page 148).

2. Mix 1/4 cup tamari, 2 teaspoons grated gingerroot, and 1 tablespoon minced garlic into the finished dough before beginning a recipe.

Cook's Note: For a fast, good-quality seitan, try Arrowhead Mills Seitan Mix (available at natural foods markets); it can be ready in five minutes.

Appendix

Weights and Measures of Common Ingredients

Ingredient	Weight	Measure
Apple (1 average)	8 ounces	1 1/2 cups, diced
Beans (1 cup raw)		
Split peas	7 ounces	2 1/2 cups, cooked
Kidney beans	6 1/2 ounces	2 cups, cooked
Garbanzos	6 ounces	2 cups, cooked
Carrot (1 average)	3 ounces	1/2 cup, diced
		2/3 cup, grated
Celery (1 stalk)	3 ounces	1/2 cup, diced
Garlic (3 cloves)	1 ounce	1 tablespoon, minced
Ginger (1/4-inch)	1 ounce	2 1/2 teaspoons, minced
Grains (1 cup raw)		
Rice	6 1/4 ounces	2 cups, cooked
Millet	7 ounces	3 cups, cooked
Quinoa	6 ounces	2 3/4 cup, cooked
Greens	4 ounces	4 1/2 cups, chopped
		1 cup cooked
Leeks (1 average)	8 ounces	2 cups, chopped
Lemon (1 average)	6 ounces	3 tablespoons juice
Mushrooms	8 ounces	3 cups, sliced
Onion (1 average)	8 ounces	1 cup, diced
Parsley (1 small bunch)	2 ounces	1/2 cup, minced
Potato (1 average)	10 ounces	2 cups, diced
Scallions (2 average)	1 ounce	1/4 cup, minced
Tomato (1 average)	8 ounces	1 cup, diced

Definitions of Terms

Acidulated water. Water to which lemon juice or vinegar is added. Light-colored fruit and vegetables are sometimes stored or cooked in acidulated water to retard discoloration.

Bain Marie. Literally translated from the French as "Mary's bath," it is a container which is filled with water into which another container (containing ingredients) is placed so that foods may be poached or warmed.

Braise. To brown a food (traditionally by frying), then cook it slowly in a small amount of flavorful liquid.

Caramelize. To cook slowly until natural sugars contained in an ingredient are released and begin to brown. Foods may be caramelized without oil if they are slowly baked. On top of the stove, foods may be caramelized by slow cooking in a small amount of oil. Surface caramelization may also be achieved by brushing an ingredient with oil before slow broiling.

Chop. To cut into pieces that are roughly square in shape. To chop most vegetables, first slice them into 1/4- to 1/2-inch-wide pieces. Stack the pieces and cut, lengthwise, into "logs," then cut crosswise into cubes. To chop onions, leeks or other layered root vegetables leave the root end intact when making cuts in the first two directions. This will help to keep the ingredient in a neat stack and facilitate chopping.

Dice. To cut into small cubes that are about 1/8- to 1/4-inch in size. This is the same process as chopping, but the pieces are generally smaller.

Julienne. To cut into squared strips. Classically they are usually squared to the size of a matchstick, but the term may be applied to larger squared strips as well. Most vegetables can be cut into julienne strips by cutting them horizontally into slices of the desired thickness, then stacking these slices and cutting them vertically into square sticks. Julienne strips may vary in length, depending on the recipe.

Mince. To chop very evenly and finely. See page 32.

Nonreactive pan. Cookware in which foods can be cooked without discoloring. Eggs and ingredients with a high acid content may react with the metal in pans made of copper or aluminum in such a way that the food becomes discolored or has a metallic smell or taste.

Reduce. To boil a liquid without a cover in order to reduce its volume through evaporation. Stocks may be reduced to 1/32 their original volume for homemade bouillon cubes, which can be frozen in ice cube trays. Once solid, they can be stored in an airtight container in the refrigerator, then reconstituted with water before adding to a recipe. If a liquid is greatly reduced, it may need to be transferred into a smaller saucepan once or twice to avoid burning.

Roll Cut. An attractive cut for long, thin vegetables such as carrots. First slice the end off the vegetable at a 45-degree slant. Roll the vegetable over 90 degrees and move it under the knife to the length of the cut you desire. Again cut the carrot at a 45-degree angle. Repeat the rolling and cutting.

Sauté. The French word *sauté* means to jump and that is what is intended when foods are sautéed. To sauté, heat a small amount of oil or butter over medium high heat until it is hot, but not smoking. Add the ingredient(s) and toss to coat with the fat. There should be a sizzling sound when the ingredient first hits the fat. Stir and toss the ingredients constantly as they cook. Foods may be removed immediately, or sautéing may be the first step in a recipe, in which case the heat will be lowered or liquid will be added for additional cooking.

Shred. To cut into very thin strips, similar to julienne strips, but much thinner. To shred ginger root, for example, cut a peeled piece of ginger root into paper-thin strips. Stack these on top of each other and cut in the opposite direction into very thin sticks. Mushrooms may be shredded by first slicing into rounds, then into strips. Leaves such as sorrel or basil are sometimes shredded by first stacking the leaves, facing the same direction, then cutting them into thin strips.

Simmer. To cook liquid at a very low boil. Tiny bubbles are visible on the surface of the liquid.

Skim. To remove scum that rises to the surface, as when a broth is first cooking.

Slice. To cut in even, thin pieces. Average slices are about 1/4 inch thick.

Sweat. To sprinkle an ingredient, usually cucumbers or eggplant, with salt as a means of drawing water and/or bitterness out of the ingredient.

Taste and adjust the seasonings. To taste a dish or sauce just before serving after all ingredients are added. The dish should be at the temperature it will be served as flavors, especially salt, vary depending on temperature. If the flavor of the dish is not precisely what is desired, small amounts of additional ingredients already found in the dish may be added.

Timbale. A mold for an individual serving of a baked or poached dish. Traditionally they are relatively small (2 to 3 inches in diameter and 2 to 4 inches in height) and are often made of steel.

Whisk. To mix with a wire whisk. Most often the term is used when a liquid is mixed into a roux for a sauce or in order to thin a semisolid ingredient, such as miso. To minimize lumping, begin by whisking the more solid ingredient and once the motion is established, gradually pour in the liquid, whisking constantly. This type of whisking action demands that the whisk be in contact with the bottom of the bowl or pan and be drawn back and forth, then round and round over the bottom of the pan.

Glossary of Ingredients

Ancho Pepper. Dried poblano peppers, ancho peppers are large, flat, and deep red to black in color. They are mildly hot with a lasting and full aftertaste.

Arame. A brown alga which is shredded into long delicate strands. It has a light flavor and texture that people who "don't eat seaweed" often enjoy. It should be quickly rinsed and soaked before adding to a recipe, but should not be cooked long as it will begin to dissolve. Arame is available at natural foods markets.

Beefsteak Leaves. Dried leaves from the beefsteak plant that have been pickled in vinegar (usually plum) or vinegar and salt. Beefsteak leaves are available at natural foods markets, or substitute crumbled dulse.

Butter. I recommend using only unsalted butter in all recipes. First, salt is added partly as a preservative in butter, so that which is salted may be less fresh. Second, if you use salted butter, you cannot control for salt in a recipe. If you do not include butter in your diet, an equal measure of vegetable oil may be substituted in most recipes. Except in some baked goods in which oils do not work, I generally do not recommend using margarine as it is a hydrogenated fat (page 17).

Chanterelle Mushrooms. Also known as girolles, chanterelles are a beautiful, light orange, trumpet-shaped mushroom. Their taste is mild and buttery, but rich. When unavailable, hedgehog mushrooms may be substituted.

Chili Paste with Garlic. A spicy seasoning/condiment often used in Chinese cooking. It is made from ground chilies, garlic, oil, and salt and is sold in Asian markets and many fine supermarkets. A very small amount will contribute a substantial amount of heat to a dish. After opening, it will keep indefinitely if refrigerated, although it slowly loses its punch.

Chili Peppers. Very hot small peppers, available dried and fresh in most supermarkets. The dried variety is best browned before being added to a dish as this helps to release and tone its flavor.

Chipotle Pepper. Smoked jalapeño peppers which are often sold dried. They lend heat and a smoky aftertaste to a dish. Available in Latin American markets.

Coconut Milk. The liquid extracted after grated coconut is ground together with water, then squeezed through cheesecloth. The meat from 1 coconut combined with 5 cups water will produce about 3 cups coconut milk. Coconut milk is also available canned in most supermarkets and Asian markets. **Light Coconut Milk** is coconut milk which has been diluted 3 parts coconut milk to 1 part water.

Daikon. Daikon or Japanese radish is a white root that resembles a large carrot in shape. It can range in size from 8 to 24 inches and should be light in color and firm.

Dulse. A purplish-red, flat-leaf sea vegetable. It may be eaten raw or quickly rinsed before being added to a dish. Dulse is available in most natural foods stores.

Epazote. An herb which grows wild throughout the western United States and Mexico. It has a strong and distinctive flavor. When added to the cooking water of dried beans, it is said to aid in digestion.

Fenugreek. A spice typically used in Indian dishes. Seeds may be ground and added to curries; dried leaves may be added to sauces and soups. Fenugreek contributes a mildly musty, yet sweet undertone to dishes. Both seeds and leaves are available in most Asian markets that stock Indian ingredients.

Fermented Black Beans. Beans that have been preserved in a salty brine, then dried and fermented. By themselves they have an overpowering salty flavor, but in small quantities, added to simmered dishes, they provide depth, dimension, and texture. They are sold in Asian markets and many fine grocery stores.

Five-Spice Powder. A seasoning mixture used in some Chinese dishes. It is made from five fragrant spices, typically star anise, Szechwan peppercorns, cinnamon, cloves, and licorice root. Available in Asian markets and fine grocery stores.

Flower Water. Water perfumed by the essence of a flower, most commonly rose or orange. Readily available in Middle Eastern markets and many natural foods stores.

Galangal. A ginger-like root that is used in Southeast Asian cooking. It is hotter but less pungent than ginger and is usually added to dishes as a smashed round, rather than minced (as is ginger). It is available in Asian markets. Gingerroot may be substituted.

Garam Masala. A fragrant blend of a number of spices, such as cinnamon, cloves, cumin, dried peppers, and cardamom, which is used in Indian cooking.

Garlic. Purple or white garlic is appropriate for recipes in this book. Elephant garlic is much milder and more onion-like in quality. When selecting garlic, all cloves should be firm and should fit snugly to the core. The papery skin should be full and crisp.

Ghee. The Indian term for clarified butter. To prepare ghee, cut 1 pound of butter into small pieces and place them in a heavy-bottomed, 1 1/2-quart saucepan. Melt the butter over a very low flame. Skim and discard the foam that rises to the surface, then set the pan aside to cool. The solids will sink to the bottom and the ghee may be poured off the top. Refrigerated in an airtight container, ghee will keep for several months. Commercially produced ghee often has a rather unpleasant and distinctive flavor, and given the fact that it is usually far more expensive than the butter itself, I recommend making your own.

Ginger. Ginger is readily available fresh, in root form, and pickled (often sold as ginger for sushi). Candied and dried ginger are not called for in any of the recipes in this book. Fresh gingerroot should be plump with tight, smooth skin. A small piece broken off the main root should have a fresh gingery scent and be an even color. Refrigerate gingerroot loose, in the vegetable drawer.

Hing (Asafoetida). A powerful seasoning used extensively throughout India. It is a resin extracted from ferula plants. When dried, its flavor and aroma have a strong sulphurous quality, and it is used in tiny quantities to mirror the sulfuric effect of onion or garlic. Use hing with extreme caution as it can be overpowering.

Jalapeño Pepper. A widely available chili pepper that is cone-shaped with a rounded tip. It is usually 2 to 3 inches long and has green to red or purple skin which may have rough brown lines on it. Jalapeños are medium-hot.

Jicama. A light brown-skinned, rounded oval root vegetable. It must be peeled. Its white flesh is crisp, juicy, and slightly sweet. It can be eaten raw in salads or other dishes or added to stir-fries and other entrées for the final minutes of cooking. Store jicama in the refrigerator, with cut edges sealed with plastic wrap.

Kombu. Kombu is a sea vegetable which is sold in 8- to 12-inch strips. It resembles a stiff, dull, gray-black piece of plastic and is used in stocks, when cooking beans, or for a seafood flavor in other dishes. Kombu is available at natural foods stores and Asian markets.

Kuzu. Kuzu is a white powdery starch used as a thickener. It is derived from the root of the kuzu plant and has been used in the Orient for centuries, where it is believed to aid digestive disorders. Kuzu is available at natural foods stores.

Leeks. Leeks look like overgrown scallions, but their flavor is comparatively mild and sweet. They are used as a base seasoning in stocks and sauces and are also delicious sautéed or steamed.

Lemon Grass. Lemon grass is often used in Southeast Asian cuisines. Sold by the stalk in Asian markets, it should be firm and fresh-looking, never brown or dried. It adds a very appealing lemony aroma to dishes. Use only the bottom 4 to 6 inches of the stems.

Lemon (Lime or Orange) Zest. Citrus zest is obtained by grating the outermost layer of skin from fresh citrus. As citrus is often highly sprayed with pesticides, always wash and dry the fruit before zesting; better yet, buy organic citrus.

Lily Buds. Lily buds may be purchased, dried, in Asian markets and fine supermarkets. They are the buds from a particular type of tiger lily flower and add interesting texture and a tang in flavor to stir-fries, steamed dishes, and stuffings.

Lime Leaves. Fresh lime leaves are used in many Asian dishes for their slightly bitter, lime undertone. They are available in Asian markets. A small amount of lime zest may be substituted.

Maple Sugar. Crystallized maple syrup becomes maple sugar. It may be used interchangeably with sugar in most recipes, though its flavor is distinctively maple. Available in many natural foods stores.

Mirin. Mirin is a sweet Japanese cooking wine made from sweet rice. The best quality mirin is made from sweet rice, rice koji, and water with no added sugar, alcohol, or chemical fermenting agents.

Miso. A fermented soybean paste that is made by mixing cooked beans with a mold (koji), salt, and water. The mixture ferments for anywhere from 2 months to 5 years. Other beans or grains may be mixed into the paste. The best misos are nonpasteurized. Different types of beans used in the miso, and variations in storage time, will result in misos with extremely different tastes. Those that are light in color tend to be lighter in taste. Experiment with different varieties to find a few that suit your tastes. Miso contains an enzyme (lactobacillus bacteria) that aids in digestion. If miso is boiled, the enzyme is killed.

Morel Mushrooms. A distinctive brown to dark brown mushroom with a hollow, cone-shaped cap. They look very spongy, but are actually rich, nutty, and meaty. They are an excellent addition to dishes that contain a variety of mushrooms. False morels—sometimes found in the wild—are deadly if eaten raw.

Non-aluminum Baking Powder. Baking powder to which no aluminum is added. Available in natural foods stores.

Nori. Thin sheets of sea vegetable made from that which is chopped, then dried on a bamboo mat. Its flavor is enhanced by toasting, passing it quickly close to a flame. Nori is available in natural foods stores and most Asian markets.

Porcini Mushrooms. Also called cepes, porcini mushrooms have a rich aroma and wholesome alluring quality. They have light brown, umbrella-shaped caps with thick, meaty stems. You are more likely to find them dried than fresh.

Quatre Épices. A French spice mixture commonly used in pâtés and sausages. You may make your own quatre épices blend by combining 1 tablespoon each: ground nutmeg, ground cinnamon, ground cloves, and finely ground black pepper.

Rice Noodles/Rice Sticks. Translucent noodles made from rice flour that, when cooked, have a delicate, slightly rubbery texture. They are available in thick and thin cut and require very little if any cooking beyond soaking in hot liquid. Rice noodles are available in Asian markets and many fine grocery stores.

Rice Sheets. Paper-thin round sheets used for wrapping spring rolls or as the outer "skin" on Tofu Roll (page 134). Rice sheets are available in 9- or 14-inch rounds. They are very fragile and should be stored flat without anything resting on top of them. (Inside a bamboo steamer is a good storage spot.)

Rice Syrup. Rice syrup is made from adding either an enzyme from sprouted barley or the sprouted barley itself to cooked rice. The resulting thick syrup resembles honey in appearance but is thicker and less intensely sweet. Rice malt syrup has a distinctive barley taste and rice syrup is mellow. Rice syrup may be substituted in equal amounts for honey, for a less sweet effect. It is available in natural foods stores.

Seitan. Used extensively in Asia as a meat substitute, seitan is the gluten that remains when wheat flour is rinsed and kneaded in water. (See page 184 for detailed instructions on preparing seitan.) Seitan is available commercially prepared, but will be precooked and seasoned. Be certain that the flavors of the precooking are appropriate for the dish in which it will be used. A quick seitan mix (manufactured by Arrowhead Mills) is also available and is an excellent resource if you do not want to dedicate the time required to prepare seitan from scratch.

Serrano Pepper. A small, slightly curved chili pepper that may range in size from 1 to 2 inches and can be green, red, or orange-brown. It is very hot and care should be taken to avoid eye contact. Serranos are sold fresh in many grocery stores. Jalapeño pepper may be substituted.

Shallots. Shallots look like red-brown-skinned, large cloves of garlic. They have a rich, onion-like flavor with an edge of garlic taste. If unavailable, substitute a mixture of 1 1/2 tablespoons chopped onion and 1 teaspoon garlic for each 1/4 cup shallots.

Shiitake Mushrooms. Known in Japan as the "perfumed" mushroom, shiitakes are commonly used in many Asian cuisines. They have large, flat tawny brown caps with cream-colored undersides. They are slightly chewy with what is sometimes considered as a "meaty" flavor. You will find shiitakes dried in Asian markets and natural foods stores and fresh in many fine supermarkets. Dried shiitake are more pungent in flavor than the fresh, and most dishes can only tolerate somewhere between 4 and 8 dried shiitakes.

Soba Noodles. Classic Japanese noodles that are flat in shape and traditionally made from 100% buckwheat. Some are made with additional flours and may be lighter in color and less expensive than traditional noodles. They are available in natural foods stores and some Asian markets.

Soy Cheese. A relatively new food found in some natural foods stores. Soy cheese comes in various flavors and, depending on the brand, may be very creamy (or even rubbery) to dry. It is made from soy milk to which caseinate and natural flavors are added. Soy cheese may be substituted for dairy cheese in all recipes.

Soy Milk. The liquid resulting from cooking ground soybeans in water. It is available commercially in various flavors. It has a chalky taste, but will only smell or taste unpleasant if it is rotten. Soy milk may be substituted in most recipes calling for cow's milk, though it can separate if it is boiled.

Soy Sauce. (See Tamari)

Straw Mushrooms. Most commonly found canned, straw mushrooms are a small variety of mushroom with dark brown-gray caps and creamy stems. They are mild in flavor.

Sun-Dried Tomatoes. Sun-dried tomatoes are available dry and packed in oil. Italian oil-packed sun-dried tomatoes are delectable but high in fat, and may be extremely expensive. You can soak dried sun-dried tomatoes in hot water for 20 minutes, then drain them and toss them with a light coating of olive oil and several slices of garlic for an excellent substitute. Refrigerate tightly covered for up to 5 days. If you plan to keep them longer, cover them completely with oil to prevent mold from growing on the tomatoes.

Szechwan Peppercorns. A widely available seasoning commonly used in Chinese cooking, Szechwan peppercorns are an open-husked peppercorn with a penetrating aroma and taste. They are best toasted before being added to dishes and you may wish to remove them before serving unless guests are familiar with their texture.

Tahini. A peanut butter-like paste made from finely ground, hulled sesame seeds. It is available toasted or untoasted (which has a raw but milder flavor) in supermarkets and natural foods stores.

Tamari and Soy Sauce. Traditional seasonings used throughout Asia in many recipes for the salty, rich taste and caramel color they contribute. Soy sauce (known also as shoyu) is traditionally made from soybeans, wheat and salt that are fermented in wooden kegs—much like wine—for at least 2 years. Traditional tamari is the liquid that rises and is skimmed from the surface of miso. Traditionally it contains no wheat and is more intensely flavored than soy sauce. Today both soy sauce and tamari have become so popular in the West that the names have not always remained true to traditional methods of preparation. Many manufacturers now label their sauces to indicate how they are prepared. Those labled "tamari shoyu" or "soy sauce" are usually prepared with wheat, and those labeled "tamari" are usually prepared without wheat. Low-sodium soy sauce is also available and is usually labled as such or "light." The best soy sauce is made from whole beans, using a double fermentation process in which no salt is added to the second fermentation. High-quality soy sauce will have no added colors or preservatives. Check the label for information on how the soy sauce was manufactured before buying.

Tamarind. Tamarind is the pod from a tall tamarind tree that grows in India and throughout Southeast Asia. The pods are peeled and seeded, then compacted into blocks before being sold. Tamarind has a very dark brown, chocolate-like color and strong, lemon-like aroma. It must be softened in hot water and strained before using. It is available in many Latin American and Asian markets.

Tempeh. A traditional food of Indonesia, tempeh is made from whole cooked soy beans which are incubated with a mold culture (*Rhizopus oligosporus*). This causes the beans to bind together. Tempeh has a full flavor and meatier texture than tofu. Other ingredients may be added to the tempeh before it ferments and these will be listed on labels. Some tempeh, that combined with sea vegetables, for example, has a delightful taste and texture, but will fall apart if used in recipes that require it to be cut thin (Tempeh Fajitas, page 99) or that require stirring over a long period of time (Tangy Tempeh Stew, page 86).

Tofu. Soy milk which has a curdling agent added to it (usually nigari). It is then drained and pressed, like cheese. Depending on these factors, its texture may be soft or firm, silken or not. It is always mild in taste.

Tofu sold fresh, often found in Asian markets, should be eaten within a few days of purchase. Packaged, refrigerated tofu will have an expiration date clearly marked on it and should be consumed by that date. Aseptic packages of silken tofu may be stored at room temperature for months before being opened. They are vary handy to have on the shelf for use in sauces. All unused portions of tofu should be refrigerated in a glass or plastic container which should be filled with fresh water daily. When tofu is sour, the water surrounding it will be cloudy, and the tofu will have a sour/rancid smell. It should not be used in this case.

All tofu, except silken varieties, may be frozen. To do so, drain the block of tofu, then slice it into 1-inch-thick blocks. Individually wrap these slices in plastic, then place them in an airtight container and freeze until solid. Tofu will keep frozen for up to 2 months. Before using, thaw the tofu in its wrapper, then place it, unwrapped, between two cutting boards. Press the boards together and weight with a heavy skillet. Drain for at least 30 minutes. Drained frozen tofu may be grated, crumbled, or diced. Its texture will be firm and spongy and will respond well to long cooking.

Tomatillos. A round green tomato-like vegetable with a distinctive light tan husk. Used in salsa and sauces. Available fresh or canned.

Tree Oyster Mushrooms. Light pearl gray to brown mushrooms that look like a fan and may come in clusters. Their flavor is mild and, when cooked, their texture is reminiscent of true oysters.

Udon Noodles. A flat Japanese wheat noodle that is about the width of linguine. They are light in color, with a delightful, chewy texture. If unavailable, linguine may be substituted. Udon noodles are available in Asian markets and most natural foods stores.

Umeboshi Paste. A paste made from ume plums (a particular type of Japanese plum) that is pickled with salt and/or shiso (salted beafsteak leaves). It is very strong in flavor, slightly sour with a tiny pucker to the taste, and very salty.

Ume Vinegar. A salty, light pink vinegar made from ume plums (see below). It will color tofu, cauliflower, or other light-colored ingredients pink if it is added to them.

Wasabi Powder. Also known as Japanese horseradish, wasabi is a light green powder which is extremely strong and penetrating in aroma and flavor. Mix dry wasabi into a paste with a small amount of warm water. Wasabi powder is available in most supermarkets and Asian markets.

Index

About the Author

Mary F. Taylor received the Grande Diplóme from L'École des Trois Gourmandes in Neuilly, France and trained at L'École LeNótre. More recently, Taylor studied classic Indian cooking while living in Mysore, South India. She spent six years working in various facets of the natural foods industry and has also been a cooking instructor and caterer. She is passionate in her pursuit of well-being and peace of mind through good food, good eating, yoga and laughter. She lives in Boulder, Colorado.

The Crossing Press
publishes many cookbooks.
For a free catalog, call toll-free
800 / 777-1048